Amnesty, Serious Crimes and International Law

Amnesty, Serious Crimes and International Law examines the permissibility of amnesties for serious crimes in the contemporary international order. In the last few decades, there has been a growing tendency to consider that amnesties are prohibited in respect of certain grave crimes. However, the question remains controversial as there is no explicit treaty ban and general amnesties continue to be frequently issued in post-conflict and transitional contexts. The first part of the book explores the use of amnesties from antiquity to the present day. It reviews amnesty traditions in ancient societies and provides a global picture of modern amnesties. In parallel, it traces the development of the accountability paradigm underpinning the current prohibitive stance on amnesties. The second part assesses the position of modern international law on amnesties. It comprehensively analyses the main arguments supporting the existence of a general amnesty ban, including the duty to prosecute international crimes, the right to redress of victims of human rights violations, international standards and trends in state practice, and the mandate of international criminal courts. The book argues that, while international legal or policy requirements restrict the freedom of states to extend amnesty in respect of serious crimes, or the effectiveness of amnesty measures in preventing the prosecution of such crimes, these restrictions do not add up to an absolute and universal prohibition.

Josepha Close is a researcher in International Law who has previously taught Law and Criminology at Middlesex University, London, UK, and is now based in Liège, Belgium.

Post-Conflict Law and Justice

International law has great relevance in post-conflict contexts, but the complexity of its role, both as a supporting and restraining factor, can be underestimated. This series explores the role of law, and in particular international law, in securing 'justice' in post-conflict contexts. The remit of the series extends to matters of law connected to, for example: post-conflict legal reforms and the development of constitutions; the establishment of the rule of law; the place of international organizations in post-conflict; peace-keeping; transitional justice mechanisms (including criminal justice); and discussion of jus post bellum. It also seeks self-reflexive works on notions of post-conflict justice, transitional justice, and similar.

Series Editors: James A. Sweeney, Lancaster University, and Matthew Saul, University of Oslo

Available titles in this series include:

International Law and Post-Conflict Reconstruction Policy
Matthew Saul and James A. Sweeney

Silenced Victims of Wartime Sexual Violence
Olivera Simic

Sexualized Crimes, Armed Conflict and the Law
The International Criminal Court and the Definitions of Rape and Forced Marriage
Hannah Baumeister

Self-Determination, International Law and Post-Conflict Reconstruction
A Right in Abeyance
Manuela Melandri

Amnesty, Serious Crimes and International Law
Josepha Close

For more information about this series, please visit: www.routledge.com/Post-Conflict-Law-and-Justice/book-series/POSTCONLAW

Amnesty, Serious Crimes and International Law

Global Perspectives in Theory and Practice

Josepha Close

Routledge
Taylor & Francis Group
LONDON AND NEW YORK

First published 2019
by Routledge
2 Park Square, Milton Park, Abingdon, Oxon OX14 4RN

and by Routledge
605 Third Avenue, New York, NY 10017

First issued in paperback 2020

Routledge is an imprint of the Taylor & Francis Group, an informa business

British Library Cataloguing-in-Publication Data
A catalogue record for this book is available from the British Library

Library of Congress Cataloging-in-Publication Data
Names: Close, Josepha.
Title: Amnesty, serious crimes and international law : global perspectives in theory and practice / Josepha Close.
Description: Abingdon, Oxon ; New York, NY : Routledge, 2019. | Series: Post-conflict law and justice | Based on author's thesis (doctoral - Middlesex University, England, 2016) issued under title: The international legal status of amnesties granted for serious crimes : historical and contemporary perspectives, | Includes bibliographical references and index.
Identifiers: LCCN 2018054236
Subjects: LCSH: Amnesty (International law)
Classification: LCC KZ7130 .C56 2019 | DDC 345/.077–dc23
LC record available at https://lccn.loc.gov/2018054236

ISBN 13: 978-0-367-72854-0 (pbk)
ISBN 13: 978-0-815-38579-0 (hbk)

Typeset in Galliard
by Integra Software Services Pvt. Ltd.

Contents

Acknowledgments

The journey for this book started in early 2012 following my first meeting with Professor William Schabas at Middlesex University, London. His support, patient guidance and kind encouragements as a PhD supervisor and mentor have made this project possible. It has been a great privilege to benefit from his teachings and wisdom throughout my doctoral studies. Dr Nadia Bernaz, my second supervisor, has also given invaluable help on many different levels towards the completion of this project, including through her comments on various drafts of the thesis and the book proposal. I am grateful to everyone at the School of Law and the Doctoral Institute at Middlesex for fostering our intellectual development in an atmosphere of mutual support and friendship. Special thanks go to my teachers, colleagues and friends for advising and encouraging me at critical moments in the writing process, particularly Professor Phoebe Okowa, Professor Ann Jacobs, Dr David Keane, Dr Anthony Cullen, Dr Giulia Pecorella and Dr Adnan Sattar. I would also like to thank Professor Carsten Stahn for his guidance and comments during my viva.

The second pivotal moment in the journey for this book was the drafting of an *amicus curiae* on the legal status of amnesties for the European Court of Human Rights in the case of *Marguš v. Croatia* (app no 4455/10). The contribution of several experts, authors of the *Belfast Guidelines on Amnesty and Accountability* (2013), gave weight and added meaning to the brief which was cited in the Court's judgment of 27 May 2014. Their work on amnesties, particularly the groundbreaking studies of Professor Louise Mallinder and Mark Freeman, have significantly influenced and inspired my research. The book has also benefited from the feedback received at Conferences in London (Queen Mary University), Belfast (Queen's University) and Oxford (the Society of Legal Scholars) in 2016. The questions and comments of students during guest lectures at Middlesex and Queen Mary Universities in 2017 also contributed to develop and refine my ideas for this project.

The third important juncture towards the completion of this book was my encounter with Professor James Sweeney at the Belfast Conference. He gave me the opportunity for writing this book and my deepest thanks go to him and Dr Matthew Saul for their support, comments and suggestions at different stages of the process. I would also like to thank the anonymous reviewers of the book proposal for their feedback and my editors at Routledge for their help in finalising the book.

Last but not least, many thanks go to my partner, Sébastien, for his unfailing support every step of the way, my parents, Pierre and Marianne, and my sisters, Odile and Marie. My daughter Zélie was born a few days after the book proposal was approved and she has been the source of so much joy, wonder and optimism throughout the writing process. This book is dedicated to her.

Table of cases

International Court of Justice

Human Rights Committee

Committee against Torture

Inter-American Human Rights System

European Human Rights System

African Commission on Human and People's Rights

International Criminal Tribunal for the former Yugoslavia

Special Court for Sierra Leone

Extraordinary Chambers in the Courts of Cambodia

International Criminal Court

Table of international instruments

International treaties

Statutory instruments of international or hybrid criminal courts

Abbreviations

ACHR	American Convention on Human Rights
ACHPR	African Charter on Human and Peoples' Rights
AHRLR	African Human Rights Law Reports
AU	African Union, formerly Organisation of African Unity (OAU)
CAR	Central African Republic
CAT	Committee against Torture
CEN-SAD	Community of Sahel-Saharan States
CETS	Council of Europe Treaty Series
CHR	Commission on Human Rights
CTF	Commission on Truth and Friendship (Indonesia/East Timor)
DR	Decisions and Reports of the European Commission on Human Rights
DRC	Democratic Republic of Congo
EAC	Extraordinary African Chambers within the Senegalese judicial system
ECCAS	Economic Community of Central African States
ECCC	Extraordinary Chambers in the Courts of Cambodia
ECHR	European Convention on Human Rights
ECOWAS	Economic Community of West African States
EHHR	European Human Rights Reports
EU	European Union
GA	General Assembly
HRC	Human Rights Committee
ICC	International Criminal Court
ICCPR	International Covenant on Civil and Political Rights
ICGLR	International Conference on the Great Lakes Region
ICJ	International Court of Justice
ICTR	International Criminal Tribunal for the former Yugoslavia
ICTY	International Criminal Tribunal for Rwanda
ICRC	International Committee of the Red Cross
ILM	International Legal Materials
IMT	International Military Tribunal
KSC	Kosovo Specialist Chambers

OAS	Organisation of American States
OIC	Organisation of Islamic Conference
OIF	Organisation Internationale de la Francophonie
OSCE	Organisation of Security and Cooperation in Europe
OTP	Office of the Prosecutor
RC	Republic of Congo
SADC	Southern African Development Community
SC	Security Council
SCC	Special Criminal Court in the Central African Republic
SCP	Serious Crimes Panels for East Timor
SCSL	Special Court for Sierra Leone
STL	Special Tribunal for Lebanon
TRC	Truth and Reconciliation Commission
UK	United Kingdom
UN	United Nations
UNHCR	United Nations High Commissioner for Refugees
UNTS	United Nations Treaty Series
US	United States
USSR	Union of Soviet Socialist Republics
RF	Russian Federation

Introduction

Amnesties have been contentious in the last few decades in so far as they extend to serious crimes of international concern, including genocide, crimes against humanity, war crimes, torture and other gross human rights violations. There has been a growing tendency for international bodies to consider that measures exempting persons accused of these crimes from punishment are contrary to international law. The UN and human rights organisations have been the most vocal in condemning such measures as part of a global policy promoting accountability for serious crimes. Whether international law prohibits amnesties in relation to serious crimes remains controversial, however, since there is no express treaty prohibition and broad amnesty laws continue to be frequently issued by states emerging from war or repression. For these and other reasons, the nature and contours of the alleged amnesty ban are unclear and continue to be debated in the case law and the literature.[1]

For instance, in a judgment of 13 November 2012 in the case of *Marguš v. Croatia*, the European Court of Human Rights declared that:

> Granting amnesty in respect of "international crimes" – which include crimes against humanity, war crimes and genocide – is increasingly considered to be prohibited by international law. This understanding is drawn from customary rules of international humanitarian law, human rights treaties, as well as the decisions of international and regional courts and developing State practice, as there has been a growing tendency for international, regional and national courts to overturn general amnesties enacted by Governments.[2]

1 See Louise Mallinder, 'The End of Amnesty or Regional Overreach? Interpreting the Erosion of South America's Amnesty Laws' (2016) 65 *International and Comparative Law Quarterly* 645; Naomi Roht-Arriaza, 'After Amnesties are Gone: Latin American National Courts and the new Contours of the Fight Against Impunity' (2015) 37(2) *Human Rights Quarterly* 341; Renée Jeffery, *Amnesties, Accountability, and Human Rights* (University of Pennsylvania Press 2014); Francesca Lessa and Leigh A Payne (eds), *Amnesty in the Age of Human Rights Accountability: Comparative and International Perspectives* (CUP 2012). The international case law on amnesties is discussed in chs 6 and 7 of this volume.

2 *Marguš v Croatia* App No 4455/10 (ECtHR, 13 November 2012) para 74.

When the Grand Chamber of the Court reconsidered this case, the author submitted an *amicus curiae* highlighting weaknesses in the view that amnesties covering serious crimes are altogether prohibited by international law.[3] In its judgment of 27 May 2014, the Grand Chamber held that '[a] growing tendency in international law is to see such amnesties [covering serious human rights violations] as unacceptable because they are incompatible with the unanimously recognised obligation of States to prosecute and punish grave breaches of fundamental human rights'.[4] However, the Court then nuanced this statement by acknowledging that amnesties might be 'possible where there are some particular circumstances, such as a reconciliation process and/or a form of compensation to the victims'.[5]

Amnesties have a long history spanning all continents. They have been used for millennia in different types of societies for a similar range of purposes, including as a means to facilitate the restoration of peace and foster reconciliation in relation to an armed conflict or a civil strife. For example, the oldest amnesty of which we have some records was included in a treaty of peace between the pharaoh of Egypt and the king of the Hittites in the thirteenth century BC.[6] In the Roman world, amnesties were frequently used for pacification, among other purposes.[7] For a period of over a thousand years, broad amnesties were also regularly proclaimed by Chinese emperors in order to restore stability and tranquillity.[8] In Europe, at the end of the medieval period, amnesty clauses started to be traditionally included in peace treaties ending major armed conflicts, a practice from which the Treaty of Versailles (1919) marked a symbolic departure.[9]

The English word amnesty comes from the old French *amnestie*, itself derived from *amnestia*, a latinised form of the Greek ἀμνηστία (amnēstia).[10] The terms amnesty and amnesia both come from the same Greek root – amnēstia – which the Etymological Dictionary of English defines as forgetfulness.[11] Accordingly, amnesty has long been understood as an act of oblivion entailing the forgetting of past wrongs. Thus, the most famous ancient amnesty, granted at the end of

3 'Legal Status of Amnesty: Third party intervention in the case of *Marguš v. Croatia*, Application no 4455/10' (29 May 2013), on file with author. The brief was drafted in collaboration with a group of international experts.

4 *Marguš v Croatia* [GC] ECHR 2014-III, para 139.

5 Ibid.

6 See Langdon and Alan H Gardiner, 'The Treaty of Alliance between Hattusili, King of the Hittites, and the Pharaoh Ramesses II of Egypt' (1920) 6(3) *The Journal of Egyptian Archaeology* 179, 197–98.

7 See Melissa Barden Dowling, *Clemency and Cruelty in the Roman World* (University of Michigan Press 2006).

8 See Brian E McKnight, *The Quality of Mercy, Amnesties and Traditional Chinese Justice* (University Press of Hawaii 1981).

9 See ch 2 of this volume.

10 Walter W Skeat, *An Etymological Dictionary of the English Language* (new edn, OUP 1924) 19.

11 Ibid.

the Athenian civil war in 403 BC, prohibited all citizens from 'recalling the misfortunes of the past' in order to restore civic harmony.[12] This pact of oblivion was sealed through the swearing of individual oaths by Athenian citizens and legal mechanisms were devised to sanction persons introducing a claim based on past wrongs.[13] To mark the erasure of the memory of the civil war, an altar was erected to Lethe – the goddess of oblivion – on the Acropolis.[14]

Amnesty continued to be associated with forgetfulness and oblivion in later times. For instance, two of the most extensive amnesties in English and French history prohibited citizens from remembering all the things that had happened during the preceding civil strife. The general pardon proclaimed by Charles II in the aftermath of the English Civil War prescribed that, in order 'to bury all Seeds of future Discords and Remembrance' of the war, all crimes committed since its start would be 'pardoned, released, indemnified, discharged and put in utter Oblivion'.[15] In France, the Edict of Nantes concluding the last religious war of the sixteenth century similarly ordered the erasure of everything that had occurred during past conflicts.[16] It also provided that people infringing this command would be punished as disrupters of the public peace.

Christian Wolff and Emer de Vattel, two eminent jurists and philosophers of the eighteenth century, described amnesty as 'complete and lasting forgetfulness of wrongs and offences previously committed' or 'perfect oblivion of the past'.[17] These definitions reflect the ancient conception of amnesty as a legal form of amnesia imposed with respect to past wrongs. Modern amnesties, however, though still designed to extinguish the penal consequences of past crimes, generally do not provide for a duty of oblivion. In fact, several recent amnesties have been conditioned on truth-telling or combined with mechanisms aiming to provide a historical record of past crimes and reckon with the suffering of the victims, typically in the form of truth commissions.[18] Forgetfulness is thus no longer an essential feature of contemporary amnesties. As observed by Louise Mallinder, 'the traditional conception of amnesty as "amnesia" is becoming

12 Nicole Loraux, *The Divided City: On Memory and Forgetting in Old Athens* (Zone Books 2002) ch 6.
13 This amnesty is discussed in ch 1 of this volume.
14 Loraux (n 12) 153–54.
15 12 Car.2, c.11 (1660), Statutes at Large.
16 Nantes Edict of 1598, arts 1 and 2. See Michel Rocard, *L'art de la paix, l'édit de Nantes* (Janine Garrisson ed, Atlantica 1997) 25.
17 Christian Wolff, *Jus Gentium Methodo Scientifica pertractatum* (Clarendon Press 1934) 502; Emer de Vattel, *The Law of Nations, Or, Principles of the Law of Nature, Applied to the Conduct and Affairs of Nations and Sovereigns* (Liberty Fund 2008) 664, para 20.
18 The most well-known truth commission was set up in South Africa following the end of apartheid and required applicants to disclose the truth about their crimes to become eligible for amnesty. On truth commissions, see Priscilla B Hayner, *Unspeakable Truths: Transitional Justice and the Challenge of Truth Commissions* (Taylor & Francis 2010). On amnesty as an instrument of truth, see Jeffery (n 1) ch 3.

increasingly outdated. Instead, states are finding innovative ways to address past crimes without burying the truth or enforcing widespread retributive justice'.[19]

Considerable evolutions have been achieved in the last century respecting the ways in which countries in transition from war or dictatorship should address their past, with an emphasis on the need to combat impunity through the prosecution of persons responsible for grave crimes. Nonetheless, amnesties remain commonplace in situations of armed conflict or political turmoil. For instance, between 2015 and 2017, amnesty provisions were included in peace agreements aiming to end conflicts in Ukraine, Colombia, Afghanistan and Libya.[20] During that period, amnesty laws were also passed or suggested in Iraq, Nepal and other countries destabilised by war or civil unrest.[21] In 2018, broad amnesties were adopted in Mali, to encourage the reintegration of rebel fighters, in Côte d'Ivoire, to promote reconciliation among political foes, and in South Sudan, to induce rebel forces to engage in peace negotiations.[22]

While amnesties are still granted at a relatively steady rate, the development of a global accountability policy in recent decades has had an impact on this practice.[23] As policymakers and human rights advocates increasingly call on states not to allow impunity for serious crimes, some recent amnesties were drafted so as to exclude these crimes. For example, the amnesty provision of the Colombian peace agreement made an exception for perpetrators of genocide, crimes against humanity, war crimes and gross human rights violations, among

19 Louise Mallinder, *Amnesty, Human Rights and Political Transitions: Bridging the Peace and Justice Divide* (Hart Publishing 2008) 14.

20 Package of Measures for the Implementation of the Minsk Agreements (Ukraine-Russia), 12 February 2015, s 5; Final Agreement for Ending the Conflict and Building a Stable and Lasting Peace (Colombia), 24 November 2016, ch 5, item 5.1.2 (II) paras 23–27; Peace deal between the government of Afghanistan and Hezb-i-Islami, 29 September 2016, art 9; Ceasefire agreement between Libya's Prime Minister Fayez al-Sarraj and General Khalifa Haftar, 25 July 2017, art 1.

21 Sara al-Qaher, 'Iraqi Parliament approves controversial amnesty law' *Al Monitor* (30 August 2016); Human Rights Watch, 'Nepal: 9-Point Deal Undermines Transitional Justice, Annul Clemency for Grave Crimes' (12 May 2016); Aislinn Laing, 'Nigeria's Buhari suggests Boko Haram amnesty for Chibok girls' *The Telegraph* (16 September 2015); 'Burkina Faso: Proposition d'amnistie des putschistes' *@rib news* (29 September 2015); 'Burundi: Nkurunziza promet l'amnistie aux insurgés qui se rendront d'ici cinq jours' *Jeune Afrique* (2 November 2015).

22 'Mali adopts "national consensus" law' *News24* (1 June 2018); 'Côte d'Ivoire: le président Ouattara annonce l'amnistie de Simone Gbagbo' *Le Monde* (6 August 2018); Denis Dumo, 'South Sudan president Kiir grants Machar, other rebels amnesty' *Reuters* (9 August 2018).

23 On the global accountability policy, see Kathryn Sikkink, 'The Age of Accountability: The Global Rise of Individual Criminal Accountability' in Francesca Lessa and Leigh A Payne (eds), *Amnesty in the Age of Human Rights Accountability: Comparative and International Perspectives* (CUP 2012); Kathryn Sikkink, *The Justice Cascade: How Human Rights Prosecutions Are Changing World Politics* (WW Norton 2012); Ellen Lutz and Kathryn Sikkink, 'The Justice Cascade: The Evolution and Impact of Foreign Human Rights Trials in Latin America' (2001) 2 *Chicago Journal of International Law* 1.

other crimes.[24] Although broad and unlimited amnesties continue to be issued, they are regularly condemned by human rights bodies, organisations and agencies. For instance, the UN Special Rapporteur on extrajudicial, summary or arbitrary executions expressed concern regarding the broad amnesty provision included in the peace agreement for Ukraine.[25] With respect to a prison release in Mali, the representative of the High Commissioner for Human Rights stressed that '[a]mnesties that prevent the prosecution of individuals who may be legally responsible for war crimes, crimes against humanity and gross violations of human rights are inconsistent with States' obligations under various sources of international law'.[26]

Claims contesting the validity of amnesties on the basis of international law have arisen relatively recently, partly because the power to enact such measures has traditionally been understood as a sovereign prerogative of states lying beyond the reach of international law. Before the emergence of an international movement against impunity in the 1990s, the mechanism of amnesty was also seen in a rather positive light. It was used as a rallying call for the release of political prisoners, prompting a non-governmental human rights organisation to choose this name in the 1960s. The humanitarian role of amnesty following internal armed conflicts was notably recognised in Article 6(5) of the Second Protocol Additional to the Geneva Conventions.[27] Its potential as a safeguard against the death penalty was also acknowledged in Article 6(4) of the International Covenant on Civil and Political Rights.[28] Further back in time, in the early modern period, amnesty was described by prominent publicists as the 'leading article' of peace treaties because of its function in ensuring that the causes for which war had been waged were permanently extinguished between the belligerents.[29]

The book explores these stages in the evolution of international opinion and practice on amnesty. As the mechanism itself and general perceptions of its utility and desirability have changed over time, the first part of the book investigates the history of amnesty, from ancient times to the present day. This historical inquiry aims to provide perspective on the contemporary international law debate on the acceptability of amnesty for serious crimes. It shows how the

24 Final Agreement for Ending the Conflict and Building a Stable and Lasting Peace (n 20) Chapter 5, item 5.1.2 (II) para 40.

25 UN Office of the High Commissioner for Human Rights, 'End of visit statement of the Special Rapporteur on extrajudicial, summary or arbitrary executions, Christof Heyns, Ukraine: Lives lost in an accountability vacuum' (18 September 2015).

26 UN News Centre, 'Mali: UN alarmed at release of human rights abusers; warns de facto amnesty contrary to international law' (11 August 2015).

27 Protocol Additional to the Geneva Conventions of 12 August 1949 relating to the Protection of Victims of Non-International Armed Conflicts (adopted 8 June 1977, entered into force 7 December 1978) 1125 UNTS 609.

28 International Covenant on Civil and Political Rights (adopted 16 December 1966, entered into force 23 March 1976) 999 UNTS 171.

29 See Wolff (n 17) 502; de Vattel (n 17) 664; Jean Louis Klüber, *Droit des gens moderne de l'Europe* (Librairie de J G Cotta, Stuttgart 1819, vol 1) 500–501.

mechanism has evolved and adapted to different time periods and types of societies. While its inherent features have remained unchanged, notwithstanding the varied forms it is susceptible to take, some of its characteristics have altered in accordance with social, political and legal developments.

Chapter 1 traces the origins and evolution of amnesty traditions in ancient societies. It reviews the contexts into which, and reasons for which, amnesties were used in the past in order to assess whether there is a degree of continuity between ancient and modern amnesties. Chapter 2 focuses on the practice of including amnesty clauses in European peace treaties from the late Middle Ages to the early twentieth century. It examines the transition from this amnesty tradition to the accountability paradigm which emerged in connection with the two world wars and underpins the current prohibitive stance of the international community towards amnesties. Whether international standards and practice are likely to evolve towards the consolidation of a general amnesty prohibition, or to allow for a more nuanced and context-specific approach, is one of the questions explored in the book.

Chapter 3 makes the transition between the historical analysis and the core part of the book considering the position of international law on amnesties. It defines amnesties and provides a global perspective on how they have been used in the recent past. It then introduces a typology of modern amnesties classifying them in two broad categories, depending on their context of adoption, and looking at the moral dilemmas to which they are associated in such contexts, explaining their controversial nature. To illustrate the diversity of amnesties, this chapter reviews a number of emblematic cases studies from different parts of the world.

The question underlying the book is whether a norm of international law prohibits the granting of amnesty for serious crimes of international concern. Answering it necessitates an analysis of the primary sources of international law as identified in article 38 of the Statute of the International Court of Justice (ICJ).[30] The most straightforward way for an amnesty prohibition to become part of international law would be through the adoption of an international convention to that effect.[31] Whereas no such instrument was adopted, it has been argued that certain treaties implicitly rule out amnesties by imposing on states obligations incompatible with these measures. The other main source of international law through which an amnesty prohibition might emerge is customary international law, defined as 'evidence of a general practice accepted as law'.[32] Establishing the existence of a customary norm would require the proof of an

30 Statute of the International Court of Justice, Annex to the Charter of the United Nations (adopted 26 June 1945, entered into force 24 October 1945) 1 UNTS XVI (ICJ Statute) art 38.

31 This was done with respect to statutory limitations through the Convention on the Non-Applicability of Statutory Limitations to War Crimes and Crimes against Humanity (adopted 26 November 1968, entered into force 11 November 1970) 754 UNTS 73.

32 ICJ Statute (n 30) art 38.

'extensive and virtually uniform' state practice, as well as the corresponding *opinio juris* of states, i.e. their belief that they are legally bound to follow the practice in question.[33] According to article 38, 'judicial decisions and the teachings of the most highly qualified publicists of the various nations' are subsidiary means to determine the existence and content of an international norm.[34]

Whether treaty law, customary law, judicial decisions and academic commentaries point to the existence of a general amnesty ban is examined in the second part of the book assessing the legality of amnesties in the contemporary international order. Each of the last four chapters considers one legal argument supporting the view that amnesties are prohibited with respect to serious crimes. These chapters are based on an analysis of different types of primary and secondary sources, including international conventions and their preparatory works, state practice, peace agreements, policy documents, expert guidelines, judicial decisions, qualitative and quantitative studies. They proceed in a chronological fashion in order to highlight possible changes over time in the position of global, regional and domestic actors regarding the acceptability of amnesty for serious crimes.

Chapter 4 addresses the argument deriving from the existence of international obligations to prosecute perpetrators of international crimes. Several multilateral treaties proscribe certain crimes of international concern and require states parties to prosecute the persons allegedly responsible. On the one hand, it is largely accepted that the grant of an amnesty would be incompatible with these prosecutorial obligations. On the other hand, states have avoided the issue of amnesty during the negotiation of international treaties, indicating a lack of consensus in this respect. The chapter analyses the content and drafting history of international conventions imposing prosecutorial requirements or bearing on the issue of amnesty. It also discusses whether a duty to prosecute international crimes may be derived from customary international law or from the *jus cogens* status of these crimes.

Chapter 5 examines the argument based on international standards and recent trends in state practice towards the limitation of amnesties. It traces the evolution of the UN position on amnesties, from a permissive approach to a strict rejection of any type of amnesty covering international crimes or serious human rights violations. It then investigates whether the practice of states and international organisations has tended to conform to these standards. On the basis of an original Peace Agreement Amnesties Database, it assesses whether amnesty provisions included in peace agreements have excluded serious crimes in the last few decades. It also reviews how amnesty laws covering serious crimes have been challenged at the domestic level and whether national

33 International Court of Justice, *North Sea Continental Shelf Cases* (Federal Republic of Germany v Denmark/ Federal Republic of Germany v Netherlands) (Merits) [1969] ICJ Rep 3, para 74.

34 ICJ Statute (n 30) art 38.

authorities have responded to these challenges by repealing, restricting or upholding the impugned measure.

Chapter 6 discusses the argument linked to the right to a remedy of victims of human rights violations. General human rights treaties require states to give effect to human rights and ensure that victims of serious violations have access to a remedy. On these bases, human rights courts and bodies have considered that states must investigate violations of fundamental rights and, in some cases, prosecute the persons responsible. Accordingly, human rights bodies have concurred on the view that amnesties preventing the investigation of serious human rights violations are contrary to international human rights law. However, they have diverged as regards the rationale of this rule and the question of whether it is absolute or admits exceptions in special circumstances. The chapter analyses their case law in order to ascertain the contours of the emerging amnesty ban in human rights law.

Chapter 7 considers the argument based on the mandate of international criminal courts to prosecute persons accused of international crimes. Some of these courts are explicitly required by their statute not to recognise amnesty as an obstacle to their jurisdiction. Besides express statutory provisions, other grounds support the view that amnesties cannot be effective in depriving international criminal bodies of jurisdiction over perpetrators of international crimes. The chapter analyses the case law of ad hoc criminal courts having been confronted with amnesty challenges and the developing approach of the International Criminal Court. It identifies the reasons on the basis of which these bodies have refused to defer to amnesty laws and what they imply as regards the international legality of amnesties in relation to international crimes.

The book argues that, while certain international legal or policy requirements restrict the freedom of states to extend amnesty with respect to serious crimes, or the effectiveness of amnesty laws in preventing the prosecution of such crimes, these restrictions do not add up to an absolute and universal prohibition. Indeed, each of these requirements and restrictions is subject to some nuances or qualifications, leaving room for certain types of amnesties to be found acceptable in compelling circumstances – such as when they are necessary as part of a peace, reconciliation or democratisation process – even though they cover serious crimes. While broad and unconditional amnesties are unlikely to be given any form of international recognition with respect to international crimes, some international actors seem prepared to accept that, in societies emerging from periods of mass violence, limited or conditional amnesties adhering to certain criteria and forming part of a broader transitional strategy may be admissible.

Part 1

The use of amnesties from antiquity to today

1 Ancient amnesties

Introduction

Amnesty has been used for millennia in diverse types of societies, the malleable nature of the mechanism having permitted its adaptation to different historical periods and legal systems. While ancient amnesties varied in terms of their name, form and characteristics in different civilisations, they were largely issued for the same range of purposes. This chapter examines their main features and the reasons for which they were adopted in order to assess whether there is some continuity between ancient and modern amnesties. The first section explores the origins of the mechanism in pharaonic Egypt, classical Athens, the Roman world and ancient China. The second section traces the development of similar amnesty traditions in France and England throughout the second millennium. It also reviews early clemency practices in the United States. The last section presents a typology of ancient amnesties identifying their common features and classifying them in different categories depending on their object and purpose.

1. The origins of amnesty

This section examines how the mechanism of amnesty was used in ancient civilisations in Egypt, Athens, Rome and China. These early forms of clemency are at the root of the modern notion of amnesty and have shaped the ways in which the mechanism was used in later times.

Early Egyptian amnesties

The most ancient amnesty provision of which we have some records was part of a treaty of peace concluded by Ramesses II, Pharaoh of Egypt, and Hattusili, King of Hatti, in the aftermath of the battle of Kadesh.[1] Following a military campaign

1 Langdon and Alan H Gardiner, 'The Treaty of Alliance between Hattusili, King of the Hittites, and the Pharaoh Ramesses II of Egypt' (1920) 6(3) *The Journal of Egyptian Archaeology* 179. See also Andrea O'Shea, *Amnesty for Crime in International Law and Practice* (Kluwer Law International 2002) 5.

in Syria, Ramesses II undertook the invasion of Kadesh, a mighty city of the Hatti kingdom. The ensuing battle between the Egyptian and Hittite armies did not have any conclusive result, so that animosity subsisted between the two nations for several years.[2] This period of antagonism was brought to an end by the conclusion of one of the first recorded international peace treaties.

Historians have placed the battle of Kadesh in 1296 BC and the subsequent peace treaty in 1280 BC.[3] The agreement's first operative clauses stated that the Egyptian and Hittite sovereigns would renew peaceful relations and grant each other mutual assistance in cases of invasion or rebellion.[4] The treaty also provided for the mutual extradition of fugitives and the amnesty of extradited people.[5] The amnesty provision was translated as follows:

> If one man flee from the land of Egypt, or two, or three, and they come to the great chief of Hatti, the great chief of Hatti shall seize them and shall cause them to be brought back to [Ramses], the great ruler of Egypt. But as for the man who shall be brought to [Ramses], the great ruler of Egypt, let not his crime be charged against him, let not his house, his wives or his children be destroyed, [let him not] be [killed], let no injury be done to his eyes, to his ears, to his mouth or to his legs, let not any [crime be charged] against him.
>
> Likewise, if a man flee from the land of Hatti, be he one, be he two, or be he three, and they come to [Ramses], the great ruler of Egypt, let [Ramses], the [great] ruler [of Egypt, cause] them to be brought to the great chief of Hatti, and the great chief of Hatti shall not charge their crime against them, and they shall not destroy his house, his wives or his children, and they shall not kill him, and they shall not do injury to his ears, to his eyes, to his mouth or to his legs, and they shall not charge any crime against him.[6]

Another amnesty was declared in Egypt in the period between 1166 and 1160 BC, supposedly to celebrate the accession of Ramesses IV to the throne.[7] The part of the paean containing it has been translated as follows:

> A beautiful day! Heaven and Earth rejoice, for Thou are the great Lord of Egypt. Those who had fled have returned to their home-towns; those who were in hiding have come forth. The hungry are sated and rejoice, the thirsty are drunk. The naked are clothed in fine linen, the ragged wear fair garments. Those who were in bonds are free again; those who were in chains rejoice.

2 For an account of the Kadesh battle, see Barbara Mertz, *Temples, Tombs and Hieroglyphs, A Popular History of Ancient Egypt* (Brockhampton Press 1999) 266–72.
3 Langdon and Gardiner (n 1) 201–205.
4 Ibid, 187–191.
5 Ibid, 192–98.
6 Ibid, 197–98.
7 H S Smith, 'A Note on Amnesty' (1968) 54 *The Journal of Egyptian Archaeology* 209, 212.

> The rebels in this land are become free men once more. High Niles are come forth from their caverns and make glad the heart of the people.[8]

In the Ptolemaic period (305–30 BC), amnesties were proclaimed 'at the beginnings of periods when a new reign or new dynastic arrangements held the promise of peaceful and beneficent rule succeeding internal strife'.[9] Four amnesties promulgated in this period have been identified: the first granted by Ptolemy V in 197 BC to celebrate his anniversary, the second by Ptolemy VI in 163 BC to reconcile the divided royal family, the third by Ptolemy VIII in 145–144 BC after a period of unrest linked to the death of Ptolemy VI, and the last by the same pharaoh in 118 BC in an attempt to end the continuing dynastic strife.[10] An extract of the last of these measures illustrates how Ptolemaic amnesties were formulated:

> King Ptolemy and Queen Cleopatra the Sister and Queen Cleopatra the Wife proclaim an amnesty to all their subjects for errors, crimes, accusations, condemnations, and charges of all kinds up to year 52, 9 Pharmouthi, except to persons guilty of wilful murder or sacrilege. And they have decreed that persons who have gone into hiding because they were guilty of theft or subject to other charges shall return to their homes and resume their former occupations, and their remaining property shall not be sold.[11]

It thus appears that amnesty was an accepted, if not common, practice in pharaonic Egypt. The mechanism was principally used for celebration, pacification and reconciliation purposes on certain festive occasions or in connection with periods of war or unrest. Under the Ptolemaic dynasty, amnesties were proclaimed by the sovereigns among a list of royal boons as a way of discharging their duty towards their people to rule benevolently and keep the peace.[12] Some of these amnesties excluded certain crimes on account of their gravity, as shown in the extract quoted above.

Amnesty in classical Athens

Historians have identified traces of five Athenian amnesties in the writings of Plutarch, Andocides, Isocrates, Aristotle and Xenophon.[13] These measures were

8 Ibid.
9 Ibid, 210.
10 Ibid, 209–10.
11 Ibid, 210.
12 Ibid.
13 Nicole Loraux, *The Divided City: On Memory and Forgetting in Old Athens* (Zone Books 2002); Alfred P Dorjahn, *Political Forgiveness in Old Athens: The Amnesty of 403 B.C.* (Northwestern University Studies in the Humanities No 13, Evanston 1946); Thomas Loening, *The Reconciliation Agreement of 403/402 B.C. in Athens: Its Content and Application* (Steiner, Stuttgart 1987); NGL Hammond, *A History of Greece to 322 B.C.* (3rd edn, Clarendon Press 1986); Peter Krentz, *The Thirty at Athens* (Cornell University Press 1982);

all enacted in times of national emergency, when the Athenian city-state was threatened by a foreign attack or internal disturbances. They were used as a political expedient to reunite and strengthen the nation before, during or after an armed conflict or civil strife.

The earliest of these amnesties was issued by Solon, whose archonship has been placed in the period between 594 and 590 BC.[14] He was mandated to draw up a new legal code and reform the Athenian system in order to resolve deep-seated economic and social tensions threatening to provoke a civil war. One of Solon's laws, as preserved by Plutarch, offered amnesty to disfranchised citizens with certain exceptions:

> All such as have been banished or detected of naughty life, before Solon made his laws, shall be restored again to their goods and good name, except those which were condemned by order of the council of the Aeropagites, or by the Ephetes, or by the king in open court, for murder, and death of any man, or for aspiring to usurp tyranny.[15]

One century later, shortly before the battle of Salamis against the Persian army (480 BC), an amnesty was granted by the archon Themistocles to Athenian exiles.[16] From the speeches of Andocides subsists an account of this amnesty:

> When Xerxes, the king of Persia, set out on his now famous expedition against Greece, the Athenians became alarmed at the magnitude of his preparations and the dangers threatening them. Consequently, they decided to recall their exiles and to reinstate them in all their civic rights, giving all an equal share in the common duties as well as in the common dangers. Thereupon they exchanged pledges and swore sacred oaths. Relying on their valor, the Athenians placed themselves in the forefront of all the Greeks and encountered the Persians at Marathon. After they had achieved this glorious victory, they did not think it proper to remember old wrongs. Although they found their city ravaged, the temples burned, and the walls and houses destroyed, yet, because of the concord among them, they acquired sovereignty over the Greeks and handed down to posterity a great and beautiful city.[17]

At the end of the Peloponnesian war (431–404 BC), Athens was threatened again by Lysander, a Spartan commander whose army besieged the city after

Gertrude Smith, 'The Prytanaeum in the Athenian Amnesty Law' (1921) 14 *Classical Philology* 345; Smith (n 7).

14 Ivan M Linforth, *Solon the Athenian* (University of California Press 1919) 27 and 46–72.

15 Eighth law of the thirteenth table of the laws of Solon, see RF Patterson (ed), *Plutarch's Lives of Solon and Nicias* (Blackie and Son Limited 1930) 39.

16 Dorjahn (n 13) 2–3; Smith, 'A Note on Amnesty' (n 7) 209; Smith, 'The Prytanaeum in the Athenian Amnesty Law' (n 13) 345.

17 Dorjahn (n 13) 2.

having destroyed the Athenian fleet at Aegospotami in 405 BC.[18] On this occasion, the archon Patrocleides extended an amnesty to disfranchised citizens, with certain exceptions, in order to reinforce the Athenian military capacity.[19] This measure did not save Athens from defeat. Following the Spartan victory, Lysander issued an amnesty recalling the very individuals who had been excluded from the decree of Patrocleides on account of their allegiance to Sparta.[20] Lysander's amnesty was very extensive and permitted the return of numerous partisans of oligarchy.

The most famous Athenian amnesty was granted in the aftermath of the civil war that opposed the oligarch rulers installed by Sparta to the Athenian democrats. After the capitulation of Athens in 404 BC, marking the end of the Peloponnesian war, Lysander established a provisional oligarchic government in the city. Thirty men were appointed to administer it, revise the laws and draw up a new constitution.[21] They were bestowed with extensive power and, from the way they exercised it, came to be called the 'Thirty Tyrants'. During the short period of their rule, they executed hundreds and banished thousands of citizens, the majority of whom fled to Thebes or neighbouring Piraeus.[22]

Under the leadership of Thrasybulus, a democrat Athenian commander, the refugees regrouped at Piraeus where, from the hill of Munichya, they successfully repelled Spartan and Athenian assailants.[23] Following the battle of Munichya, the oligarchic city party was divided into two clans. Whereas the Thirty and their followers migrated to the satellite city of Eleusis, the moderates stayed in Athens and elected a new board of ten men to represent them. Meanwhile, the Spartan King Pausania instituted himself as mediator of the conflict and succeeded in reconciling the moderates of the city with the exiled democrats. A peace agreement was negotiated between them providing for the establishment of two separate states in Attica: one at Eleusis where the supporters of the Thirty would emigrate, and the other at Athens where the democrats and moderates would form a government.[24]

The reconciliation agreement of 403 BC extended a general amnesty in the form of a ban on 'recalling the misfortunes of the past', solemnised through the swearing of individual oaths by all Athenian citizens ('I shall not recall the misfortunes').[25] Those performing a public function pledged a specific oath: for instance, senators promised not to conduct trials in conflict with the amnesty.[26] While the benefits of the amnesty were extended to all citizens,

18 Ibid, 3–4; Hammond (n 13) 417–18.
19 Ibid; Loening (n 13) 41; Smith (n 7) 2.
20 Dorjahn (n 13) 4–5.
21 Hammond (n 13) 443–44; Krentz (n 13) 48–56 and 78–82.
22 Ibid.
23 Hammond (n 13) 444–45; Krentz (n 13) 89–93; Dorjahn (n 13) 17–18.
24 Hammond (n 13) 446; Krenz (n 13) 102–103; Loening (n 13) 30–34.
25 Loraux (n 13) 141, 146 and 149.
26 Dorjahn (n 13) 12 and 34.

a clause of the treaty specified that the Thirty could only avail themselves of it after having accounted for their actions before the Athenian juries.[27] The amnesty sealed the reconciliation between the two rival factions and ensured continuity in the city-state through the rehabilitation of former agents of oligarchy.[28] For instance, after having submitted himself to account, the former oligarch Rhinon was reinstated and ultimately became general of the Athenian army.[29]

Athenian leaders relied on different methods to guarantee the effectiveness of the amnesty. Thrasybulus and the moderate politician Archinus regularly exhorted citizens to abide by their oath. Aristotle recounted that the latter convinced the Senate to put to death a man who had acted against the spirit of the amnesty, so that 'nobody afterwards ever remembered old wrongs'.[30] Archinus also instituted a special plea enabling persons accused in violation of the amnesty to oppose the illegal action.[31] If this preliminary objection was sustained, the original action was declared inadmissible and the plaintiff was condemned to a fine. On a more symbolic level, in order to mark the erasure of the memory of the civil war and impress clemency in the Athenian subconscious, the anniversary day of the conflict was removed from the calendar and an altar was raised to Lethe – the Greek goddess of oblivion – on the Acropolis.[32]

A contemporary of the amnesty process, Isocrates recalled that '[a]fter we came together and exchanged the solemn pledges, we have lived so uprightly and so like citizens of one country that it seemed as if no misfortune has ever befallen us'.[33] The stability that endured in Athens for several decades after the conclusion of the treaty has been seen as an indicator of the success of the amnesty. The choice of the democrats to emphasise reconciliation and focus on the reconstitution of the city, rather than dwelling on past wrongs, has been praised by many classical and modern commentators. Aristotle wrote that Athenian democrats 'used their past misfortunes in the most beautiful and most civic manner'.[34] More recently, Balogh observed that:

> We are here concerned with the first amnesty in the Greek world that was as perfect in both form and content as could be. It achieved a new harmony amongst the people of Athens, torn by passion and hatred. Wherever it may

27 Loraux (n 13) 150 and 152; Hammond (n 13) 446; Krentz (n 13) 102–103; Dorjahn (n 13) 34; Loening (n 13) 30–34 and 40–49.

28 Loraux (n 13) 148 and 150.

29 Ibid; Dorjahn (n 13) 37–38; Loening (n 13) 99–102.

30 Dorjahn (n 13) 37–38; Loening (n 13) 99–102; Loraux (n 13) 152.

31 Dorjahn (n 13) 37–38; Loening (n 13) 99; Loraux (n 13) 128.

32 Loraux (n 13) 15 and 153–54.

33 Ibid, 153.

34 Ibid.

be necessary to restore civic peace in a state after revolutions and counter-revolutions, this Greek example should be considered and imitated![35]

Roman clemency

In the Roman world, legal institutions of clemency started to be developed at the beginning of the Principate, in the first century BC.[36] Before that, clemency was mostly exercised on the battlefield as a tool to reduce wartime violence and an incentive to induce opponents to surrender. The extension of clemency to defeated forces became a common, though discretionary, practice of Roman military commanders in the third century BC.[37] It consisted in setting the enemy people free in exchange for an acknowledgement of their submission and allegiance to Rome. Julius Caesar often granted clemency to conquered barbarians during his campaigns in Gaul.[38] This practice conformed to the Roman conception of clemency implying the lower status of the recipient and his eternal debt to the grantor. Caesar expanded this notion by offering clemency to Pompey's defeated troops and allies in the context of the civil war that opposed both consuls. Although the rank and file received his mercy with gratitude, some circles of the elite perceived it as an affront. It has been suggested that Caesar's imposition of clemency on his peers was one of the factors that led to his assassination.[39]

In the aftermath of the death of Caesar in 44 BC, Cicero persuaded the Senate to extend an amnesty to his murderers.[40] This measure was intended to appease tensions but it provoked more disorder as a substantial part of the population and the army was hostile to Caesar's assassins and to the Senate. Caesar's adoptive son, Octavian, proclaimed himself as his father's avenger and formed a triumvirate with Mark Antony and Lepidus in 43 BC. With the support of the army, he forced the Senate to override the amnesty decree and enact a law condemning the murderers. The triumvirs then engaged in a retaliatory war against the republicans and defeated most of their forces at Philippi in 42 BC.[41] Following the deaths of Cassius and Brutus, the conspiracy's leaders, Octavian and Mark Antony adopted a more lenient policy and granted amnesty to most republican soldiers and supporters. In 39 BC, a

35 Elemér Balogh, *Political Refugees in Ancient Greece, From the Period of the Tyrants to Alexander the Great* (Witwatersrand University Press 1943) 63.

36 Jacques Foviaux, *La rémission des peines et des condamnations: Droit monarchique et droit moderne* (Presses Universitaires de France, Paris 1970) 21–23.

37 Melissa Barden Dowling, *Clemency and Cruelty in the Roman World* (University of Michigan Press 2006) 17.

38 Ibid, 20–26.

39 Ibid, 33.

40 Ibid, 31–32; Foviaux (n 36) 24.

41 Dowling (n 37) 45.

general amnesty was finally offered to all those who had not yet benefited from the triumvirs' clemency.[42]

Octavian became the first Roman Emperor, or Princeps, Augustus. In the first years of his reign, he adopted clemency policies on different levels in order to heal past divisions and restore harmony in the Roman nation.[43] He thus established himself as a merciful and considerate monarch. These qualities gave rise to a tradition entailing the pardon of all prisoners upon Augustus' entry into Rome. During the Augustan period, the Roman frontiers were considerably expanded. It was an era of great optimism as it was believed that the Roman armies could conquer the whole world. Clemency was a crucial part of Rome's imperialist policies as it permitted the peaceful incorporation of new populations into the empire.[44] The Roman poet Virgil, a contemporary of Augustus, described clemency as an essential element of Rome's greatness and one of the two pillars upon which rested the empire, together with conquest.[45]

The transformation of clemency from a wartime expedient to a peacetime central quality was operated during the first years of the Roman Empire. Representations of the Princeps' clemency started to appear on coins, in temples, and on artistic and popular objects.[46] Images of Augustus also came to be legally recognised as places of asylum.[47] During that period, some legal institutions of clemency started to be developed or refined in the judicial sphere, such as *indulgentia* and *venia*.[48] The concept of *indulgentia*, originally a broad notion encompassing diverse manifestations of kindness, came to be associated with individual or collective measures of grace granted by the Emperor to annul the effect of an indictment or condemnation.[49] *Venia*, for its part, evolved as a category of measures activated in the courts when equity warranted a more lenient treatment than the strict application of the law.[50] *Abolitio* emerged later on as a legal action capable of terminating all judicial proceedings. The *abolitiones publicae*, in particular, corresponded to general amnesties and were often granted as part of religious festivities and imperial celebrations.[51]

Augustus' successor, Tiberius, perpetuated the clemency tradition in public life and on the battlefield.[52] Caligula and Nero, however, refused to embrace the dominant clemency ethic, rather leaning towards severity or cruelty.[53] At the beginning

42 Ibid, 52–54.
43 Ibid, 72–74.
44 Ibid.
45 Ibid, 105.
46 Ibid, ch 4.
47 Ibid, 161–62.
48 Foviaux (n 36) 21–27.
49 Ibid; Dowling (n 37) 64–66.
50 Ibid; Dowling (n 37) 239–42.
51 Foviaux (n 36) 24–26.
52 Dowling (n 37) 170–81.
53 Ibid, 189–213.

of Nero's reign, the Roman elite manifested particular interest in the young Emperor's merciful dispositions. In his philosophical essay 'De Clementia', Seneca the Younger, Nero's tutor, sought to demonstrate to his pupil that it was in the interest of a ruler to behave clemently:

> So clemency does not just bring rulers more honour but greater safety too. It is the glory of empires at the same time as being their surest means of protection. After all, why does it happen that kings get to grow old and to hand on their kingdoms to their children and grandchildren, but that the power of tyrants is accursed and short-lived? … it is clemency that makes the significant difference between the king and the tyrant, even though each of them is fenced around by weapons to the same degree. But the one uses the weapons which he possesses to protect the peace, the other possesses weapons to curb great hatred with great terror – and yet he does not look with any confidence on the very hands to which he has entrusted himself.[54]

Seneca developed compelling arguments to promote clemency as an essential virtue and challenge the classical Stoic argument presenting mercy as a retreat from justice:

> Clemency has a freedom of decision. It forms its judgments not according to the letter of the law but according to what is right and good. And it is allowed to acquit or to set the damages in a case at any level it likes. It does none of these things with the attitude that its action is less than justice requires but with the attitude that its decision is the most just course of action possible.[55]

However, his advice did not have much impact on the conduct of the grown-up Emperor, whose reign has been associated with tyranny and ended in suicide. In the decades following Nero's death, the merciful character of the sovereign remained an important indicator of his fitness to rule in public opinion and emperors continued to advertise their clemency through their coinage, constructions and proclamations.[56] While some of Nero's successors have been known for their cruelty, like Domitian and Commodus, other Roman emperors like Trajan and Gallienus adopted an open policy of clemency.[57]

In the third century AD, as the Senate, the magistrates and popular assemblies were gradually deprived of their judicial authority, the power of clemency became the sole prerogative of the Roman emperor.[58] The Christian Church nevertheless

54 Susanna Braud, *Seneca: De Clementia* (Oxford University Press 2009) 115.
55 Ibid, 151.
56 Dowling (n 37) ch 6.
57 Ibid, 220–69.
58 Foviaux (n 36) 25–26; Pierre Duparc, *Origines de la grâce dans le droit pénal romain et français du Bas-Empire à la Renaissance* (Librairie du Recueil Sirey, Paris 1942) 24–25.

retained a right of intercession in favour of criminals who took refuge in places of worship and it exerted a growing influence on Roman emperors.[59] Accordingly, during the fourth century, general amnesties were regularly offered to celebrate religious events, particularly on the occasion of Easter (*abolitio paschalis*). In the late Roman Empire, the terms *indulgentia generalis, venia generalis* and *abolitio generalis* were variably used to refer to general amnesties.[60] These collective acts of grace were often issued for pacification purposes following rebellion or civil unrest. For example, Honorius and Arcadius extended a general amnesty to the crisis-torn province of Lycie in 396.[61] Amnesties were also regularly granted on the occasion of imperial festivities. The first Christian Emperor Philip thus proclaimed a general amnesty to celebrate the millennium of the foundation of Rome in 248.[62]

The scope and effect of collective clemency measures were determined by the emperor. Amnesties could be total or partial, with or without retroactive effect and restitution of rights or possessions. Certain crimes were considered as unforgivable, though this varied according to the discretion of every particular emperor.[63] The Church had some influence in this regard and the most systematic lists of unforgivable crimes appeared in the *abolitio paschalis.* Those measures of grace consistently excluded at least four crimes that the Catholic Church regarded as being beyond pardon, i.e. lese-majesty, homicide, adultery and abduction.[64]

Roman institutions of clemency did not disappear after the collapse of the Western Roman Empire in AD 476. The Roman emperors' barbaric successors, notably Franks, Burgundians and Visigoths, continued to apply Roman standards for the regulation of public life and soon exercised a grace prerogative resembling very much its Roman model.[65] The Church played an important role in the preservation of the Roman clemency system.

Great acts of grace in ancient China

For more than a thousand years, amnesties were a prominent feature of the Chinese traditional justice system. The origin of this clemency policy can be traced back to the founding of the Western Chou dynasty in 1027 BC.[66] In ancient China, it was

59 Duparc (n 58) 26–29.
60 Ibid, 31–32; Foviaux (n 36) 26.
61 Duparc (n 58) 32.
62 Ibid.
63 Ibid, 33–36.
64 Ibid.
65 The Visigoth-Roman law (the Alaric's breviary) promulgated in 506 and inspired by Roman codes of law provided for *abolitio publica* and for an equivalent of *venia*, see Duparc (n 58) 38–41.
66 Brian E McKnight, *The Quality of Mercy, Amnesties and Traditional Chinese Justice* (University Press of Hawaii 1981) 2.

believed that if the king behaved in a merciful and benevolent way towards his subjects, they would be encouraged to adopt the same attitude with respect to their inferiors. Pursuant to the Chou's Decree of Heaven theory, as the intermediary between heaven and men, the ruler was mandated to promote the well-being of his subjects. He was to display qualities of justice and mercy in order 'to bring order out of disorder, to cleanse those who had separated themselves from propriety so that they could again participate in the general life'.[67] The proclamation of a general amnesty at the beginning of his reign was a good way for a sovereign to demonstrate his fitness to rule.

In the third century BC, Kao-tsu acceded to the throne as the first Emperor of the Han dynasty (206 BC–220 AD).[68] Establishing a pattern that was to be followed for several centuries, he began his reign by declaring a broad amnesty. Kao-tsu proclaimed eight more general amnesties during his ten-year reign, all of them applicable to the whole Chinese territory. These acts of grace were granted for three types of reasons.[69] First, amnesties were issued in order to mark an event affecting the whole nation, such as the naming of an heir to the throne or the death of a member of the imperial family. Second, some of these measures pursued specific political or military goals, like the enlargement of the national army. Finally, acts of grace were offered to restore peace and tranquillity in regions torn by war or insurrection. For example, in 202 BC, Kao-tsu pardoned all individuals involved in the preceding civil war.

Kao-tsu's successors continued to grant empire wide amnesties at great frequency. With Emperor Ching (157–141 BC), a new cause for the proclamation of acts of grace emerged alongside the development of Han Confucianism.[70] According to this doctrine, closely tied to Chinese cosmology and numerology, human behaviour should be as much as possible in harmony with the natural order. This was especially applicable to the sovereign and high officials whose task was to guide the people. Most amnesties were thus introduced in the spring, the season of growth and life. Acts of grace were also issued in connection with natural phenomena, such as eclipses or earthquakes, with the same intention to conform to the laws of nature and restore the order of things.[71]

67 Ibid, 3.
68 Ibid, 15–16.
69 Ibid, 16–20.
70 Ibid, 21–22.
71 Ibid, 16–19. In the seventh and the eighth century in Japan, general amnesties were similarly frequently issued in connection with the occurrence of auspicious omens and natural phenomena. This practice arose from a Buddhist tradition, the *hojo-e*, which instructed Buddhists to practise regularly the liberation of living beings, see Marinus Willem de Visser, *Ancient Buddhism in Japan Sutras and Ceremonies in Use in the Seventh and Eighth Centuries AD and Their History in Later Times* (Librairie Orientaliste Paul Geuthner, Paris 1928) 197–236.

Every Han emperor and empress issued acts of grace, some of them proclaiming one in every single year of their reign.[72] In ancient China, while the most extensive grants of clemency were called *ta-she*, translating as 'great acts of grace' or general amnesties, ordinary measures of clemency were called *she*, corresponding to amnesties of a more limited scope. Limited amnesties were also issued by the Han dynasty, though less frequently than general ones. Until the end of the T'ang dynasty in 907 AD, there was consistency in the imperial practice of enacting acts of grace.[73] According to McKnight, 'the most striking characteristic [of the clemency system in this period] is continuity rather than change. Whole phrases are passed from dynasty to dynasty'.[74] From 280 to 907 AD, general amnesties were granted on average once every two years.[75] A *ta-she* decree promulgated in 729 by Emperor Hsüan-tsung illustrates the way in which those acts were formulated:

> Now, imperial Heaven has cared for my T'ang. With a worshipful heart I seek to make it prosper for my descendants. As to this good fortune in the receiving of blessings, how could I confine the benefits of such grace to me, the one man? [Such grace] ought to be extended to the whole world. Let a great act of grace be proclaimed to all under Heaven. Let all those liable for crimes committed prior to dawn of the twenty-second day, eleventh month, seventeenth year of K'ai-yuan, without distinguishing whether [their crimes] were serious or not, [whether their crimes] have already been discovered or not, whether [their cases] have been decided or not, including those who would not be freed by an ordinary amnesty, be completely freed.[76]

Great acts of grace in the post-Han era usually applied to the whole empire. Their principal effect was to free all or most criminals, erase their sentence and expunge their criminal record. This was a manifestation of the emperor's power 'to wash people free of their taint', giving them a chance to renew themselves and start afresh.[77] As a consequence, it was prohibited to bring charges against persons who had benefited from a great act of grace, the sanction in the T'ang being the trial of the claimant for the crime specified in the suit.[78] As in the *ta-she* decree quoted above, the benefits of general amnesties were usually available to all criminals without distinguishing on the basis of the gravity of their crime. However, certain great acts of grace explicitly excluded specific crimes.

72 For example, the latter Han emperors Shang-ti, Chung-ti and Shao-ti granted a general amnesty once a year, see McKnight (n 66) 25.

73 Ibid, ch 2.

74 Ibid, 43.

75 Ibid, 71.

76 Ibid, 44–45.

77 Ibid, 48.

78 This practice already existed in the Han period, see McKnight (n 66) 47.

The crimes that were considered as the most serious, which were called the 'Ten Abominations', were sometimes deemed implicitly excluded.[79]

The Sung dynasty (960–1279) perpetuated the clemency tradition by issuing one great act of grace every two years.[80] The emperors of the northern state of Liao who governed north China from 907 to 1125 also issued great acts of grace but less frequently, on average every six or seven years.[81] Subsequent Chinese dynasties followed this new pattern of granting general amnesties on a more exceptional basis. Under the last dynasty, the Ch'ing (1644–1912), the clemency policy was further limited by the criminal code which listed a long series of unforgivable crimes that were to be excluded from imperial acts of grace.[82]

What remained of the clemency system in the fourteenth to the nineteenth century is not comparable to what existed during the preceding millennium in the Chinese Empire:

> A great empire which opened the gates of its jails every few years, forgave those uncaught, wiped all outstanding cases from the books, dismissed those in process of trial, pardoned men sentenced to death, and often sent home its exiles.[83]

The clemency system that evolved in China from the third century BC to the thirteenth century AD is quite unique in the great leniency it exhibited towards criminals. Its ideological, philosophical and religious underpinnings partly explain why it was developed and how it worked as such. Still, it is difficult to imagine how a system which released its criminals every other year could have been functional. Yet, according to McKnight, 'the system worked to an astonishing degree most of the time'.[84]

2. Western clemency traditions

This section traces the history of the French, English and American systems of clemency. Beyond terminological differences, the mechanisms forming part of these systems were very similar in terms of their rationale, scope and effect. Analogies may also be drawn between the ways in which the executive and legislative powers of these countries struggled for the control of the clemency prerogative.

79 The Ten Abominations referred to the crimes of plotting rebellion, plotting great sedition, plotting treason, contumacy, depravity, great irreverence, lack of filial piety, discord, unrighteousness and incest, see ibid, 60.

80 Ibid, 75.

81 Ibid, 94–96.

82 Ibid, 109–10.

83 Ibid, 112.

84 Ibid.

The power of grace in France

Early Frankish dynasties

From the fall of the Roman Empire to the twelfth century, Merovingian kings and their Carolingian successors reigned over France. Under these Frankish dynasties, acts of grace could be granted by the king, the Roman Catholic Church and certain non-royal authorities.[85] The Alaric's Breviary, a Visigoth-Roman law of AD 506 providing for *abolitio publica* and other Roman measures of clemency, was spread throughout Europe in the sixth and seventh centuries.[86] It inspired subsequent French compilations such as the Epitome Monachi, issued in the eighth century, which referred to Easter amnesties (*abolitio paschalis*).

The Church still exerted a great deal of influence in this period and it worked for the conservation of Roman clemency traditions. While collective acts of grace were regularly granted on the occasion of religious festivities, individual pardons were often granted following clerical intercession.[87] Beyond the sphere of influence of the Church, but still in continuity with Roman emperors, early French kings proclaimed general amnesties to celebrate royal events and consolidate peace after internal revolts. For example, Louis the Pious granted an amnesty to insurgents in 831 and Charles the Bald offered a general amnesty to the refractory people of Aquitaine in 856. Starting in the reign of Charles the Bald (840–877), there was a gradual weakening of the monarchical power and, along with the collapse of central and regional authorities, the justice system disintegrated.[88] The king, unable to maintain order and ensure justice, lost his power of grace. As a result, private vengeance arrangements became the norm up to the end of the eleventh century.[89]

Centralisation of the clemency power

Central and regional authorities were restored in the twelfth century and the justice system was reorganised under the influence of Roman law, still propagated by the Church. The reunion of these conditions brought about the reappearance of the power of grace, originally shared by the king with secular and ecclesiastic authorities as well as municipal magistrates.[90] However, while the king rapidly extended the scope of his clemency power to the whole kingdom, the power of the lords remained limited to their area of jurisdiction.[91]

85 Duparc (n 58) 38–60; Foviaux (n 36) 30–31.
86 Duparc (n 58) 41–51.
87 Ibid.
88 Foviaux (n 36) 31.
89 Ibid; Duparc (n 58) 54–59.
90 Duparc (n 58) 60–77.
91 Ibid; Jacques Monteil, *La grâce en droit français moderne* (Librairies techniques, Paris 1959) 15.

French kings often granted collective graces as part of religious or royal festivities.[92] In continuity with the Augustan period, from the thirteenth century onwards it became a royal custom to issue an amnesty on the occasion of what was called a *joyeux advenement* in order to celebrate the accession or first entry of the king into a French town.[93] General amnesties, sometimes called *abolitions générales* in keeping with their Roman model, were also frequently enacted in connection with international or internal armed conflicts. For example, the disruptions caused by the Hundred Years War (1337–1453) prompted the royal authorities to declare several consecutive amnesties, including the regent's ordinance of 1360 which remitted all sentences for crimes connected with the war.[94] These amnesties were sometimes extended to whole cities or provinces caught in the troubles.[95]

Certain non-royal authorities were competent to accord graces in the twelfth and thirteenth centuries, albeit on a more limited scale than the king. In the Middle Ages, the power of clemency was linked to the justice prerogative. Accordingly, every person who possessed the privilege of jurisdiction – secular and religious authorities, magistrates and collectivities – could exercise clemency to some extent.[96] The power of certain high authorities, like the great vassals of the French Crown, was of such magnitude that they could dispose of their prerogative of grace and, for instance, delegate it. By contrast, the jurisdiction of ecclesiastic justices in criminal matters was limited, materially to crimes against the faith and personally to people benefiting from the clergy privilege. Within these boundaries, the bishop was the judge of his diocese, competent to condemn and pardon.

Throughout the fourteenth to the sixteenth century, two important changes transformed the French system of grace. On the one hand, non-royal authorities gradually lost their clemency power to the benefit of the king. This evolution culminated with the Blois ordinance of 1498 whereby Louis XII affirmed the power of grace as an exclusive royal prerogative:

> Combien que a nous seul et a nos successeurs rois de France appartienne de donner graces, pardons et remissions, et avec ce que nous avons plusieurs droits singuliers et privilégiéz qui sont a nous et a nos successeurs rois de France réservéz en signe de souveraineté; néantmoins aucuns de nos lieutenans et gouverneurs, et aussi leurs lieutenans par nous etablis en plusieurs contrées de nostre royaume, ont entrepris et s'efforcent, sous couleur

92 Duparc (n 58) 110–19.

93 Louis X, Charles V, Charles VII and Louis XI notably offered collective graces in such circumstances, see Duparc (n 58) 112; Monteil (n 91) 18.

94 Duparc (n 58) 120–23.

95 For example: Amiens in 1358, Neufchateau in 1367, Paris in 1413, Figeac in 1444, Périgueux in 1446, Arras, Coutances and Montaigu-en-Laonnois in 1449, and Bordeaux in 1453, see ibid.

96 Duparc (n 58) 146–58; Monteil (n 91) 15.

> d'aucun pouvoir qu'ils disent avoir obtenu de nous … donner graces, rémissions et pardons … Pour ces causes révoquons … leurdit pouvoir.[97]

On the other hand, individual graces accorded for lack of responsibility were separated from other clemency measures and recognised as a special category of graces, called *lettres de rémission* (remission letters). This distinction was codified in the Villers-Cotterets ordinance of 1539 providing that, in cases of homicides committed in self-defence or by necessity, clemency could be granted in chancery through an expeditious procedure.[98] These types of measures of grace were thus removed from the exclusive competence of the king.

Categories of grace

The French clemency system became more complex and specialised during the sixteenth century. Graces continued to be granted according to tradition – upon the celebration of religious or royal events and on the first entry of the king into a town – but several evolutions were realised. Most importantly, different categories of grace emerged, distinguished on the basis of the nature of the crime committed, the degree of culpability of the offender and the intended effect of the measure.[99] As mentioned above, the remission letters concerned cases of non-culpability and could be granted by royal officials through accelerated procedures. The *lettres d'abolition* (abolition letters) had a broader scope of application as they could cover any crime and did not necessitate the proof of an excuse or legal justification. They amounted to collective or individual amnesties, the effect of which was to suppress the 'memory' of the infraction altogether. The *lettres de pardon* (pardon letters) were similar to the abolition letters but concerned only minor offences that were not punishable by death. The effect of these three categories of grace was to remit the entire sentence and preclude any further proceedings. The effect of other types of grace, such as the commutation and rehabilitation letters, was merely to reduce the sentence or remove the condemnation's defamatory consequences. These distinctions were codified in the ordinance of 1670 which reorganised French criminal law and procedure.[100]

Pacification amnesties

During the sixteenth and the seventeenth century, French kings granted general amnesties for pacification purposes following religious or civil strife. The sixteenth century was marked by a series of wars between the catholic and

97 Blois Ordinance of 1498, art 70. See Duparc (n 58) 83; Monteil (n 91) 16.
98 Duparc (n 58) 84–87.
99 Foviaux (n 36) 51–57 and 83–91.
100 Duparc (n 58) 86–87.

protestant faiths (1562–1598).[101] At the end of each of these religious conflicts, a pacification edict containing a broad amnesty clause was enacted, the edicts together forming the tolerance legislation.[102] The amnesty formula of the Saint-Germain edict of 1570, referring to the need to erase the memory of everything happened during the conflict, was taken up by several subsequent pacification legislation:

> Que la mémoire de toutes choses, passées d'une part et d'autre et dès et depuis les troubles advenus en nostredit royaume et à l'occasion d'iceux, demeure estainte et assopie comme de chose non advenue.[103]

Pacification edicts generally covered all acts committed in connection with religious strife, annulling both condemnation and sentence.[104] The amnesty provision included in the Nantes edict of 1598 – the last of the tolerance legislation and the only one that endured – had the most extensive effects. In order to ensure the erasure of the memory of the conflict, it prohibited prosecutors, public and private persons from introducing any kind of legal action in this respect or mentioning things covered by the amnesty. It also decreed that those who quarrelled, offended or provoked one another in connection with these events would be punished as disturbers of the public peace:

> Premièrement, que la mémoire de toutes choses passées d'une part et d'autre, depuis le commencement du mois de mars 1585 jusqu'à notre avènement à la couronne et durant les autres troubles précédents et à leur occasion, demeurera éteinte et assoupie, comme de chose non advenue. Et ne sera loisible ni permis à nos procureurs généraux, ni autres personnes quelconques, publiques ni privées, en quelque temps, ni pour quelque occasion que ce soit, en faire mention, procès ou poursuite en aucune cours ou juridictions que ce soit.
>
> Défendons à tous nos sujets, de quelque part et qualité qu'ils soient, d'en renouveler la mémoire, s'attaquer, ressentir, injurier, ni provoquer l'un l'autre par reproche de ce qui s'est passé, pour quelque cause et prétexte que ce soit, en disputer, contester, quereller ni s'outrager, ou s'offenser de fait ou de parole, mais se contenir et vivre paisiblement ensemble comme frères, amis et concitoyens, sur peine aux contrevenants d'être punis comme infracteurs de paix et perturbateurs du repos public.[105]

101 Janine Garrisson, *L'édit de Nantes: chronique d'une paix attendue* (Fayard, Paris 1998).

102 Edicts of Amboise (1563), Longjumeau (1568), Saint-Germain (1570), Boulogne (1573), Baulieu (1576), Poitiers (1577), peace of Fleix (1580), edict of Mantes (1591), declaration of Saint-Germain (1594) and edict of Nantes (1598), see ibid.

103 Foviaux (n 36) 71.

104 Ibid, 87–90.

105 Michel Rocard, *L'art de la paix, l'édit de Nantes* (Janine Garrisson ed, Editions Atlantica, Biarritz 1997) 25.

In the seventeenth century, general amnesties were also relied on to pacify crisis-torn regions.[106] These amnesties were issued through ordinances and usually covered crimes committed in connection with the events object of the measure. For instance, several amnesty ordinances were proclaimed during and following the Fronde, a civil war fought between 1648 and 1653.[107] Like the pacification edicts, pacification ordinances annulled both condemnation and sentence.

Distinction between the power of grace and the power to amnesty

The power to grant collective and individual graces remained an exclusively royal prerogative until the French Revolution of 1789, in the aftermath of which the legislative power was entrusted to an elected assembly. On 14 September 1791, the new Parliament enacted a general amnesty law covering all acts related to the Revolution, thereby affirming its right to amnesty.[108] The power of grace, for its part, was abolished by the Criminal Code of October 1791.[109] Several reasons led to its revocation, notably a resolve to restrain the power of the king and the fact that some of the grounds for which pardons were hitherto granted had become legal causes of exception or justification in the new criminal code.[110] The pardoning power was reinstated by a *senatus-consulte* of 1802 which entrusted it to the first Consul Napoleon.[111] The additional act to the imperial constitution of 22 April 1815 further bestowed on Bonaparte, now Emperor, the power to grant amnesties.[112] Whereas the grace prerogative was retained by subsequent heads of state, whether kings, emperors or presidents, amnesty remained a legislative power under republican regimes but reverted to the sovereign in autocracies. It was thus vested in the Parliament by the constitution of 1848 and returned to Napoleon III by a *senatus-consulte* of 1852 following the restoration of the empire.[113]

Amnesty was affirmed as a republican symbol in connection with the insurrection of the Paris Commune in the spring of 1871.[114] In the aftermath of these events, there were calls for a general amnesty of the thousands of Parisians

106 Foviaux (n 36) 73–74.

107 For example: the Amnesty Declaration of April 1650 covering the facts that occurred in Paris on 11 December 1649 and those that followed in Dijon; the King's edict of 1652 according general amnesty following the troubles of Paris, see ibid.

108 Foviaux (n 36) 90; Stéphane Gacon, *L'amnistie, De la Commune à la guerre d'Algérie* (Editions du Seuil, Paris 2002) 29.

109 Article 13 of the 1791 French Criminal Code, see Monteil (n 91) 19.

110 Ibid, 19–21; Foviaux (n 36) 92.

111 Monteil (n 91) 22; Gacon (n 108) 30.

112 Foviaux (n 36) 95.

113 Ibid.

114 For an account of the history of the amnesty for the Paris Commune, see Jean T Joughin, *The Paris Commune in French Politics, 1871–1880: The History of the Amnesty of 1880* (Johns Hopkins Press 1955). See also Gacon (n 108) pt 2.

implicated in the uprisings. However, only discretionary and discriminatory pardons were accorded by the government on a case-by-case basis so long as monarchist and conservative elements controlled the legislative and executive powers. The question of amnesty aroused public opinion and generated much debate, campaigning and political agitation up to 21 June 1880, when the eventual adoption of an amnesty law by the republican Parliament finally closed this divisive chapter of French history.

The pardoning power in England

The king's mercy

During the Anglo-Saxon period, after the Roman occupation of England and prior to the Norman Conquest, English medieval society was organised in kinships and functioned without a centralised justice system.[115] Offences were sanctioned through the payment of a fine, or *wergild*, as compensation to the victims. However, certain serious crimes were recognised as unamendable and called for public penalties.[116] The king's jurisdiction to grant pardons and commute sentences was originally limited to these graver offences.[117] However, throughout the tenth and eleventh centuries, as the system of punishment was reorganised and sanctions became harsher, the scope of the pardon prerogative was gradually extended to temper this new severity. This willingness to moderate the impact of the transformation of the justice system on the population was also apparent in the royal practice of respecting the victims' claim for compensation even though the penalty of the offender was graciously remitted.

The royal power of clemency appeared in Anglo-Saxon statutory rolls under the reign of King Ine of Wessex (668–725 AD) whose laws provided that '[i]f any one fight in the king's house, let him be liable in all his property, and be it in the king's doom whether he shall or shall not have life'.[118] The laws of Alfred (871–901), Ethelred (978–1016) and Cnut (1017–1035) also placed at the mercy of the king those who would fight in his house.[119] Other categories of offenders could benefit from royal clemency. For instance, thieves were

115 Luke Owen Pike, *A History of Crime in England* (Smith Elder and Co 1873, vol 1) ch 1.

116 Naomi D Hurnard, *The King's Pardon for Homicide before AD 1307* (Clarendon Press 1969) 1.

117 At the end of the Anglo-Saxon period, unamendable crimes included murder, plotting against kings or lords, acts of violence in the army, assaults upon houses, arson, obvious theft, harbouring an excommunicate or outlaw, coining and fighting in the king's court, see Hurnard (n 116) 1–2.

118 William F Duker, 'The President's Power to Pardon: a Constitutional History' (1977) 18(3) *William and Mary Law Review* 475, 476; Stanley Grupp, 'Some Historical Aspects of the Pardon in England' (1963) 7 *The American Journal of Legal History* 51, 53–54.

119 Ibid.

allowed to rely on the king's mercy by the laws of Athelstan (924–940) and Edgar (959–975).[120] The laws of Ethelred provided that 'the moneyers who work within a wood, or elsewhere; that they be liable in their lives, unless the King will be merciful to them'.[121]

Until a more advanced period, several authorities including lords, magistrates and clerics shared the clemency power with the king. According to Pike, 'every shire was a little kingdom in itself, jealous of its own local privileges'.[122] Prominent among those privileges was the prerogative of private jurisdiction, to which the clemency power was generally attached. The most common and efficient way to obtain a pardon, even when appealing to the king, was to secure the intercession of clerics or other powerful personalities. As in medieval France, the Church exercised a strong influence and permitted a segment of the population to escape normal punishment through the benefit of clergy.[123]

The English system of individual pardons

Following the Norman Conquest, William the Conqueror (1066–1087) maintained the law as it stood regarding the pardon prerogative. However, according to Jensen, he 'brought from Normandy the view that clemency was an exclusive privilege of the king'.[124] His son Henry I (1100–1135) strengthened the royal pardoning power by establishing that all offenders responsible for serious crimes would fall exclusively within the scope of the king's mercy.[125] King John (1199–1216) was very generous in his offers of pardons, as were his successors Henry III (1216–1272), Edward I (1272–1307) and Edward II (1307–1327).[126]

Different types of inducement could be useful in securing a royal pardon, depending on the gravity of the crime and the social rank of the offender. When the crime had been committed with malice or when no cause of excuse or justification could be advanced, it was generally necessary to get the support of an influential personage and to pay a large amount of money. Certain kings, such as Richard II (1377–1399), were known for their rapacity in this regard.[127] The procedure was more straightforward in relation to accused persons who could present some cause of justification for their acts, such as self-defence, misadventure, or insanity. In medieval England, such circumstances were not recognised as legal defences but as legitimate causes to be pardoned.[128] When commissioners or

120 Ibid.
121 Ibid.
122 Pike (n 115) 84.
123 Ibid, 297–99.
124 Christen Jensen, *The Pardoning Power in the American States* (University of Chicago Press 1922) 1.
125 Duker (n 118) 477–78.
126 Hurnard (n 116) 35–40 and 217–19.
127 Grupp (n 118) 59.
128 Ibid; Duker (n 118) 479.

magistrates recommended a case to the king's mercy in view of extenuating circumstances, the actual granting of pardon became a matter of mere formality within the competence of the chanceries, as was the case in France with respect to remission letters.[129]

The English system of collective pardons

Under the reigns of Edward I the crusader, his son Edward II and grandson Edward III (1327–1377), pardon was employed as an instrument of conscription.[130] In this respect, Pike related that:

> As soon as war was declared, it was the custom to issue a proclamation in which a general pardon of all homicides and felonies was granted to everyone who would serve for a year at his own cost. The terms were readily accepted, and the King increased his force by a number of men who would perhaps be inferior to none in courage, though they might not improve the discipline of the army. The rolls according abound with instances in which a pardon was alleged for military service, and allowed without dispute.[131]

Other reasons prompted English monarchs to bestow clemency on large categories of people. On the one hand, collective pardons were often issued at the end of wars or insurrections in order to restore peace to the realm.[132] General pardons were granted for pacification purposes in the reigns of Richard II (1377–1399),[133] Henry VII (1485–1509),[134] Charles II (1660–1685),[135] William and Mary (1689–1702),[136] Georges I (1714–1727),[137] and Georges II (1727–1760).[138] These acts were similar in many respects to the French

129 Hurnard (n 116) 42–46 and 223–25.

130 Hurnard (n 116) 219; Duker (n 118) 478; Grupp (n 118) 58–59.

131 Pike (n 115) 294.

132 Grupp (n 118) 59.

133 6 Rich.2, St.1, c.13 (1382) Statutes at Large: 'The King's Pardon to his Subjects after the late Insurrection'; 6 Rich.2, St.2, c.1 (1383): 'A more large Pardon granted by the King to the offenders in the late Insurrection'.

134 1 Hen.7, c.6 (1485): 'A Pardon granted to all them who assisted the King in his Wars against Richard, Duke of Gloucester' (after the Wars of the Roses).

135 12 Car. 2, c.11 (1660): 'An Act of Free and General Pardon, Indemnity and Oblivion' (after the English Civil War).

136 2 W & M, sess.1, c.10 (1690): 'An Act for the King's and Queen's most gracious, general, and free Pardon' (after the revolution of 1688).

137 7 Geo.1, St.1, c.19 (1720): 'General Pardon of all Crimes (not excepted) committed before the 24th of July 1721. Excepted, All who on the 24th of July 1721 were in the Service of the Pretender' (after the first insurrection in Scotland).

138 20 Geo. 2, c.52 (1747): 'An Act for the King's most Gracious, General and Free Pardon' (after the second insurrection in Scotland).

pacification amnesties. The most extensive general pardon was enacted in 1660 after the restoration of Charles II following the English Civil War:

> The King's most excellent Majesty taking into his gracious and serious Consideration the long and great Troubles, Discords and Wars that have for many Years past been in this Kingdom, and that divers of his Subjects are by Occasion thereof, and otherwise fallen into and be obnoxious to great Pains and Penalties; (2) Out of a hearty and pious Desire to put an End to all Suits and Controversies that by Occasion of the Late Distractions have arisen or may arise between all his Subjects; (3) and to the Intent that no crime whatsoever committed against his Majesty or his Royal Father, shall hereafter rise in Judgment, or be brought in Question, against any of them to the least Endamagement of them, Either in their Lives, Liberties, Estates, or to the Prejudice of their Reputations, by any Reproach or Term of Distinction; (4) and to bury all Seeds of future Discords and Remembrance of the former, as well in his own Breast as in the Breasts of his Subjects one towards another … (6) and be it enacted by the King's most excellent Majesty, with the Advice and Consent of the Lords and Commons, in this present Parliament assembled, First, That all and all Manner of Treasons, Misprisions of Treasons, Murthers, Felonies, Offences, Crimes, Contempts and Misdemeanores, counselled, commanded, acted or done since the first Day of January in the Year of our Lord [1637], by any Person or Persons before the twenty-fourth Day of June in the Year of our Lord [1660], other than the Persons hereafter by Name excepted, … be pardoned, released, indemnified, discharged and put in utter Oblivion.[139]

On the other hand, general pardons were also traditionally proclaimed to celebrate royal events or express the sovereign's benevolence. Most kings and queens from the reign of Richard II (1377–1399) to that of Georges I (1714–1727) granted at least one act of 'free and general pardon'.[140] The most generous sovereigns in this regard were Henry IV (1399–1413), who granted

139 12 Car.2, c.11 (1660).

140 1 Rich.2, c.10 (1377); 13 Rich.2, St.2, c.1 (1389); 21 Rich.2, c.14 and c.15 (1397); 1Hen.4, c.20 (1399); 2 Hen.4, c.13 (1400); 5 Hen.4, c.15 (1403); 9 Hen.4, c.10 (1407); 4 Hen.5, c.8 (1416); 27 Hen.6, c.6 (1448); 28 Hen.6, c.3 (1449); 21 Hen.8, c.1 (1529); 22 Hen.8, c.15 and c.16 (1530); 23 Hen.8, c.19 (1531); 26 Hen.8, c.18 (1534); 32 Hen.8, c.49 (1540); 35 Hen.8, c.18 (1543); 1 Edw.6, c.15 (1547); 2&3 Edw.6, c.39 (1548); 3&4 Edw.6, c.24 (1549); 7 Edw.6, c.14 (1554); 5 Eliz., c.31 (1562); 8 Eliz., c.18 (1565); 13 Eliz, c.28 (1570); 18 Eliz., c.24 (1576); 23 Eliz., c.16 (1581); 27 Eliz., c.30 (1585); 29 Eliz., c.9 (1587); 31 Eliz., c.16 (1589); 35 Eliz., c. 14 (1593); 39 Eliz., c.28 (1597); 43 Eliz., c. 19 (1601); 3 Jac.1, c.27 (1605); 7 Jac.1, c.24 (1609); 21 Jac.1, c.35 (1623); 25 Car.2, c.5 (1672); 6&7 W.3, c.20 (1695); 7 Ann, c.22 (1708); 3 Geo.1, c.19 (1716) Statutes at Large.

four general pardons in his fourteen-year rule, and Elizabeth I (1558–1603), who issued eleven general pardons during her forty-five years of reign. These amnesties were introduced with the primary aim of displaying the sovereign's mercy in order to attract the gratitude and obedience of his or her subjects. These intentions are illustrated by the wording of 7 Ann, c.22 (1708):

> Being graciously inclined to encourage and invite all her loving Subjects to live and continue in their due Obedience to her Majesty, rather by Acts of Grace and Mercy than by a severe Execution of Justice; and having especial Trust and Confidence in her said Subjects, that they will with more Cheerfulness and Affection apply Themselves to the Discharge of their respective Duties towards her Majesty, and her Government, when they shall be released and freed from the many Pains, Penalties, and Forfeitures to which they are now liable, hath thought fit to grant her general and free Pardon, in a large and more bountiful Manner than hath heretofore been done.

Parliamentary attempts to curtail the royal pardon prerogative

The liberal use of the mercy prerogative by successive English monarchs provoked agitation in Parliament. Throughout the fourteenth century, the lords attempted to restrict the royal pardoning power to cases where extenuating circumstances had been proved.[141] For example, the Statute of Northampton enacted in 1328 provided that:

> Whereas Offenders have been greatly encouraged, because the Charters of Pardon have been so easily granted in Times past, of Manslaughters, Robberies, Felonies and other Trespasses against the Peace; it is ordained and Enacted, That such Charter shall not be granted, but only where the King may do it by his Oath, that is to say, where a Man slayeth another in his own Defense, or by Misfortune.[142]

These parliamentary attacks did not prove very effective and British sovereigns continued to regard their pardoning power as absolute, like their prerogative to dispense their subjects of the application of the law. Whatever restrictions had been imposed on the royal clemency power were removed by an act of 1535 restoring the exclusive and absolute pardon prerogative of the Crown:

> Be it enacted by authority of this present Parliament that no person or persons of what estates or degrees soever they be of, from the first day of July which shall be in the year of our Lord 1536 shall have any power or

141 Duker (n 118) 479–87.
142 Ibid, 483.

> authority to pardon or remit any treasons, murders, manslaughters or any kinds of felonies ... or any outlawries for such offenses afore rehearsed, committed, perpetuated, done, or divulged, or hereafter to be committed ... by or against any person or persons in any parts of this Realm, Wales, or the Marches of the same; but that the King's Highness, his heirs and successor Kings of this realm, shall have the whole and sole power and authority thereof united and knit to the Imperial Crown of this Realm, as of good right and equity it appertaineth, any grants, usages, prescriptions, act or acts of Parliament, or other things to the contrary thereof notwithstanding.[143]

The royal mercy prerogative remained unfettered until the end of the seventeenth century. In 1678, a constitutional crisis provoked by the king's pardon of the Earl of Danby following the latter's impeachment by the Commons, brought back the pardoning power in public debates.[144] The royal prerogative was thereafter successfully curtailed by Parliament in three respects.[145] The first limitation was incorporated into the Habeas Corpus Act of 1679 which prohibited mercy when a king's subject had caused another to be imprisoned outside the realm. Ten years later was enacted the Bill of Rights which deprived the Crown of its power to suspend, disregard or dispense from the application of the law. Finally, the Act of Settlement of 1700 provided that royal pardons could not be pleaded to an impeachment by the Commons. In 1726, Parliament was eventually entrusted with a pardon prerogative concurrent to that of the Crown, the latter remaining strong even within its new bounds.

The Indian mutiny

The most wide-ranging act of clemency issued by the British Crown in the nineteenth century related to the Indian insurrection of 1857. In the aftermath of this crisis, Parliament passed the Government of India Act dissolving the East India Company and transferring the administration of the Indian territories to the British Government.[146] On 1 November 1858, Queen Victoria issued a Proclamation granting to Indian citizens a status equivalent to that of British subjects as well as a number of rights and a general amnesty.[147] The Proclamation deplored 'the evils and misery which have been brought upon India' and confirmed pardons granted by the Governor-General 'with a view to stop the

143 Willard Harrison Humbert, *The Pardoning Power of the President* (American Council on Public Affairs, Washington D.C. 1941) 10; Duker (n 118) 476.

144 Duker (n 118) 487–96; James N Jorgensen, 'Clemency and Pardons Note' (1992–1993) 27 *University of Richmond Law Review* 345, 350–52.

145 Ibid; Grupp (n 118) 57; Humbert (n 143) 11.

146 21 & 22 Victoria, c. 106 (2 August 1858).

147 Proclamation of the Queen to the Princes, Chiefs & People of India, The Calcutta Gazette (Allahabad, 1858).

further effusion of blood, and to hasten the Pacification of Our Indian Dominions'.[148] Furthermore, it extended clemency to all offenders, with three exceptions: persons who had directly taken part in the murder of British subjects, those having knowingly given asylum to murderers, and the leaders and instigators of the revolt.[149] The amnesty provision was formulated as follows:

> To all others in Arms against the Government, We hereby promise unconditional Pardon, Amnesty, and Oblivion of all Offences against Ourselves, Our Crown and Dignity, on their return to their homes and peaceful pursuits. It is Our Royal Pleasure that these Terms of Grace and Amnesty should be extended to all those who comply with their Conditions before the First Day of January next.[150]

The pardon prerogative in the United States

A British legacy

When the British Empire was expanded to North America in the seventeenth century, the Crown's pardoning power was delegated to the executive authorities of the colonies, as extensive as it was understood in Britain at the time.[151] For example, the governor of Virginia was granted 'full and absolute Power and Authority to correct, punish, pardon, govern, and rule' by the Virginia Charter of 1609.[152] Similar language was employed in the New England Charter of 1620, the Massachusetts Bay's Charter of 1629 and the Maine Charter of 1664. Following the American War of Independence, however, the executive clemency power was restricted in most states. On the one hand, it was entrusted to the legislative branch or made dependent upon its assent in the majority of states and, on the other, it was excluded in cases of impeachment, treason or murder in some states.[153] The only colonial governors who retained an unfettered and exclusive mercy prerogative were those of New York, Delaware, Maryland, North Carolina and South Carolina.

The pardoning power in the American constitution

The pardoning power was not mentioned in the principal plans presented at the Philadelphia Constitutional Convention of 1787. However, the drafts of Charles

148 Ibid.
149 Ibid.
150 Ibid.
151 Humbert (n 143) 11–13.
152 Duker (n 118) 497–98.
153 Humbert (n 143) 13–14; Duker (n 118) 500–501; Daniel T Kobil, 'The Quality of Mercy Strained: Wresting the Pardoning Power from the King' (1991) 69 *Texas Law Review* 569, 590.

Pinckney and Alexander Hamilton proposed to entrust it to the chief executive of the United States, excluding cases of impeachment or treason.[154] The former suggestion was adopted and incorporated in the second article of the US constitution in those terms: '[The President] shall have Power to Grant Reprieves and Pardons for Offenses against the United States, except in Cases of Impeachment'.[155] Three amendments relating to the pardoning power had been advanced and defeated during the Convention's debates.[156] The first required the consent of the Senate prior to the grant of a presidential pardon and obtained only one favourable vote. A second proposal to prohibit reprieves before conviction was rejected on the ground that pre-trial leniency measures could be useful in encouraging accomplices to testify. The last and most controversial amendment related to the crime of treason. Several delegates were concerned that the president might use his pardoning power to shield revolutionary elements with whose cause he sympathised.[157] Notwithstanding general agreement as to the danger of entrusting one man with so great a power, it was not possible for the delegates to agree on the body that should share the pardoning power with the president.

During the period preceding the ratification of the constitution by American states, little debate was held regarding the presidential pardoning power. In the Virginia Convention, arguments were advanced against the vesting of the prerogative in the president alone, the possibility of pardon for treason or before conviction.[158] However, these misgivings were overcome by the persuasive speeches of the proponents of an unfettered executive clemency power. For instance, Alexander Hamilton argued that:

> It is not to be doubted that a single man of prudence and good sense is better fitted, in delicate conjunctures, to balance the motives which may plead for and against the remission of the punishment, than any numerous body whatever … But the principal argument for reposing the power of pardoning in … the Chief Magistrate is this: in seasons of insurrection and rebellion there are often critical moments when a well-timed offer of pardon to the insurgents or rebels may restore the tranquillity of the commonwealth; and which, if suffered to pass unimproved, it may never be possible afterwards to recall. The dilatory process of convening the legislature, or one of its branches, for the purpose of obtaining its

154 Humbert (n 143) 15.
155 United States Constitution (adopted 17 September 1787, entered into force 4 March 1789) art 2, s 2.
156 Humbert (n 143) 15–20; Duker (n 118) 501–502.
157 Ibid; Kobil (n 153) 590–92.
158 Ibid; Duker (n 118) 504–506.

> sanction to the measure, would frequently be the occasion of letting slip the golden opportunity.[159]

The constitutional pardon clause remained unchanged at the conclusion of the ratifying Conventions. The power to grant reprieves and pardons was thus established as an exclusive prerogative of the chief executive, reminiscent of the system of clemency that prevailed in England up to the seventeenth century. The British legacy of the presidential pardoning power was acknowledged by Chief Justice Marshall in the first Supreme Court decision dealing with this issue:

> As this power has been exercised from time immemorial by the executive of that nation whose language is our language, and to whose judicial institutions ours bear a close resemblance, we adopt the principles respecting the operation and effect of a pardon, and look into their books for the rules prescribing the manner in which it is to be used by the person who would avail himself of it.[160]

First presidential pardons

As explained by Hamilton, the executive clemency power notably aimed to facilitate the restoration of peace and tranquillity in situations of civil unrest. This objective prompted the first American President George Washington to proclaim 'a full, free, and entire pardon' to all persons having participated in the Whiskey Rebellion of 1794, on the condition that they pledge allegiance to the laws of the United States.[161] The second general pardon was issued by the second American President John Adams in connection with the so-called House Tax Insurrection in Pennsylvania.[162] The leaders of the insurrection had been condemned to death but, against the advice of his ministers, Adams ordered the proclamation of:

> [A] general pardon of all treasons and conspiracies to commit treasons, heretofore committed in the three offending counties, in opposition to the law laying taxes on houses … that tranquillity may be restored to the minds of those people, if possible.[163]

159 Duker (n 118) 505–506; LCK, 'The Power of the President to Grant a General Pardon or Amnesty for Offences against the United States' (1869) 17(10) *The American Law Register* 577, 582.

160 *United States v. Wilson*, 32 U.S. (7 Pet.) 150 (1833).

161 The Whiskey Rebellion took place in Pennsylvania in 1794 in reaction to the new taxation on distilled spirits; see LCK (n 159) 582–84.

162 This rebellion erupted in connection with a new law levying taxes on houses, land and slaves; see ibid.

163 Ibid.

The next act of general pardon was issued in 1807 by Thomas Jefferson and applied to army deserters who would surrender in a delay of four months.[164] Several pardons of this type, though unconditional, were granted by James Madison in relation to the war of 1812 against the British Empire.[165] The most wide-ranging and controversial amnesties issued in the United States were proclaimed during and after the American Civil War by Presidents Abraham Lincoln and Andrew Johnson. They gave rise to tensions between the executive and legislative powers regarding the capacity of the president to extend general pardons without the assent of Congress.

Amnesties of the American Civil War

Given the considerable number of American citizens involved in the Confederacy's struggle for independence from the United States, the penalty of death – which had been the sanction for treason since 1790 – came to be considered as too severe by the federal authorities.[166] Moreover, the crime of treason did not permit them to adequately differentiate between the various degrees of culpability of persons involved in the revolutionary war. In order to adapt the law to the circumstances, Congress enacted the Confiscation Act on 17 July 1862.[167] This Act distinguished between different types of rebellious acts, amounting or not to treason, and made fine and imprisonment applicable penalties for the least serious of these offences. It also provided that:

> The President is hereby authorized at any time hereafter, by proclamation to extend to any persons who may have participated in the existing rebellion in any state or part thereof, pardon and amnesty, with such exceptions and at such time and on such conditions as he may deem expedient for the public welfare.[168]

This provision reaffirmed the clemency power already vested in the president by the constitution. President Lincoln used it as early as February 1862 to order the release of all political prisoners who would swear an oath of allegiance to the US.[169] On 8 December 1863, he offered a general pardon in the following terms:

164 Norman Weisman, 'A History and Discussion of Amnesty' (1972) 4 *Columbia Human Rights Law Review* 529, 531; Daniel M Migliore, 'Amnesty: An Historical Justification for its Continuing Viability' (1972–1973) 12 *Journal of Family Law* 63, 65.

165 Ibid.

166 Jonathan Truman Dorris, *Pardon and Amnesty under Lincoln and Johnson* (University of North Carolina Press 1953) 3–7; Robert Bruce Murray, *Legal Cases of the Civil War* (Stackpole Books 2003) 237.

167 Dorris (n 166) 6–7.

168 Ibid; Stephen C Neff, *Justice in Blue and Grey: A Legal History of the Civil War* (Harvard University Press 2010) 223; Murray (n 166) 237.

169 Dorris (n 166) 10–11.

> Therefore, I Abraham Lincoln … do proclaim, declare, and make known to all persons who have, directly or by implication, participated in the existing rebellion, except as hereinafter excepted, that a full pardon is hereby granted to them and each of them with restoration of all rights of property, except as to slaves and in property cases where rights of third parties shall have intervened, and upon the condition that every such person shall take and subscribe an oath and thence-forward keep and maintain said oath inviolate.[170]

From the benefits of this amnesty were excluded the leaders of the Confederacy, the magistrates and Congressmen having aided the rebellion, military and naval high-ranking officers, and the persons who had unlawfully treated coloured persons.[171] The main goal of Lincoln's pardon policy was to weaken the Confederate army by encouraging defections. It worked to some extent since, by the end of the war, tens of thousands of rebel soldiers had availed themselves of the amnesty.[172] However, the proclamation was deemed too liberal by Congress and even by his author, who issued a second proclamation in March 1864 excluding prisoners of war from the amnesty offer.[173]

After the assassination of Lincoln on 14 April 1865, his Vice President Andrew Johnson ascended to the presidency. As soon as 29 May 1865, he proclaimed his first general amnesty. Although this act was similar to Lincoln's general pardon, it contained twice as much exceptions.[174] The excluded persons, however, were not deprived of any hope of mercy since a section of the proclamation provided that:

> Special application may be made to the President for pardon by any person belonging to the excepted classes, and such clemency will be liberally extended as may be consistent with the facts of the case and the peace and dignity of the United States.[175]

President Johnson was generous in granting pardons to the persons excluded from the amnesty proclamation, to the dissatisfaction of Congress.[176] The Republican

170 Ibid, 33–36; John Martin Davis and George B Tremmel, *Parole, Pardon, Pass and Amnesty Documents of the Civil War: An Illustrated History* (McFarland and Company 2014) 54–55; Neff (n 168) 223; Murray (n 166) 237.

171 Dorris (n 166) 35; Davis and Tremmel (n 170) 54.

172 Dorris (n 166) 67–73; Davis and Tremmel (n 170) 92; Neff (168) 224.

173 Dorris (n 166) 45–46 and 56–58.

174 Ibid, 108–12; Davis and Tremmel (n 170) 112–13; Neff (n 168) 224.

175 Dorris (n 166) 112.

176 According to Neff (n 168), Johnson granted approximately nine tenths of the pardon requests, see 224. See also Dorris (n 166) ch 14; Davis and Tremmel (n 170) 123–25.

radicals feared a government alliance between Democrats and pardoned secessionists if the latter were reinstated in representative functions.[177] Therefore, after their victory in the elections of 1866, radical congressmen took actions to curtail the President's clemency power.[178] In December 1866, Congress repealed the section of the Confiscation Act empowering him to grant amnesty by proclamation. In March 1867, it annulled the political benefits of presidential pardons. Finally, in March 1868, it passed a 'law of disfranchisement' excluding a vast number of Southerners from the privilege of voting and holding office.

In September 1867, emphasising the tense political situation enduring in the South, Johnson proclaimed a second general amnesty.[179] This measure excluded only three categories of persons: the leaders of the Confederacy, those accused of treason and people having unlawfully treated federal prisoners of war. Like previous amnesties, it was conditional upon the taking of an oath of allegiance to the US. The number of persons unaffected by presidential clemency after this second amnesty, amounting to a few hundreds, was reduced to a dozen by the nearly universal amnesty proclaimed by the President in July 1868.[180] This third amnesty contained only one exception, excluding persons charged with treason, and did not require the swearing of an oath of loyalty. Johnson completed his oeuvre on Christmas day, 1868, by granting 'unconditionally and without reservation, to all and to every person, who directly or indirectly, participated in the late insurrection or rebellion a full pardon and amnesty for the offence of treason against the United States'.[181] While it took only a little more than three years for every person involved in the insurrection, including its leaders, to be pardoned by the President, disfranchised Southerners had to wait thirty more years before Congress enacted a universal amnesty removing all political disabilities.[182]

3. A typology of ancient amnesties

This overview of the forms of clemency that existed in ancient societies reveals the perennial nature of amnesty. Several unconnected ancient civilisations had recourse to it for the same range of purposes and these amnesty traditions endured for long periods of time, despite regime change or system collapse. While ancient amnesties had different names, forms and characteristics, most of them shared four distinctive features. After identifying these core characteristics, this section classifies ancient amnesties in different categories depending on the type of purpose for which they were issued.

177 Dorris (n 166) 320.
178 Ibid, ch 14.
179 Ibid, 343–44; Neff (n 168) 224–25; Davis and Tremmel (n 170) 132.
180 Dorris (n 166) 352–56; Neff (n 168) 224–25; Davis and Tremmel (n 170) 132.
181 Dorris (n 166) 357.
182 Ibid, ch 16.

The first distinctive feature of ancient amnesties is that they were declared by a sovereign authority, whether a monarch, an elected body or political leader. In most of the societies studied, amnesties were proclaimed by omnipotent rulers such as pharaohs, emperors and kings. While some of these monarchs originally shared the clemency power with lesser secular or ecclesiastic authorities, it was soon consolidated as an exclusive prerogative of the sovereign granted at his or her discretion. In early democracies in classical Athens and the Roman Republic, elected representatives were competent to grant amnesties. In modern democracies, the prerogative was either entrusted to the legislative assembly, as in France following the revolutions of 1789 and 1848, or maintained as an executive power, as in the United Kingdom and the United States.[183]

The second characteristic feature of ancient amnesties, which permits to distinguish them from other clemency measures such as pardons, is that they applied to categories of people as opposed to individuals. In ancient Egypt and Athens, amnesties were usually granted to exiles or disfranchised people. In the Roman and Chinese Empires, as well as in France and England, they were extended to convicted people and prisoners on certain festive occasions or following periods of conflict or unrest. Amnesties issued in relation to an armed conflict primarily benefited insurgents, rebels or defeated soldiers. While some amnesties were all-inclusive, others excluded certain categories of crimes or persons. As regards excluded crimes, they corresponded to offences regarded as the most serious in the society in question. For example, certain Chinese amnesties regularly excluded a series of crimes called the 'Ten Abominations' because of their perceived seriousness. Some Roman amnesties similarly excluded certain categories of offences listed as unforgivable. Alternatively, certain ancient amnesties excluded specific persons, usually the leaders of a coup or insurrection. Although legal rules were adopted for the purpose of limiting the scope of amnesties in some ancient societies, they were not always respected by those holding the amnesty prerogative.

The third common element concerns the primary effect of ancient amnesties, which was to exempt their beneficiaries from the legal consequences deriving from the commission of a criminal offence. While some amnesties covered ordinary crimes, others applied to political offences committed in the context of a rebellion against the state. The moment at which the measure intervened, and the extent of its benefits, varied. In France, the Roman and Chinese Empires, differently named clemency measures were used at different moments in the criminal process and had different effects. However, most ancient amnesties resulted in the elimination of the penal consequences attached to a criminal act, removing sentence and conviction as well as expunging the recipient's criminal record. In some cases, this was contingent on the fulfilment of a condition by

183 The British prerogative of mercy is still nominally a royal prerogative, see Andrew Novak, *Comparative Executive Clemency: The Constitutional Pardon Power and the Prerogative of Mercy in Global Perspective* (Routledge 2016) ch 2.

the applicant. For example, most of the amnesties passed in connection with the American Civil War required applicants to swear an oath of allegiance to the US. The Athenian amnesty of 403 BC was also conditional on the swearing of a solemn oath and required the Thirty Tyrants, additionally, to account for their deeds before the Athenian juries.

The last characteristic of most ancient amnesties is that they were issued in connection with a special event or time period, either a festive event like a royal celebration or a troubled period like a war. Different types of amnesties were introduced in connection with different sorts of events. Four categories of amnesties have been identified depending on the main purpose they pursued, which was usually connected to the event or period in relation to which they were adopted.

The first category comprises measures issued in relation to an armed conflict or period of unrest in order to restore peace and stability. Pacification amnesties aimed to draw a line on the past to enable a divided society to move beyond a period of violence. Accordingly, they often entailed the erasure of the memory of wrongs committed in connection with the events in question and sometimes explicitly prohibited citizens to mention or allude to these events. For example, the amnesty granted through the Athenian reconciliation treaty of 403 BC required citizens to promise that they would not recall the misfortunes of the past. The amnesty provision included in the Nantes edict of 1598 AD also provided for the erasure of all things that had happened during past conflicts and prohibited French citizens from making reference thereto. Pacification amnesties were issued in all the societies examined, often in a recurring pattern. Throughout French and British history, they were relied on to facilitate the restoration of peace and foster reconciliation following international conflicts or internal revolts. US presidents also resorted to amnesties in connection with periods of disorder or conflict including the American Civil War. As a matter of fact, amnesties were issued after most periods of conflict or unrest of some importance in all the societies studied.

The second category includes amnesties granted to celebrate imperial, royal or religious events. Celebration amnesties were linked to the cult of the sovereign and thus mostly proclaimed in autocracies. In legal systems where power was concentrated in one person, clemency was an important attribute of the ruler which counterbalanced his or her absolute power to punish. Upon festive occasions, such as the accession or anniversary of the sovereign, general amnesties were offered to the subjects of the realm as part of the national rejoicing. For example, in the Roman Empire, general amnesties were extended upon imperial celebrations (*abolitio publicae*) and religious festivities (*abolitio paschalis*). During the reign of the first Princeps Augustus, it became a custom to grant a general pardon upon his entry into Rome. This tradition was kept up in medieval France where collective acts of grace were issued upon the accession or first entry of a king into a French town (*joyeux advenement*). In the same vein, successive English monarchs granted acts of general pardon in order to display their benevolence to their subjects and as a means of securing their loyalty and obedience. In ancient China, general amnesties (*ta-she*) were offered to celebrate events in the imperial family and in accordance with philosophical teachings bearing on the relation of men with nature. The doctrine of Han Confucianism thus entailed the grant of amnesties in certain appropriate seasons or on the occurrence of natural phenomena.

The third category encompasses amnesties adopted in order to achieve a particular military or political goal, such as enlarging the army or inducing an enemy to surrender. Expedient amnesties were primarily used in connection with periods of war or national emergency. For example, several Athenian amnesties were extended to exiles and disfranchised people in order to reinforce the military capacity of the city-state and reunite the population against an imminent attack. Similarly, general pardons were used in England as an instrument of conscription throughout the thirteenth and fourteenth centuries. In the Roman world, military commanders resorted to clemency in order to induce enemy troops to surrender and integrate foreign populations into the empire when combat was over. Expedient amnesties were also used to sway public opinion in periods of crisis, e.g. following the death of Julius Caesar or the insurrection of the Paris Commune. It may be assumed that expedient amnesties were sometimes disguised as benevolent amnesties in order to elicit public sympathy and support in periods of trouble.

The last category of measures, including both amnesties and pardons, were granted in order to alleviate the harshness of the justice system. These measures of relief were necessary to permit a degree of flexibility in legal systems which did not recognise grounds of non-culpability such as self-defence and insanity as legal defences or mitigating circumstances. In some ancient societies, they were also used to circumvent the application of the law in the interest of equity or when special circumstances justified the use of mercy. In the Roman Empire, legal institutions of clemency such as *indulgentia* and *venia* allowed the judges or the emperor to exercise discretion in cases where equity appeared to warrant a more lenient treatment than the strict application of the law. In France, the remission, abolition and pardon letters enabled the king and other royal authorities to forego punishment when a cause of excuse was pleaded or circumstances called for clemency. Similarly, in medieval England, some extenuating circumstances were recognised as legitimate causes for pardons.

There is a high degree of continuity between ancient and modern amnesties in term of their purposes. Indeed, amnesties continue to be broadly issued for the same types of reasons which prompted their adoption in the past. In the last few decades, amnesties have frequently been adopted in situations of armed conflict or civil strife for pacification and reconciliation purposes.[184] In such contexts, they are commonly used as expedients to induce rebel forces to

184 See chs 3 and 5 in this volume.

surrender or engage in peace talks.[185] Amnesties also continue to be proclaimed for celebration purposes in some countries, usually in monarchical systems or regimes with authoritarian tendencies.[186] Most penal codes throughout the world now provide for self-defence, duress and diminished responsibility as legal defences, rendering this type of corrective clemency measures somewhat obsolete. However, amnesties still occasionally operate as measures of relief in relation to a change in public policy or a decriminalisation of certain conducts.[187] They are also sometimes used to relieve prison overcrowding, release political prisoners or persons sentenced to death.[188]

Conclusion

As was the case in ancient societies, amnesties are still commonly issued to foster peace and reconciliation, celebrate national events, achieve strategic military or political objectives, or provide relief from the rigours of the law. The acceptability of amnesties from a moral or ethical standpoint might depend on the legitimacy of their particular purpose. For instance, while amnesties may be justifiable in so far as they aim to alleviate the effect of harsh laws or facilitate the termination of an armed conflict, they may be less so when they are used by repressive regimes to manipulate public opinion or secure impunity for grave crimes. As regards the legality of amnesties in the contemporary international order, however, it is less the legitimacy of their purpose than their validity in so far as they apply to certain crimes that has been in question. Indeed, in

185 See e.g. Andrew G Reiter, 'Examining the Use of Amnesties and Pardons as a Response to Internal Armed Conflicts' (2014) 47(1) *Israel Law Review* 133.

186 For example, the king of Morocco traditionally extends graces to celebrate national anniversaries, see 'Maroc: 188 personnes ayant participé à la révolte du Rif graciées par le roi' *Le Monde* (21 August 2018). In December 2013, President Putin submitted to the Russian Parliament a broad amnesty bill to mark the twentieth anniversary of the Russian constitution. This celebration amnesty led to the release of thousands of dissidents and political prisoners, see Luke Harding and Francesca Ebel, 'Pussy Riot and Arctic 30 Amnesty is a Putin Masterstroke Ahead of Olympics' *The Guardian* (18 December 2013).

187 For example, following the legalisation of cannabis in California, the District Attorney expunged thousands of convictions for the recreational use of that drug, see Chloe Aiello, 'The San Francisco DA Will Dismiss Thousands of Marijuana-Related Convictions in an Unprecedented Move' *CNBC* (31 January 2018). Proposals to grant an amnesty to persons convicted for cannabis use have also been made in Canada in link with the legalisation of the drug, see Leyl and Cecco, 'Canada Plans to Legalize Weed – But Will Those Convicted of Crimes Get Amnesty?' *The Guardian* (8 May 2018). In Mexico, President López Obrador has called for an amnesty for certain categories of drug-related offences in a new strategy to tackle violent drug crimes, see Martha Pskowski, 'The Radical Amnesty Plan of Mexico's Next President' *The New Republic* (2 July 2018).

188 See e.g. Sinisa Jakov Marusic, 'Macedonia Plans Amnesty to Ease Pressure on Jails' *Balkan Insight* (21 September 2017); 'Ethiopian parliament approves amnesty for political prisoners' *Al Jazeera* (21 July 2018); John Namkwahe, 'Tanzania: Magufuli Grants Presidential Amnesty to 61 Death Row Inmates' *AllAfrica* (9 December 2017).

accordance with the development of an accountability paradigm over the last century, it is increasingly considered that amnesties are prohibited for serious crimes of international concern. If an international norm prohibiting the grant of amnesty for this type of crimes has emerged, it would restrict the freedom of states to enact general and unlimited amnesties, regardless of whether their purpose is legitimate or not.

2 At the end of war

From the amnesty tradition to the accountability paradigm

Introduction

The same pacification purpose which prompted rulers in ancient civilisations to declare general amnesties following armed conflicts gave rise to a practice of including amnesty clauses in European peace treaties in the late Middle Ages. This practice was followed for several centuries before being departed from at the end of the two world wars, in recognition of the principle that major criminals of war should be prosecuted rather than amnestied. This chapter examines the transition from the amnesty tradition to the accountability paradigm underpinning contemporary claims that amnesties are prohibited with respect to serious crimes. The first section looks at the context into which the amnesty tradition emerged and reviews the amnesty provisions of major European peace treaties. It also considers the reasons underlying this practice according to prominent publicists of the period. The second section examines the evolution of the laws of war in the same period, focusing on the emergence of a right to punish war criminals under international law and early instances of post-war trials. It concludes with an analysis of the peace settlements of the world wars foregrounding the development of the principle of individual liability for crimes against international law.

1. Amnesty as a traditional component of peace treaties

Emergence of the practice

Amnesty emerged as a component of European peace treaties during the fifteenth century. This development took place in the context of the progressive decay of the European medieval legal and religious orders based on the supremacy of the Holy Roman Emperor and the Pope over monarchies and autonomous cities.[1] Throughout the fourteenth and fifteenth centuries, while principalities gained in

1 Randall Lesaffer, 'Peace Treaties from Lodi to Westphalia' in Randall Lesaffer (ed), *Peace Treaties and International Law in European History* (CUP 2004); Frederick H Russel, *The Just War in the Middle Ages* (CUP 1975) 292–308.

strength and influence so as to eventually accede to the level of sovereign powers, the hitherto predominant just war doctrine appeared increasingly unsuitable to the new international configuration.[2] According to this doctrine, which provided a justification for war during feudal times, discrimination was to be exercised between warring parties. The unjust belligerent, as opposed to the party recognised as having a just cause for waging war, was to be declared responsible for the war and punished for the damages inflicted as a result.[3] The appearance of amnesty clauses in peace treaties in the fifteenth century and their implicit recognition of the belligerents as equals, in disregard of the just war doctrine, evidenced the strengthening of the power of sovereign princes and presaged the collapse of imperial and papal authorities.[4]

The Arras Treaty of 1482 ending the war between the Austrian Hapsburg and France included a clause declaring the '*absolution totale, rapel de tous bans, defauts et contumaces au Sujets d'une party et d'autre, de quelconques cas, delits, crimes, ou offenses que l'on pourrait leur imposer*'.[5] The Treaties of Conflans (1465), Péronne (1468) and Senlis (1493) contained similar amnesty clauses aiming to extinguish the consequences of the war for the belligerent parties and their subjects.[6] By signing these treaties, the parties agreed not to seek revenge by judicial or other means for injuries and damages suffered as a result of the war.

The practice of incorporating amnesty clauses in European peace treaties intensified in the sixteenth century to become commonplace in the following centuries.[7] These amnesty provisions entailed not only a complete and reciprocal forgiveness of all wrongful acts committed as part of the hostilities but also that none of the belligerents was to be assigned responsibility for the war. The seventeenth century witnessed the formation of the modern European state system resting on the fundamental principles of sovereignty and equality of states.[8] Sovereign states were no longer bound by any higher political or

2 Russel (n 1) 292–308; Philippe Contamine, *War in the Middle Ages* (Blackwell 1984) 286–87.

3 Lesaffer (n 1) 38–39. On the just war doctrine, see Joachim von Elbe, 'The Evolution of the Concept of the Just War in International Law' (1939) 33 *American Journal of International Law* 665–88; Maurice Keen, *The Laws of War in the Late Middle Ages* (Routledge & Kegan Paul 1965) ch 5.

4 Lesaffer (n 1) 38–39.

5 Randall Lesaffer, 'The Westphalia Peace Treaties and the Development of the Tradition of Great European Peace Settlement prior to 1648' in Randall Lesaffer (ed), *Peace Treaties and International Law in European History* (CUP 2004) 87.

6 Lesaffer, 'Peace Treaties from Lodi to Westphalia' (n 1) 39.

7 Lesaffer, 'The Westphalia Peace Treaties and the Development of the Tradition of Great European Peace Settlement prior to 1648' (n 5) 87–88; Heinz Duchhardt, 'Peace Treaties from Westphalia to the Revolutionary Era' in Randall Lesaffer (ed), *Peace Treaties and International Law in European History* (CUP 2004) 49; Alfred Maurice De Zayas, 'Westphalia, Peace of (1648)' in Rudolph Bernhardt (ed), *Encyclopaedia of Public International Law* (Max Planck Institute for Comparative Public Law and International Law 2000, vol 4) 1468.

8 Lesaffer, 'The Westphalia Peace Treaties and the Development of the Tradition of Great European Peace Settlement prior to 1648' (n 5) 88–89.

religious authority and thus free to wage war and peace without justification. They had equal standing on the international scene and regulated their mutual relations on the basis of reciprocity. This reciprocity was notably manifested through the inclusion of peace, friendship and amnesty provisions in peace agreements.[9]

Peace treaties between western European powers

The decline of the Holy Roman Empire

The Peace of Westphalia (1648) marked the beginning of the new European secular order based on a balance of power between sovereign states.[10] It put an end to the religious conflicts that had devastated Europe for over a century and culminated in the Thirty Years War. In the aftermath of this particularly destructive and protracted conflict, the parties were committed to the establishment of lasting peace and the definitive settlement of religious dissensions. Hence, the first two articles of the Treaties of Münster (Holy Roman Empire and Sweden) and Osnabrück (Holy Roman Empire and France), together forming the Peace of Westphalia, provided for universal peace, perpetual amity and a general amnesty of all things related to the war.[11] The amnesty clause of the Westphalia Treaties was the most elaborate so far and included an obligation for the parties and their subjects to 'bury in eternal oblivion' everything happened during the conflict:

> That there shall be on the one side and the other a perpetual Oblivion, Amnesty, or Pardon of all that has been committed since the beginning of these Troubles, in what place, or what manner soever the Hostilitys have been practis'd, in such a manner, that nobody, under any pretext whatsoever, shall practice any Acts of Hostility, entertain any Enmity, or cause any Trouble to each other; neither as to Persons, Effects and Securitys, neither of themselves or by others, neither privately nor openly, neither directly nor indirectly, neither under the colour of Right, nor by the way of Deed, either within or without the extent of the Empire, notwithstanding all Covenants made before to the contrary: That they shall not act, or permit to be acted, any wrong or injury to any whatsoever; but that all that has pass'd on the one side, and the other, as well before as during the War, in Words, Writings, and Outrageous Actions, in Violences, Hostilitys, Damages and

9 Heinhard Steiger, 'From Paris to Versailles' in Randall Lesaffer (ed), *Peace Treaties and International Law in European History* (CUP 2004) 84.

10 Fred L Israel (ed), *Major Peace Treaties of Modern History 1648–1967* (Chelsea House Publications 1967, vols 1–4) 3–5; Charles L Phillips and Alan Axelrod, *Encyclopaedia of Historical Treaties and Alliances* (Fitzroy Dearborn 2001, vols 1–2) 34–35; De Zayas (n 7) 1465–69.

11 Israel (n 10) 7–10; Clive Parry (ed), *The Consolidated Treaty Series* (Oceana Publications, Dobbs Ferry N.Y. 1969–1986, vol 1) 198–201 and 319–22.

> Expences, without any respect to Persons or Things, shall be entirely abolish'd in such a manner that all that might be demanded of, or pretended to, by each other on that behalf, shall be bury'd in eternal Oblivion.[12]

The Treaty of the Pyrenees (1659) ending the war between the Spanish Hapsburg and France also contained an amnesty clause.[13] The next major European conflict opposed France, whose main objective was the control of the Spanish Netherlands, to England, the United Netherlands and Sweden.[14] The Dutch war gave rise to two peace treaties, the second of which – the Treaty of Nijmegen (1678) – provided for an amnesty.[15] The subsequent Treaty of Ryswick (1697) was concluded between Louis XIV of France and William III of England to bring an end to the war of the League of Augsburg.[16] It also provided for the traditional amnesty formula requiring the parties' subjects to forget all offences and damages connected to the war:

> That all Offences, Injurys, Damages, which the said King of Great Britain and his Subjects, or the said most Christian King and his Subjects have suffer'd from each other during this War, shall be forgotten, so that neither on account of them, or for any other cause or pretence, neither Party, or the Subjects of either, shall hereafter do, cause or suffer to be done any Hostility, Enmity, Molestation or Hindrance to the other, by himself or others, secretly or openly, directly or indirectly, by colour of Right or way of Fact.[17]

The Peace of Utrecht (1713) concluding the Spanish Succession War contained an amnesty provision identical to that of the Ryswick Treaty.[18] The Utrecht Treaty settled the conflict between the main belligerents (England, the Netherlands, Austria, France and Spain). However, the Holy Roman Emperor Charles V maintained a hostile stance towards Louis XIV until their signing of the Treaty of Rastatt (and Baden) in September 1714.[19] The latter typically extended a 'perpetual Pardon and Amnesty' for 'all that has been done since the beginning of the war'.[20]

The European equilibrium of forces established by the Peace of Utrecht subsisted until 1740, when the death of the heirless Emperor Charles VI generated

12 Israel (n 10) 9–10.
13 Ibid, 3–5 and 55 (art 4); Phillips and Axelrod (n 10) 50–52.
14 Israel (n 10) 117–19.
15 Ibid, 121–29 (art 3); Phillips and Axelrod (n 10) 53–55.
16 Israel (n 10) 117–19; Phillips and Axelrod (n 10) 59–60; Hannis Taylor, *A Treatise on Public International Law* (Callaghan and Company 1901) 103–106.
17 Israel (n 10) 146 (art 3).
18 Ibid, 179 (art 3); Phillips and Axelrod (n 10) 78–81; Taylor (n 16) 106–107.
19 Phillips and Axelrod (n 10) 82.
20 Israel (n 10) 243 (art 2).

disputes regarding the Hapsburg succession.[21] The Austrian succession war affected the whole of Europe and had further ramifications in India and North America where England, France and Spain fought over colonial territories. In 1748, the belligerents had arrived at such a state of exhaustion that they agreed on the Treaty of Aix-la-Chapelle, which extended a general amnesty to all the parties' subjects.[22]

The Treaties of Hubertsburg and Paris, both concluded in February 1763, brought an end to the Seven Years War.[23] This conflict primarily opposed Great Britain and France in relation to their overseas territories but also involved Prussia, Austria and Russia on the Continent. Both peace settlements included an amnesty clause, that contained in the Hubertsburg Treaty (Austria and Prussia) being particularly wide-ranging:

> Both sides shall grant a general amnesty and totally wipe from their memory all hostilities, losses, damages and injuries whatever their nature, committed or sustained on either side during the recent disturbances. Hostilities shall nevermore be alluded to nor shall any compensation be claimed under any pretext or in any name. No subject on either side shall ever be troubled but shall enjoy this amnesty and all its effects to the full, despite the decrees sent out and published; all orders for confiscation shall be withdrawn and goods confiscated or sequestrated shall be returned to their owners, from whom they were taken during the recent disturbances.[24]

The Napoleonic wars

In the wake of the French Revolution, Napoleon was appointed first Consul of France and waged several wars of expansion. The Treaties of Campo-Formio (1797), Amiens (1802) and Pressburg (1805) recognised his conquests and the defeats of the three successive coalitions formed by his adversaries (Austria, Russia, Great Britain, Prussia, Spain and the Netherlands).[25] The first two of these peace settlements contained an amnesty clause.[26] So did the Tilsit Treaty of July 1807 which gave Napoleon virtual control over Europe and restored peace between France and Russia.[27] The Treaty of Schönbrunn (1809), also

21 Ibid, 263–67; Phillips and Axelrod (n 10) 90–92; Taylor (n 16) 107–109.

22 Israel (n 10) 272 (art 2).

23 Ibid, 263–67; Phillips and Axelrod (n 10) 92–93; Taylor (n 16) 109; E Robson, 'The Seven Years War' in *The New Cambridge Modern History* (CUP 1957, vol 7) 465–86.

24 Israel (n 10) 330 (art 2).

25 Israel (n 10) 427–32.

26 Ibid, 438 (art 16) and 451 (art 13, para 4).

27 Ibid, 472 (art 10); Phillips and Axelrod (n 10) 182–84; Jacques Godechot, Beatrice F Hyslop and David L Dowd, *The Napoleonic Era in Europe* (Holt, Rinehart and Winston 1971) 123–25.

providing for an amnesty, marked the failure of Austria's attempt to form an alliance with Prussia against France.[28] However, when the French *Grande Armée* invaded Russia in June 1812, thereby voiding the Tilsit Treaty, Russia, Prussia, Austria and Sweden formed a fourth coalition to liberate Europe from French imperium. Napoleon's army was subjugated by these forces at the Leipzig Battle of Nations in October 1813. After further setbacks, the French Emperor eventually admitted defeat, relinquished power and departed for Elba under the terms of the Treaty of Paris (1814).[29] This agreement declared a general amnesty casting into oblivion all acts connected to the Napoleonic wars:

> The High Contracting Parties, desirous to bury in entire oblivion the dissensions which have agitated Europe, declare and promise that no Individual, of whatever rank or condition he may be, in the Countries restored and ceded by the present Treaty, shall be prosecuted, disturbed, or molested, in his person or property, under any pretext whatsoever, either on account of his conduct or political opinions, his attachment either to any of the Contracting Parties, or to any Government which has ceased to exist, or for any other reason, except for debts contracted towards Individuals, or acts posterior to the date of the present Treaty.[30]

The parties to the Treaty of Paris agreed to send plenipotentiaries to Vienna in order to settle European dissensions and prevent further troubles. The Vienna Congress of 1815 instituted a new balance of power and reiterated the offer of a 'full, general, and special Amnesty' to all individuals involved in the past troubles.[31] In March 1815, Napoleon escaped from Elba and attempted to regain his dominion over Europe. Following his final defeat at Waterloo, the allies concluded the second Treaty of Paris (1815) providing for the reduction of France to its former boundaries, the payment of an indemnity and the exile of the fallen Emperor to St. Helena, where he died a few years later.[32] This peace treaty did not include the habitual amnesty clause. In France, however, the restored Louis XVIII issued an ordinance on 24 July 1815 extending amnesty to the insurgents having rallied to Napoleon, with certain exceptions.[33]

28 Israel (n 10) 427–32; Phillips and Axelrod (n 10) 185–92 (art 10).

29 Ibid.

30 Israel (n 10) 509 (art 16).

31 Israel (n 10) 523; Phillips and Axelrod (n 10) 196; Fritz Münch, 'Vienna Congress (1815)' in Rudolph Bernhardt, *Encyclopaedia of Public International Law* (Max Planck Institute for Comparative Public Law and International Law 2000, vol 4) 1286–89.

32 Phillips and Axelrod (n 10) 193–95.

33 Gary Jonathan Bass, *Stay the Hand of Vengeance: The Politics of War Crimes Tribunals* (Princeton University Press 2000) 46–47.

The Italian and German unification processes

Following the Congress of Vienna and the demise of Napoleon began the Italian unification process.[34] The Kingdom of Sardinia sought the support of France to liberate itself from Austrian occupation. In return for territorial gains, the French accepted combining forces with the Sardinians and pushing Austria out of Italy. The Treaty of Zurich (1859) recognised Italy's victory and included the following amnesty clause:

> In order to contribute, with all their efforts, to the pacification of men's minds, His Majesty the King of Sardinia and His Majesty the Emperor of Austria declare and promise that, in their respective Territories, and in the Countries restored or ceded, no Individual compromised on the occasion of the late events in the Peninsula, of whatever class or condition he may be, shall be prosecuted, disturbed, or troubled in his person or in his property, on account of his political conduct and opinions.[35]

As to the German unification process, the first war was fought by Prussia and Austria against Denmark in relation to the succession to the duchies of Schleswig and Holstein.[36] The Danes delivered them to the temporary German allies through the Treaty of Vienna (1864) which granted a general amnesty.[37] A few years later, joining their forces to weaken Austria's territorial domination, Italy and Prussia engaged in the Seven Weeks War (1866). This conflict was concluded by the Treaty of Vienna (between Austria and Italy) whereby Italy gained Venetia, and the Treaty of Prague (between Austria and Prussia) whereby Prussia acquired Schleswig and Holstein. Both included an amnesty provision worded similarly to that of the Zurich Treaty.[38] In 1870, the North German Confederation's Chancellor Bismarck induced Napoleon III to open hostilities against Prussia. The Franco-Prussian war resulted in the defeat of Napoleon III, the establishment of France's Third Republic and of Bismarck's coveted German Empire.[39] It was ended by the Treaty of Frankfurt (1871) which offered a general amnesty.[40]

Peace treaties between western and eastern European powers

The decline of the Ottoman Empire

The dominance of the Ottoman Empire in eastern Europe started to be challenged by European powers at the turn of the eighteenth century. Pursuant to

34 Israel (n 10) 597–602.
35 Ibid, 610 (art 22).
36 Ibid, 597–602.
37 Ibid, 622–23 (art 23).
38 Ibid, 642 (art 23) and 631–32 (art 10, para 3).
39 Phillips and Axelrod (n 10) 310.
40 Israel (n 10) 652 (art 2).

the Treaties of Carlowitz (1699) and Passarowitz (1718), the Turks were compelled to transfer large portions of territory to Austria, including Hungary and Transylvania, some of which they regained through the Treaty of Belgrade (1739) which extended a general amnesty to all the parties' subjects.[41] In the following decades, Russia became the main beneficiary of the Ottoman Empire's decline. Its increasing ascendancy in the eastern territories was acknowledged in the Treaty of Kutschuk Kaïnardji (1774) whose first article declared that: 'in virtue of this sincere renewal of friendship, the two Parties promise a reciprocal amnesty and a general pardon, without any exception whatsoever, for all of their subjects who might have committed any wrong against one Party or the other'.[42]

Half a century later, Russia waged war against the Ottomans, officially to support Greece's and Serbia's claims for autonomy.[43] The Russian army was successful until the plague decimated its ranks and compelled Nicholas I to negotiate peace with Mahmud II. The Treaty of Adrianople (1829) also granted a general amnesty.[44] In 1833, the Russian and Ottoman sovereigns concluded a pact of military alliance and non-aggression through the Treaty of Constantinople.[45] Hostilities nevertheless resumed in the 1850s, with France and England strategically joining the Ottoman side in the Crimean War.[46] This tripartite alliance overpowered Russia on the battlefield and constrained the latter to accept the terms of the Paris Treaty (1856) which restored the territorial integrity of the Ottoman Empire and offered the traditional amnesty.[47] However, the Russian Emperor did not admit defeat and engaged in another war against the Ottomans in 1877, purportedly to promote Bulgaria's independence.[48] This objective was achieved by the Treaty of San Stefano (1878) which also granted a general amnesty to all Ottoman subjects implicated in the war.[49]

European powers, particularly England and Austria, felt threatened by Russia's victory over Turkey and the large autonomous state of Bulgaria.[50] Therefore, they convened a Congress at Berlin in 1878 to submit the San Stefano Treaty to scrutiny. As a result, the size of Bulgaria was reduced, Romania and Serbia were declared independent and Russia's territorial acquisitions were partly revoked. A new treaty between the Russian and Ottoman Emperors was

41 Israel (n 10) 863–67, 901–902 (art 8).
42 Ibid, 914.
43 Ibid; Phillips and Axelrod (n 10) 297–98.
44 Israel (n 10) 937–38 (art 13).
45 Ibid, 943–46; Phillips and Axelrod (n 10) 294–96.
46 Israel (n 10) 863–67; Phillips and Axelrod (n 10) 302; Taylor (n 16) 119–20.
47 Israel (n 10) 948 (art 5).
48 Israel (n 10) 863–67; Phillips and Axelrod (n 10) 313–14; Taylor (n 16) 125–26.
49 Israel (n 10) 968 (art 17).
50 Ibid, 863–67; Sina Van den Bogaert, 'Berlin Congress (1878)' in R Wolfrum (ed), *The Max Planck Encyclopedia of Public International Law* (OUP 2012) 900–906.

concluded the following year at Constantinople, reaffirming the engagements adopted at the Berlin Congress and those provisions of the San Stefano Treaty that had not been invalidated by the latter, including the amnesty clause:

> A full and general amnesty is secured to all Ottoman subjects who shall have become compromised during the late events in the provinces of European Turkey, and all persons either detained on that account, or sent into exile or removed from their country, shall immediately be restored to the enjoyment of their liberty.[51]

The Balkan wars and the dissolution of the Ottoman Empire

By the beginning of the twentieth century, the Balkan region was characterised by struggles for independence from Ottoman, Russian and Austrian influences as well as territorial conflicts between the newly autonomous states. In 1911, the Ottoman Empire was confronted with Italy's claim to the territory presently known as Libya and, on the other hand, the uprisings marking the outbreak of the first Balkan war.[52] The Italo-Turkish war was concluded by the Treaty of Lausanne (1912) establishing Libya as an Italian protectorate and granting a 'full amnesty' to its inhabitants.[53]

The first Balkan war opposed the Balkan League (Serbia, Greece, Bulgaria and Montenegro) to the Ottoman Empire, the latter being rapidly overwhelmed by the allied armies.[54] Under the Treaty of London (1913), a large part of Ottoman territory was ceded to the states forming the Balkan League. However, they could not agree on its division amongst themselves, the fate of Macedonia being particularly contentious. These disputes led to the second Balkan war between Bulgaria and its former allies, with Romania and Turkey intervening on the side of the League. Following the defeat of Bulgaria against these combined forces, three peace treaties were negotiated to resolve the separate territorial disputes: the Treaty of Bucharest in August 1913 (Bulgaria, Greece, Romania and Serbia), the Treaty of Constantinople in September 1913 (Turkey and Bulgaria) and the Treaty of Athens in November 1913 (Turkey and Greece). The latter two included a general amnesty provision, that of the Athens Treaty stipulating that:

> The two high contracting parties accord full and complete amnesty to all persons involved in the political occurrences prior to the present treaty. Consequently, no individual shall be pursued, disturbed, or molested in person or property or in the exercise of his rights, because of acts relating

51 Israel (n 10) 1001 (art 9).
52 Phillips and Axelrod (n 10) 408–10.
53 Ibid; Israel (n 10) 1006.
54 Israel (n 10) 863–67.

> in any manner whatever to the war, and all judicial sentences and administrative measures based upon facts of that nature shall be ipso facto annulled.[55]

The Ottoman Empire was partitioned by the Allies in the Treaty of Sèvres (1920) in the wake of the First World War. This settlement placed Middle Eastern territories under British or French mandate and submitted the Turkish economy to the Allies' control.[56] Rather than providing for an amnesty, it contained penalty clauses establishing 'the right of the Allied Powers to bring before military tribunals persons accused of having committed acts in violation of the laws and customs of war'.[57]

The Ottoman Sultan proceeded to the trial of a number of former government officials in special court-martials in Constantinople.[58] However, the public execution of the first death sentence sparked a movement of revolt. The Turks, resenting the severe peace terms imposed by the Treaty of Sèvres, took side with revolutionary leader Mustapha Kemal who sought to distance Turkey from the Ottoman Empire. He refused to sign the peace treaty, which never entered into force. When the Greek army invaded Turkey, Kemal gathered forces to repel its advance and, with the help of Russia, eventually drove foreign powers out of Anatolia.[59] The Turkish Republic was established by the Treaty of Lausanne (1923) to which was appended the following amnesty declaration:

> No person who inhabits or who has inhabited Turkey, and reciprocally no person who inhabits or who has inhabited Greece, shall be disturbed or molested in Turkey and reciprocally in Greece, under any pretext whatsoever, on account of any military or political action taken by him, or any assistance of any kind given by him to a foreign Power signatory of the treaty of peace signed this day, or to the nationals of such Power … Full and complete amnesty shall be respectively granted by the Turkish Government and by the Greek Government for all crimes or offences committed during the same period which were evidently connected with the political events which have taken place during that period.[60]

55 Ibid, 1023 (art 6) and 1040 (art 3).
56 Phillips and Axelrod (n 10) 462.
57 Israel (n 10) 2134–35 (arts 226 and 230)
58 Jennifer Balint, 'The Ottoman State Special Military Tribunal for the Genocide of the Armeniens: "Doing Government Business"' in Kevin Jon Heller and Gerry Simpson (eds), *The Hidden Histories of War Crimes Trials* (OUP 2013); David M Crowe, *War Crimes, Genocide, and Justice: A Global History* (Palgrave Macmillan 2014) 101–114; Vahakn N Dadrian, 'The Turkish Military Tribunal's Prosecution of the Authors of the Armenian Genocide: Four Major Court-Martial Series' (1997) 11 *Holocaust and Genocidal Studies* 28.
59 Israel (n 10) 1225–34; Phillips and Axelrod (n 10) 551–54.
60 'Declaration of Amnesty' (1924) 18(2) *American Journal of International Law* (Supplement: Official Documents) 92–94.

International peace treaties

Though the amnesty tradition was most prevalent in Europe in the period studied, it was not limited to this region. In the eighteenth and nineteenth centuries, some peace treaties involving American, Asian and African nations included amnesty provisions as well. For instance, the peace settlement negotiated by the United States with the Delaware tribe in 1778 during the American War of Independence provided in its first article that 'all offences or acts of hostilities by one, or either of the contracting parties against the other, be mutually forgiven, and buried in the depth of oblivion, never more to be had in remembrance'.[61] The Paris Treaty of 1783 whereby Great Britain recognised the independence of the United States also extended a general amnesty.[62]

In Asia, the Treaty of Nanking (1842) concluding the first Opium War between China and Great Britain offered a 'full and entire amnesty' to all Chinese and British subjects compromised during the conflict.[63] Half a century later, China and Japan confronted each other in the Korean war of independence. This conflict was settled by the Treaty of Shimonoseki (1895) whereby China recognised Korea's independence and ceded parts of its territory to Japan.[64] This treaty granted an amnesty to prisoners of war, Japanese military offenders and Chinese subjects who had sided with Japan during the war.[65]

On the African continent, the Treaty of Vereeniging (1902) concluding the second Boer War between Great Britain and the two Afrikaner governments of South Africa – the South African Republic and the Orange Free State – also included an amnesty.[66] The measure was extended to the Burghers for their involvement in the war in exchange for their surrender to the British colonial power. By contrast with previous European peace treaties, this amnesty provision excluded from its scope acts 'contrary to the usage of war'.[67]

Amnesty as a necessary element of peace treaties

Reflecting the prevalence of amnesty in international peace settlements from the seventeenth to the early twentieth century, prominent publicists of this period considered it as a necessary element implied in every peace treaty. In the seventeenth century, Hugo Grotius considered that:

> Unless there is an express stipulation to the contrary, it is understood that, in all treaties of peace, there is an implied assent that no actions are to be

61 Phillips and Axelrod (n 10) 122.
62 Israel (n 10) 345–49 (art 6); Phillips and Axelrod (n 10) 125–28.
63 Israel (n 10) 1062 (art 9); Phillips and Axelrod (n 10) 299–300.
64 Phillips and Axelrod (n 10) 316–17.
65 Israel (n 10) 1106 (art 9).
66 Ibid, 1146 and 1051–57 (art 4); Phillips and Axelrod (n 10) 322–23.
67 Ibid.

> brought for losses occasioned by the accidental calamities of war, either to states or individuals. For those are natural consequences of a state of hostilities: and it is supposed that in doubtful cases, no belligerent would consent to be convicted of injustice.[68]

In the eighteenth century, Christian Wolff explained the essential role played by amnesty in the conclusion of peace:

> Since in a treaty of peace neither party convicts the other of wrong, and since when peace has been made as regards that cause for which the war was waged, war cannot again be renewed, consequently the war and whatever was done in it is consigned to perpetual oblivion and everlasting silence, and since an amnesty is complete and lasting forgetfulness of wrongs and offences previously committed; in a treaty first of all there must be an agreement for an amnesty, and this is contained in every treaty of peace as such, even if there should be no agreement for it … Indeed, unless this may be considered as certain, the war cannot be said to be ended when peace is concluded, since from it enmities survive liable to renew the war, which the common safety of nations demands should be completely ended, and the common safety is certainly the highest law in the supreme state, just as it is in each individual states.[69]

Other distinguished commentators of the eighteenth and nineteenth centuries referred to amnesty as a critical element of peace treaties. For example, Emer de Vattel observed that:

> An amnesty is a perfect oblivion of the past; and the end of peace being to extinguish all subjects of discord, this should be the leading article of the treaty: and accordingly, such is at present the constant practice. But though the treaty should be wholly silent on this head, the amnesty, by the very nature of peace, is necessarily implied in it.[70]

68 Hugo Grotius, *De jure belli ac pacis libri tres* (A C Campbell tr, Hyperion Press 1979) 390–91.

69 Christian Wolff, *Jus Gentium Methodo Scientifica pertractatum* (Clarendon Press 1934) 502.

70 Emer de Vattel, *The Law of Nations, or, Principles of the Law of Nature, Applied to the Conduct and Affairs of Nations and Sovereigns* (Liberty Fund 2008) 664, para 20. See also Jean Louis Klüber, *Droit des gens moderne de l'Europe* (Librairie de J G Cotta, Stuttgart 1819, vol 1) 500–501, para 324 ('Une clause essentielle dans tout traité de paix, et par conséquent supposée tacite, si elle n'est point exprimée et que le traité en dispose autrement, c'est l'amnistie (lex oblivionis). On entend par-là la déclaration des deux parties d'après laquelle elles regardent leur inimitiés comme entièrement terminées et abolies, et se promettent réciproquement qu'elles ne serviront jamais de cause ni de prétexte à une nouvelle guerre. Ce qui n'a point été cause, ni objet de la guerre, n'est point compris dans l'amnistie.')

In the beginning of the twentieth century, Lassa Oppenheim expounded the practice as follows:

> Since a treaty of peace is considered a final settlement of war, one of the effects of every peace treaty is the so-called amnesty – that is, an immunity for all wrongful acts done by the belligerents themselves, the members of their forces and their subjects during the war, and due to political motives. It is usual, but not at all necessary, to insert an amnesty clause in a treaty of peace. Therefore, unless the contrary is expressly stipulated in the treaty, so-called war crimes which were not punished before the conclusion of peace may no longer be punished after its conclusion. Individuals who have committed such war crimes, and have been arrested for them, must be liberated.[71]

The grant of general amnesties at the end of armed conflicts entailed that persons having committed war-related offences could no longer be prosecuted. More generally, by application of a post-war tabula rasa principle, all actions for losses and damages incurred as a result of the war were forfeited as a consequence of the conclusion of peace. Though this was the accepted practice, the victorious party could derogate from it and, for instance, require the surrender of war criminals as part of the peace terms. Indeed, according to Oppenheim:

> [A]lthough the Treaty of Peace brings to an end the right to prosecute war criminals, no rule of International Law prevents the victorious belligerent from imposing upon the defeated State the duty, as one of the provision of the armistice or of the Peace Treaty, to surrender for trial persons accused of war crimes. In this, as in other matters, the will of the victor is the law of the Treaty.[72]

71 Lassa Oppenheim, *International Law: A Treatise* (7th edn, Longmans 1948) vol 2, 611–12.

72 Lassa Oppenheim, *International Law: A Treatise* (6th edn, Longmans 1944) vol 2, 457–58. Following the Second World War, a judge of the International Military Tribunal for the Far East – Chief Justice Stone of the US Supreme Court – similarly observed '[i]t has been pointed out that, "In so far as the application of the usages of war to war crimes is concerned, the jurisdiction of the enemy courts only exists as long as the war lasts. After the war, war crimes can only be prosecuted if they constitute ordinary crimes" and "The most serious shortcoming of customary International Law consists in its limitation for the duration of war of national jurisdiction in war crimes which are not simultaneously ordinary crimes." The position under customary International Law seems, therefore, to be that whereas (as was recognised by the Supreme Court and by general international practice following the recent war) jurisdiction over war crimes exists without limitation beyond the cessation of fighting and up to the conclusion of peace, jurisdiction continues after this point only over such offences as are also infringements of the municipal law of the state whose courts are trying the alleged offender. ... This position under customary International Law can, of course, be altered by international agreement; " ... the belligerents have to make up their mind at the peace conference whether they wish to bury the past by a general amnesty, leave the matter unsettled or institute proceedings in time of peace, a procedure which, as a derogation of customary

The following section examines the origins of war crimes jurisdiction under international law and early instances when victorious belligerents considered the holding of trials at the end of war in derogation to the amnesty tradition.

2. Development of the accountability paradigm

The origins of war crimes jurisdiction under international law

The laws of war in the late Middle Ages

The laws of war in medieval Europe were based on the rules of chivalry governing the conduct of knights.[73] These rules were primarily determined by reference to customary usage or practices regarded as accepted from old times by learned knights and heralds. The code of knights, together with the written rules of civil and canon law regulating matters arising from war, formed the law of arms applicable in the whole Christendom regardless of soldiers' allegiances.[74] Medieval wars were unsparing towards non-combatants. Canon law attempted to restrain wartime violence by instituting days in which fighting was prohibited and an immunity for certain categories of non-combatants.[75] The code of knights also prescribed that the weak and innocent, including women, children, the aged and the sick, should not be harmed.[76] However, during the Hundred Years War (1337–1453), pillage, excesses and brutality towards non-combatants remained the rule, particularly because soldiers in those times were not adequately or regularly paid.[77]

International Law, requires the sanction of an international agreement between the States concerned."' See United Nations War Crimes Commission, *Law Reports of Trials of War Criminals* (HM Stationery Office 1948, vol 4) 76.

73 Keen, *Laws of War in the Late Middle Ages* (n 3) ch 2; Theodor Meron, *Henry's Wars and Shakespeare's Laws, Perspectives on the Law of War in the Later Middle Ages* (Clarendon Press 1993) 7–13; James Johnson, *Just War Tradition and the Restraint of War* (Princeton University Press 1981) ch 5; Christopher Allmand, *The Hundred Years War* (CUP 1988) 111–13.

74 Ibid.

75 Johnson (n 73) ch 5; Meron (n 73) 91–92; Russel (n 1) 61–70.

76 Johnson (n 73) 135–39; Meron (n 73) 91–92. Some royal ordinances of war also provided for the immunity of non-combatants, see Maurice Keen, 'Richard II's Ordinances of War of 1385' in Rowena E Archer and Simon Walker (eds), *Rulers and Ruled in Late Medieval England* (Hambledon Press 1995) 37; Anne Curry, 'The Military Ordinances of Henry V: Texts and Contexts' in Chris Given-Wilson, Ann Kettle and Len Scales (eds), *War, Government and Aristocracy in the British Isles, c. 1150–1500* (Boydell Press 2008) 227 and 230; Christopher Allmand, 'The War and Non-Combatants' in Kenneth Fowler (ed), *The Hundred Years War* (Mac Millan Press 1971) 168–80; Meron (n 73) ch 8.

77 Meron (n 73) 123–24; Keen, *Laws of War in the Late Middle Ages* (n 3) 192; Allmand, 'The War and Non-Combatants' (n 76) 168–69; Keen, 'Richard II's Ordinances of War of 1385' (n 76).

Justiciable matters arising out of war in the late Middle Ages typically included disputes over ransom or armorial bearings.[78] They were usually dealt with by the officers of the host during a particular campaign. Alternatively, courts of chivalry such as the English Court of Chivalry and the Parliament of Paris had permanent jurisdiction over matters of war.[79] Courts of chivalry were competent to adjudicate on criminal cases involving treason or lese majesty. The crime of treason was understood broadly as any act carried out in breach of a soldier's honour or good faith.[80] It was generally punished by death and degradation from all knightly honours.

Maurice Keen refers to a number of criminal cases tried by military courts in the fifteenth century.[81] The violations of the law of arms for which defendants were judged in these cases do not quite correspond to our modern conception of war crimes. For example, in 1418 a Frenchman was sentenced to death by Henry V because he had negotiated the surrender of a French town to the English invaders whilst it was still supplied in food and arms, an act that was considered a breach of the code of knighthood and a grave form of treason.[82] Yet, two medieval military trials initiated out of a feeling of outrage at violations of the laws of humanity resonate with modern atrocity trials. The first concerned Sir William Wallace, a Scottish knight who stood accused of having waged war against his liege lord in 1305.[83] However, according to Georg Schwarzenberger, it was not this charge that prompted Sir Wallace's trial and condemnation but rather his conduct in the war:

> Even judged by the rather low standards which, in fourteenth century warfare, were observed towards non-combatants, Wallace appears to have gone far beyond ordinary license and to have engaged in a war of extermination against the English population, "sparing neither age nor sex, monk nor nun."[84]

The second is the Breisach trial of 1474, widely regarded as the ancestor of modern international war crimes trials.[85] It took place before the outbreak of

78 Maurice Keen, 'The Jurisdiction and Origins of the Constable's Court' in John Gillingham and JC Holt (eds), *War and Government in the Middle Ages* (Boydell Press 1984) 159; Meron (n 73) 12.

79 Maurice Keen, 'Jurisdiction and Origins of the Constable's Court' (n 78); Allmand, *Hundred Years War* (n 73) 112; Meron (n 73) 12.

80 Honoré Bonet, *The Tree of Battles* (Liverpool University Press 1949) ch 10; Keen, *Laws of War in the Late Middle Ages* (n 3) ch 4.

81 Keen, *Laws of War in the Late Middle Ages* (n 3) ch 4; Keen, 'Jurisdiction and Origins of the Constable's Court' (n 78).

82 Keen, *Laws of War in the Late Middle Ages* (n 3) 46–47.

83 Georg Schwarzenberger, 'The Judgment of Nuremberg' (March 1947) 21(3) *Tulane Law Review* 329, 330.

84 Ibid.

85 Georg Schwarzenberger, *International Law as Applied by International Courts and Tribunals* (Stevens & Sons Limited 1968, vol 2) 462–66; M Cherif Bassiouni, *Crimes Against*

the Burgundian wars opposing the Duke of Burgundy, Charles the Bold, to the King of France, Louis XI. Under an agreement with the Archduke of Austria, Charles had been entrusted with the administration of the town of Breisach.[86] He had appointed Peter von Hagenbach as governor of the town and, in carrying out his duties, the latter perpetrated acts of brutality and rapacity against the town's inhabitants, including murder, rape, arbitrary taxation and confiscation. Outraged by his conduct, neighbouring kingdoms, city-states and cantons formed an alliance against Charles. Taking advantage of an uprising in Breisach, the allied powers captured his henchman and tried him before a tribunal composed of judges representing each power. Among other charges, Hagenbach was accused of having 'trampled under foot the laws of God and man'.[87] His defence of superior orders was rejected and he was condemned to death and deprived of his knighthood.

The customary right to punish enemy war criminals

Until the codification of the laws of war in the nineteenth century, the conduct of belligerents was primarily regulated through usage, custom and military codes or ordinances. The main customary rules related to the just war doctrine, the good faith that was to be observed between belligerents and the status of land, property and persons coming into enemy hands during the war.[88] The killing of non-combatants and prisoners of war was considered unrighteous and cruel but was not per se prohibited by the law of nations.[89] Grotius, for example, prescribed that:

> An enemy, therefore, who considers, not what human laws permit, but what is his duty, what is righteous and pious, will spare hostile blood: and will never inflict death, except either to avoid death, or evils like death, or to punish crimes which are capital in desert. And even to some who have deserved that, he will remit all, or at least, capital punishment, either out of humanity, or for some other plausible causes.[90]

Humanity in International Criminal Law (Martinus Nijhoff Publishers 1992) 197; Gregory S Gordon, 'The Trial of Peter Von Hagenbach: Reconciling History, Historiography and International Criminal Law' in Kevin Jon Heller and Gerry Simpson (eds), *The Hidden Histories of War Crimes Trials* (OUP 2013) 13.

86 Schwarzenberger, *International Law as Applied by International Courts and Tribunals* (n 85) 462–66; Gordon (n 85).

87 Ibid. For a discussion of whether these charges correspond to modern-day war crimes and crimes against humanity, see Gordon (n 85) 41–46.

88 Hugo Grotius, *The Rights of War and Peace* (CUP 1853).

89 See Jean-Mathieu Mattei, *Histoire du droit de la guerre (1700–1819)* (Presses Universitaires d'Aix-Marseille 2006, vol 1) 695–701 and 729–36.

90 Grotius (n 88) 374.

However, in continuity with the canon laws and chivalric rules which granted immunity to certain categories of non-combatants in the late Middle Ages, from the sixteenth century onwards certain military codes or 'Articles of war' proscribed the ill-treatment of women and clerics, such as those decreed by Emperor Maximilian in 1508 or King Gustavus II of Sweden in 1621.[91]

Two primary means of enforcement of the laws of war were available to belligerents in the seventeenth through to the nineteenth century. In the first place, when a soldier had committed a grave breach of the laws of war and came into the custody of the adversary during the war, it was the latter's right to punish the wrongdoer by death or any other sanction deemed appropriate.[92] In the alternative, faced with enemy soldiers violating the laws of war, a belligerent was entitled to resort to reprisals or, in other words, to disregard the same laws of war towards the transgressors. However, as mentioned above, there were no legally enforceable international standards prohibiting excesses towards non-combatants. Emer de Vattel explained the situation as follows:

> [W]henever it is certain and evident that such a measure, such an act of hostility, is necessary in general for overpowering the enemy's resistance, and attaining the end of a lawful war, – that measure, thus viewed in a general light is, by the law of nations, deemed lawful in war, and consistent with propriety, although he who unnecessarily adopts it when he might attain his end by gentler methods, is not innocent before God and his own conscience. In this, lies the difference between what is just, equitable, irreprehensible in war, and what is only allowed between nations, and suffered to pass with impunity.[93]

According to de Vattel, principles of justice and humanity required the sparing of enemy combatants who laid down their arms, except in one specific situation:

> It is when that enemy has been guilty of some enormous breach of the law of nations, and particularly when he has violated the laws of war. This refusal of quarter is no natural consequence of the war, but a punishment for his crime, – a punishment which the injured party has the right to inflict.[94]

This right to punish enemy combatants guilty of serious violations of the laws has been identified as the legal foundation of war crimes jurisdiction

91 Schwarzenberger, *International Law as Applied by International Courts and Tribunals* (n 85) 15–16; Kenneth Ogren, 'Humanitarian law in the Articles of War decreed in 1621 by King Gustavus II Adolphus of Sweden' (1996) 36 (313) *International Review of the Red Cross* 438.

92 Grotius (n 88) 377–78.

93 de Vattel (n 70) 542.

94 Ibid, 544.

under international law.[95] However, the punishment of soldiers' excesses was by no means a generalised or systematic practice:

> If sometimes the furious and ungovernable soldier carries his brutality so far as to violate female chastity, or to massacre women, children and old men, the officers lament those excesses: they exert their utmost efforts to put a stop to them; and a prudent and humane general even punishes them whenever he can.[96]

In any event, once peace had been concluded, it was generally accepted that all actions for damages done to persons or property in relation to the war were forfeited. This was usually explicitly stated in the treaty of peace by means of a general amnesty extinguishing the belligerents' jurisdiction over enemy combatants. This post-war tabula rasa principle was deemed essential in order to ensure that former enmities had been eradicated and would not be used as a pretext for a new conflict.[97]

An inchoate form of post-war justice

Following the French defeat at Waterloo, the victorious powers were divided as to how to deal with Napoleon and his supporters.[98] The Prussians, who had borne the brunt of the war, resented the French and would have opted for executing Napoleon but for the refusal of the British. The latter preferred to see the fallen emperor tried for treason before French courts. However, the Bourbons were anxious at the perspective of a show trial that risked diminishing even further their already tenuous public support. Napoleon was seen by the allies as more of an enemy that must be dealt with than a war criminal in the modern sense of the term. He was accused of treason to the French Crown but not of having violated the laws of war, apart from Prussia which insisted on the mistreatment of Prussian prisoners of war.

The compromise solution advocated and enforced by the British was to banish Napoleon to St. Helena. With respect to the conspirators who had made his return possible, the British urged Louis XVIII to submit them to exemplary punishment in order to put a definitive end to Frenchmen's revolutionary tendencies. Under pressure from his foreign advisors, the King agreed to exclude, from his amnesty ordinance of 24 July 1815, the most dangerous traitors and agitators. The act accordingly stipulated that 57 listed conspirators would

95 Ibid; Oppenheim (n 72) 457–58; E van Sliedregt, *The Criminal Responsibility of Individuals for Violations of International Humanitarian Law* (TMC Asser Press 2003) 2; Jackson Nyamuya Maogoto, *War Crimes and Realpolitik: International Justice from World War I to the Twenty-First Century* (Lynne Rienner Publishers 2004) 17.

96 de Vattel (n 70) 549.

97 See Grotius (n 88) 418–19; Wolff (n 69) 502; de Vattel (n 70) 664; Klüber (n 70) 324.

98 See Bass (n 33) ch 2.

stand military trial or be exiled.[99] In the end, however, only three military commanders were tried and sentenced to death for treason, all the others managing to escape.

The exile of Napoleon and the trial by French courts of a few of his generals were a far cry from the Nuremberg international proceedings and modern war crimes trials. Significant progress was nonetheless achieved on two fronts. On the one hand, the victorious powers refrained from simply executing the enemy leader, the treatment usually reserved to defeated foes at the time. On the other hand, the British pushed for the holding of trials after the conclusion of the war, an unprecedented initiative since peace agreements usually precluded war-related legal proceedings. This was a first step towards more legalism in dealing with vanquished enemy leaders in the aftermath of destructive war. According to Bass, 'popular outrage and even a weak legalism forced even the unsentimental architects of the Vienna system to act in ways that contradicted their own understanding of the national interest'.[100] When deciding on the fate of the defeated Kaiser Wilhelm II at Versailles one century later, the Allies would refer to this precursor attempt to institute post-war trials.

The codification of the laws of war

A few decades later, the first international efforts to codify the laws of war led to the adoption of a number of treaties regulating specific aspects of the conduct of hostilities.[101] The Lieber Military Code of 1863, promulgated by President Lincoln during the American Civil War, prefigured later international instruments regulating the laws of war in a more comprehensive manner.[102] It contained certain provisions on war crimes such as article 44 prescribing that:

> All wanton violence committed against persons in the invaded country, all destruction of property not commanded by the authorized officer, all robbery, all pillage or sacking, even after taking a place by main force, all rape, wounding, maiming, or killing of such inhabitants, are prohibited under the penalty of death, or such other severe punishment as may seem adequate for the gravity of the offense.[103]

99 Ibid; Marcel Doher, *Proscrits et exilés après Waterloo* (J Peyronnet & Cie, Paris 1965) 22–23, 37; Jean-Marc Largeaud, *Napoléon et Waterloo: la défaite glorieuse de 1815 à nos jours* (Boutique de l'histoire, Paris 2006) 174–76.

100 Bass (n 33) 39.

101 For example, the Paris Declaration Respecting Maritime Law of 1856 and the Geneva Convention for the Amelioration of the Condition of the Wounded in Armies in the Field of 1864, see Oppenheim (n 72) 179–80.

102 Instructions for the Government of Armies of the United States in the Field, General Order N° 100, 24 April 1863, see Dietrich Schindler and Jin Toman, *The Laws of Armed Conflicts* (Martinus Nihjoff Publisher 1988) 3–21.

103 Ibid, 3–8.

The Lieber Code was used as a basis for the Hague Conference of 1899 which adopted a Convention (II) with Respect to the Laws and Customs of War on Land.[104] This treaty was revised at the second Hague Conference of 1907 and became Convention (IV) respecting the Laws and Customs of War on Land.[105] Both conventions required belligerent powers to regulate the conduct of their armed forces.[106] The 1907 convention also importantly established the international responsibility of states for breaches committed by their troops, entailing the payment of compensation to the state of nationality of the victim.[107] In keeping with the traditional view of states as the primary subjects of international law, these international duties to respect the laws of war were not imposed directly on the individuals concerned but through the medium of the international responsibility of states.[108] The introduction of a legal basis for holding belligerents responsible for breaches committed by their armed forces induced states to incorporate the laws of war into their municipal law and ensure the repression of war crimes at the domestic level.

Several provisions of the Hague Conventions were designed to restrict unnecessary violence on the battlefield. For example, the use of weapons causing superfluous injuries, the ill treatment of prisoners of war and the abuse of power over civilians of an occupied country were prohibited. Acts violating these conventional rules of warfare constituted war crimes that the adverse belligerent power was entitled to punish during the war pursuant to customary international law. As regards this right to punish, Oppenheim explained that:

> The right of the belligerent to punish, during the war, such war criminals as fall into his hands is a well-recognised principle of International Law. It is a right of which he may effectively avail himself after he has occupied all or part of the enemy territory, and is thus in a position to seize the war criminals who happen to be there. He may, as a condition of the armistice, impose upon the authorities of the defeated State the duty to hand over persons charged with having committed war crimes, regardless of whether such persons are present in the territory actually occupied by him or in the

104 Ibid, 49–53; Crowe (n 58) 86–92.

105 Schindler and Toman (n 102) 53–57; James Brown Scott (ed), *The Hague Conventions and Declarations of 1899 and 1907* (OUP 1915).

106 Convention (II) with Respect to the Laws and Customs of War on Land, art 1; Convention (IV) respecting the Laws and Customs of War on Land, art 1, see Schindler and Toman (n 102) 62.

107 Convention (IV) respecting the Laws and Customs of War on Land, art 3, see Schindler and Toman (n 102) 62.

108 Elizabeth Zoller, 'The Status of Individuals under International Law' in George Ginsburgs and Vladimir Nikolaevich Kudriavtsev, *The Nuremberg Trial and International Law* (Martinus Nijhoff Publishers 1990) 99–102.

> territory which, at the successful end of hostilities, he will be in a position to occupy. For in both cases the accused are, in effect, in his power.[109]

Schwarzenberger suggested that this right to punish enemy war criminals was originally an individualised form of reprisals.[110] On this basis, he explained the three main characteristics of war crimes jurisdiction under international law at the time, namely: that it was optional, that the type of punishment to be imposed was at the discretion of the belligerent, and that jurisdiction terminated with the conclusion of peace. According to that commentator, the punishment of war criminals and the payment of compensation to the victim state were understood as the criminal and civil sanctions of the rules of warfare.[111]

The settlement of the First World War: departure from the amnesty practice

In the early days of the First World War, German troops carried out atrocities in Belgium. The sack of Louvain, during which hundreds of civilians were killed and the ancient part of the city burned down, provoked indignation in the Allied countries.[112] Citizens called on their government to require the post-war punishment of the German Kaiser and his soldiers responsible for serious crimes. Accordingly, French military courts tried several German prisoners responsible for violations of the laws of war during the first years of the conflict.[113] In response, the Germans retaliated against captured French soldiers. In the same vein, angered by German indiscriminate submarine warfare, British military leaders detained captured U-boat crew members and threatened to try them as war criminals, thereby provoking German reprisals against British prisoners of war.[114]

These reprisal and counter-reprisal tactics soon proved unproductive. The idea of post-war trials had more success among British leaders, who set up a government committee to gather evidence on German war crimes.[115] In relation to Turkish crimes, the French, British and Russian governments issued a joint declaration to the Ottoman Sultan in 1915 describing the massacres of Armenians carried out by the Young Turks as crimes 'against humanity and civilization' whose perpetrators would be held personally responsible

109 Oppenheim (n 72) 457–58.
110 Schwarzenberger (n 85) 453–55.
111 Ibid.
112 James F Willis, *Prologue to Nuremberg: The Politics and Diplomacy of Punishing War Criminals of the First World War* (Greenwood Press 1982) 9–11.
113 Ibid, 13; James W Garner, 'Punishment of Offenders against the Laws and Customs of War' (1920) 14 *The American Journal of International Law* 70, 76–77.
114 Willis (n 112) 17; Leonard Charles Frederick Turner, *The First World War* (Frederick Warne & Co 1967) 12–13, 28–29.
115 Willis (n 112) 21–22.

irrespective of their official status.[116] However, a fundamental pre-condition to the holding of post-war trials was an overwhelming victory of the Allies. Accordingly, commitments to the idea fluctuated depending on the fortunes of the war. The disastrous Somme offensive in the autumn of 1916 brought the Allies' morale down. Thus, when the Germans deported tens of thousands of Belgian, French and Pole civilians to work as forced labour in Germany, no new threats of war crimes trials were issued by the Allies.[117]

The conflict stagnated without decisive advance on either side until the collapse of the exhausted Czarist Russia in 1917. Following violent upheavals in St Petersburg in early March 1917, the Czar abdicated, leaving power in the hands of an unpopular provisional government unable to match the Bolshevik party's appealing programme of peace and social reform.[118] By the autumn, Lenin and Trotsky were able to gather enough support to take control of the government, marking the end of the Russian Empire. Several reasons prompted them to negotiate an armistice with Germany and its allies (the Central Powers) including the alarming state of Russia's economy, the menace of an impending civil war and the need to consolidate the Bolshevik regime. The young Soviet Republic was thus compelled to accept the harsh peace terms of the Brest-Litovsk Treaty (3 March 1918).[119] A supplementary agreement concluded on the same day extended a general amnesty to both parties' nationals.[120]

The entry into the war of the United States in the summer of 1918 precipitated the Central Powers' defeat. Despite previous declarations by some Allied governments to the effect that the German Kaiser and his soldiers would be prosecuted for their crimes, the armistice agreement of 11 November did not mention post-war trials.[121] The day before it was signed, Wilhelm II fled to the Netherlands, which had remained neutral during the war and granted him asylum.[122]

The Allies convened a peace conference in Paris in January 1919 to determine the terms to be imposed on the defeated powers. The Paris Conference created a Commission on the Responsibility of the Authors of the War and on Enforcement of Penalties composed of two members from each of the major powers (France, Great Britain, Italy, the US and Japan) and one member from the lesser powers (Belgium, Greece, Poland, Romania and Serbia).[123] It was mandated to determine

116 Bass (n 33) 117; Balint (n 58) 83.

117 Willis (n 112) ch 2; Howard S Levie, *Terrorism in War: The Law of War Crimes* (Oceana Publications, Dobbs Ferry N.Y. 1993) 21.

118 Turner (n 114) 27–36; Israel (n 10) 1225–34; Phillips and Axelrod (n 10) 419–24.

119 Turner (n 114) 37; Sally A Boniece, 'Brest-Litovsk, Peace of (1918)' in R Wolfrum (ed), *The Max Planck Encyclopedia of Public International Law* (OUP 2012) 1051–54.

120 Parry (n 11) vol 223, 103–104 (arts 23 to 27)

121 Bass (n 33) 63; Turner (n 114) 40–41; Phillips and Axelrod (n 10) 425–27.

122 Turner (n 114) 41.

123 Commission on the Responsibility of the Authors of the War and on Enforcement of Penalties (1920) 14(1/2) *American Journal of International Law* 95, 95–98.

the responsibility of the authors of the war, the violations of the laws and customs of war committed by the Central Powers' armed forces, their degree of criminal responsibility and the possibility of establishing an international tribunal to deal with persons responsible for offences against the law of nations.[124]

The Commission found that the responsibility for the war rested on the Central Powers, primarily on Germany and Austria, secondarily on Turkey and Bulgaria.[125] It established a long list of war crimes perpetrated by their armed forces and stressed that 'there is no reason why rank, however exalted, should in any circumstances protect the holder of it from responsibility when that responsibility has been established before a properly constituted tribunal. This extends even to the case of heads of states'.[126] The Commission observed that granting immunity to head of states:

> [W]ould involve laying down the principle that the greatest outrages against the laws and customs of war and the laws of humanity, if proved against him, could in no circumstances be punished. Such a conclusion would shock the conscience of civilized mankind.[127]

Hence, it declared that:

> All persons belonging to enemy countries, however high their position may have been, without distinction of rank, including Chiefs of States, who have been guilty of offences against the laws and customs of war or the laws of humanity, are liable to criminal prosecution.[128]

With respect to the constitution of an international tribunal, the Commission made a distinction between, on the one hand, violations of the laws of war and humanity and, on the other, acts having provoked the war.[129] It recommended the establishment of an international tribunal to try the former types of offences, stressing that 'all enemy persons alleged to have been guilty of offences against the laws and customs of war and the laws of humanity shall be excluded from any amnesty to which the belligerents may agree'.[130] As regards the latter category of acts, however, the Commission noted that 'a war of aggression may not be considered as an act directly contrary to positive law, or one which can be successfully brought before a tribunal such as the Commission is authorised to consider under its terms of reference'.[131] While it suggested that the Peace

124 Ibid, 95.
125 Ibid, 98.
126 Ibid, 116.
127 Ibid.
128 Ibid, 117.
129 Ibid, 118.
130 Ibid, 123.
131 Ibid, 118.

Conference should formally condemn these acts, it advised against their prosecution before a criminal tribunal.[132]

The Commission's conclusions and recommendations reflected the agreement of European Allies regarding the need to punish German war criminals, assign responsibility for the war to the Kaiser and establish an international tribunal having jurisdiction over violations of the laws of war and humanity. The American delegates, however, dissented on several points and felt the need to append to the Commission's report a minority opinion.[133] In the first place, they objected to the Commission's reference to the laws of humanity on the ground that they were not, by contrast with the laws of war, susceptible to objective determination or accepted as binding by the society of nations.[134] Secondly, in common with the Japanese delegates, the Americans were not prepared to accept the principle that heads of states could be liable to criminal prosecution. Finally, they objected to the creation of an international tribunal, an institution for which there was no precedent and whose judgments would be based on ex post facto laws. As an alternative, the American delegates proposed the establishment of mixed military tribunals to deal with war crimes affecting more than one country.

The provisions of the Versailles Treaty (28 June 1919) dealing with penalties reflected a compromise between the European and American positions. Article 227 provided for the creation of a special tribunal composed of one judge from each of the major powers to try Wilhelm II for 'a supreme offence against international morality and the sanctity of treaties'.[135] In deference to the American objection, this formulation did not refer to the Kaiser's criminal responsibility for initiating the war. Nonetheless, it was the first time in the history of nations that a head of state was assigned personal responsibility at the international level in such a legalistic manner. In practical terms, however, these efforts were to no avail as the Netherlands refused to extradite the Kaiser to the Allies.

Article 228 of the Versailles Treaty established the victors' right to try members of the Central Powers' armed forces accused of war crimes before national or mixed military tribunals and required Germany to surrender such persons to the Allies.[136] Political expediency also prevailed on that front as there was no mention either of the laws of humanity or of an international tribunal. And again, the provision had no practical effect since the German government refused to extradite war criminals, invoking the instability of post-war German society and the risk of a military coup in the event article 228 should be complied with.[137] The Allies reluctantly renounced their right to enforce the war crimes

132 Ibid, 118–20.
133 Ibid, 127–52.
134 Ibid, 134.
135 Phillips and Axelrod (n 10) 137.
136 Ibid, 437.
137 Willis (n 112) ch 7; Bass (n 33) ch 3.

provision on the condition that a number of designated war criminals be prosecuted before German courts. Although some trials were effectively held at Leipzig, they were found highly unsatisfactory by the Allies, the convictions being few, the sentences very light and the number of accused managing to escape high.[138] Nevertheless, as pointed out by Willis:

> For the first time, a major international peace treaty had established the principle in international law that war crimes punishment was a proper conclusion of peace, that the termination of war did not bring a general amnesty as a matter of course.[139]

The Versailles Treaty also marked a departure from previous peace practice in that it imposed the payment of war reparations on the Central Powers as a punitive measure, the reparation clause being tied with the clause establishing the responsibility of Germany for the initiation of the war (articles 232 and 233).[140] Starting in the beginning of the nineteenth century, certain peace treaties stipulated that the defeated party was to pay for the war expenses of the victor as an indemnity. However, this was not understood as a form of sanction imposed on the vanquished belligerent prior to the Versailles Treaty.[141] Previous peace treaties did not put blame on one party for its conduct before or during the war. Rather, by virtue of the principles of sovereignty and equality of states, they opted for peace, friendship and amnesty clauses. This departure was consistent with the provision of the Hague Convention of 1907 establishing the responsibility of states for breaches of the laws of war committed by their armed forces and a concomitant obligation to compensate the state victim of the violations.[142]

The Treaty of Sèvres (1920), complementing the Treaty of Versailles with regard to the Ottoman Empire, contained a war crimes provision modelled on article 228 and a clause permitting the prosecution of persons responsible for the Armenian genocide.[143] Anticipating the will of the Allies and wishing to conciliate them, Turkish authorities had embarked on the trial of several Young Turk leaders in April 1919, one year before the signing of the treaty.[144] These proceedings led to the conviction of several government officials and were

138 Law Officers' Department, 'German War Crimes Trials: Report of the Proceedings before the Supreme Court in Leipzig' (1922) 16 *The American Journal of International Law* 628–640; Willis (n 112) ch 8; Bass (n 33) ch 3.

139 Willis (n 112) 85. Maogoto similarly states that '[i]n a dramatic break with precedent, the treaties were to contain penal provisions as opposed to blanket amnesties', see n 95 at 50.

140 Phillips and Axelrod (n 10) 438; Turner (n 114) 46–48.

141 Steiger (n 9) 85–86.

142 De Zayas (n 7) 148–50.

143 Israel (n 10) 2134–35 (arts 226 and 230).

144 Balint (n 58) 96–99; Dadrian (n 58); Crowe (n 58) 101–14; Willis (n 112) 153–63; Bass (n 33) ch 4.

initially seen as promising by the Allies. However, they were hampered by the Allied-sanctioned Greek occupation of the Anatolian city of Smyrna, which began in May 1919. The atrocities committed by Greek forces in this context significantly damaged the Allies' credibility and provided fuel to the patriotic movement gathering under the lead of Mustapha Kemal in opposition to any form of collaboration with the Allies.[145] In this climate of unrest, most of those arrested or sentenced for crimes connected to the war were released by Turkish prison authorities, the remaining prisoners being taken into British custody and transferred to the islands of Mudros and Malta.

Britain's interest in prosecuting Turkish atrocities was primarily motivated by the ill-treatment that British soldiers endured at the hands of the Young Turks during the war.[146] British public opinion was also sensitive to the plight of Christian Armenians. By the time the Sultan finally signed the Treaty of Sèvres in August 1920, the other Allies had distanced themselves from Turkish post-war trials and the British remained alone in pushing for prosecution. British military authorities arrested a number of Turkish suspects throughout 1919 and 1920 and transferred them to Malta.[147] However, Turkish nationalists retaliated by capturing several British soldiers, the release of whom was conditioned upon the liberation of Turkish detainees. British authorities eventually agreed to this bargain in December 1921, marking the end of Allied efforts to prosecute major criminals of the First World War. As has been seen, the Treaty of Lausanne concluded by Mustapha Kemal with the Allies in 1923 supplanted the treaty of Sèvres and provided for the traditional amnesty of all acts connected to the war.[148]

The settlement of the Second World War: establishment of the principle of individual liability for international crimes

During the first years of the Second World War, the Allies expressed outrage at the atrocities committed by Nazi forces in Europe and announced their intention to punish these crimes at the end of the war.[149] On 1 November 1943, the three main Allied Powers (the United States, the Soviet Union and the United Kingdom) issued the Moscow Declaration setting out the pattern for the post-war punishment of Nazi criminals:

145 Ibid.
146 Balint (n 58) 84; Bass (n 33) ch 4; Willis (n 112) 153–63.
147 Ibid; Crowe (n 58) 113.
148 'Declaration of Amnesty' (n 60).
149 United Nations War Crimes Commission, *History of the United Nations War Crimes Commission and the Development of the Laws of War* (HM Stationery Office 1948) 87–94; George Ginsburgs, 'The Nuremberg Trial: Background' in George Ginsburgs and Nikolaevich Kudriavtsev (eds), *The Nuremberg Trial and International Law* (Martinus Nijhoff Publishers 1990).

> At the time of the granting of any armistice to any Government which may be set up in Germany, those German officers and men and members of the Nazi Party who have been responsible for or have taken a consenting part in the above atrocities, massacres and executions will be sent back to the countries in which their abominable deeds were done in order that they may be judged and punished according to the laws of these liberated countries and of the Free Governments which will be erected therein ... The above declaration is without prejudice to the case of the major criminals whose offenses have no particular geographical location and who will be punished by a joint decision of the Government of the Allies.[150]

As a preparation for these prosecution efforts, the Allies established a United Nations War Crimes Commission charged to investigate the crimes committed by Axis forces. The mandate of the Commission was initially limited to war crimes committed against Allied nationals but was later extended to cover acts of aggression and crimes against stateless persons and nationals of the Axis countries, the latter designated as crimes against humanity.[151]

A few months after the end of the war, an agreement 'for the Prosecution and Punishment of the Major War Criminals of the European Axis' was concluded in London by the three major Allied powers and the provisional government of France.[152] The London Agreement reaffirmed the Moscow Declaration and provided for the creation of an International Military Tribunal (IMT) competent to try major criminals of the Axis forces, which was set up at Nuremberg in November 1945.[153] The Charter of the IMT was the first international instrument to institute individual criminal responsibility for war crimes, crimes against humanity and crimes against peace.[154] The recognition of crimes against humanity as an international crime was groundbreaking since crimes committed by a state against its own nationals were hitherto considered to fall within the sphere of domestic law. Developing another aspect of international criminal law, the Charter excluded the immunity of heads of state and senior government officials for international crimes.[155] In parallel to the Nuremberg IMT, an International Military Tribunal was

150 United Nations War Crimes Commission (n 149) 107–108.

151 Ibid, 169–87; Arieh J Kovachi, *Prelude to Nuremberg, Allied War Crimes Policy and the Question of Punishment* (University of North Carolina Press 1998) chs 4 to 6.

152 Agreement for the Prosecution and Punishment of the Major War Criminals of the European Axis (signed 8 August 1945, entered into force 8 August 1945) 82 UNTS 280 (London Agreement). See Kovachi (n 151) ch 6.

153 London Agreement (n 152) art 1.

154 Charter of the International Military Tribunal, Annex to the London Agreement (n 152) art 6.

155 Ibid, art 7.

established in Tokyo by the Supreme Commander of the Allied Powers for Japan, US General MacArthur, to prosecute major war criminals of the Far East.

According to Professor Zoller:

> The Nuremberg and Tokyo trials were certainly a major departure from classical international law insofar as individuals were for the first time in the record of the law of nations tried and punished by an international judicial body in accordance with international rules.[156]

Defendants before the Nuremberg IMT raised the argument that international law was not concerned with the acts of individuals but solely with the acts of states. Moreover, they claimed that the doctrine of sovereign immunity prevented individuals acting on behalf of a state from being held criminally responsible for such acts. Responding to these assertions, the Nuremberg Tribunal famously stated that:

> Crimes against international law are committed by men, not by abstract entities, and only by punishing individuals who commit such crimes can the provisions of international law be enforced ... The very essence of the Charter is that individuals have international duties which transcend the national obligations of obedience imposed by the individual state. He who violates the laws of war cannot obtain immunity while acting in pursuance of the authority of the state if the state in authorizing action moves outside its competence under international law.[157]

The IMT thus established that international law imposes duties upon individuals, without the interposition of domestic law, and that the breach of these duties entails individual criminal liability.

The Nuremberg Charter provided the legal basis for the power of the IMT, an emanation of the four victorious Allies and, to a certain extent, of the international community, to try the nationals of the defeated powers accused of crimes under international law.[158] According to the Tribunal:

> The making of the Charter was the exercise of the sovereign legislative power by the countries to which the German Reich unconditionally surrendered; and the undoubted right of these countries to legislate for the occupied territories has been recognized by the civilized world.[159]

156 Zoller (n 108) 101.

157 International Military Tribunal (Nuremberg), Judgment and Sentences (1 October 1946), reprinted in (1947) 41 *American Journal of International Law* 172, 221.

158 In addition to the four victorious Allies, nineteen states signed the Nuremberg Charter.

159 International Military Tribunal (Nuremberg), Judgment and Sentences (n 157) 216.

The Charter was not intended to be an instrument of general application, its article six circumscribing the personal jurisdiction of the IMT to persons 'acting in the interests of the European Axis countries'.[160]

In the wake of the conclusion of the London Agreement, the victorious powers established an Allied Control Council to govern the occupation of Germany by the Allied military authorities. On 20 December 1945, the Council enacted Control Council Law No. 10 empowering the occupying authorities to try suspected war criminals and other serious offenders within their respective zone of occupation.[161] This law reproduced the provision of the Nuremberg Charter establishing the criminal responsibility of persons responsible for war crimes, crimes against humanity and crimes against peace. The last paragraph of the provision stipulated that accused persons:

> Shall not be entitled to the benefits of any statute of limitation in respect to the period from 30 January 1933 to 1 July 1945, nor shall any immunity, pardon or amnesty granted under the Nazi regime be admitted as a bar to trial or punishment.[162]

This clause was meant to ensure that the laws and policies of the National Socialist regime tending to the exoneration of Nazi criminals would not bar their conviction and punishment by Allied military authorities. However, in so far as it only related to measures taken by Nazi authorities, it did not restrict the freedom of the occupying authorities or of the new German government to exempt convicted persons from punishment.

As a matter of fact, in the aftermath of the Second World War, a number of Nazi and fascist criminals benefited from amnesties or pardons. In West Germany, two amnesty laws covering minor Nazi offences were enacted in 1949 and 1954 by the new Parliament.[163] In addition, pardons were granted by the Allied military authorities to a number of heavily implicated Nazi criminals in the 1950s, some of whom had been convicted by the IMT.[164] In Japan, American military authorities similarly offered immunity to a number of prominent war criminals as well as to the Japanese Emperor.[165] The new governments of the main wartime

160 Charter of the International Military Tribunal, Annex to the London Agreement (n 154) art 6.

161 Control Council Law No 10, Punishment of Persons Guilty of War Crimes, Crimes Against Peace and Against Humanity (20 December 1945) 3 Official Gazette Control Council for Germany 50–55 (1946) (CCL No 10) art 3; United Nations War Crimes Commission (n 149) 461–62.

162 CCL No 10 (n 161) art 2(5).

163 Norbert Frei, *Adenauer's Germany and the Nazi Past, the Politics of Amnesty and Integration* (Columbia University Press 2002) chs 1 and 2; John H Herz, 'Denazification and Related Policies' in Neil J Kritz (ed), *Transitional Justice, How Emerging Democracies Reckon with Former Regimes* (United States Institute of Peace Press 1995, vol 2).

164 See Frei (n 163) chs 5, 6, 7 and 9.

165 See Zachary Kaufman, 'Transitional Justice for Tōjō's Japan: The United States Role in the Establishment of the International Military Tribunal for the Far East and other Transitional

allies of Germany – Austria and Italy – also introduced sweeping amnesty laws that extinguished the criminal liability of perpetrators of international crimes among other offenders.[166] A number of individuals responsible for atrocity crimes during World War II thus benefited from amnesties, pardons or penal practices leading to their release and rehabilitation. The Allies were not overly preoccupied by these practices and in some instances themselves proceeded to the release of major criminals. In the end, the windup of the question of war criminals and their reintegration into society did not take much longer than ten years in the countries most concerned with the rise of Nazism and fascism.

The principles of international law recognised in the Nuremberg Charter were affirmed by the UN General Assembly in Resolution 95(I) of 11 December 1946, which contributed to making them a part of general international law. The General Assembly then created the International Law Commission with the mandate, inter alia, to formulate the principles of international law recognised in the Nuremberg Charter and the IMT judgment.[167] The first principle established that '[a]ny person who commits an act which constitutes a crime under international law is responsible therefore and liable to punishment'.[168] The sixth principle provided that crimes against peace, war crimes and crimes against humanity as defined in the IMT Charter and Judgment are 'punishable as crimes under international law'.[169] The International Law Commission's draft conferred a general scope of application to the principle of individual liability for crimes under international law and entitled states to prosecute persons responsible for these crimes outside of the World War II context.

Justice Mechanisms for Japan after World War II' (2014) 27 *Emory International Law Review* 755; Yves Beigbeder, *Judging War Criminals, The Politics of International Justice* (Palgrave Macmillan 1999) 50–57.

166 On the Italian post-war amnesty, see Roy Domenico, *Italian Fascists on Trial 1943–1948* (University of North Carolina Press 1991) ch 7; Filippo Focardi and Lutz Klinkhammer, 'The Question of Fascist Italy's War Crimes: The Construction of a Self-Acquitting Myth (1943–1948)' (2004) 9(3) *Journal of Modern Italian Studies* 330; Michele Battini, 'Sins of memory: reflections on the lack of an Italian Nuremberg and the administration of international justice after 1945' (2004) 9(3) *Journal of Modern Italian Studies* 349. On Austrian post-war amnesties, see Siegfried Beer, 'Hunting the Discriminators: Denazification in Austria, 1945–1957' in Guðmundur Hálfdanarson (ed), *Racial Discrimination and Ethnicity in European History* (Edizioni PLUS 2003); Gerhard Botz, 'Janus-Headed Austria, Transition from Nazism as Restoration, Continuity and Learning Process' in Stein Ugelvik Larsen (ed), *Modern Europe after Fascism, 1943–1980s* (Columbia University Press 1998, vol 1); Dieter Stiefel, 'Has the course of denazification been determined by "economic necessities"?' in Stein Ugelvik Larsen (ed), *Modern Europe after Fascism, 1943–1980s* (Columbia University Press 1998, vol 1).

167 UN General Assembly Resolution 177 (II) (21 November 1947).

168 Principles of International Law recognized in the Charter of the Nürnberg Tribunal and in the Judgment of the Tribunal, with commentaries, Yearbook of the International Law Commission, 1950, vol 2, 374–78.

169 Ibid.

Conclusion

Most of the peace treaties concluded between European powers from the seventeenth to the beginning of the twentieth century contained a general amnesty clause. The reciprocity that these provisions entailed reflected the development of the principle of sovereignty and equality of states upon which the modern European state system was founded. Distinguished commentators of this period regarded amnesty as an essential element of peace treaties necessary to ensure that all the causes for which war had been waged were permanently extinguished. In the absence of an express provision to the contrary, an amnesty clause was therefore considered to be implicitly included in every treaty of peace.

Peace agreement amnesties expunged all forms of responsibility in relation to war-related offences, including serious crimes. They reflected a post-war tabula rasa principle entailing that all actions for losses and damages occasioned by the war were forfeited at its end. During the war, however, customary law entitled belligerents to try and punish enemy soldiers having violated the laws of war who came in their custody. This right to punish enemy combatants has been identified as the foundation of war crime jurisdiction under international law. Alongside reprisals, it constituted the primary means of enforcement of the laws of war prior to their codification in the Hague Conventions at the turn of the twentieth century. Until then, international law did not strictly prohibit excesses towards non-combatants and this type of wartime offences was rarely punished.

While jurisdiction over wartime offences conventionally terminated with the conclusion of peace, victorious belligerents could derogate from this usage and require the surrender of war criminals for the purpose of prosecution in the peace treaty. There was a precursor attempt in this sense at the end of the Napoleonic wars, when the victorious powers demanded the exile of Napoleon and the trial of his most prominent followers. However, the fallen Emperor was dealt with in a political more than legal fashion and, though a few of his generals were tried by domestic military courts, they were convicted of offences against the French monarchy rather than international crimes. The Treaty of Versailles was the first of its kind to require the prosecution of a defeated power's head of state and members of his armed forces accused of war crimes before internationally constituted tribunals. The Treaty of Sèvres also provided for the right of the Allied Powers to try Turkish nationals suspected of having committed serious crimes during the war. These penalty provisions eventually remained dead letters since the climate in post-war Germany and Turkey did not permit the imposition of war crime trials by the Allies. Nonetheless, the formal rejection of amnesty for major criminals of war and the call for their prosecution at the international level reflected a change of mentality that would revolutionise the law in that area.

In the aftermath of World War II, the victorious powers agreed on the creation of two international military tribunals at Nuremberg and Tokyo to try major criminals of the defeated forces. The Charters of these tribunals unprecedentedly established their jurisdiction over war crimes, crimes against humanity and crimes against peace. The Nuremberg and Tokyo trials broke with the traditional tabula rasa principle, reflecting the emergence of a new post-war paradigm requiring that perpetrators of serious wartime offences should be held criminally responsible. Accountability following World War II was largely one-sided since it only targeted the nationals of the defeated powers, thus attracting criticisms of victors' justice. However, in subsequent years, the principle of individual liability for crimes under international law was affirmed by the UN General Assembly and the International Law Commission, thereby elevating it to the status of a principle of general international law. In the following decades, the international community's resolve to enforce that principle led to the adoption of international conventions requiring states to prosecute international crimes regardless of whether they were committed in war or peacetime. International criminal courts and tribunals have also been established in order to ensure the prosecution of these crimes when national authorities fail to do so.

The peace settlements of the two world wars thus operated a transition between the centuries-old post-war amnesty tradition and the emergence of a global accountability paradigm. In the aftermath of World War I, the Commission on Responsibilities created by the Paris Conference formally rejected the grant of amnesty to persons responsible for war crimes and crimes against humanity, calling for their prosecution before an international tribunal. The peace settlement of World War II effectively provided for the creation of an International Military Tribunal at Nuremberg to prosecute major criminals of war. These proceedings, in turn, led to the recognition by the international community that individuals responsible for international crimes are liable to punishment under international law. The Nuremberg trial has served as a model of post-conflict justice and inspired the development of the disciplines of international criminal law and transitional justice, both of which place emphasis on accountability for serious crimes. In a context of growing demands for prosecution and punishment following periods of mass violence, amnesties have been subject to increasing scrutiny. While they continue to be frequently resorted to in post-conflict or transitional situations, a number of international instruments adopted since the end of World War II have been relied on to challenge their legality in so far as they apply to crimes under international law.

3 Modern amnesties and moral dilemmas

Introduction

This chapter defines amnesties and provides a global perspective on how they have been used in recent decades. The first section explores their historical origin and identifies their distinctive features. It also examines their legal basis in modern legal systems and the types of crimes for which they are commonly granted. The second section reviews the types of contexts into which and rate at which amnesties have been issued in the last few decades according to recent empirical studies. The last section introduces a typology of modern amnesties classifying them in two broad categories – pacification or transitional amnesties – depending on their context of adoption. It discusses the moral dilemmas to which they are associated in these contexts, explaining their controversial nature. It then reviews different types of amnesties within each category through emblematic case studies from different parts of the world. These cases illustrate how amnesties can vary in terms of their legitimacy and effectiveness depending on factors such as their mode of adoption, objectives, scope or design. Their diversity along these lines cautions against one-size-fits-all approaches to the problem of amnesty in post-conflict or transitional contexts.

1. Defining amnesty

The origin of amnesty as a sovereign power

In a study on amnesty laws, UN Special Rapporteur Louis Joinet noted that:

> Amnesty is an outgrowth of the right of pardon, an act of individual clemency of theocratic origin. The divine nature of pardon was related to the sacred character of the King, whether the latter was himself a god or an intermediary between the gods and men.[1]

1 UN Sub-Commission on the Prevention of Discrimination and Protection of Minorities, 'Study on amnesty laws and their role in the safeguard and promotion of human rights',

Indeed, the power to grant pardons and amnesties historically belonged to the sovereign. Egyptian pharaohs, Roman and Chinese emperors, French and English kings all exercised a prerogative of mercy encompassing the power to grant pardons to individuals and amnesties to classes of individuals. This power was linked to their justice prerogative and could be delegated to lower authorities possessing the privilege of jurisdiction such as lords, vassals, religious or military authorities. With the advent of democratisation in modern times, while pardon generally remained a power of the head of state, the amnesty prerogative was typically vested in the legislature.[2] In France, for instance, following the revolution of 1789, the power of amnesty was separated from the power of grace and entrusted to the Parliament.[3]

Distinguishing amnesty from pardon

Contemporary definitions of amnesty describe it as a form of pardon. For example, the Oxford English Dictionary defines amnesty as 'an official pardon given to people convicted of political offences' and Black's Law Dictionary as 'a pardon extended by the government to a group or class of persons, usually for a political offense'.[4] The two mechanisms are often assimilated because they have the same object, i.e. to exempt offenders from the normal application of the law. However, they differ in several respects.

According to the Max Planck Encyclopaedia of Public International Law, '[w]hile pardons usually cancel a penalty individually after conviction, amnesties are more general in scope, applying usually to a greater number of offenders having committed specific offences, and preventing or terminating prosecutorial investigations'.[5] This definition sheds light on the three main features distinguishing amnesty from pardon. First, while pardons are granted on an individual basis, amnesties generally extend to categories of individuals. Second, whereas pardons intervene after conviction, amnesties are more often issued before the initiation of the criminal process, precluding investigation as well as prosecution. Finally, though pardons dismiss or commute the sentence, they do not as a rule affect the condemnation, whereas amnesties usually remove the prospect of prosecution, conviction and sentence, sometimes also expunging the legal record of the offence.

Preliminary report by Mr. Louis Joinet, Special Rapporteur (21 June 1985) UN Doc E/CN.4/Sub.2/1985/16, para 9.

2 Leslie Sebba, 'The Pardoning Power: A World's Survey' (1997) 68 (1) *Journal of Criminal Law and Criminology* 83, 118.

3 Stéphane Gacon, *L'amnistie: De la Commune à la guerre d'Algérie* (Editions du Seuil, Paris 2002) 29.

4 *Oxford English Dictionary* (seventh edn, OUP 2012); Bryan A Gardiner (ed), *Black's Law Dictionary* (ninth edn, 2009).

5 Anja Seibert-Fohr, 'Amnesties' in R Wolfrum (ed), *The Max Planck Encyclopaedia of Public International Law* (OUP 2012).

The distinction is not always clear-cut and there are exceptions to these general principles. For example, amnesties are sometimes granted after conviction and do not always preclude investigatory proceedings or civil suits.[6] The use of different terminologies in different legal systems further complicates the matter. Common law systems do not traditionally use the term amnesty, understanding it as no more than a general or collective form of pardon. For instance, in relation to a presidential amnesty issued following the American Civil War, the US Supreme Court observed that:

> The constitution does not use the word 'amnesty,' and except that the term is generally employed where a pardon is extended to whole classes or communities, instead of individuals, the distinction between them is one rather of philological interest than of legal importance … All the benefits which can result to the claimant from both pardon and amnesty would equally have accrued to him if the term 'pardon' alone had been used in the proclamation of the president.[7]

Conversely, the continental legal tradition distinguishes between amnesties and pardons, ascribing an additional value to the former on account of their sweeping, non-discriminatory and propitiatory character:

> Amnesty, under this [European] interpretation, was more than pardon because it wiped the record clean; it conjured the rebellious act into the realm of nonexistence. And it left – by law, at any rate – no lingering taint. Persons freed from prison or exile under an amnesty were restored to the full enjoyment of their civil and political rights. Finally, one of the most important distinguishing characteristics of an amnesty was the fact that it treated not of special cases but of whole categories, for it was in effect the deed itself which was being amnestied, not the doers. Such was the pure theory of amnesty.[8]

The constitutional footing of amnesty

The power to grant amnesty and pardon is generally rooted in national constitutions. Of the 193 UN member states, 186 have a constitution providing for the power to extend amnesties and/or pardons.[9] Among them, 105 refer to both

6 For example, amnesties passed for the purpose of releasing political prisoners usually intervene after a part of their sentence has been served.

7 *Knote v. United States*, 95 U.S. 149, 153 (1877) quoted in WW Thornton, 'Pardon and Amnesty' (1885) 6(4) *Criminal Law Magazine* 457, 458–59.

8 Jean T Joughin, *The Paris Commune in French Politics, 1871–1880: The History of the Amnesty of 1880* (Johns Hopkins Press 1955) 54.

9 This subsection draws on *Constitue*, a database of the constitutions of the world developed by the Comparative Constitutions Project <www.constituteproject.org> accessed 7 November 2018. The seven constitutions which do not refer to amnesty or pardon are those of

powers. Of those 105 constitutions, 79 entrust the amnesty prerogative to the legislative assembly and the pardoning power to the head of state. Among the constitutions mentioning only one type of clemency measure, 77 refer solely to pardon and four solely to amnesty. The former include the constitutions of the 53 member states of the Commonwealth, with the exception of Australia and Canada, whose constitutions do not mention clemency at all, Cameroon, Mozambique and South Africa, whose constitutions also refer to amnesty. Since common law countries conceive of amnesty as a general pardon, the absence of reference to the former in their constitution does not mean that the mechanism does not exist in those systems but merely that it is deemed to form part of the pardoning power. For instance, the provision of the US constitution empowering the president to grant 'reprieves and pardons' has been used on several occasions as the legal basis for declarations of amnesty.[10]

There are 21 constitutions indicating the crimes which may or may not be the object of an amnesty or pardon. While eight of them provide that amnesty may only be granted for political crimes,[11] the remaining 13 precisely identify the crimes ineligible for clemency measures.[12] For example, Turkey's constitution prohibits the grant of amnesty or pardon with respect to offences against the forest. On a different note, the constitutions of Chile, Iraq and Brazil exclude terrorist offences from the permissible scope of clemency measures. As regards crimes under international law such as genocide, war crimes and crimes against humanity, the constitutions of seven countries exclude all or some of them from the reach of amnesty laws.[13]

Andorra, Australia, Bosnia-Herzegovina, Canada, Syria, Saudi Arabia and Yemen. However, amnesties have been passed in at least some of these countries, including Bosnia-Herzegovina, Syria, Saudi Arabia and Yemen, see Leigh A Payne, Tricia D Olsen, and Andrew G Reiter, *Transitional Justice Database Project* <www.tjdbproject.com> accessed 7 November 2018.

10 Constitution of the United States of America 1789 (rev 1992), art 2(2). See LCK. 'The Power of the President to Grant a General Pardon or Amnesty for Offences against the United States' (1869) 17(10) *The American Law Register* 577, 582–84.

11 Constitutions of Colombia 1991 (rev 2013), arts 150(17) and 201(2); Costa Rica 1949 (rev 2011), art 121(21); Dominican Republic 2010, art 93(1)(p); Greece 1975 (rev 2008), art 47 (3); Guatemala 1985 (rev 1993), art 171(g); Haiti 1987 (rev 2012), art 147; Honduras 1982 (rev 2013), art 205(16); and Panama 1972 (rev 2004), art 159(6).

12 Constitutions of Angola 2002, art 61; Brazil 1988 (rev 2014), art 5(XLIII); Chile 1980 (rev 2014), art 9; Costa Rica 1949 (rev 2011), art 121(21); Ecuador 2008 (rev 2011), art 80; El Salvador 1983 (rev 2003), art 244; Ethiopia 1994, art 28; Iraq 2005, art 73; Niger 2010, art 72; Spain 1978 (rev 2011), art 102; Tonga 1875 (rev 1988), art 37; Turkey 1982 (rev 2011), art 169; and Venezuela (Bolivarian Republic of) 1999 (rev 2009), art 29.

13 Constitutions of Angola 2002, art 61(genocide and crimes against humanity); Brazil 1988 (rev 2014), art 5(XLIII) (torture, terrorism and drug trafficking); Ecuador 2008 (rev 2011), art 80 (genocide, crimes against humanity, war crimes, forced disappearance and aggression); Ethiopia 1994, art 28 (genocide, crimes against humanity, torture, summary executions and forcible disappearances); Iraq 2005, art 73 (international crimes, terrorism, financial and administrative corruption); Niger 2010, art 72 (imprescriptible crimes); and Venezuela

The scope of amnesties

Black's Law Dictionary provides that, '[u]nlike an ordinary pardon, amnesty is usually addressed to crimes against state sovereignty – that is, to political offences with respect to which forgiveness is deemed more expedient for the public welfare than prosecution and punishment'.[14] With regard to amnesty clauses included in peace agreements, it specifies that they usually apply to 'offences such as treason, sedition, rebellion, and even war crimes'.[15]

It is generally accepted that amnesties are primarily concerned with political offences. However, this concept is rather flexible and may potentially encompass any crime provided that the perpetrator had a political motive, belonged to a political organisation or acted within a broader political context.[16] Indeed, according to Christine Van Den Wijngaert, the notion of political crime is a 'label which, as soon as a number of criteria are fulfilled, may be attached to every crime'.[17] In practice, therefore, the fact that the material scope of application of an amnesty is limited to political offences does not necessarily imply that the measure excludes serious crimes against individuals or crimes under international law.[18]

Amnesties generally cover offences committed in relation with a particular event or within a specific time-frame, such as an armed conflict, dictatorship, coup d'état or rebellion. Hence their focus on political, as opposed to ordinary, crimes. They can apply broadly and unconditionally to all crimes committed in connection with the events in question (blanket amnesties), cover only certain types of offences or exclude certain crimes (limited amnesties). Some amnesties require recipients to adhere to certain conditions or perform specific obligations before becoming eligible, such as renouncing violence and surrendering weapons, disclosing the truth about past crimes or repairing the harm done to the victims (conditional amnesties).[19] Amnesties may also be distinguished depending on their beneficiaries. They can apply to both sides in an armed conflict or

(Bolivarian Republic of) 1999 (rev 2009), art 29 (crimes against humanity, serious violations of human rights and war crimes).

14 *Black's Law Dictionary* (n 4).

15 Ibid.

16 Louise Mallinder, *Amnesty, Human Rights and Political Transitions: Bridging the Peace and Justice Divide* (Hart Publishing 2008) 135–44; Christine Van Den Wyngaert, *The Political Offence Exception to Extradition: The Delicate Problem of Balancing the Rights of the Individual and the International Public Order* (Kluwer, Deventer 1980) 95–96.

17 Van den Wyngaert (n 16) 96.

18 For example, the South African Truth and Reconciliation Commission was empowered to grant amnesty with respect to crimes associated with a political objective, including serious human rights violations.

19 On the types of conditions which can be included and the ways in which amnesties can be designed to maximise respect for international law and human rights, see *The Belfast Guidelines on Amnesty and Accountability* (Transitional Justice Institute, University of Ulster 2013); Mark Freeman, *Necessary Evils: Amnesties and the Search for Justice* (CUP 2009) pt 2; Mallinder (n 16) ch 4.

political confrontation. Alternatively, they can be directed specifically at opponents of the state or state agents. While amnesties passed by a repressive regime in order to exonerate its own agents (self-amnesties) are frequently denounced by civil society and international organisations, limited or conditional amnesties adopted through an inclusive democratic process usually enjoy a greater degree of legitimacy.

Amnesties applying exclusively to offences against the state such as treason, rebellion and sedition are not controversial and are even encouraged by international law following internal armed conflicts.[20] The international law debate on the permissibility of amnesties concerns those applying to crimes deemed so grave that they are prohibited by international norms. The argument is that, by permitting the perpetrators of these crimes to escape accountability, amnesties defeat the purpose of these norms, some of which explicitly require prosecution. Amnesties have been most heavily criticised in relation to the core crimes under international criminal law – genocide, crimes against humanity and war crimes – and serious human rights violations such as torture and enforced disappearances. The main arguments supporting the view that a general ban on amnesties for those crimes has emerged under international law are examined in the following chapters.

2. The prevalence of amnesties

The practice of states in issuing amnesties has started to be analysed empirically in the second half of the 2000s. Following in the footsteps of Louise Mallinder, who created an Amnesty Law Database compiling information on over 500 amnesties processes in 130 countries since the Second World War, several scholars have documented large numbers of amnesties adopted around the world in the last half century.[21] Some of these studies focus on amnesties, like Renée Jeffery's analysing 636 amnesties implemented between 1974 and 2007.[22] Other scholars have assembled datasets compiling information on amnesties and other transitional justice or post-conflict mechanisms. The major work in the field of transitional justice is the Transitional Justice Database

20 Protocol Additional to the Geneva Conventions of 12 August 1949 relating to the Protection of Victims of Non-International Armed Conflicts (adopted 8 June 1977, entered into force 7 December 1978) 1125 UNTS 609, art 6(5).

21 Mallinder (n 16). See also Louise Mallinder, 'Global Comparison of Amnesty Laws' in M Cherif Bassiouni (ed), *The Pursuit of International Criminal Justice: A World Study on Conflicts, Victimization and Post- Conflict Justice* (Intersentia 2010); Louise Mallinder, 'Amnesties' Challenge to the Global Accountability Norm? Interpreting Regional and International Trends in Amnesty Enactment' in Francesca Lessa and Leigh A Payne (eds), *Amnesty in the Age of Human Rights Accountability: Comparative and International Perspectives* (CUP 2012) 69.

22 Renée Jeffery, *Amnesties, Accountability, and Human Rights* (University of Pennsylvania Press 2014).

Project documenting over 900 transitional justice mechanisms implemented between 1970 and 2007, including more than 600 amnesties.[23] Some databases are more specific in focus, like Vinjamuri and Boesenecker's study examining mechanisms included in peace agreements from 1980 to 2006 (Peace Agreements Database) and Binningsbø et al.'s dataset analysing measures adopted following and relating to an armed conflict from 1946 to 2006 (Post-Conflict Dataset).[24] For the purpose of this research, a Peace Agreement Amnesties Database has been created containing information on 145 amnesty provisions included in peace agreements between 1970 and 2017.[25]

According to Mallinder, recourse to amnesties has increased since the end of the Second World War and 'amnesty laws are not relied upon solely in certain parts of the world, but in fact occur across the globe'.[26] Jeffery has also observed that 'the average number of amnesties implemented each year has steadily increased' in recent decades, with peaks in their popularity in the late 1970s (24 amnesties in 1977), early 1980s (23 in 1981), early 1990s (39 in 1991) and early 2000s (28 in 2003).[27] Her study reveals that amnesties are generally adopted in relation to an armed conflict or a period of state repression, more often in the former type of context.[28] This is corroborated by the Transitional Justice Database.[29] As regards amnesties adopted as part of the settlement of an armed conflict, the Peace Agreement Amnesties Database shows that their use has remained relatively steady since 1990, at an average rate of 4.8 per year.

Analysing trends in the use of different types of amnesties over time, Jeffery finds that:

> [T]he durability of amnesties between 1974 and 2007 can be attributed to the continued popularity of amnesties designed to quell civil unrest and end rebel violence, and the increased popularity of those intended to facilitate the signing of a peace agreement or to contribute to postconflict truth and healing.[30]

23 Payne, Olsen and Reiter, *Transitional Justice Database Project* (n 9). On the results of this project, see Tricia D Olsen, Leigh A Payne and Andrew G Reiter, *Transitional Justice in Balance: Comparing Processes, Weighing Efficacy* (United States Institute of Peace Press 2010). For a subset of the database focusing on amnesties granted in relation to internal armed conflicts, see Andrew G Reiter, 'Examining the Use of Amnesties and Pardons as a Response to Internal Armed Conflicts' (2014) 47(1) *Israel Law Review* 133.

24 Leslie Vinjamuri and Aaron P Boesenecker, 'Accountability and Peace Agreements, Mapping trends from 1998 to 2006' (September 2007) *Centre for Humanitarian Dialogue* (Peace Agreements Database); Helga Malmin Binningsbø et al., 'Armed conflict and post-conflict justice, 1946–2006: A dataset' (2012) 49(5) *Journal of Peace Research* 731 (Post-Conflict Dataset).

25 The Peace Agreement Amnesties Database (in appendix) is discussed in ch 5 of this volume.

26 Mallinder, *Amnesty, Human Rights and Political Transitions* (n 16) 19–20.

27 Jeffery (n 22) 36–37.

28 Ibid, 39.

29 Olsen, Payne and Reiter, *Transitional Justice in Balance* (n 23) 36.

30 Jeffery (n 22) 46–47.

According to her database, the three purposes for which amnesties were most frequently granted in the period of inquiry were (1) to facilitate the release of political prisoners after an armed conflict, (2) to end violence by non-state armed groups and (3) to quell unrest following civil disturbances.[31] By contrast, self-amnesties designed to shield state agents from accountability were identified as the least common form of amnesties, accounting for fewer than eight percent of all amnesties included in the database.[32] Along the same line, Mallinder's study and the Transitional Justice Database indicate that amnesties are more commonly extended to opponents of the state than to state agents.[33]

Comparing the use of amnesties with other transitional justice mechanisms, the authors of the Transitional Justice Database have found that '[a]mnesty is the most frequently used form of transitional justice, accounting for half of all the mechanisms adopted'.[34] The Peace Agreements Database, the Post-Conflict Dataset and the Peace Agreement Amnesties Database also shed light on the prevalence of amnesties in peace agreements and post-conflict situations.[35] They show that blanket amnesties have been more frequent than limited or conditional amnesties in these contexts.[36] According to the Post-Conflict Dataset, amnesties are granted more often following civil wars than low-intensity armed conflicts.[37] They are also more likely when conflicts terminate through negotiations rather than military victory.[38]

A common finding of several studies is that recent amnesties have often been combined with other mechanisms in transitional situations, including trials and truth commissions.[39] One way to link amnesties to other mechanisms is through the inclusion of conditions within the former requiring beneficiaries to engage with other transitional measures, a technique that has gained in popularity.[40] According to Mallinder, the types of conditions most often attached to amnesties relate to surrender and disarmament or to reparation.[41]

31 Jeffery (n 22) 38–40.
32 Ibid, 41.
33 Olsen, Payne and Reiter, *Transitional Justice in Balance* (n 23) 36–37; Mallinder, *Amnesty, Human Rights and Political Transitions* (n 16) 84.
34 Olsen, Payne and Reiter, *Transitional Justice in Balance* (n 23) 39.
35 Peace Agreements Database (n 24) 16–18; Post-Conflict Dataset (n 24) 735; Peace Agreement Amnesties Database in appendix.
36 Ibid.
37 Post-Conflict Dataset (n 24) 737.
38 Ibid, 738.
39 Peace Agreements Database (n 24) 19; Olsen, Payne and Reiter, *Transitional Justice in Balance* (n 23) 105.
40 Mallinder, *Amnesty, Human Rights and Political Transitions* (n 16) ch 4.
41 Ibid, 155.

3. A typology of modern amnesties

Scholars have organised amnesties on the basis of different criteria.[42] For example, Jeffery has created nine categories of amnesties based on their general aim, political purpose and type of beneficiaries.[43] Amnesties are very diverse in terms of their form, aims, mode of adoption, scope and design, complicating attempts at classification. Indeed, according to Mark Freeman:

> The difference between certain amnesties is so vast, in fact, that it is almost nonsensical to compare them. A corrective amnesty passed in good faith by a democratically elected government is, for example, on a completely different moral and legal plane from a general and unconditional self-amnesty adopted without public debate by an authoritarian regime. In short, no two amnesties – and no two contexts of amnesty – are exactly alike.[44]

Nonetheless, amnesties are most often issued in relation to two types of situations: an armed conflict or a democratic transition. In both types of contexts, they aim to protect categories of persons from accountability for offences committed during a period that is coming to an end, either a war or a repressive regime. They do so with a view to facilitate a transition towards peace or democracy by drawing a line on the past. This section organises modern amnesties in two broad categories – pacification amnesties and transitional amnesties – based on their context of adoption (a peace or a democratisation process) with a view to examine how different types of measures within each category benefit from varying degrees of legitimacy or effectiveness depending on certain factors.

There is some permeability between these two categories. Indeed, while opposition to state repression can rapidly escalate into armed confrontations akin to small-scale internal conflicts, fully fledged wars are often rooted in political violence and inequalities.[45] For example, the amnesties granted in South Africa at the end of apartheid constituted both a key element in the peace process that ended the confrontations between the government and liberation movements, and a necessary precondition to ensure that military and security forces would support the democratic transition. Though there are overlaps between the two categories, this typology permits a better visualisation of the

42 Jeffery (n 22). See also Reiter (n 23); Ronald C Slye, 'The Legitimacy of Amnesties Under International Law and General Principles of Anglo-American Law: Is a Legitimate Amnesty Possible?' (2002) 43 Virginia Journal of International Law 173; William W Burke-White, 'Reframing Impunity: Applying Liberal International Law Theory to an Analysis of Amnesty Legislation' (2001) 42 *Harvard International Law Journal* 467.

43 Jeffery (n 22) 39.

44 Freeman (n 19) 13.

45 The COW typology of war sets the threshold for civil wars at a minimum of 1000 annual battle-deaths. However, other approaches adopt a lower threshold, such as the UCDP datasets using a threshold of 25 annual fatalities for small-scale conflicts. This lower threshold can be crossed by armed confrontations triggered by state repression.

main contexts into which amnesties are commonly issued and of the different sets of competing goals underlying their controversial nature in both types of situations. Each category of amnesties also involves different problems and possible solutions as regards their legitimacy.

Pacification amnesties

As seen in the first two chapters, amnesty has been relied on as a pacification instrument for many centuries. While it traditionally featured in peace treaties settling international armed conflicts, it has become more common in the settlement of internal armed conflicts between state and non-state armed groups.[46] In such contexts, amnesties can be issued during the war in order to provide an incentive to rebels groups for engaging in peace talks, as part of the peace agreement to reassure the parties and encourage them to commit to the peace process, or following the end of the conflict to neutralise spoilers and consolidate peace.[47]

Pacification amnesties are primarily used as a bargaining tool to entice rebel groups to negotiate or commit to peace when the state is unable to defeat them through military means. Accountability for wartime offences, including crimes against the state committed by rebel groups and human rights violations perpetrated on both sides, often represents a stumbling block during peace talks. There is no easy solution between, on the one hand, a commitment to full-scale accountability necessitating a strong military position or international presence and risking to alienate the parties, and, on the other hand, the promise of a blanket amnesty entrenching the impunity of human rights violators, undermining respect for the rule of law and human rights. As observed by Ian Martin, a UN representative having served in several peacekeeping missions in different parts of the world:

> There is no avoiding the dilemma for negotiators: maintaining the principle of accountability may well raise the initial hurdle to a peaceful transition, even if it serves its eventual sustainability … A determination to uphold to the fullest the principle of accountability may imply a greater dependence on military action; conversely, a desire to seek only a peaceful solution may imply being unable to assert the accountability of those who are prepared to prolong the fighting to evade justice. This is unwelcome, but has to be recognized by those who would wish to endorse military interventions or solutions only as a last resort, or who are simply realistic about their difficulty in practice.[48]

46 See the Peace Agreement Amnesties Database in appendix, discussed in ch 5 of this volume.

47 On the different types of amnesties used in relation to internal armed conflicts, see Reiter (n 23).

48 Ian Martin, 'Justice and Reconciliation: Responsibilities and Dilemmas of Peace-makers and Peacebuilders' in Alice H Hankin (ed), *The Legacy of Abuses: Confronting the Past, Facing the Future* (Conference Report, The Aspen Institute 2002) 81.

The question of whether to secure peace through amnesty, thereby ending the bloodshed but impairing future efforts to deliver justice, or insist on accountability in order to safeguard the rule of law and human rights despite the risk to prolong the conflict, has generated much debate in the literature.[49] On one side of this controversy is the view that there can be no peace without justice, encapsulated in this statement by one of its leading proponent: '[i]f peace is not intended to be a brief interlude between conflicts, then in order to avoid future conflict, it must encompass what justice is intended to accomplish: prevent, deter, punish, and rehabilitate'.[50] Advocates of this position stress that peace and justice are complementary rather than competing goals and that the former cannot be accomplished without the latter. They contend that, in order to achieve sustainable peace and end the cycles of retributive violence, it is imperative to establish a measure of criminal accountability in the aftermath of mass violence. A movement against impunity for serious crimes driven by the UN and global human rights organisations has been gaining steam over the last two decades, one of its rallying call being that amnesties covering international crimes are not acceptable, even as a tool to negotiate the end of an armed conflict.[51]

On the other side of the peace and justice divide are proponents of a more flexible position recognising the desirability of accountability for serious crimes but maintaining that the need for peace should override other considerations in the midst of violent armed conflicts. For instance, William Schabas has observed that:

49 See e.g. Freeman (n 19); William Schabas, 'No Peace Without Justice? The Amnesty Quandary' in William Schabas, *Unimaginable Atrocities: Justice: Politics and Rights at the War Crimes Tribunals* (OUP 2012) 173; Payam Akhavan, 'Are International Criminal Tribunals a Disincentive to Peace? Reconciling Judicial Romanticism with Political Realism' (2009) 31(3) *Human Rights Quarterly* 624; Jack Snyder and Leslie Vinjamuri, 'Trials and Errors: Principle and Pragmatism in Strategies of International Justice' (Snyder and Vinjamuri 2004) 28 *International Security* 5; Mark J Osiel, 'Why Prosecute? Critics of Punishment for Mass Atrocity' (2000) 22 *Human Rights Quarterly* 118; M Cherif Bassiouni, 'Searching for Peace and Achieving Justice: The Need for Accountability' (1996) 59(4) *Law and Contemporary Problems* 9; Juan E Méndez, 'Accountability for Past Abuses' (1997) 19(2) *Human Rights Quarterly* 255; Stephen J Stedman, 'Spoiler Problems in Peace Processes' (1997) 22 *International Security* 5; Michael P Scharf, 'Swapping Amnesty for Peace: Was There a Duty to Prosecute International Crimes in Haiti?' (1996) 31(1) *Texas International Law Journal* 1; Richard Goldstone, 'Exposing Human Rights Abuses: A Help or Hindrance to Reconciliation' (1995) 22 *Hastings Constitutional Law Quarterly* 607; Anthony D'Amato, 'Peace vs Accountability in Bosnia' (1994) 88 (3) *American Journal of International Law* 500.

50 Bassiouni (n 49) 13.

51 United Nations Security Council (UNSC), Report of the Secretary General, 'The rule of law and transitional justice in conflict and post-conflict societies' (23 August 2004) UN Doc S/2004/616; Office of the United Nations High Commissioner for Human Rights, 'Rule-of-Law Tools for Post-Conflict States: Amnesties' (UN Publication 2009); Priscilla Hayner, 'Negotiating justice: Guidance for mediators' *Centre for Humanitarian Dialogue* (February 2009); Human Rights Watch 'Selling Justice Short: Why Accountability Matters for Peace' (7 July 2009).

> Those who argue that prosecution should not be sacrificed in a peace bargain should be prepared to answer for the alternative, which can never be ruled out, namely a return to conflict *because* of the inability of negotiators to be able to promise the rebel leaders that if they lay down their arms they will not be prosecuted.[52]

According to some scholars, the first steps towards preventing atrocities and promoting the rule of law in situations of armed conflict involve brokering 'politically expedient bargains' between adverse parties, which may necessitate recourse to amnesty in order to contain spoilers.[53] Once such deals are struck, efforts may then be concentrated on establishing institutions upholding the rule of law and human rights for the future. These pragmatists have warned that 'attempting to implement universal standards of criminal justice in the absence of these political and institutional preconditions risks weakening norms of justice by revealing their ineffectiveness and hindering necessary political bargaining'.[54] Other scholars have challenged the claim that criminal justice is the only appropriate response to mass atrocities, suggesting ways in which carefully crafted amnesties may contribute to both peace and justice by complementing selective prosecution strategies and encouraging offenders to engage with alternative accountability mechanisms.[55]

Illustrating the peace vs justice dilemma: the case of northern Uganda

In northern Uganda, both amnesty and criminal justice were successively relied on in order to end the protracted armed conflict opposing the government to several rebel groups, the most prominent of which is known as the Lord's Resistance Army (LRA). Between the late 1980s and the mid-2000s, the conflict claimed thousands of lives and led to the displacement of over a million people. The LRA became infamous for using terror tactics against civilians, including the cutting off of limbs and the large-scale abduction of children.

The Ugandan government followed an ambivalent strategy to end the war in the 1990s, including large-scale military operations to capture the LRA leadership and half-hearted peace talks.[56] In 1998, the Acholi Religious Leaders Peace Initiative and other civil society organisations began campaigning for a peaceful resolution of the conflict through amnesty and traditional reconciliation mechanisms.[57] Besides an overwhelming desire for peace, two factors have been

52 Schabas (n 49) 196.

53 Snyder and Vinjamuri (n 49) 6. On the problems presented by spoilers in peace processes, see Stedman (n 49).

54 Snyder and Vinjamuri (n 49) 6.

55 See *The Belfast Guidelines on Amnesty and Accountability* (n 19).

56 Tim Allen and Koen Vlassenroot, 'Introduction' in Tim Allen and Koen Vlassenroot (eds), *The Lord's Resistance Army: myth and reality* (Zed Book 2010).

57 Gilbert M Khadiagala, 'The Role of the Acholi Religious Leaders Peace Initiative (ARLPI) in Peace Building in Northern Uganda' (USAID, March 2001) Case Study 2; Louise Mallinder,

put forward to explain the widespread support for an amnesty process in northern Uganda. First, the Acholi culture is said to favour the resolution of disputes through restorative, rather than retributive, justice mechanisms such as traditional forgiveness and cleansing ceremonies.[58] Second, since a large part of the LRA is made up of abducted children forced to engage in criminal acts, it has been argued that prosecutions would not serve the interests of justice.[59]

The Amnesty Act (2000) was adopted unanimously by the Ugandan Parliament on 7 December 1999. It extends to any Ugandan citizen being or having engaged in war or armed rebellion against the government since 1986 on the condition that applicants renounce the conflict and surrender weapons to the authorities.[60] Upon fulfilment of these conditions, an Amnesty Commission issues reporters with an amnesty certificate and a reinsertion package. It has been estimated that over 26,000 returning fighters from different armed groups have benefited from the law since 2000, irrespective of the gravity of their crimes.[61] The amnesty law has played a critical role in encouraging defections from the LRA and other armed groups, helping former combatants to reintegrate their communities and promoting reconciliation in Ugandan society. It was extended several times and continues to enjoy strong support among the population of northern Uganda.[62]

In 2004, unable to defeat the LRA militarily or induce its leaders to negotiate peace, the government referred the situation in northern Uganda to the International Criminal Court (ICC).[63] The Office of the Prosecutor unsealed arrest warrants against five LRA commanders in 2005, following which the rebels

'Uganda at a crossroads: narrowing the amnesty?' Working Paper no 1, *Beyond Legalism: Amnesties, Transition and Conflict Transformation* (Queen's University Belfast, March 2009) 19–22.

58 Refugee Law Project, 'Peace First, Justice Later: Traditional Justice in Northern Uganda' Working Paper no 5 (July 2005); Cecily Rose, 'Looking Beyond Amnesty and Traditional Justice and Reconciliation Mechanisms in Northern Uganda: A Proposal for Truth-Telling and Reparations' (2008) 28(2) *Boston College Third World Law Journal* 344.

59 Refugee Law Project, 'Whose Justice? Perceptions of Uganda's Amnesty Act 2000: The Potential for Conflict Resolution and Long-Term Reconciliation' Working Paper no 15 (February 2005) 9.

60 Amnesty Act, 2000, ss 3.1 and 4.

61 Barney Afako, 'Undermining the LRA: Role of Uganda's Amnesty Act' (August 2012) Conciliation Resources; Kasper Agger, 'The End of Amnesty in Uganda: Implications for LRA Defections' (Enough Project, August 2012); Samuel Okiror, 'Forgive and forget? Amnesty dilemma haunts Uganda' *Irin* (12 June 2015).

62 The Amnesty Act (Extension of Expiry Period) Instrument, 24 May 2013. See Parliament of Uganda, Report of the Committee on Defence and Internal Affairs on the petition on the lapsing of part II of the Amnesty Act, 2000 (August 2013). In June 2015, the Amnesty Act was extended for a further period of two years, see Okiror, 'Forgive and forget? Amnesty dilemma haunts Uganda' (n 61).

63 Payam Akhavan, 'The Lord's Resistance Army Case: Uganda's Submission of the First State Referral to the International Criminal Court' (2005) 99 *American Journal of International Law* 403.

accepted engaging in peace talks with the government at Juba.[64] As both events coincided, the ICC prosecutor and some commentators credited the intervention of the Court for the progress in the Ugandan peace process.[65] However, the LRA leaders protested against the ICC indictments and conditioned their commitment to the peace process upon their withdrawal. Representatives of Ugandan civil society attempted to persuade the ICC Prosecutor's Office to take a step back in order to preserve the Juba opportunity.[66] Though President Museveni expressed his readiness to defer to the LRA's demand, the organs of the Court were not prepared to rescind the arrest warrants. In a Conference address in 2007, Prosecutor Luis Moreno-Ocampo declared that:

> Arrest warrants are decisions taken by the judges in accordance with the law, they must be implemented. I call upon States Parties and other stakeholders to remain in all circumstances aware of the mandate given to the Court; there can be no political compromise on legality and accountability.[67]

As a result, the Ugandan government was no longer able to make a reliable promise of amnesty to the rebels in exchange for their surrender and commitment to peace. The leader of the LRA ultimately failed to show up to the peace agreement's signing ceremony, thus marking the end of the Juba process and the resumption of violence against civilians.[68] This turn of events brought several commentators to criticise the inflexible position of the ICC in northern Uganda, including Schabas who observed that '[i]f international justice is brought to bear on situations like that of northern Uganda because it can help promote peace, perhaps it should be prepared to stand down when criminal prosecution becomes an obstacle to peace'.[69]

64 See Ronald R Atkinson, 'The realists in Juba? An analysis of the Juba peace talks' in Tim Allen and Koen Vlassenroot (eds), *The Lord's Resistance Army, Myth and Reality* (Zed Books 2010) 205; Thomas Unger and Marieke Wierda, 'Pursuing Justice in Ongoing Conflict: A Discussion of Current Practice' in Kai Ambos, Judith Large and Marieke Wierda (eds), *Building a Future on Peace and Justice: Studies on Transitional Justice, Peace and Development* (Springer 2009) 270.

65 'Opening Remarks, Luis Moreno-Ocampo, Fifth Session of the Assembly of State Parties' (23 November 2006) 2–3; Unger and Wierda (n 64) 270; Akhavan, 'The Lord's Resistance Army Case' (n 63) 416–20.

66 ICC Press Release, 'Statements by ICC Chief Prosecutor and the visiting Delegation of Acholi leaders from northern Uganda' (18 March 2005).

67 Address by Luis Moreno-Ocampo, Building a Future on Peace and Justice Conference (Nuremberg, 25 June 2007).

68 Atkinson (n 64) 221–22.

69 Schabas (n 49) 196; Freeman (n 19) 86 ('[T]he retention of the ICC arrest warrants – and, by corollary, the prevention of any reliable amnesty arrangement – appear to be direct contributors to the situation of ongoing human misery and suffering in areas of LRA occupation'). See also Adam Branch, 'Uganda's Civil War and the Politics of ICC Intervention' (2007) 21 *Ethics and International Affairs* 179.

Blanket amnesties: the cases of Mozambique and Angola

Following their independence from Portugal in 1975, Mozambique and Angola became engulfed in civil wars between the new governments formed by the liberation movements and rebel armed groups. These conflicts reproduced the Cold War dynamic with the governments – the Frelimo party in Mozambique and the MPLA in Angola – supported by the Soviet Union, and the rebel movements – the Mozambican Renamo and the Angolan UNITA – backed by the United States and the apartheid regime of South Africa. Both wars gave rise to the grant of successive amnesties, usually offered by the governments to induce the rebels to disarm or pave the way for peace talks.[70] The Mozambican and Angolan armed conflicts, each of which caused hundreds of thousands of deaths, were finally brought to an end by two comprehensive peace settlements – the 1992 General Peace Agreement for Mozambique and the 2002 Luena Peace Agreement for Angola – brokered with substantial international involvement and support from the UN.[71] Both peace agreements provided for a blanket amnesty covering all crimes committed during the conflicts.[72]

Whereas the amnesties issued during the Mozambican and Angolan civil wars had only a limited impact on the resolution of the conflicts, those granted as part of the final peace agreements have been described as key elements in the countries' transition towards peace, reconciliation and democracy.[73] Besides the amnesty provision, which represented the parties' main strategy towards reconciliation, the peace agreements placed emphasis on demobilisation and democratisation. In both cases, the rebel movements became political parties represented in Parliament and their armed forces were either integrated into the national armed forces or reintegrated into civilian life.[74] The rehabilitation of former combatants and victims was facilitated by traditional justice and reconciliation mechanisms such as community and individual cleansing ceremonies.[75] These grassroots practices were premised on leaving the violent past behind to repair broken relationships and rebuild communities.

70 See Jeffery (n 22) 107–109, 111–13; Mallinder, 'Global Comparison of Amnesty Laws' (n 21); José Doria, 'Angola: A Case Study in the Challenges of Achieving Peace and the Question of Amnesty or Prosecution of War Crimes in Mixed Armed Conflicts' (2002) 5 *Yearbook of International Humanitarian Law* 3, 8–18.

71 General Peace Agreement for Mozambique, 4 October 1992 (GPA); Memorandum of Understanding between the Government of the Republic of Angola and UNITA, 4 April 2002 (Luena Agreement).

72 GPA (n 71) Protocol 1.1, implemented through Law no 15/92 (13 October 1992); Luena Agreement (n 71) ch 2, art 2.1, implemented through Law no 4/02 (4 April 2002).

73 See Helena Cobban, *Amnesty after Atrocity: Healing Nations after Genocide and War Crimes* (Paradigm Publishers 2007) 150; Doria (n 70) 48–49; Jeffery (n 22) 112–13; Snyder and Vinjamuri (n 49) 34.

74 Doria (n 70) 27–31; Cobban (n 73) 150–55.

75 See Alcinda Honwana, 'Children of War: Understanding War and War Cleansing in Mozambique and Angola' in Simon Chesterman (ed), *Civilians in War* (Lynne Rienner Publishers 2001); Victor Igreja, 'Multiple Temporalities in Indigenous Justice and Healing Practices in

Although widespread atrocities were committed in both conflicts, there was no attempt to institute war crimes tribunals or truth commissions in either country. In Mozambique, the lack of mobilisation for post-conflict justice has been attributed to a collective feeling of guilt, an overwhelming urge for peace and a willingness to move beyond past wrongs in order to concentrate on reconciliation, reintegration and reconstruction.[76] Reflecting on the post-war years in Angola and the absence of calls for accountability for the crimes of the civil war, Joris van Wijk observed that:

> While many advocates of doing justice such as the United Nations, Western countries and rights based NGOs in general terms continue to state that granting amnesty to perpetrators of war crimes is unacceptable, they in actual practice do seem to acknowledge that it might in the specific situation of Angola be better to keep silent about its culture of impunity. Seen in the light of the current overall positive situation in Angola, this is not surprising. They may feel that at this moment it is better to let the past in Angola rest. Just like the Angolan government, they might feel that prosecuting war criminals who currently hold important positions in the Angolan administration might only stir up political antagonism, negatively impact political and economic interests and endanger the current peace. Publicly calling for justice could only destabilize the country.[77]

As regards Mozambique, recent developments have tempered positive assessments of the amnesty's role in securing lasting peace. Two decades after the conclusion of the General Peace Agreement, there has been a resurgence of violence between Frelimo and Renamo in certain parts of the country.[78] A ceasefire agreement providing for a general amnesty was concluded in 2014 but low-scale confrontations have resumed.[79] Peace talks are ongoing at the time of writing and a further settlement is expected before the presidential elections of 2019.[80]

Mozambique' (2012) 6 *The International Journal of Transitional Justice* 404; Lyn S Graybill, 'Pardon, punishment, and amnesia: three African post-conflict methods' (2004) 25(6) *Third World Quarterly* 1117.

76 See Cobban (n 73) 161–82; Graybill (n 75) 1124–27.

77 Joris van Wijk, 'Amnesty for War Crimes in Angola: Principled for a Day?' (2012) 12 *International Criminal Law Review* 743, 759.

78 Victor Igreja, 'Amnesty Law, Political Struggles for Legitimacy and Violence in Mozambique' (2015) 9 *International Journal of Transitional Justice* 239, 240 and 256–58; Stephanie Regalia, 'The Resurgence of Conflict in Mozambique: Ghosts from the Past and Brakes to Peaceful Democracy', *Observatoire de l'Afrique australe et des Grands Lacs*, Note no 14 (Ifri 2017).

79 Regalia (n 78) 24; Igreja, 'Amnesty Law, Political Struggles for Legitimacy and Violence in Mozambique' (n 78) 258; Manuel Mucari, 'Mozambique government, Renamo opposition sign peace deal' *Reuters* (25 August 2014).

80 Manuel Mucari, 'Mozambique opposition leader promises to sign peace deal by November' *Reuters* (1 September 2017); 'Mozambique president presses peace deal with opposition' *The Herald* (20 February 2018).

According to Victor Igreja, the resumption of hostilities between the former adversaries reflects the absence of genuine reconciliation due to the continuing failure to address the memories of the civil war.[81]

Limited amnesties: the cases of the Democratic Republic of Congo and Burundi

Lengthy peace processes in Burundi and the Democratic Republic of Congo (DRC) have similarly given rise to the grant of limited amnesties complying with international standards against impunity for serious crimes. Since their independence in the early 1960s, both countries have oscillated between armed conflicts pitting government forces against various rebel groups and periods of precarious peace. The Congolese and Burundian conflicts were particularly destructive and entailed the commission of massive and systematic human rights violations along political and ethnic lines, as in neighbouring Rwanda. Though armed violence halted in the first half of the 2010s, the refusal of both countries' presidents to step down at the end of their constitutional term provoked political upheavals and there has been growing international concern regarding patterns of gross human rights violations committed by government forces in recent years.[82]

In the late 1990s, the international community started to provide assistance towards the negotiation of a cessation of hostilities in the DRC and Burundi. These mediation efforts led to the conclusion of a series of ceasefire and peace agreements in the 2000s, all of which provided for an amnesty for acts of war expressly excluding international crimes.[83] In the DRC, the rebels' proposal for a broad amnesty was opposed not only by international peace negotiators but also by the government. The latter objected to pardoning the insurgents, even for narrowly conceived political crimes, and abstained from demanding immunity for its own forces, presumably on account of its confidence in the inertia of the Congolese justice system when it comes to military crimes.[84] In Burundi,

81 Igreja (n 78).

82 International Crisis Group, 'Time for Concerted Action in DR Congo', Africa Report N°257 (4 December 2017); ICC Press Release, 'ICC judges authorise opening of an investigation regarding Burundi situation' (9 November 2017); UN Human Rights Council, 'Report of the United Nations Independent Investigation on Burundi established pursuant to Human Rights Council resolution S-24/1' (20 September 2016) UN Doc A/HRC/33/37.

83 The major ceasefire and peace agreements for the DRC are the Lusaka Ceasefire Agreement of 19 July 1999; the Global and Inclusive Agreement on Transition in the Democratic Republic of Congo, Final Act of 2 April 2003 (Sun City Agreement) and the 'Actes d'Engagements' for South and North Kivu of 23 January 2008. Those for Burundi are the Arusha Peace and Reconciliation Agreement of 28 August 2000 (Arusha Agreement); the Global Cease-Fire Agreement with the CNDD-FDD of 2 November 2003 and the Comprehensive Cease-Fire Agreement with the PALIPEHUTU-FNL of 7 September 2006.

84 Laura Davis and Priscilla Hayner, 'Difficult Peace, Limited Justice: Ten Years of Peacemaking in the DRC' *International Center for Transitional Justice* (March 2009) 16; Laura Davis,

acting as mediator in the early stages of the peace process, Nelson Mandela advocated for a general amnesty and the release of all political prisoners.[85] However, both the government and the rebels were initially set against this idea in so far as it amounted to leaving the crimes committed by the other side unpunished. In order to preserve the possibility of criminal accountability for the most serious crimes, the UN and international human rights organisations consistently insisted on an exception for international crimes in any type of clemency measure adopted in Burundi or the DRC.[86]

The first major peace agreements concluded in both countries provided for the creation of two accountability institutions: on the one hand, a national truth and reconciliation commission, and on the other, an international criminal court (DRC) or an international judicial commission of inquiry (Burundi).[87] More than a decade after the conclusion of the relevant accords, the international judicial mechanisms still remain to be established, though the DRC government referred the situation in its country to the ICC in 2004.[88] The agreements' provisions relating to the establishment of a truth commission were implemented in both countries. However, while the DRC's Truth and Reconciliation Commission ended in 2006 before having heard a single case, Burundi's was only recently set up in controversial circumstances.[89] In the absence of an intervention by the international community to set up a war crimes court, there have been few prosecutions for wartime atrocities, at the exception of those undertaken by the ICC against a handful of Congolese perpetrators.[90] This lack of accountability has brought commentators to observe that the justice provisions

'Power Shared and Justice Shelved: The Democratic Republic of Congo' (2013) 17(2) *The International Journal of Human Rights* 289, 299.

85 Caroline Sculier, 'Négociations de paix au Burundi: Une justice encombrante mais incontournable' *Centre for Humanitarian Dialogue* (May 2008) 33.

86 Sculier (n 85) 37–39; Stef Vandeginste, 'Bypassing the Prohibition of Amnesty for Human Rights Crime under International Law: Lessons Learned from the Burundian Peace Process' (2011) 29(2) *Netherlands Quarterly of Human Rights* 189, 201–202; Davis and Hayner (n 84) 16–20.

87 Sun City Agreement (n 83) Annex I, Resolutions ICD/CPR/04 and DIC/CPR/05; Arusha Agreement (n 83) protocol 1, art 6(10).

88 However, the temporal jurisdiction of the ICC is limited to crimes committed after the entry into force of the Rome Statute in 2002, thus excluding the international crimes committed during the Congolese wars of the 1990s.

89 Davis and Hayner (n 84) 21–22; Stef Vandeginste, 'Burundi's Truth and Reconciliation Commission: How to Shed Light on the Past while Standing in the Dark Shadow of Politics?' (2012) 6 *International Journal of Transitional Justice* 355; Sydney Leclercq, 'Injustice through Transitional Justice? Subversion Strategies in Burundi's Peace Process and Postconflict Developments' (2017) 11 *International Journal of Transitional Justice* 525.

90 On prosecutions of international crimes by Congolese courts and the ICC, see Davis and Hayner (n 84) 25–30; Davis (n 84) 297–98. On the lack of accountability for war crimes in Burundi, see Human Rights Watch, 'Burundi: Seek Justice for War Crimes Victims, Gatumba Massacre Anniversary Marked by Ongoing Impunity' (13 August 2009).

and the limitation of amnesty in the Congolese and Burundian peace agreements failed to have any impact in practice.[91]

The international community's strict position on amnesties gave rise to tensions during the peace negotiations in both the DRC and Burundi.[92] However, it has not been capable of curbing the long-standing tradition of impunity in either country so far. The difficulty in implementing transitional justice mechanisms in these countries has been attributed to a number of factors, including the weakness and lack of independence of their judicial systems, the endemic corruption and the delaying tactics used by powerful domestic actors opposing accountability efforts.[93] With regard to the DRC, Laura Davis and Priscilla Hayner additionally observed that:

> It has been trying to implement policies of peace even while war has continued or been constantly threatened in other parts of the country (or even in the same region with other armed groups). Even while concluding each cease-fire or peace agreement, the DRC was never fully at peace, and the humanitarian impact has been extraordinarily grave. These conditions have influenced each set of decisions and made it difficult for any actor to advance the priority of accounting for the crimes of yesterday when further atrocities are threatened every day.[94]

With respect to Burundi, the failure of accountability for wartime atrocities is also due to two bypassing mechanisms which have effectively circumvented the principle of limited amnesty promoted by the UN.[95] The first of these mechanisms involves a law enacted in 2003 to incorporate the crimes of genocide, war crimes and crimes against humanity into Burundian law.[96] It was drafted so as to permit their prosecution solely for the future, specifying that international crimes committed before the law's promulgation were subject to the jurisdiction of the international commission of inquiry contemplated by the 2000 Arusha Agreement.[97] Since this commission was not, and will probably never, be established, the only remaining option to obtain accountability for the atrocity crimes committed before 2003 is to prosecute them as ordinary crimes pursuant to domestic law. However, this method is barred by temporary immunities granted by the successive peace accords to facilitate the participation of exiled rebel leaders in political and military power-sharing agreements.[98] These immunities – the second

91 Davis and Hayner (n 84) 15; Vandeginste (n 86) 191–92; Sculier (n 85) 48.

92 Davis and Hayner (n 84) 17–18; Vandeginste (n 86) 201; Sculier (n 85) 37–39.

93 Davis and Hayner (n 84) 25–27; Davis (n 84); Vandeginste (n 86) 203–204; Sculier (n 85) 39–40, 48–49.

94 Davis and Hayner (n 84) 38.

95 See Vandeginste (n 86) 202–209; Leclercq (n 89).

96 Loi no 1/004 du 8 mai 2003 portant répression du crime de génocide, des crimes contre l'humanité et des crimes de guerre.

97 Ibid, art 33(1).

98 Vandeginste (n 86) 205–209; Sculier (n 85) 34–38.

bypassing mechanism – have proved to be anything but temporary and their scope was extended until they covered not only the leaders and combatants of all rebel groups but also the national security forces and even convicted civilians.[99] The combination of these techniques has effectively secured the impunity of all persons responsible for serious crimes in the Burundian armed conflict, thus producing the same effect as a blanket amnesty. According to Stef Vandeginste, the way in which post-conflict justice has been neutralised in Burundi suggests that:

> [W]hen it comes to promoting 'sustainable peace', dirty deals between political and military elites with blood stained hands are only cosmetically affected by the international normative environment. Negotiating and implementing peace agreements is, first and foremost, a matter of making interests meet and seen from that angle, normative constraints are a nuisance that can be creatively circumvented.[100]

Conditional amnesties: the cases of South Africa and Colombia

The South African apartheid system and the violent confrontations to which it gave rise were brought to an end through negotiations between the National Party (NP) government and the principal liberation movement, the African National Congress (ANC).[101] The talks lasted several years until the victory of the ANC in the first South African democratic elections of April 1994, which led to the formation of a Government of National Unity including representatives from the NP. At the outset of the negotiations, as a gesture of good faith, the NP released political prisoners and extended amnesty in several forms to members of the liberation movements, including through an Indemnity Act of 1990.[102] According to Jeremy Sarkin, 'individuals were released throughout the four years of negotiations, but it was sometimes unclear in terms of which provision those releases occurred. Sometimes it was not clear whether those releases were done in terms of any law at all'.[103] State officials and security forces had already benefited from several indemnity legislations and immunity provisions

99 Ibid. See also Stef Vandeginste, 'Museveni, Burundi and the Perversity of *Immunité Provisoire*' (2016) 10(3) *International Journal of Transitional Justice* 1, 6 (noting that temporary immunities continue to apply in Burundi).

100 Vandeginste (n 86) 211.

101 For a brief account of the apartheid system and the South African transition, see Cobban (n 73) 80–98.

102 Indemnity Act no 35 of 18 May 1990. See Jeremy Sarkin, *Carrots and Sticks: The TRC and the South African Amnesty Process* (Intersentia 2004) 36–49; Adam Sitze, *The Impossible Machine: A Genealogy of South Africa's Truth and Reconciliation Commission* (University of Michigan Press 2013) 25–27; Peter Parker, 'The Politics of Indemnities, Truth Telling and Reconciliation in South Africa: Ending Apartheid Without Forgetting' (1996) 17 (1–2) *Human Rights Law Journal* 1, 1–5; John Dugard, 'Reconciliation and Justice: The South African Experience' (1998) 8 *Transnational Law and Contemporary Problems* 277, 291.

103 Sarkin (n 102) 39.

throughout the years of apartheid.[104] Nonetheless, the government passed a Further Indemnity Act in 1992 enabling the President to grant immunities to state agents on a discretionary and confidential basis.[105] The issue of amnesty remained contentious throughout the negotiating process. While there is wide agreement that the South African transition would not have been possible had the ANC insisted on criminal accountability for the crimes of the regime, liberation movements strongly opposed the idea of a blanket and unconditional amnesty.

The interim constitution of December 1993 was adopted by a multi-party forum known as CODESA (Conference for a Democratic South Africa).[106] It aimed to provide a 'historic bridge' between the divisions of the past and a future founded on respect for human rights and democracy on the basis that there was 'a need for understanding but not for vengeance, a need for reparation but not for retaliation, a need for *ubuntu* but not for victimisation'.[107] Accordingly, the interim constitution prescribed that an amnesty would be granted for crimes committed with a political objective in the course of the conflict, leaving the modalities to be determined by the new Parliament.[108] This provision was implemented in the Promotion of National Unity and Reconciliation Act of 1995, which created a Truth and Reconciliation Commission (TRC) mandated 'to promote national unity and reconciliation in a spirit of understanding which transcends the conflicts and divisions of the past'.[109]

The TRC comprised three committees: one dealing with human rights violations, one with reparation and rehabilitation, and one with amnesty. The latter was empowered to grant amnesty with respect to politically motivated offences, including gross human rights violations, providing that the applicant accepted responsibility for their acts and made a full disclosure of all relevant facts in a public hearing.[110] The TRC Act required the Amnesty Committee to publish the names of the perpetrators and the crimes for which they had been granted amnesty.[111] According to the statistics, full amnesty was granted to 1167 individuals, most of whom had committed gross human rights violations.[112]

104 Ibid, 47; Parker (n 102) 1; Sitze (n 102) 25.

105 Further Indemnity Act no 151 of 1992. See Sarkin (n 102) 43–44; Parker (n 102) 2–6.

106 On CODESA, see Richard Spitz and Matthew Chaskelson, *The Politics of Transition: A Hidden History of South Africa's Negotiated Settlement* (Hart Publishing 2000).

107 Constitution of the Republic of South Africa (1993) ch 16.

108 Ibid. The amnesty provision was incorporated in the South African constitution of 1996 by Schedule 6, art 22(1).

109 Promotion of National Unity and Reconciliation Act 34 of 1995 (TRC Act), ss 2 and 3.

110 Ibid, s 20. S 19(3)(b) required the Amnesty Committee to hold a public hearing when gross human rights violations were concerned. On the functioning and findings of the amnesty committee, see Sarkin (n 102).

111 TRC Act (n 109) s 20(6).

112 For an analysis of the number of amnesties granted by the TRC, see Sarkin (n 102) 107–48. On the statistics of amnesty application, see also Martin Coetzee, 'An Overview of the TRC

The TRC process was a milestone in the evolution of transitional justice in general and the concept of amnesty in particular. At a time when the literature on transitional justice was dominated by debates on the wisdom of pursuing accountability versus amnesty in the aftermath of repressive rule, the South African experience concretised the idea that there was a 'third way' between wholesale prosecutions following the Nuremberg model and blanket amnesties imposing national amnesia.[113] It popularised the notion of conditional amnesty imposing requirements on applicants. The combination of amnesty-granting and truth-seeking functions within the same institution, and the conditioning of the former on submission to the latter, was unprecedented and momentous for the development of transitional justice. This model has been replicated by several truth commissions in post-conflict contexts.[114] The TRC process also gave rise to a new understanding of amnesty as an instrument to unearth, rather than bury, the past. By enticing the perpetrators to disclose all relevant facts about their crimes, the promise of amnesty permitted the revelation of the truth to a larger extent than would otherwise have been possible given the difficulties in accessing evidence or witnesses in relation to apartheid crimes. By requiring human rights violators to admit responsibility in a public hearing, this system also enforced a degree of accountability, provided a sense of catharsis to the South African society and a form of reparation to the victims.

The decades-long armed conflict in Colombia was similarly brought to an end by negotiations between the adversaries. The Colombian peace process has been ongoing since the 1980s between the government, paramilitary groups and left-wing guerrillas. It gave rise to several peace agreements, some of which entailed recourse to broad amnesties.[115] The Justice and Peace Law of 2005 provided the framework for the demobilisation of paramilitary forces. Unlike previous Colombian pacification legislation, it recognised the right of the victims of the conflict to truth, justice and reparations. It also provided for a degree of accountability through a system of reduced prison sentences for paramilitaries

Amnesty Process' in Charles Villa-Vicencio and Erik Doxtader (eds), *The Provocations of Amnesty: Memory, Justice and Impunity* (Africa World Press 2003) 193–94.

113 Alex Boraine, 'Truth and Reconciliation in South Africa: The Third Way' in Robert I Rotberg and Dennis Thompson (eds), *Truth v. Justice: The Morality of Truth Commissions* (Princeton University Press 2000) 175; Desmond Tutu, *No Future without Forgiveness* (Rider, London 1999) ch 2.

114 For example, truth commissions empowered to grant amnesty have been established in Liberia, Timor-Leste, the Solomon Islands, Kenya and Nepal.

115 On the Colombian peace process, see Helen Alviar Garcia and Karen Engle, 'The Distributive Politics of Impunity and Anti-Impunity: Lessons from Four Decades of Colombian Peace Negotiations' in Karen Engle, Zinaida Miller and DM Davis (eds) *Anti-Impunity and the Human Rights Agenda* (CUP 2016) 216; Lisa J Laplante and Kimberly Theidon, 'Transitional Justice in Times of Conflict: Colombia's Ley de Justicia y Paz' (2006) 28 *Michigan Journal of International Law* 49.

who renounced violence and contributed to fact-finding and reparation.[116] Negotiations between the government and the most prominent rebel armed group, the Revolutionary Armed Forces of Colombia (FARC), began in 2012. A comprehensive peace agreement was eventually signed by the belligerents in 2016, with strong support from the international community. After being rejected by a narrow margin in a national referendum, a revised version of the accord was ratified by the Colombian Congress on 30 November 2016. Along the line of the Justice and Peace law, this accord creates a system including elements of truth, justice, amnesty, reparation and non-repetition to deal with the legacy of the conflict.

From the beginning of the negotiations, the FARC made clear that their commitment to the peace process depended on the possibility to benefit from leniency measures permitting them to avoid imprisonment.[117] The 2016 peace agreement is remarkable for the complex system it elaborates in order to encourage the armed group to commit to peace while also upholding the rights of the victims.[118] It creates two transitional institutions: a Commission on Truth, Coexistence and Non-Repetition mandated to investigate the armed conflict and provide a forum to the victims, and a Special Jurisdiction for Peace competent to deal with serious crimes committed during the conflict. The agreement also introduces an amnesty extending to political and related crimes but excluding international crimes and gross human rights violations.[119] Perpetrators of serious crimes may, however, receive an alternative sentence permitting them to avoid serving prison time if they acknowledge responsibility for their crimes and commit to non-repetition at the beginning of the proceedings before the special tribunal.[120] Alternative sentences entail restrictions on their liberty of movement and residence as well as five to eight years of reparative labour according to an individual or collective project devised in consultation with the victims and monitored by the tribunal.[121] While offenders failing to come forward in time are liable to serve the same term under normal prison conditions, those who do not recognise their responsibility face terms of imprisonment of fifteen to twenty years.[122]

This sophisticated transitional justice system aims, inter alia, to establish the truth about human rights violations committed during the Colombian conflict, repair the harm done to the victims, facilitate the reintegration of combatants

116 Garcia and Engle (n 115) 228–31; Laplante and Theidon (n 115) 79–81; Catalina Diaz, 'Colombia's Bid for Justice and Peace' in Kai Ambos, Judith Large and Marieke Wierda (eds), *Building A Future on Peace and Justice* (Springer 2009) 488–89.

117 Garcia and Engle (n 115) 232–33.

118 Final Agreement for Ending the Conflict and Building a Stable and Lasting Peace, 24 November 2016.

119 Ibid, chapter 5, item 5.1.2 (II) paras 23–25, 38–41.

120 Ibid, item 5.1.2 (III) paras 45–47, 60, 75.

121 Ibid, item 5.1.2, para 75 (I)

122 Ibid, item 5.1.2, para 75 (III).

and foster reconciliation. Although the alternative sentence scheme falls short of criminal imprisonment, it goes a long way towards addressing the rights of the victims. On the one hand, it may be equated with a conditional amnesty in so far as it requires offenders to fulfil certain conditions in order to avoid criminal imprisonment. Like the South African TRC process, it enables perpetrators of serious crimes to benefit from a lenient treatment if they engage in truth-telling and admit responsibility. On the other hand, suspected perpetrators are tried by a judicial tribunal and receive a criminal sentence consisting in restrictions on rights and freedom for a term of several years. This scheme also goes further than the South African TRC by requiring convicted perpetrators to repair the damages done by the war, get involved with the communities most affected by it and work towards economic and social development.[123] This ongoing experiment in transitional justice shows that leniency measures may be used in creative ways and combined or sequenced with other judicial and non-judicial mechanisms in order to facilitate the achievement of peace, reconciliation and reintegration while complying with international standards on accountability, truth and reparation.

Transitional amnesties

Transitional amnesties are issued in connection with a process of political transition from an authoritarian regime to a democracy. As a condition of their surrender of power, authoritarian rulers often require guarantees of immunity for the abuses committed by their agents:

> The more brutal, inhumane, and extensive were the repressive actions, the more their actual perpetrators – the institutions involved and those persons who collaborated in them or supported them – feel threatened and will tend to form a bloc opposing any transition. Where they cannot prevent the transition, they will strive to obtain iron-clad guarantees that under no circumstances will "the past be unearthed"; failing to obtain that, they will remain a serious threat to the nascent democracy.[124]

Hence, amnesties are frequently passed in relation to political transitions, either by the authoritarian regime itself before leaving power or by the newly elected government in response to threats by undemocratic forces capable of destabilising the transition. The treatment to be reserved for former state agents responsible for widespread human rights violations presents a dilemma to emerging

123 Possible restorative projects include reparation programmes for displaced people, environmental protection, infrastructure building and repair in rural or urban areas, programmes to substitute crops used for illicit purposes and to clear and dispose of anti-personal mines and explosive devices, see ibid.

124 Guillermo O'Donnell and Philippe C Schmitter, *Transitions from Authoritarian Rule: Tentative Conclusions about Uncertain Democracies* (John Hopkins University Press 1986) 29.

democracies. On the one hand, securing their impunity through amnesty or pardon would send a signal running counter to the very principles of democracy and the rule of law underpinning the new political order. On the other hand, the pursuit of accountability for past crimes risks provoking a backlash from supporters of the outgoing regime, which often include large segments of the military and security forces wielding enough power to derail the transition.

This quandary has been one of the most debated issues in the field of transitional justice, which emerged in reaction to the waves of democratic transitions that swept Latin America and Europe in the last decades of the twentieth century.[125] The question of whether to forgive and forget or prosecute and punish atrocity crimes committed by a predecessor regime has also been considered by democratisation analysts.[126] The majority of scholars in both circles have emphasised the need to hold to account at least some of the persons considered most responsible for past crimes in order to uphold the rule of law and democratic values, deter future violations and provide closure to the victims and the society as a whole. However, it has also been generally accepted that the prosecution of all persons implicated in past abuses may not be possible due to the political constraints limiting the margin of manoeuver of fledgling democracies. For instance, Diane Orentlicher, one of the leading proponents of a duty to prosecute in transitional contexts, has conceded that:

> To the extent that the purpose of prosecutions is to vindicate the authority of the law and deter repetition of recent crimes, it is not necessary that a transitional government prosecute all who participated in a previous system of violations. These and other objectives served by post-transition prosecutions can be accomplished with exemplary trials, provided the criteria used to select defendants do not vitiate the justifying aims of prosecutions by, for

125 Neil J Kritz, *Transitional Justice: How Emerging Democracies Reckon with Former Regimes* (United States Institute of Peace Press 1995); Naomi Roht-Arriaza and Javier Mariezcurrena, *Transitional Justice in the Twenty-First Century: Beyond Truth versus Justice* (CUP 2006); Juan E Méndez, 'In Defense of Transitional Justice' in A James McAdams (ed), *Transitional Justice and the Rule of Law in New Democracies* (University of Notre Dame Press 1997) 1; José Zalaquett, 'Balancing Ethical Imperatives and Political Constraints: The Dilemma of New Democracies Confronting Past Human Rights Violations' (1992) 43 *Hastings Law Journal* 1425; Diane F Orentlicher, 'Settling Accounts: The Duty to Prosecute Human Rights Violations of a Prior Regime' (1991) 100(8) *Yale Law Journal* 2537; Carlos S Nino, 'The Duty to Punish Past Abuses of Human Rights Put Into Context: The Case of Argentina' (1991) 100 *Yale Law Journal* 2619; Naomi Roht-Arriaza, 'State Responsibility to Investigate and Prosecute Grave Human Rights Violations in International Law' (1990) 78 *California Law Review* 449; Jaime Malamud-Goti, 'Transitional Governments in the Breach: Why Punish State Criminals' (1990) 12(1) *Human Rights Quarterly* 1.

126 O'Donnell and Schmitter (n 124) 15–36; Samuel P Huntington, *The Third Wave: Democratization in the Late Twentieth Century* (University of Oklahoma Press 1991) 211–31; James McAdams, *Transitional Justice and the Rule of Law in New Democracies* (University of Notre Dame Press 1997).

> example, cynically targeting scapegoats. Once the chief aims of criminal law enforcement are achieved, further prosecutions have "diminishing returns" and may reverse progress toward consolidating a democratic transition.[127]

In his landmark study on democratic transitions, Samuel Huntington cautioned against the prosecution of officials of a departing regime in cases where it has not been militarily defeated and retains substantial power because '[t]he political costs of such an effort will outweigh any moral gains'.[128]

Political constraints in democratic transitions: the case of Argentina

Argentina's transitional process illustrates the dangers inherent in efforts by a new democratic government to prosecute agents of a former authoritarian regime responsible for atrocity crimes. In the early 1980s, discredited by its defeat in the Malvinas war, corruption and human rights scandals, the Argentinean military junta announced general elections.[129] They were won by the human-rights oriented candidate, Raul Alfonsin, whose campaign included a pledge to investigate past abuses and bring to justice the architects of state terror.[130] Accordingly, the new government established a national commission to investigate and document the systematic human rights violations perpetrated by the military regime.[131] In addition, on the initiative of the executive, the Argentinean Congress annulled an amnesty law passed by the military regime in 1983 to prevent the prosecution of crimes committed during the so-called Dirty War.[132] The removal of this legal obstacle permitted the trial of several military generals bearing the brunt of responsibility for state repression before the Federal Court of Appeals of Buenos Aires in 1985.[133]

The intention of President Alfonsin was to limit criminal prosecutions to those most responsible for past atrocities in order to protect the democratic order against military backlashes.[134] However, the government lost control of the process and Argentinean courts were rapidly overwhelmed by cases filed by victims and human rights organisations against military officers. As a result, agitation grew within the armed forces and the risk of a military coup became

127 Orentlicher (n 125) 2598–99.
128 Huntington (n 126) 231.
129 Nino (n 125) 2622–23.
130 Ibid; Kritz (n 125) vol 2, 323–24.
131 Argentina Comision Nacional sobre la Desaparicion de personas, *Nunca Mas (Never Again): A Report by Argentina's National Commission on Disappeared People* (Faber 1986).
132 Law no 22924 (22 September 1983). See Engstrom and Gabriel Pereira, 'From Amnesty to Accountability: The Ebb and Flow in the Search for Justice in Argentina' in Francesca Lessa and Leigh A Payne (eds), *Amnesty in the Age of Human Rights Accountability: Comparative and International Perspectives* (CUP 2012) 97, 100.
133 See Paula K Speck, 'The Trial of the Argentine Junta: Responsibilities and Realities' (1987) 18 *University of Miami Inter-American Law Review* 491.
134 Nino (n 125) 2623–27.

imminent. Responding to this mounting threat, the government took action to curtail the prosecution of military officers. First, it instructed the prosecutors to speed up the proceedings and concentrate on the highest-ranking perpetrators.[135] Second, it introduced a law establishing a sixty-day deadline for the lodging of new charges against the military.[136] This so-called 'full stop law' unexpectedly provoked an avalanche of new human rights cases and reinforced the determination of the judiciary to see through them all. The feared military response materialised in April 1987 with a revolt by radicalised middle- and low-ranking officers opposed to the continuation of the trials.[137] This crisis prompted the government to introduce a law creating an irrevocable presumption that all military officers not formally endowed with decision-making power had acted pursuant to superior orders and, therefore, could not be held responsible for their actions.[138] In practice, this so-called law of due obedience provided immunity to all but a few high-ranking military officers.

The last year of Alfonsin's mandate was marred by a terrorist attack against a military barrack and a growing rupture between his party and the Argentinean human rights network. His successor, Carlos Menem, granted presidential pardons to all persons convicted or undergoing trial for crimes connected with the Dirty War, even those condemned for having orchestrated state terror.[139] The Argentinean experience evinces the difficulties faced by nascent democracies attempting to reckon with a violent past. The conditions for accountability in Argentina were optimal as the military regime had been defeated in war, the executive and judiciary branches were willing to go forward with prosecution, there was a strong human rights network and widespread public support for criminal justice. However, it was not possible to overcome the obstacles presented by undemocratic forces in the immediate aftermath of the transition. As a result, impunity prevailed in this first phase of the Argentinean journey towards democracy.[140]

Self-amnesties: the cases of Chile and Peru

In Chile, power was captured by a military junta headed by General Augusto Pinochet in September 1973. Under his authority, a secret counterinsurgency unit was created for the purpose of eliminating opposition to the regime through executions, forced disappearances and torture.[141] In April 1978, the

135 Kritz (n 125) vol 2, 360–63.

136 Law no 23492 (24 December 1986).

137 Nino (n 125) 2628–29; Engstrom and Pereira (132) 104–105.

138 Law no 23521 (4 June 1987).

139 Nino (n 125) 2630; Engstrom and Pereira (n 132) 108.

140 On the eventual repeal of the Argentinean amnesty measures and the fate of other amnesties discussed in this section, see ch 5 in this volume.

141 Robert J Quinn, 'Will the Rule of Law End? Challenging Grants of Amnesty for the Human Rights Violations of a Prior Regime: Chile's New Model' (1994) 62 *Fordham Law Review* 905, 912–13 and 915–17; Edward C Snyder, 'The Dirty Legal War: Human Rights and the

regime issued an amnesty decree covering all crimes committed since the coup.[142] According to Robert Quinn, '[w]hile superficially benefiting all sides, in practice the decree excluded most opponents of the government, in part because many had already been killed, disappeared, or were in exile. Primarily military personnel and their agents benefited from the amnesty decree'.[143] In 1980, a new constitution contemplating a progressive transition towards democracy was drafted by the military regime, some of its provisions endowing the amnesty decree with constitutional status.[144]

Through a national plebiscite held in 1988, the Chilean people voted Pinochet out of the presidency and expressed their desire for a democratic transition. Patricio Aylwin was elected president in 1990, his agenda including a commitment to investigate the crimes of the military and remove the obstacle to justice presented by the 1978 amnesty decree.[145] Shortly after the presentation of his programme, a military commander issued a statement declaring that the repeal of the amnesty would violate the constitution and endanger the democratic transition. Pinochet himself announced that, if one of his men was touched, 'the rule of law would end'.[146] Since the dictatorship continued to benefit from substantial popular support following the transition, the new government had to proceed within the bounds of the 1980 constitution, including the amnesty and a provision entitling Pinochet to retain his function as commander-in-chief of the armed forces and become senator-for-life upon retirement.[147] In this highly controlled democratisation process with a strong authoritarian legacy, emphasis was placed on truth and reparation rather than criminal accountability in the immediate post-transition phase.

In Peru, the 1980s was plagued by terrorist attacks from the insurgent group Sendero Luminoso and the Tupac Amaru Revolutionary Movement. The military response involved the commission of systematic human rights violations including summary executions and disappearances. The last years of the decade were marked by increasingly violent campaigns by both sides in the internal conflict, the growing dominance of the military and the emergence of clandestine paramilitary groups.[148] A political unknown, Alberto Fujimori, capitalised on these dire circumstances to propel himself into the presidency on the basis of a

Rule of Law in Chile 1973–1995' (1995) 2 *Tulsa Journal of Comparative and International Law* 253, 258–64.

142 Decree Law no 2191 (18 April 1978).

143 Quinn (n 141) 918; Snyder (n 141) 268–69.

144 Quinn (n 141) 914; Snyder (n 141) 279.

145 Jorge Correa Sutil, 'Dealing with Past Human Rights Violations: The Chilean Case After Dictatorship' (1992) 67 *Notre Dame Law Review* 1455, 1460–62.

146 Ibid; Jorge Correa Sutil, '"No Victorious Army Has Ever Been Prosecuted ..." The Unsettled Story of Transitional Justice in Chile' in James McAdams, *Transitional Justice and the Rule of Law in New Democracies* (University of Notre Dame Press 1997) 132.

147 See Cath Collins, 'Human Rights Trials in Chile during and after the "Pinochet Years"' (2010) 4 *International Journal of Transitional Justice* 67, 70–75.

148 Rebecca K Root, *Transitional Justice in Peru* (Palgrave Macmillan 2012) 22–26.

populist agenda. In the name of fighting terrorism, he gradually extended his power and control over the national security apparatus, within which was created a clandestine death squad to eliminate opposition to the regime.[149] This group carried out notorious massacres in the first years of Fujimori's rule, notably at Barrios Altos and La Cantuta.[150] A parliamentary committee formed to investigate the Barrios Altos massacre was discontinued on account of the self-coup instigated by Fujimori in April 1992.[151] Further attempts to bring to justice members of the death squad were defeated by the adoption of an amnesty law. According to Susana Villarán:

> It was precisely at this moment – when the center of power was being investigated by a prosecutor and a judge – that the Peruvian Congress, in the early morning hours of 14 June 1995, secretly approved an amnesty law. The language for the law had been transmitted directly from the Government Palace, and there was no congressional debate. This law exonerated from any responsibility the military and police forces and civilians who had committed or participated in any human rights violations between 1980 and 1995. As a result, the few investigations that had been opened up to that point were set aside.[152]

A Peruvian judge's subsequent attempt to challenge the constitutionality of the law and its compatibility with human rights treaties was obstructed by the enactment of a second amnesty law prohibiting judicial review of the first and rendering its application by the judiciary obligatory.[153]

The Chilean and Peruvian amnesties are typical self-amnesties issued at the instigation of a repressive regime responsible for widespread and systematic human rights violations with the direct aim of shielding its agents from accountability. None of them were adopted pursuant to democratic processes or following public consultations, so that they enjoyed little public support or legitimacy. While the Chilean amnesty law maintained the appearance of being granted in the interest of the country's democratic transition, the Peruvian self-amnesties lacked even this pretext. Not all amnesties relating to periods of state repression, however, are enacted in such a unilateral and undemocratic fashion. The

149 Ibid, 34–35; Lisa J Laplante, 'Outlawing Amnesty: The Return of Criminal Justice in Transitional Justice Schemes' (2009) 49(4) *Virginia Journal of International Law* 915, 945–53.

150 Ibid. See *Barrios Altos v Peru* (Judgment) Inter-American Court of Human Rights Series C No 75 (14 March 2001); *La Cantuta v Peru* (Judgment) Inter-American Court of Human Rights Series C No 162 (29 November 2006).

151 Root (n 148) 28–29; Laplante (n 149) 945–53.

152 Susana Villarán de la Puente, 'Peru' in *Victims Unsilenced: The Inter-American Human Rights System and Transitional Justice in Latin America* (Due Process of Law Foundation 2007) 115.

153 Laws nos 26479 (14 June 1995) and 26492 (28 June 1995).

amnesty laws adopted as part of the transitional processes in Spain and Brazil, for instance, benefited from substantial popular support.

Amnesties resulting from popular demands: the cases of Spain and Brazil

The Spanish amnesty law of October 1977 covered all crimes committed during the Spanish civil war (1936–1939) and Franco's authoritarian regime (1939–1975).[154] When the bill was passed in the new democratic Parliament, over ninety percent of the Chamber of Deputies voted for it.[155] During the debate, it was described by different parties as 'the only means of consolidating peace', 'the sole measure which might close that chapter of civil wars and crusades' and 'the ethical-political premise for democracy, which fervently seeks to overcome and go beyond the divisions which divided and set us against each other in the past'.[156] The absence of calls for accountability during the Spanish transition has been attributed to the traumatic memory of the civil war and a consensus that 'first, all those involved were equally guilty and, secondly, the tragedy must never again be repeated'.[157] This translated into mass mobilisations in favour of a broad amnesty throughout 1976 and 1977 including strikes, demonstrations, rallies and marches organised by political movements and a wide spectrum of civil society organisations.[158] According to Paloma Aguilar, '[t]he political amnesty was considered by many to be the sine qua non for the establishment of democracy in Spain, the foundation of symbolic reconciliation between victors and vanquished'.[159] The 1977 law entailed the release of political prisoners, the rehabilitation and provision of indemnities to those having fought against authoritarian rule, and a blanket immunity for state agents covering the worst abuses of the Franco regime.[160]

The Brazilian amnesty law of 1979 has been described as the 'cornerstone of Brazil's political transition'.[161] It was adopted following years of campaigning by civil society groups for the release of political prisoners and the return of

154 Law no 46/77 (15 October 1977).

155 Paloma Aguilar, *Memory and Amnesia: The Role of the Spanish Civil War in the Transition to Democracy* (Berghahn Books 2002) 198.

156 Ibid, 196–97.

157 Paloma Aguilar, 'Collective Memory of the Spanish Civil War: The Case of the Political Amnesty in the Spanish Transition to Democracy' (1997) 4(4) *Democratization* 88, 90. See also Omar G Encarnacion, 'Reconciliation after Democratization: Coping with the Past in Spain' (2008) 123(3) *Political Science Quarterly* 435.

158 Aguilar, 'Collective Memory of the Spanish Civil War' (n 157) 90–92, 98–102.

159 Ibid, 104.

160 Paloma Aguilar, 'Justice, Politics, and Memory in the Spanish Transition' in Alexandra Barahona De Brito, Carmen Gonzalez Enriquez and Paloma Aguilar (eds), *The Politics of Memory and Democratization: Transitional Justice in Democratizing Societies* (OUP 2001) 102–104.

161 Paulo Abrão and Marcelo D Torelly, 'Resistance to Change: Brazil's Persistent Amnesty and its Alternatives for Truth and Justice' in Francesca Lessa and Leigh A Payne (eds), *Amnesty*

exiled activists. This movement gained prominence nationwide in the second half of the 1970s, culminating in the creation of the Brazilian Committee for Amnesty in 1978.[162] The amnesty law was enacted as part of a process of progressive political liberalisation by the Brazilian military dictatorship (1964–1985). The law was introduced by the regime and was accordingly more restrictive as regards political offences than advocated by popular movements.[163] Though it primarily benefited state agents responsible for human rights abuses, most actors of the opposition and civil society supported the amnesty as a step towards reconciliation and democratisation.[164]

A constitutional amendment reaffirming the amnesty was adopted by the Brazilian National Assembly in 1985.[165] The democratic constitution of 1988 expanded its scope by making it applicable to a longer time period and to categories of persons excluded from the 1979 law. In the following decades, measures were adopted to complement the amnesty, including a law acknowledging the state's responsibility for the crimes of the dictatorship, a reparation programme for victims of political persecution, a truth commission and a commission on disappearances.[166] Thus, according to Fabia Veçoso:

> [W]hen the context of the Brazilian amnesty is taken into account, it becomes clear that almost all elements that seek to protect the victims' rights are present. The absence of trials in Brazil did not imply the total disregard of the victims' rights, nor the absence of strategies to deal with the violence of the military rule. On the contrary, it is possible to assert that amnesty in Brazil promoted the realization of human rights in a long-term perspective.[167]

Amnesties enjoying some degree of legitimacy: the cases of Uruguay and South Africa

At both ends of the spectrum of transitional amnesties may be placed those issued unilaterally by an authoritarian regime to benefit state agents, like the measures adopted in Argentina and Chile, and those enacted in response to

in the Age of Human Rights Accountability: Comparative and International Perspectives (CUP 2012) 153.

162 Ibid, 154; Fabia Fernandes Carvalho Veçoso, 'Whose Exceptionalism? Debating the Inter-American View on Amnesty and the Brazilian Case' in Karen Engle, Zinaida Miller and DM Davis (eds), *Anti-Impunity and the Human Rights Agenda* (CUP 2016) 193–94; Nina Schneider, 'Impunity in Post-authoritarian Brazil: The Supreme Court's Recent Verdict on the Amnesty Law' (2011) 90 *European Review of Latin American and Caribbean Studies* 39, 42–44.

163 Law no 6683/79 (28 August 1979). See Veçoso (n 162) 195–97.

164 Schneider (n 162) 43.

165 Veçoso (n 162) 197; Abrão and Torelli (n 161) 154.

166 Veçoso (n 162) 198–200; Abrão and Torelli (n 161) 153–64.

167 Veçoso (n 162) 204.

public demands, like the Spanish and Brazilian amnesty laws. Somewhere in the middle are transitional amnesties which, though passed to accommodate outgoing repressive regimes, have a degree of public legitimacy. Uruguay's amnesty law of December 1986 may be placed in this category.[168] It was adopted in response to military unrest provoked by attempts to prosecute human rights violations committed by security forces during the Uruguayan dictatorship (1973–1985).[169] However, it was ratified in two national plebiscites at twenty years of interval, indicating the continued support of the measure by a majority of voters. The first referendum was called by civil society groups and held in 1989 following several months of intensive campaigning for truth and justice.[170] The population mobilised massively with a participation rate of 84%, 55% of whom were in favour of retaining the law.[171] According to commentators:

> [T]he view that the referendum functioned to seal the problem of the legacy of human rights violations, from a political and legal point of view, has been widespread. Moreover, the fact that civil society mobilized widely and had the chance to challenge the decision by the political class has given further legitimacy to the formal method of resolving such problems.[172]

The second referendum of 2009 endorsed the amnesty law by a narrow margin, despite the decision of Uruguay's Supreme Court declaring its unconstitutionality a few days before.[173]

The South African amnesty-for-truth deal was not ratified through a referendum but the law implementing it was adopted through democratic procedures and following large-scale public consultations.[174] During the peace talks between the government and the ANC, the former attempted to impose the passage of a blanket and unconditional amnesty on the latter.[175] However, ANC leaders resisted this pressure and reserved the right for the new Parliament to decide the conditions on which amnesty would be granted.[176] The TRC Act

168 Law no 15848 (21 December 1986).

169 See Francesca Lessa, 'Barriers to Justice: The Ley de Caducidad and Impunity in Uruguay' in Francesca Lessa and Leigh A Payne (eds), *Amnesty in the Age of Human Rights Accountability: Comparative and International Perspectives* (CUP 2012) 123, 127–30.

170 Ibid, 130–131; Luis Roniger and Mario Sznajder, 'The Legacy of Human Rights Violations and the Collective Identity of Redemocratized Uruguay' (1997) 19 *Human Rights Quarterly* 55, 64–73; Lessa (n 169) 131.

171 Ibid, 64–65.

172 Roniger and Sznajder (n 170) 59.

173 Jo-Marie Burt, Gabriela Fried Amiliviay and Francesca Lessa, 'Civil Society and the Resurgent Struggle against Impunity in Uruguay (1986–2012)' (2013) 7 *International Journal of Transitional Justice* 306, 317–19.

174 TRC Act (n 109).

175 Sarkin (n 102) 41; Parker (n 102) 3.

176 The epilogue of the Interim Constitution of 1993 provides that 'amnesty shall be granted in respect of acts, omissions and offences associated with political objectives and committed in

was elaborated through an inclusive process enabling civil society organisations, political parties and individuals to make submissions to the parliamentary committee responsible for drafting the bill and thus influence the design of the future TRC.[177] In addition, efforts were made to consult cross-sectional segments of the public through seminars, workshops and a national conference.[178] When the TRC Act was adopted in Parliament, it was vigorously debated in both chambers and received the support of all but two political parties.[179]

Conclusion

A comparison of the distinctive features of ancient and modern amnesties reveals several points of continuity.[180] Amnesties are still issued by sovereign authorities in order to exempt categories of offenders from criminal liability, generally in relation to a period of armed conflict or civil unrest. There is, however, one important respect in which the concept of amnesty has altered in recent decades. Whereas the mechanism used to be associated with a duty of oblivion, it is less closely tied to the notion of amnesia today. Modern amnesties still aim to foreclose the possibility of prosecution for offences committed in connection with certain events, but they no longer entail an obligation to suppress the memory of these events. Some amnesties are even designed to entice offenders to tell the truth and admit responsibility so as to permit the establishment of a historical record of past crimes. This new function to facilitate the recovery of the truth and the memory of certain events demonstrates the capacity of the mechanism to evolve and adapt to the needs of modern societies in which truth has come to be recognised as a fundamental right.

Recent empirical studies indicate that there has been an increase in the number of amnesties issued worldwide since the Second World War. They reveal that amnesty is the mechanism that is most commonly relied on in situations of transition from war or authoritarian rule. It is more often extended to opponents of the state than state agents and, in relation to armed conflicts, is more likely following negotiated settlements than military victories. While the most popular types of amnesties are those granted to release political prisoners and end armed violence by rebel groups, self-amnesties aiming to secure the impunity of authoritarian agents represent only a small fraction of modern amnesties. In post-conflict contexts, blanket amnesties are the most frequent.

the course of the conflicts of the past. To this end, Parliament under this Constitution shall adopt a law determining a firm cut-off date … and providing for the mechanisms, criteria and procedures, including tribunals, if any, through which such amnesty shall be dealt with at any time after the law has been passed'.

177 Alex Boraine, *A Country Unmasked: Inside South Africa's Truth and Reconciliation Commission* (OUP 2000) ch 2; Sarkin (n 102) 53.

178 Boraine (n 177) 50–52.

179 Ibid, 71.

180 On ancient amnesties, see ch 1 in this volume.

However, in recent years, amnesties have tended to become more limited or tailored in accordance with international standards by excluding serious crimes, being combined with accountability mechanisms or imposing conditions on applicants.

Amnesties have varying degrees of legitimacy and effectiveness in achieving their goal to ease a peace or democratic process depending on several factors, including their context and mode of adoption, scope, design and intended beneficiaries. Pacification amnesties generally enjoy a higher degree of legitimacy than transitional amnesties because they usually cover crimes committed by both sides in an armed conflict or solely by opponents of the state. They are often introduced by a peace agreement, thus resulting from negotiations between adversaries rather than unilateral action. During peace negotiations, they may be key in order to induce the belligerents to commit to the peace process, facilitate the disarmament, demobilisation and reintegration of rebel combatants, and enable power-sharing between the parties, as in Mozambique and Angola. Amnesties may also be issued unilaterally by the state in the midst of an armed conflict to encourage defections by rebel fighters, promote their reintegration into their communities and foster reconciliation, as in Uganda. Pacification amnesties may be adopted in response to pressure by rebel groups, as in the DRC, or public demands, as in Uganda. They are usually introduced through an act of Parliament, often in furtherance of a peace agreement.

While blanket amnesties covering serious crimes are condemned by policymakers and human rights advocates, the cases of Mozambique and Angola show that they are capable of contributing to the overriding objective of restoring peace and stability. Both countries have known over a decade of peace following the conclusion of comprehensive settlements including a blanket amnesty, though the failure to deal with the legacy of the war may have contributed to provoking a resumption of violence two decades later in Mozambique. On the other hand, the cases of Burundi and the DRC show that, although the limitation of pacification amnesties to exclude serious crimes preserves the possibility of justice in the long-term, it may not facilitate accountability, nor peace, in the short-term. International pressure to restrict the scope of amnesties often complicates peace negotiations, thus running the risk of prolonging conflicts. In addition, in the absence of political will towards the prosecution of serious crimes at the domestic level, limited amnesties may in practice operate as blanket amnesties, as occurred in Burundi. Some of the tensions between peace and justice arising in relation to armed conflicts may be overcome through the use of conditional amnesties, as in South Africa, or alternative sentence schemes, as in Colombia, permitting to uphold the rights of the victims to truth and reparation while also achieving a degree of accountability.

Transitional amnesties are often associated with self-amnesties because they are typically passed at the instigation of an authoritarian regime in order to exonerate its agents responsible for widespread abuses against civilians. The cases of Argentina, Chile and Uruguay illustrate different ways in which impunity may be imposed by an outgoing regime and maintained following the democratic transition through an amnesty law passed under threats of authoritarian reversal by undemocratic forces. The self-amnesty issued in Peru ranked even lower in terms of its legitimacy since it was not even justified by an impending democratisation process. By contrast, some transitional amnesties have been adopted in response to popular mobilisation campaigns in favour of the release of political prisoners and the return of exiles, as in Spain and Brazil. As a concession to the regime, those amnesties also provided immunity to state agents responsible for serious crimes. They were nonetheless endowed with a high degree of domestic legitimacy at the time of their adoption because they represented a step towards the liberalisation of the regime, democratisation and reconciliation.

Amnesties vary widely along different lines. It is difficult to set out general rules regarding their legitimacy and efficacy in fulfilling their goals because they are highly context-dependent. What can be gathered from this review of different types of amnesties is that the more inclusive and adversarial their elaboration and adoption process is, the more legitimate they are at the local level. Whether they are supported by international and domestic actors will also depend on the extent to which they provide protection for perpetrators of serious crimes and impose conditions on applicants permitting a degree of accountability, truth and reparation. The question of the effectiveness of amnesties in facilitating the restoration of peace or the establishment of democracy is more complex since many factors besides the presence or not of an amnesty and its particular type participate to the positive or negative outcome of a transitional process. Such an outcome may also vary considerably at different points in time. However, the cases studied show that even blanket amnesties may in some circumstances contribute to peace or democracy taking hold following periods of generalised violence, as in Angola and Spain. Amnesties that are combined with or conditional on participation to transitional justice mechanisms are more desirable since they enable transitional societies to reckon with their past, thereby enhancing the prospect of long-term sustainable peace. Notwithstanding these general observations, the diverse ways in which amnesties may be crafted or implemented in different types of contexts caution against one-size-fits-all approaches, advocating instead for a consideration of their merits on a case-by-case basis.

Part 2

Assessing the legality of amnesties in the contemporary international order

4 The obligation to prosecute

Introduction

The view that international law prohibits amnesties for serious crimes of international concern has garnered considerable support in the last few decades. It is grounded in several arguments, the most prominent of which relates to the obligation to prosecute certain crimes contained in international conventions. There are scant references to amnesty in multilateral treaties, none of them prohibiting or discouraging this mechanism. Though there is no explicit treaty prohibition, it has been argued that amnesties are incompatible with international duties to prosecute perpetrators of international crimes. This chapter examines conventions relating to the repression of international crimes and their bearing on the permissibility of amnesty for these crimes. Through an analysis of the *travaux préparatoires* of these instruments, it aims to clarify the intention of their drafters with respect to the issue of amnesty.

The first section briefly retraces the development of the principle of individual liability for international crimes. Sections 2 and 3 examine the treaty obligations to prosecute genocide and grave breaches of the laws of war applicable in international armed conflicts. Section 4 considers whether the international convention prohibiting the application of statutory limitations to war crimes and crimes against humanity has a bearing on the issue of amnesty, both mechanisms representing potential obstacles to the prosecution of international crimes. Section 5 investigates the drafting history of one of the only two treaty provisions referring directly to amnesty, article 6(5) of the second protocol additional to the Geneva Conventions, which encourages the grant of amnesty at the end of non-international armed conflicts.[1] Sections 6 and 7 examine the treaty obligations to prosecute torture and enforced disappearances. Section 8 questions whether treaty requirements to prosecute implicitly prohibit the grant of amnesties. Finally, section 9 considers whether customary law imposes a duty to prosecute

1 The other treaty provision referring to amnesty is article 6(4) of the International Covenant on Civil and Political Rights (adopted 16 December 1966, entered into force 23 March 1976) 999 UNTS 171 (ICCPR) providing that '[a]mnesty, pardon or commutation of the sentence of death may be granted in all cases'. It is discussed in ch 6 in this volume.

international crimes, particularly those for which there is no treaty-based repression regime, i.e. crimes against humanity and war crimes committed in non-international armed conflicts.

Most treaty requirements to prosecute international crimes were introduced before the 1990s. However, claims asserting that amnesties may not be granted in relation to these crimes only started to emerge in public discourse during that decade. The time gap between both sets of events – the creation of the international obligations and the emergence of claims contesting the validity of amnesties on that basis – suggests that other developments contributed to the view that amnesties covering serious crimes are contrary to international law. Accordingly, while this chapter concentrates on the argument deriving from duties to prosecute international crimes, the next three chapters consider other legal bases supporting this view.

1. The principle of individual liability for crimes under international law

Before the two world wars, the principle of the responsibility of individuals for international crimes was not clearly articulated. International law entitled states to punish certain crimes offending international rules but it did not directly assign criminal liability to the perpetrators, leaving that task to municipal legislators.[2] In the aftermath of the First World War, a Commission created by the Paris Peace Conference recognised the criminal liability of individuals responsible for war crimes and crimes against humanity.[3] Though this principle had only limited practical impact in the post-World War I context, it laid the ground for the major international law developments realised at the end of World War II. The efforts of the victorious powers to ensure the prosecution of major Nazi criminals gave rise to the establishment by the international community that war crimes, crimes against humanity and crimes against peace are crimes under international law whose perpetrators incur individual criminal responsibility.[4] While this principle entitles all states to prosecute persons responsible for these crimes, it does not require them to do so. However, in the decades following the Second World War, several international conventions were adopted for the purpose of ensuring the repression of certain grave crimes

2 See text to n 107–108 in ch 2 of this volume.

3 Commission on the Responsibility of the Authors of the War and on Enforcement of Penalties (1920) 14(1/2) *American Journal of International Law* 95, 117.

4 Charter of the International Military Tribunal, Annex to the Agreement for the Prosecution and Punishment of the Major War Criminals of the European Axis (signed 8 August 1945, entered into force 8 August 1945) 82 UNTS 280; UN General Assembly Resolution 95(I) (11 December 1946); Principles of International Law recognized in the Charter of the Nürnberg Tribunal and in the Judgment of the Tribunal, with commentaries, Yearbook of the International Law Commission, 1950, vol II, 374–78.

through their proscription at the international level and the imposition on states parties of an obligation to prosecute alleged perpetrators.

2. The obligation to prosecute genocide

The Convention on the Prevention and Punishment of the Crime of Genocide (Genocide Convention) was the first human rights convention adopted by the UN on 9 December 1948.[5] Its first article provides that 'genocide, whether committed in time of peace or in time of war, is a crime under international law' which the contracting parties 'undertake to prevent and to punish'. Article 2 defines genocide as a series of acts committed against persons belonging to a national, ethnical, racial or religious group with the intent to destroy this group as such in whole or in part. Article 5 requires states parties to criminalise and provide effective penalties for acts of genocide. Article 6 prescribes that:

> Persons charged with genocide or any of the other acts enumerated in Article 3 **shall** be tried by a competent tribunal of the State in the territory of which the act was committed, or by such international penal tribunal as may have jurisdiction with respect to those Contracting Parties which shall have accepted its jurisdiction.[6]

The drafters of this provision agreed on the use of the word 'shall' in order to stress the obligation of the territorial state to prosecute the perpetrator if it did not hand him over to an international tribunal.[7] This obligation to prosecute only binds the state on the territory of which genocide was committed, though other states might decide to assert jurisdiction over suspected perpetrators on a different legal basis.

The Genocide Convention affirms in several places that persons responsible for genocide shall be punished (articles 1, 3 and 4). It also specifies that they must be tried by a competent tribunal (article 6) according to domestic legislation providing for effective penalties (article 5). Thus, while its drafting history does not refer to amnesties, the insistence of the convention on prosecution and punishment would seem incompatible with measures whose effect is to bar the possibility of criminal proceedings.[8] Hence, there is general agreement among scholars that states parties to the Genocide Convention may not extend an

5 Convention on the Prevention and Punishment of the Crime of Genocide (adopted 9 December 1948, entered into force 12 January 1951) 78 UNTS 277.

6 Ibid (emphasis added).

7 UN Economic and Social Council, Ad Hoc Committee on genocide, summary records of the twentieth meeting (4 May 1948) UN Doc E/AC.25/SR.20, 2. On the drafting history of article 6, see William Schabas, *Genocide in International Law: The Crime of Crimes* (CUP 2009) 411–16.

8 On the drafting history of the Convention, see Hirad Abtahi and Philippa Webb, *The Genocide Convention: The Travaux Préparatoires* (Martinus Nijhoff Publishers 2008).

amnesty to persons having committed genocide on their territory without breaching their prosecutorial commitment.[9]

3. The obligation to prosecute grave breaches of the Geneva Conventions

The four Geneva Conventions of 12 August 1949 were the first multilateral treaties to institute a system for the repression of grave breaches of the laws of war committed in international armed conflicts.[10] This initiative originated in the realisation that most domestic penal legislations either did not contain provisions enabling the repression of war crimes or penalised these acts only when committed by nationals.[11] The absence of a uniform system for the repression of grave breaches was identified as one of the reasons for which the laws of war had been violated on so many occasions during World War II. Accordingly, in preparation for a Diplomatic Conference convened at Geneva in 1949, a group of experts from the International Committee of the Red Cross (ICRC) drafted penalty provisions with three objectives in mind: induce states to incorporate the laws of war into their municipal law, identify the grave breaches of those laws that should be criminalised in all penal systems, and institute a system of universal jurisdiction over these grave breaches in order to ensure their effective repression.[12]

The first of these goals was achieved by the first paragraph of articles 49/50/129/146 of the Geneva Conventions, modelled on article 5 of the Genocide Convention. It provides that '[t]he High Contracting Parties undertake to enact any legislation necessary to provide effective penal sanctions for persons committing, or ordering to be committed, any of the grave breaches of the present Convention defined in the following Article'.[13] The second objective was realised through the enumeration of acts constituting grave breaches of each convention in articles 50/51/130/147, including wilful killing, torture, inhuman treatment

9 Anja Seibert-Fohr, *Prosecuting Serious Human Rights Violations* (OUP 2009) ch 4; John Dugard, 'Dealing With Crimes of a Past Regime. Is Amnesty Still an Option?' (1999) 12 *Leiden Journal of International Law* 1001; Michael P Scharf, 'The Letter of the Law: The Scope of the International Legal Obligation to Prosecute Human Rights Crimes' (1996) 59(4) *Law and Contemporary Problems* 41; Diane F. Orentlicher, 'Settling Accounts: The Duty to Prosecute Human Rights Violations of a Prior Regime' (1991) 100 *Yale Law Journal* 2537.

10 Geneva Conventions (I) for the Amelioration of the Condition of the Wounded and Sick in Armed Forces in the Field, (II) for the Amelioration of the Condition of Wounded, Sick and Shipwrecked Members of Armed Forces at Sea, (III) relative to the Treatment of Prisoners of War, (IV) relative to the Protection of Civilian Persons in Time of War (adopted 12 August 1949, entered into force 21 October 1950) 75 UNTS 31/85/135/287 (Geneva Conventions).

11 Final Record of the Diplomatic Conference of Geneva of 1949, vol 2(B), Summary Records of the 29th meeting of the Special Committee, 85.

12 Revised and New Draft Conventions for the Protection of War Victims: Remarks and Proposals, ICRC (Geneva, February 1949) 18–22.

13 Geneva Conventions (n 10).

and serious bodily injury. The third aim was accomplished by the second paragraph of articles 49/50/129/146 instituting universal jurisdiction over grave breaches of the conventions:

> Each High Contracting Party shall be under the obligation to search for persons alleged to have committed, or to have ordered to be committed, such grave breaches, and shall bring such persons, regardless of their nationality, before its own courts. It may also, if it prefers, and in accordance with the provisions of its own legislation, hand such persons over for trial to another High Contracting Party concerned, provided such High Contracting Party has made out a prima facie case.[14]

During the negotiation of this provision, the Italian delegate proposed to limit the obligation to search for and bring to justice perpetrators of grave breaches to the parties to a given armed conflict.[15] However, the Netherlands' representative insisted on a principle of universality requiring all contracting parties to prosecute or extradite suspects coming into their custody, and the Italian amendment was withdrawn.[16] Pursuant to a French proposal, it was decided to insert a requirement that the state demanding the extradition of a suspected offender must establish a prima facie case in the extradition request.[17] Nonetheless, the Netherlands' delegate made clear that, in accordance with the *aut dedere aut judicare* principle, 'if a Contracting Party does not hand over an accused person, it has to bring him to trial before its own courts'.[18] This alternative obligation to prosecute or extradite leaves little room for an amnesty to be extended to perpetrators of grave breaches in compliance with the Geneva Conventions.

The third paragraph of articles 49/50/129/146 limits the scope of the obligation to enact legislation and prosecute or extradite to the grave breaches identified in articles 50/51/130/147. The drafters considered these offences as so grave that 'no legislator would object to having [them] included in the penal code'.[19] The criminalisation and repression of other breaches of the conventions were left

14 Ibid.

15 Final Record of the Diplomatic Conference of Geneva of 1949, vol 2(B), Summary Records of the 30th meeting of the Special Committee, 87.

16 Ibid; Final Record of the Diplomatic Conference of Geneva of 1949, vol 2(B), Fourth Report drawn up by the Special Committee of the Joint Committee, 115–16.

17 Ibid.

18 Final Record of the Diplomatic Conference of Geneva of 1949, vol 2(B), Fourth Report drawn up by the Special Committee of the Joint Committee, 115. According to Cherif Bassiouni, '[t]he expression "aut dedere aut judicare" is commonly used to refer to the alternative obligation to extradite or prosecute which is contained in a number of multilateral treaties aimed at securing international cooperation in the suppression of certain kinds of criminal conducts'. See M Cherif Bassiouni and Edward M Wise, *Aut Dedere Aut Judicare: The Duty to Extradite or Prosecute in International Law* (Martinus Nijhoff Publishers 1995) 3.

19 Final Record of the Diplomatic Conference of Geneva of 1949, vol 2(B), Fourth Report drawn up by the Special Committee of the Joint Committee, 115.

to the discretion of national authorities.[20] Another important limitation of the grave breaches regime is that it is only applicable in international armed conflicts. During the negotiation of common article 3 to the Geneva Conventions, the only provision addressing situations of non-international armed conflicts, it was emphasised that the conventions are not applicable to this type of conflict in the absence of an express stipulation to that effect.[21] The extension of the grave breaches regime to internal armed conflicts was not seriously envisaged during the Conference.

4. The prohibition of statutory limitations for war crimes and crimes against humanity

The idea of a convention prohibiting statutory limitations for international crimes arose out of a concern that the time limit for the prosecution of Nazi criminals would expire in several European countries, including the Federal Republic of Germany, in the late 1960s. A draft resolution to ban statutory limitations for war crimes and crimes against humanity was thus submitted by Poland to the UN Commission on Human Rights in 1965.[22] This new agenda item gave rise to lengthy debates within the Commission, notably on the question of whether statutory limitations were applicable to crimes under international law.[23] On the one hand, several delegations took the view that crimes should be punished to the full extent unless otherwise provided by law.[24] Since international instruments establishing jurisdiction over international crimes, such as the Nuremberg Charter and the Geneva Conventions, did not provide for statutory limitations, it was argued that such limitations were not applicable to war crimes and crimes against humanity. On the other hand, it was pointed out that the application of rules of prescription to all criminal offences is a fundamental legal principle in a number of countries.[25] Certain delegates thought that the silence of international instruments on this matter was ambiguous and could be interpreted as leaving states free to determine whether time limits applied to international crimes or not.

20 Ibid; see the third paragraph of arts 49/50/129/146 of the Geneva Conventions (n 10).

21 Final Record of the Diplomatic Conference of Geneva of 1949, vol 2(B), Seventh Report drawn up by the Special Committee, 36–37.

22 Draft resolution submitted by Poland to the Commission on Human Rights (CHR), 'Question of punishment of war criminals and of persons who have committed crimes against humanity' (25 March 1965) UN Doc. E/CN.4/L.733/Rev.1. Crimes against humanity were added to war crimes upon a suggestion by France, see UN CHR, report on the 21st session (March-April 1965) UN Doc E/4024, paras 12 and 514.

23 UNCHR, report on the 21st session (March-April 1965) UN Doc E/4024, paras 529–52; UNCHR, report on the 22nd session (March-April 1966) UN Doc E/4184, paras 223–89; UNCHR, report on the 23rd session (February-March 1967) UN Doc E/4322, paras 135–85.

24 UNCHR, report on the 22nd session (March-April 1966) UN Doc E/4184, para 241.

25 Ibid, paras 239–44.

While recognising the need to prohibit statutory limitations for the gravest crimes in the future, some delegations were concerned by suggestions that the convention would apply with retroactive effect.[26] This issue presented difficulties for several states and prompted the Greek delegation to introduce the following amendment:

> If the crimes mentioned … have already been amnestied or come under statutory limitation at the time of ratification of this Convention, in accordance with the domestic law of a Contracting Party, that Party shall … ensure the non-applicability of statutory limitation to any such crimes committed in the future.[27]

According to the delegate of the USSR, this amendment was 'in flat contradiction' with the principle underlying the Convention.[28] He stressed that '[t]he whole purpose of the draft convention would be undermined if an amnesty or a statutory limitation, applied before the adoption of the convention was allowed to stand'.[29] The Greek delegate replied that, when past crimes had already been covered by statutory limitations, such limits were part of the rule of law and should thus be upheld.[30] He emphasised that, since the draft convention would be the first instrument to set aside statutory limitations for grave crimes, it was crucial to make it acceptable to as many states as possible. The representatives of Argentina, Italy, Guatemala, Peru and Sweden expressed support for the Greek amendment.[31] The French delegate, for his part, suggested that the problem of retroactivity could be overcome by allowing reservations to the convention. He also observed that it would be inappropriate to refer to domestic amnesty measures in an instrument affirming the international character of certain crimes.[32]

The problem of reconciling the non-applicability of statutory limitations to international crimes with the principle of non-retroactivity of the criminal law could not be resolved within the Commission.[33] It was entrusted to a working

26 UNCHR, summary record of the 921st meeting (10 March 1967) UN Doc E/CN.4/SR.921, 8–9; UNCHR, summary record of the 931st meeting (17 March 1967) UN Doc E/CN.4/SR.931, 9–11; UNCHR, report on the 23rd session (February-March 1967) UN Doc E/4322, paras 167–68.

27 Amendment to the preliminary draft convention on the non-applicability of statutory limitation to war crimes and crimes against humanity submitted to the Commission of Human Rights by Greece (9 March 1967) UN Doc E/CN.4/L.917. See UNCHR, report on the 23rd session (February-March 1967) UN Doc E/4322, para 151; UNCHR, summary record of the 921st meeting (10 March 1967) UN Doc E/CN.4/SR.921, 8.

28 UNCHR, summary record of the 931st meeting (17 March 1967) UN Doc E/CN.4/SR.931, 7.

29 Ibid.

30 Ibid, 8.

31 Ibid, 9–16.

32 Ibid, 16.

33 UNCHR, report on the 23rd session (February-March 1967) UN Doc E/4322, paras 179–81.

group which also failed to reach a decision on the Greek amendment.[34] The issue resurfaced in the Third Committee of the General Assembly with an amendment by Norway proposing to give effect to the convention only with respect to crimes for which statutory limitations had not expired as yet.[35] This amendment was very controversial and the delegation eventually accepted to withdraw it in a spirit of conciliation.[36] However, a similar Norwegian proposal was reintroduced in a subsequent meeting of the Third Committee.[37] As previous amendments touching on the issue of retroactivity, it generated divisions and was eventually rejected by 40 votes to 18, with 33 abstentions.[38]

The Convention on the Non-Applicability of Statutory Limitations to War Crimes and Crimes against Humanity was adopted by the General Assembly on 26 November 1968.[39] Its first article provides that statutory limitations shall not apply to war crimes and crimes against humanity 'irrespective of the date of their commission'. Thus, the final version of the convention did not take into account the reservations expressed by several states about the retroactive nature of the prohibition. Divergences of opinion on this and other issues prevented many states from voting for the convention in the General Assembly and subsequently ratifying it. The treaty was adopted by 58 votes (less than half of the UN membership at the time) to seven, with 36 abstentions.[40] According to a commentator, '[m]ore opposing votes were cast against the adoption of this convention than were voted in opposition to any prior international human rights instrument'.[41] As of June 2018, only 55 states have ratified the convention.[42]

The retroactive nature of the convention placed states in which statutory limitations had already expired with respect to international crimes in a difficult position. In explaining their vote, several delegations identified this issue as one of

34 UNCHR, Report of the Joint Working Group on the draft convention concerning the non-applicability of statutory limitations to war crimes and crimes against humanity (7 December 1967) UN Doc A/C.3/L.1503.

35 UN General Assembly (UNGA), Third Committee, summary record of the 1567th meeting (10 October 1968) UN Doc A/C.3/SR.1567, paras 8–9.

36 UNGA, Third Committee, summary record of the 1568th meeting (10 October 1968) UN Doc A/C.3/SR.1568, paras 1–33.

37 UNGA, Third Committee, summary record of the 1571st meeting (14 October 1968) UN Doc A/C.3/SR.1571, para 9.

38 Ibid, para 58.

39 Convention on the Non-Applicability of Statutory Limitations to War Crimes and Crimes against Humanity (adopted 26 November 1968, entered into force 11 November 1970) 754 UNTS 73.

40 General Assembly, Official Records of the 23rd session, 1727th plenary meeting (26 November 1968) UN Doc A/PV.1727, para 75.

41 Robert H. Miller, 'The Convention on the Non-Applicability of Statutory Limitations to War Crimes and Crimes against humanity' (1971) 65 *American Journal of International Law* 476, 477–78

42 The European Convention on the Non-Applicability of Statutory Limitations to Crimes against Humanity and War Crimes (adopted 25 January 1974, entered into force 27 June 2003) CETS No. 082 has been ratified by only three states as of 7 November 2018.

the reasons for which they had abstained or voted against the convention. For example, the Belgian delegate observed that, while his country attached great importance to the principle underlying the convention, 'it would in any case be impossible for Belgium to adopt a text sanctioning the absolute retroactivity of any penal provision, no matter what it might be'.[43] Among the delegations who did not vote in favour of the convention were most Latin American and central European states, including many of those who had suffered from Nazi atrocities during the Second World War.

Several European states appeared concerned by the risk that the relative equilibrium and stability restored to their country two decades after the end of World War II would be jeopardised by the setting aside of time limits already in effect. As reflected in the Greek and Norwegian amendments, and the substantial support they garnered, a number of governments felt uneasy about a legal provision liable to unsettle the compromise solutions adopted in their countries to deal with the large number of persons implicated in wartime offences, including statutory limitations, pardons and amnesties. It may be surmised that opposition of at least equal intensity to that encountered as regards the removal of statutory limitations already expired would have been met had the draft convention included amnesties among the measures retroactively prohibited by international law.

While statutory limitations take effect automatically as a result of the passage of a specific time period and are of general application, amnesties are extraordinary measures applying solely to certain categories of offenders in relation to specific events. However, both types of mechanisms have the same effect, that is, to extinguish criminal liability for past crimes. As the rationale underlying the convention was to ensure the effective punishment of war crimes and crimes against humanity, its elaboration provided states with an opportunity to prohibit amnesties – another legal mechanism liable to impede the prosecution of international crimes – alongside statutory limitations. However, though the issue of amnesty was raised during the negotiation of the convention, it was deliberately sidestepped, presumably because it would have generated dissensions susceptible to derail the negotiation process.

5. The encouragement of amnesties at the end of internal armed conflicts

The Second Protocol Additional to the Geneva Conventions, adopted on 8 June 1977, supplements their article 3 in the protection of victims of non-international armed conflicts.[44] It establishes minimal guarantees to be observed by state and

43 General Assembly, Official Records of the 23rd session, 1727th plenary meeting (26 November 1968) UN Doc A/PV.1727, para 18. The representatives of Austria, Denmark, El Salvador, Italy, Japan, Norway, Portugal, the United Kingdom, the United States and Sweden also referred to this issue.

44 Protocol Additional to the Geneva Conventions of 12 August 1949 relating to the Protection of Victims of Non-International Armed Conflicts (adopted 8 June 1977, entered into force 7 December 1978) 1125 UNTS 609 (Second Protocol).

non-state armed forces in the treatment of persons who do not take part or have ceased to take part in internal armed conflicts. The First Protocol, adopted on the same day, develops the law applicable in international armed conflicts and extends the obligation to prosecute or extradite imposed by the Geneva Conventions to a new set of grave breaches.[45] By contrast, the Second Protocol does not require the prosecution of serious violations committed in internal armed conflicts. Article 6 of this instrument, dealing with penal prosecutions, provides that:

1. This Article applies to the prosecution and punishment of criminal offences related to the armed conflict.
2. No sentence shall be passed and no penalty shall be executed on a person found guilty of an offence except pursuant to a conviction pronounced by a court offering the essential guarantees of independence and impartiality. In particular:

    (a) The procedure shall provide for an accused to be informed without delay of the particulars of the offence alleged against him and shall afford the accused before and during his trial all necessary rights and means of defence;
    (b) No one shall be convicted of an offence except on the basis of individual penal responsibility;
    (c) No one shall be held guilty of any criminal offence on account of any act or omission which did not constitute a criminal offence, under the law, at the time when it was committed; nor shall a heavier penalty be imposed than that which was applicable at the time when the criminal offence was committed; if, after the commission of the offence, provision is made by law for the imposition of a lighter penalty, the offender shall benefit thereby;
    (d) Anyone charged with an offence is presumed innocent until proved guilty according to law;
    (e) Anyone charged with an offence shall have the right to be tried in his presence;
    (f) No one shall be compelled to testify against himself or to confess guilt.

3. A convicted person shall be advised on conviction of his judicial and other remedies and of the time-limits within which they may be exercised.
4. The death penalty shall not be pronounced on persons who were under the age of eighteen years at the time of the offence and shall not be carried out on pregnant women or mothers of young children.

45 Protocol Additional to the Geneva Conventions of 12 August 1949 relating to the Protection of Victims of International Armed Conflicts (adopted 8 June 1977, entered into force 7 December 1978) 1125 UNTS 3, art 85.

5. **At the end of hostilities, the authorities in power shall endeavour to grant the broadest possible amnesty to persons who have participated in the armed conflict, or those deprived of their liberty for reasons related to the armed conflict, whether they are interned or detained.**[46]

Article 6 originated in three proposals made by the ICRC during a conference of government experts convened in preparation for the Diplomatic Conference on the Reaffirmation and Development of International Humanitarian Law Applicable in Armed Conflicts held in Geneva from 1974 to 1977.[47] The first proposal dealt with the penalties imposed on rebel combatants for their mere participation to the conflict. By taking up arms against their government, rebel fighters commit an offence under domestic law for which they are liable to be punished, sometimes by death, by contrast with regular combatants who benefit from an immunity for lawful acts of war, including the killing of enemy combatants. To remedy this imbalance between state and non-state armed forces, the ICRC proposed to introduce a principle whereby rebel combatants would not be punished for the mere fact of having taken part in hostilities against the government. The second proposal addressed the problem of summary executions and suggested to suspend all executions for the duration of the hostilities. The third proposal contemplated the proclamation of a general amnesty at the end of the conflict on the basis of the following considerations:

> At the end of hostilities, it is desirable that normal life should be resumed as soon as possible. Hence, it would be fitting to generalize the proclamation of general amnesty, in the interest of both the victims and the authorities who will have to restore order and reconcile all elements of a divided people.[48]

The ICRC noted that these proposals were not intended 'to eliminate penal prosecution of war criminals, i.e. of combatants who may have committed some grave breach of the humanitarian law applicable in non-international armed conflicts'.[49] However, it observed that the investigation, trial and punishment of such offences should conform to basic judicial guarantees. The second and third paragraphs of article 6 were adopted by the Diplomatic Conference without much debate to further this aim of establishing minimal standards to be respected in the prosecution of persons accused of violating the laws of war in internal conflicts.[50] The fourth and fifth paragraphs of article 6 correspond to the second and third proposals made by the ICRC during the conference of

46 Second Protocol (n 44) art 6 (emphasis added).

47 Conference of Government Experts on the Reaffirmation and Development of International Humanitarian Law Applicable in Armed Conflicts, first session (May–June 1971) vol 5, 56–60.

48 Ibid, 59.

49 Ibid, 60.

50 On the drafting history of paragraphs 2 and 3, see Official Records of the Diplomatic Conference on the Reaffirmation and Development of International Humanitarian Law applicable in

government experts. The first drafts of article 6 contained other paragraphs that were deleted during the Conference. In order to shed light on the rationale and scope of the amnesty paragraph according to its drafters, it is necessary to examine the evolution of these other provisions and the reasons why they were rejected.

The initial ICRC draft submitted to the first committee of the Diplomatic Conference contained the following paragraphs:

ICRC draft

3. The death penalty pronounced on any person found guilty of an offence in relation to the armed conflict shall not be carried out until the hostilities have ceased.
4. The death penalty shall not be pronounced for an offence in relation to the armed conflict committed by persons below eighteen years of age and shall not be carried out on pregnant women.
5. In case of prosecutions carried out against a person only by reason of his having taken part in hostilities, the court, when deciding upon the sentence, shall take into consideration, to the greatest possible extent, the fact that the accused respected the provisions of the present Protocol.
6. At the end of hostilities, the authorities in power shall endeavour to grant amnesty to as many as possible of those who have participated in the armed conflict, in particular those whose liberty has been restricted for reasons in relation to the armed conflict, whether they are interned or detained.[51]

During the first discussion of this provision in Committee I, the delegations made a number of comments.[52] With respect to paragraphs 3 and 5 establishing safeguards for persons condemned for their participation to the conflict, the delegate of Pakistan declared that the right of non-discrimination protected by the laws of his country would be jeopardised by a situation whereby 'a citizen who had rebelled against the Government [in wartime] could avoid punishment when his fellow citizen in peacetime would be prosecuted for similar activities'.[53] He affirmed that '[i]n his country insurgents would be executed, and any attempt to impose international legislation such as that contained in article [6] would, in his opinion, constitute interference with the sovereign rights of States'.[54] Similarly, the representative of Iran stated that 'Iranian law was very severe in its

Armed Conflict (Geneva, 1974–1977) vol 4, 35–36; vol 10, 107–108; vol 9, 297–303; vol 7, 92–94.

51 Official Records of the Diplomatic Conference on the Reaffirmation and Development of International Humanitarian Law applicable in Armed Conflict (1974–1977) vol 1, pt 3, 36.

52 Ibid, vol 8, 357–65.

53 Ibid, vol 8, 360.

54 Ibid.

attitude towards anyone who sought to overthrow the legal Government by force or who advocated such action' and that '[w]hile his delegation could accept the rule in paragraph 3 in the case of international armed conflicts, it could not do so in the case of non-international armed conflicts'.[55]

In her general comment on the article as a whole, the delegate of Mongolia expressed concern regarding the silence of the protocol on the question of foreign mercenaries having committed crimes in non-international conflicts.[56] She suggested that article 6 should provide for the prosecution and punishment of foreign mercenaries and perpetrators of crimes against humanity. The delegate of the Soviet Union echoed this concern by observing that 'there was one category of persons who should not receive protection, namely, persons guilty of crimes against humanity and genocide, including foreign mercenaries participating in armed conflicts'.[57] Accordingly, the Soviet Union and a number of its satellite states proposed to add a paragraph 7 to the article providing that: 'Nothing in the present Protocol shall be invoked to prevent the prosecution and punishment of persons charged with crimes against humanity or who participate in the conflict as foreign mercenaries'.[58]

On a different note, the delegates of Spain and Nigeria were in favour of deleting paragraph 6 because they considered that the power to grant amnesty was a prerogative of domestic authorities which should not be regulated in an international instrument.[59] In the same vein, the Italian delegate observed that the question of whether or not it would be opportune to offer an amnesty should be left to the state's authorities.[60] He thus proposed to add a sentence at the end of the paragraph providing that: 'if no amnesty is granted, the authorities in power shall consider, case by case, the possibility of remitting the whole or part of the penalty inflicted during the conflict'.[61] For their part, the delegations of Belgium, the Netherlands and New Zealand proposed the insertion of a new paragraph to the effect that '[a]nyone sentenced shall have the right to seek pardon or commutation of the sentence. Amnesty, pardon or commutation of the sentence of death may be granted in all cases'.[62] This provision replicated article 6(4) of the International Covenant on Civil and Political Rights.[63] At the end of the discussion, it was decided to refer the article to a working group, which amended it as follows:

55 Ibid.
56 Ibid, vol 8, 363–64.
57 Ibid, vol 8, 365.
58 Ibid, vol 4, 34.
59 Ibid, vol 8, 361–62.
60 Ibid, vol 8, 364.
61 Ibid.
62 Ibid, vol 4, 35–36.
63 ICCPR (n 1).

Working group draft

4. The death penalty pronounced against a person convicted of an offence other than a war crime or a crime against humanity shall not be carried out until the end of the armed conflict.
5. The death penalty shall not be pronounced on persons below eighteen years of age at the time of the offence and shall not be carried out on pregnant women and mothers of young children.
6. In case of prosecutions carried out against a person only by reason of his having taken part in hostilities, the court, when deciding upon the sentence shall take into consideration, to the greatest possible extent, the fact that the accused respected the provisions of the present Protocol.
7. Anyone sentenced shall have the right to seek pardon or commutation of the sentence. Amnesty, pardon or commutation of the sentence of death may be granted in all cases.
8. At the end of hostilities, the authorities in power shall endeavour to grant amnesty to as many as possible of those who have participated in the armed conflict, or those whose liberty has been restricted for reasons in relation to the armed conflict, whether they are interned or detained.[64]

The fourth paragraph of the working group draft was the result of a compromise between the amendment sponsored by the Soviet Union, quoted above, and the third paragraph of the ICRC draft providing for the suspension of the execution of death sentences during the conflict.[65] When the Committee considered the working group draft, a number of delegations manifested their opposition to this paragraph, mainly on the ground that its reference to the death penalty was unacceptable, even with regard to perpetrators of war crimes and crimes against humanity.[66] Accordingly, the Canadian delegate proposed to delete the paragraph and add a sentence providing for the suspension of the execution of death sentences at the end of paragraph 6.[67] The Soviet delegate did not oppose the deletion of the paragraph but declared that its delegation 'was convinced that the text elaborated by Committee I could not be construed as enabling war criminals, or those guilty of crimes against peace and humanity, to evade severe punishment in any circumstances whatsoever'.[68] The following draft paragraphs were submitted to the plenary assembly:

64 Official Records of the Diplomatic Conference on the Reaffirmation and Development of International Humanitarian Law applicable in Armed Conflict (1974–1977) vol 10, 143–45.
65 Ibid, vol 9, 301–302; vol 10, 143–45.
66 Ibid, vol 9, 307–23.
67 Ibid, vol 9, 302.
68 Ibid, vol 9, 319.

Committee draft

4. The death penalty shall not be pronounced on persons below eighteen years of age at the time of the offence and shall not be carried out on pregnant women and mothers of young children.
5. In case of prosecutions carried out against a person only by reason of his having taken part in hostilities, the court, when deciding upon the sentence, shall take into consideration, to the greatest possible extent, the fact that the accused respected the provisions or the present Protocol. In no such case shall a death penalty be carried out until the end of the armed conflict.
6. Anyone sentenced shall have the right to seek pardon or commutation of the sentence. Amnesty, pardon or commutation of the sentence of death may be granted in all cases.
7. At the end of hostilities the authorities in power shall endeavour to grant amnesty to as many as possible of those who have participated in the armed conflict, or those whose liberty has been restricted for reasons in relation to the armed conflict, whether they are interned or detained.[69]

The fourth paragraph of the committee's draft was adopted by the plenary assembly without debate.[70] The discussion concentrated on paragraphs 5 and 7. With regard to the former, the delegate of Pakistan observed that it was incompatible with the laws of several states and that its retention would significantly limit the number of accessions to the Second Protocol.[71] The paragraph was rejected by 26 votes to 12, with 49 abstentions.[72] The delegates of Austria, Belgium, Cyprus, Denmark, the Federal Republic of Germany, Finland, Ireland, Portugal, Turkey and Switzerland explained that they had abstained from voting in order to ensure the broadest possible accession to the Second Protocol.[73] The representatives of Madagascar, Norway, Sweden, France and the Holy See, who had voted for the retention of paragraph 5, expressed their regret at the deletion of this humanitarian provision.[74] Paragraph 6 was rejected as well by 17 votes to 16, with 49 abstentions, without debate or explanations of vote.[75]

With respect to paragraph 7, the discussion in the plenary assembly related to its relevance and legal force. A number of delegates questioned its importance 'since provisions of that nature were included in the legislation of all States'.[76] In the view of the Canadian and Syrian delegates, the amnesty paragraph was not an essential provision since it 'was merely a recommendation, in which

69 Ibid, vol 10, 131–33.
70 Ibid, vol 7, 94.
71 Ibid, vol 7, 92–95.
72 Ibid, vol 7, 95.
73 Ibid.
74 Ibid, vol 7, 95–96.
75 Ibid, 96.
76 Ibid, vol 7, 92–94.

authorities were exhorted to grant the broadest possible amnesty to persons who had participated in the armed conflict'.[77] The representative of Nigeria 'saw no need for the retention of paragraphs 6 and 7, which pertained mainly to administrative matters and were within the competence of Heads of State'.[78] Conversely, the delegates of Norway and of the Ukrainian Soviet Socialist Republic thought that paragraph 7 'contained an extremely important provision which should be retained in Protocol II'.[79] It was eventually adopted by 37 votes to 15, with 31 abstentions. The article as amended was adopted as a whole by consensus.[80]

Some delegations felt the need to explain their vote on the amnesty paragraph. The representatives of Nigeria, Saudi Arabia and Spain, having cast a negative vote, stressed that they perceived the provision as an encroachment on state sovereignty and on the discretionary prerogative of domestic authorities to decide whether or not an amnesty would be appropriate in specific circumstances.[81] For instance, the Spanish delegate observed that:

> The adoption of measures of clemency in general and of an amnesty in particular is necessarily subject, as regards application, to considerations of expediency which can be neither appreciated nor foreseen by the drafters of a text like the one under consideration; for the same reasons, such measures fall within the exclusive competence of States, which, bearing always in mind the common good of the community they govern, can alone decide whether or not an amnesty is conducive to the restoration of public peace.[82]

On a related note, the delegates of Kenya, Cameroon and Zaire observed that the amnesty provision was superfluous in an international instrument since the domestic legislation of many countries contained provisions of this type. They made clear that they understood article 6(5) as a mere recommendation lacking mandatory force which 'rests on the humanitarian spirit of political leaders'.[83] Nonetheless, they did not cast a negative vote, and some of them supported its adoption, because of its humanitarian purpose. According to the delegate of Zaire:

> Our vote for this provision was based largely both on profound humanitarian considerations, and also and above all on national considerations. For we are convinced that in the interests of a young nation's unity, it is essential to establish a climate of understanding, and to encourage the widest degree of

77 Ibid, vol 7, 93–94.
78 Ibid, vol 7, 93.
79 Ibid, vol 7, 92 and 94.
80 Ibid, vol 7, 96.
81 Ibid, vol 7, 102–103.
82 Ibid, vol 7, 103.
83 Ibid, vol 7, 101–105.

> reconciliation in order to bring back into the fold those strayed members of the flock who unwittingly contribute to the destruction of their nation in order to please outsiders. As the very principle of amnesty is included among the various other constitutional rules of Zaire, my delegation believes that the adoption of paragraph 7 can only strengthen that principle.[84]

Confirming the role of the amnesty paragraph as a tool of pacification, the ICRC Commentary of 1987 explained that its object was 'to encourage gestures of reconciliation which can contribute to re-establishing normal relations in the life of a nation which has been divided'.[85] However, in the 1990s, the ICRC expressed the view that article 6(5) was never intended to cover serious violations of international law since it had been conceived as a mere 'combatant immunity' applying solely to rebels having respected the laws of war.[86] In a 2005 study on customary rules of international humanitarian law, the ICRC accordingly added an exception to the amnesty paragraph excluding war criminals.[87] In support of this exception, the ICRC study relies on instances of state practice and on the above-quoted declaration by the Soviet Union delegation to the effect that article 6 could not be construed as enabling war criminals or persons responsible for crimes against peace or humanity to evade punishment.[88] This restrictive interpretation has been adopted by human rights courts in the last decade.[89]

In support of this interpretation, it may be recalled that the ICRC proposal which formed the basis of the discussion on the amnesty paragraph in the Diplomatic Conference emphasised that it was not meant to prevent the prosecution of grave breaches of the laws of war in internal armed conflicts. This position, however, was not reflected in the attitude of states during the negotiation of article 6. The only references to the prosecution of grave crimes committed in internal conflicts were made by the delegations of Mongolia, the Soviet Union and some of its satellite states in the early part of the debate in Committee I.

84 Ibid, vol 7, 105.

85 Yves Sandoz, Christophe Swinarski and Bruno Zimmermann (eds), *Commentary on the Additional Protocols of 8 June 1977 to the Geneva Conventions of 12 August 1949* (Martinus Nijhoff Publishers 1987) 1402.

86 See Douglass Cassel, 'Lessons from the Americas: Guidelines for International Response to Amnesties for Atrocities' (1996) 59 *Law and Contemporary Problems* 197, 218 quoting a letter from the head of the ICRC legal division. The same position is referred to in Naomi Roht-Arriaza and Lauren Gibson, 'The Developing Jurisprudence on Amnesty' (1998) 20 *Human Rights Quarterly* 843, 865.

87 Jean-Marie Henckaerts and Louise Doswald-Beck (eds), *Customary International Humanitarian Law* (CUP & ICRC 2005) vol 1, 611.

88 Ibid, 612. See text to n 68.

89 *The Massacres of El Mozote and nearby places v El Salvador* (Merits, Reparations and Costs) Inter-American Court of Human Rights Series C No 252 (25 October 2012) paras 284–86; *Marguš v Croatia* App No 4455/10 (ECtHR, 27 May 2014) paras 210–11. On a broad interpretation of article 6(5) by domestic courts, see Roht-Arriaza and Gibson (n 86).

These proposals tied the issue to the problem of foreign mercenaries intervening in internal conflicts and did not gather any support from other states. An amendment introduced by the Soviet delegation to ensure 'the prosecution and punishment of persons charged with crimes against humanity or who participate in the conflict as foreign mercenaries' was rejected early on. A further Soviet amendment providing that death sentences should not be executed during the conflict except with respect to perpetrators of war crimes and crimes against humanity was also opposed by several states.[90] Its deletion gave rise to the statement referred to by the ICRC in support of its restrictive interpretation of article 6(5).

Since the amnesty paragraph is worded in inclusive terms ('the broadest possible amnesty', 'whether they are interned or detained'), it seems that if states had understood it as excluding certain categories of offenders, they would have said so explicitly. As there is no provision in the Second Protocol imposing the prosecution of grave breaches, it could not be assumed that serious violations committed during the course of an internal conflict would be prosecuted pursuant to international law in the absence of stipulation in this sense. As a matter of fact, prior to the 1990s, it was usually considered that war crimes could only be committed in international armed conflicts.[91]

During the negotiation of article 6, the amnesty provision was controversial for some reasons but not because states believed that international law limited their freedom to grant amnesties. To the contrary, the most recurrent cause of opposition to the paragraph was that it represented an encroachment of international law on the sovereign prerogative of states to decide whether or not to grant an amnesty in specific circumstances. Several delegations stressed that the power to issue amnesties had always fallen within the exclusive competence of domestic authorities and was a discretionary power that only those authorities could exercise in a suitable and timely manner. Accordingly, it does not appear that, at the time of the adoption of the Second Protocol, states believed that their amnesty prerogative was or should be regulated by international law. In fact, a number of delegations adopted the amnesty provision on the understanding that it was merely a non-binding recommendation. Several states also expressed the view that amnesty was a desirable course of action at the end of non-international armed conflicts because of its humanitarian role and its potential to facilitate reconciliation.

The most controversial issue throughout the debates on article 6 was the treatment to be reserved to rebel combatants for their participation in an internal conflict. While the ICRC and several states supported the adoption of measures providing safeguards to non-state fighters, other states were firmly opposed to the idea of granting any form of leniency to rebels combatants. The latter group of states eventually prevailed and the paragraphs aiming to provide guarantees to insurgents were deleted. The claim that article 6(5) was intended

90 See text to n 64–66.

91 See Eve La Haye, *War Crimes in Internal Armed Conflicts* (CUP 2008) ch 4.

to apply solely to rebel combatants having respected international law seems inconsistent with the deletion of these paragraphs. As no consensus could be found on provisions enjoining states to accord a favourable treatment to rebel combatants, including a requirement that their sentence reflect the fact that they had respected international law and the postponement of the execution of death sentences during the conflict, it appears unlikely that states would have voted for the amnesty provision if the understanding was that it would only benefit those same combatants. It seems more likely that states understood article 6(5) as a general provision applying to all persons involved in an internal conflict, including those fighting on the government's side.

A thorough scrutiny of the *travaux préparatoires* of article 6(5) does not support the view that its drafters intended it as a provision excluding certain categories of offenders. Its drafting history rather seems to confirm a literal interpretation of the provision as applying broadly to all persons having taken part in an internal conflict without distinctions or exceptions. Nonetheless, according to the ICRC, the interpretation of article 6(5) excluding war criminals has become part of customary international law.[92] In support of this customary rule, the 2005 ICRC study refers to instances where the passage of an amnesty was encouraged by the UN in the aftermath of an internal armed conflict, such as following the conflicts in South Africa and Angola.[93] However, the amnesties issued in relation to those conflicts included one or more international crimes: the crime against humanity of apartheid as regards the South African amnesty, war crimes and crimes against humanity as regards some Angolan amnesties.[94] The fact that these measures were nonetheless supported by the UN appears to contradict the view that amnesties covering grave crimes are always seen as unacceptable in the context of efforts to end internal armed conflicts.[95]

6. The obligation to prosecute torture

The Convention against Torture and Other Cruel, Inhuman or Degrading Treatment or Punishment (Torture Convention) was adopted by the UN General Assembly on 10 December 1984.[96] Its first article defines torture as 'any act by which severe pain or suffering, whether physical or mental, is intentionally inflicted on a person … at the instigation of or with the consent or acquiescence of a public official or other person acting in an official capacity'.[97] Article 2 requires contracting states to prevent torture and stresses that such acts may not be justified under any circumstance. Article 4 imposes on national authorities an

92 Henckaerts and Doswald-Beck (n 87) 611–14.
93 Ibid, 612.
94 On the amnesties passed in South Africa and Angola, see ch 3 in this volume.
95 On the evolving position of the UN on amnesties, see ch 5 in this volume.
96 Convention against Torture and Other Cruel, Inhuman or Degrading Treatment or Punishment (adopted 10 December 1984, entered into force 26 June 1987) 1465 UNTS 85.
97 Ibid.

obligation to criminalise acts of torture and make them 'punishable by appropriate penalties which take into account their grave nature'.[98] Under article 5, states are required to exercise jurisdiction over such acts when committed on a territory under their jurisdiction or by a national, and entitled to do so when the victim is a national. This provision also establishes universal jurisdiction over torture by requiring states on the territory of which suspected torturers are found to prosecute or extradite them following the *aut dedere aut judicare* principle. According to article 7:

> The State Party in the territory under whose jurisdiction a person alleged to have committed any offence referred to in article 4 is found shall in the cases contemplated in article 5, if it does not extradite him, submit the case to its competent authorities for the purpose of prosecution.[99]

Some scholars have observed that the phrase 'submit the case to its competent authorities for the purpose of prosecution' falls short of an obligation to prosecute and punish.[100] During the negotiation of article 7, a proposal to add the words 'without exception and without undue delay' to strengthen the obligation was rejected.[101] However, according to several commentators, this softer phrasing in comparison to the obligation to punish imposed by the Genocide Convention was merely intended to acknowledge the right of suspects to be presumed innocent and the discretion of domestic prosecutors in assessing evidence in support of a case.[102] Although article 16 extends the obligation to prevent torture contained in article 2 to acts of cruel, inhuman or degrading treatment or punishment, the convention does not require states to prosecute these lesser forms of torture.

Neither the Torture Convention nor its drafting history make any mention of amnesty. However, the Committee against Torture established to monitor its implementation has generally condemned amnesties extending to acts of torture. Its first case involving this issue was brought against Argentina in 1989 by individuals challenging the legality of two laws preventing the prosecution of alleged torturers.[103] The Committee ruled that the communications were inadmissible *ratione temporis* because the impugned events had taken place before the entry

98 Ibid.

99 Ibid (emphasis added).

100 Orentlicher (n 9) 2604; Louise Mallinder, *Amnesty, Human Rights and Political Transitions: Bridging the Peace and Justice Divide* (Hart Publishing 2008) 127–28.

101 Manfred Nowak and Elizabeth McArthur, *The United Nations Convention Against Torture, A Commentary* (OUP 2008) 361.

102 Ibid, 361–62; J Herman Burgers and Hans Danelius, *The United Nations Convention against Torture: A Handbook on the Convention against Torture and Other Cruel, Inhuman or Degrading Treatment or Punishment* (Martinus Nijhoff Publishers 1988) 138; Scharf (n 9) 47.

103 *OR, MM and MS v Argentina*, Communications nos 1/1988, 2/1988 and 3/1988, Report of the Committee against Torture (CAT) (1990) UN Doc A/45/44, Annex V, 108.

into force of the convention.[104] However, it considered *in obiter* that the laws were 'incompatible with the spirit and purpose of the Convention' and urged Argentina to ensure the victims access to compensation and redress.[105]

In its general comment on article 2, the Committee underlined that the prohibition against torture is absolute and may not be derogated from under any circumstance.[106] It also declared that 'amnesties or other impediments which preclude or indicate unwillingness to provide prompt and fair prosecution and punishment of perpetrators of torture or ill-treatment violate the principle of non-derogability'.[107] In its general comment on article 14 protecting the right of victims to a remedy, the Committee considered amnesties to also be incompatible with this provision because they 'pose impermissible obstacles to a victim in his or her efforts to obtain redress and contribute to a climate of impunity'.[108]

Accordingly, the Committee has on many occasions urged states to repeal amnesty laws providing immunity to perpetrators of torture. In the last two decades, for example, it criticised amnesty laws in Azerbaijan, Kyrgyzstan, Peru, Chile, Indonesia, Algeria, Macedonia, El Salvador, Spain, Senegal, and Sierra Leone.[109] However, it notably abstained to do so with respect to certain amnesties capable of being applied to torture. In its report on South Africa of 2006, the Committee commended the state 'for the peaceful transition from the apartheid regime and the establishment of a democratic South African society' and for 'the remarkable work of the Truth and Reconciliation Commission and its role in the peaceful transition in the State party'.[110] While it noted that impunity remained prevalent for acts of torture perpetrated during the apartheid era, it did not refer to the fact that the Truth and Reconciliation Commission operated on

104 Ibid, paras 7.2–7.4.

105 Ibid, para 9.

106 UNCAT, 'General Comment no 2, Implementation of article 2 by States Parties' (24 January 2008) UN Doc CAT/C/GC/2/CRP. 1/Rev.4, para 5.

107 Ibid.

108 UNCAT, 'General Comment no 3, Implementation of article 14 by State Parties' (13 December 2012) UN Doc CAT/C/GC/3, paras 38 and 41.

109 UNCAT Report, GAOR 55th session, sup No 44 (1999–2000) UN Doc A/55/44, paras 59(g), 68(e) and 74(e); UNCAT, 'Concluding Observations on Chile' (2004) UN Doc CAT/C/CR/32/5, para 6(b); UNCAT, 'Concluding observations on Chile' (2009) UN Doc CAT/C/CHL/CO/5, para 12; UNCAT, 'Concluding observations on Indonesia' (2008) UN Doc CAT/C/IDN/CO/2, para 27; UNCAT, 'Concluding observations on Algeria' (2008) UN Doc CAT/C/DZA/CO/3, para 11; UNCAT, 'Concluding observations on The former Yugoslav Republic of Macedonia' (2008) UN Doc CAT/C/MKD/CO/2, para 5; UNCAT, 'Concluding observations on El Salvador' (2009) UN Doc CAT/C/SLV/CO/2, para 15; UNCAT, 'Concluding observations on Spain' (2009) UN Doc CAT/C/ESP/CO/5, para 21; UNCAT, 'Concluding observations on Senegal' (2013) UN Doc CAT/C/SEN/CO/3, para 9; UNCAT, 'Concluding observations on Sierra Leone' (2014) UN Doc CAT/C/SLE/CO/1, para 9. See also UNCAT, 'Concluding observations on Colombia' (2010) UN Doc CAT/C/COL/CO/4, para 14.

110 UNCAT, 'Conclusions and recommendations on South Africa' (2006) UN Doc CAT/C/ZAF/CO/1, paras 5 and 18.

the basis of an exchange between truth and amnesty.[111] In its report on Uganda of 2005, the Committee acknowledged the difficulties faced by the state in relation to the armed conflict in the northern part of the country and expressed concern about the impunity generally enjoyed by perpetrators of torture.[112] However, it refrained from mentioning the unlimited amnesty law enacted in Uganda in 2000 to encourage defections by rebel fighters and bring an end to the war.[113] This lack of consistency in the condemnation of amnesty laws extending to international crimes might be taken as an indication that certain amnesties are seen as more legitimate than others.

7. The obligation to prosecute enforced disappearances

The International Convention for the Protection of All Persons from Enforced Disappearances (Disappearance Convention) was adopted on 20 December 2006 and entered into force on 23 December 2010.[114] Article 2 of the convention defines the crime of enforced disappearance as:

> [T]he arrest, detention, abduction or any other form of deprivation of liberty by agents of the State or by persons or groups of persons acting with the authorization, support or acquiescence of the State, followed by a refusal to acknowledge the deprivation of liberty or by concealment of the fate or whereabouts of the disappeared person, which place such a person outside the protection of the law.[115]

Under articles 4 and 7, states parties must criminalise this offence and make it 'punishable by appropriate penalties which take into account its extreme seriousness'.[116] Like the Torture Convention, this convention requires the territorial state and the state of nationality of the offender, and entitles the state of nationality of the victim, to exercise jurisdiction over suspected perpetrators.[117] It also establishes universal jurisdiction over the crime by requiring all states on the territory of which suspects are found to prosecute or extradite them to a third state or to an international criminal tribunal.[118] Replicating the wording

111 Ibid, para 18. On the South African Truth and Reconciliation process, see ch 3 in this volume.
112 UNCAT, 'Conclusions and recommendations on Uganda' (2005) UN Doc CAT/C/CR/34/UGA, paras 4 and 8.
113 On the Ugandan amnesty, see ch 3 in this volume.
114 International Convention for the Protection of All Persons from Enforced Disappearance (adopted 20 December 2006, entered into force 23 December 2010) 2716 UNTS 3. As of 7 November 2018, it had been ratified by 59 states.
115 Ibid.
116 Ibid.
117 Ibid, art 9(1).
118 Ibid, art 9(2).

of the Torture Convention, article 11 provides that when a state party decides not to extradite a suspect, it must 'submit the case to its competent authorities for the purpose of prosecution'.[119]

Like other conventions proscribing international crimes, the Disappearance Convention is silent on the question of amnesty.[120] This silence has more significance in relation to this convention, however, because a provision excluding amnesties was expressly considered in the course of its elaboration. The drafting history of the Disappearance Convention began with the Declaration on the Protection of All Persons from Enforced Disappearances adopted by the UN General Assembly on 18 December 1992.[121] Article 18 of this non-binding declaration provides that:

1. Persons who have or are alleged to have committed [the crime of enforced disappearance] shall not benefit from any special amnesty law or similar measures that might have the effect of exempting them from any criminal proceedings or sanction.
2. In the exercise of the right of pardon, the extreme seriousness of acts of enforced disappearance shall be taken into account.[122]

In its general comment on this provision, the UN Working Group on Enforced and Involuntary Disappearances emphasised that amnesties and similar measures are not acceptable, even when endorsed by a national plebiscite.[123] However, it acknowledged that the declaration 'allows limited and exceptional measures that directly lead to the prevention and termination of disappearances ... even if, prima facie, these measures could appear to have the effect of an amnesty law or similar measure that might result in impunity'.[124] This limited allowance for leniency measures was envisaged for situations 'where systematic or massive violations of human rights have occurred as a result of internal armed conflict or political repression' and 'legislative measures that could lead to finding the truth and reconciliation through pardon might be the only option to terminate or prevent disappearances'.[125] Even in such cases, the working group stressed that a number of conditions should be fulfilled by the measures in question, including the imposition of alternative criminal sanctions, the conduct of a

119 Ibid.
120 See also the Inter-American Convention on Forced Disappearance of Persons (adopted 9 June 1994, entered into force 28 Mars 1996) 33 ILM1429, which does not refer to amnesty.
121 Declaration on the Protection of All Persons from Enforced Disappearances, Resolution 47/133 (18 December 1992) UN Doc A/RES/47/133.
122 Ibid, art 18.
123 Report of the Working Group on Enforced or Involuntary Disappearances, UN Doc E/CN.4/2006/56 (27 December 2005) 17–18.
124 Ibid, 18, para 4.
125 Ibid, 19, para 5.

thorough investigation permitting the establishment of the truth, the access of the victims to a form of redress, and the provision of guarantees of termination and non-repetition of the practice.[126]

The original draft of the Disappearance Convention included a provision prohibiting amnesties modelled on article 18 of the declaration.[127] During the negotiation of this provision, certain participants observed that it would represent a step forward in the development of international law since no similar provision appeared in any binding international instrument.[128] However, other delegates stressed that amnesties could constitute 'necessary elements of processes of national reconciliation'.[129] The issue was controversial and successive proposals to include an article denying validity to amnesties or pardons with respect to enforced disappearances were rejected.[130] It was eventually decided to remove all references to amnesties and pardons from the convention.[131]

8. Whether treaty-based obligations to prosecute implicitly prohibit amnesties

There is broad agreement among international judges and scholars on the view that treaty norms requiring states to prosecute international crimes implicitly remove the possibility of amnesty with respect to those crimes.[132] The reasoning is that, because the main effect of amnesties is to foreclose criminal proceedings,

126 Ibid, paras 7–8.

127 Art 17 of the 1998 draft Convention provided that '[t]he perpetrators or suspected perpetrators of and other participants in the offence of forced disappearance or the acts referred to in article 2 of this Convention shall not benefit from any amnesty measure or similar measures prior to their trial and, where applicable, conviction that would have the effect of exempting them from any criminal action or penalty'. See UNCHR, Report of the sessional working group on the administration of justice (19 August 1998) UN Doc E/CN.4/Sub.2/1998/19, 28.

128 UNCHR, Report of the intersessional open-ended working group to elaborate a draft legally binding normative instrument for the protection of all persons from enforced disappearance (23 February 2004) UN Doc E/CN.4/2004/59, para 75.

129 Ibid, para 76.

130 Ibid, paras 73 and 74. See also Tullio Scovazzi and Gabriella Citroni, *The Struggle against Enforced Disappearance and the 2007 United Nations Convention* (Martinus Nijhoff Publishers 2007) 320–29.

131 Report of the intersessional open-ended working group to elaborate a draft legally binding normative instrument for the protection of all persons from enforced disappearance (n 128) paras 79–80.

132 See *Prosecutor v Nuon Chea, Ieng Sary, Ieng Thirith and Khieu Samphan*, Decision on Ieng Sary's Rule 89 Preliminary Objections, 002/19-09-2007/ECCC/TC (3 November 2011) paras 38–39; *Prosecutor v Morris Kallon and Brima Bazzy Kamara*, Decision on Challenge to Jurisdiction: Lomé Accord Amnesty, SCSL-04–15-PT-060 (13 March 2004) paras 82 and 84. See also Scharf (n 9) 43–48; Orentlicher (n 9) 2562–67; Seibert-Fohr (n 9) ch 4; Ronald C Slye, 'The Legitimacy of Amnesties Under International Law and General Principles of Anglo-American Law: Is a Legitimate Amnesty Possible?' (2002–2003) 43 *Virginia Journal of International Law* 173, 182–84.

states accepting to be bound by an obligation to prosecute certain crimes cannot at the same time preserve their prerogative to amnesty the said crimes. In support of this view, it has been emphasised that treaty norms prohibiting international crimes are absolute and cannot be derogated from in any circumstances, as explicitly stated in some of the relevant conventions.[133] The grant of an amnesty for the prohibited crimes might also be seen as contrary to the object and purpose of these conventions, i.e. to prevent and deter those crimes.[134]

The view that treaty-based obligations to prosecute international crimes implicitly prohibit the grant of amnesty to the alleged perpetrators of these crimes is consistent with the letter and drafting history of the Genocide, Geneva and Torture Conventions. These instruments clearly require states parties to prosecute the crimes they prohibit and do not provide for an amnesty exception. The inclusion of such an exception was not considered in the course of their elaboration. However, the attitude of states during the negotiation of other international conventions concerned with the repression of international crimes, in the course of which the issue of amnesty was raised, does not indicate an intention to relinquish their amnesty prerogative, rather to the contrary. States could have ruled out the grant of amnesty with respect to international crimes in the Convention prohibiting statutory limitations for war crimes and crimes against humanity. The issue of amnesty was mentioned by some states during the drafting process, the mechanism being similarly liable to impede the prosecution of these crimes, but it was not dwelt on, presumably on account of its controversial nature. The only multilateral treaty negotiation process in the course of which amnesties were discussed at some length was the elaboration of article 6(5) of the Second Protocol. In that context, states showed a reluctance to permit the regulation of their amnesty power in a binding international instrument. Thus, they insisted on the fact that the provision was a mere recommendation and emphasised the sovereign and discretionary nature of the prerogative.

The clearest sign that states do not equate a commitment to prosecute with a renunciation to their right to amnesty transpired during the drafting of the Disappearance Convention. While a previous UN declaration and the original draft of the convention included an article excluding amnesty for enforced disappearances, states could not reach agreement on this provision. Thus, although the convention requires states parties to prosecute enforced disappearances, this does not imply a prohibition of amnesties. It is not clear whether the same

133 Torture Convention (n 96) art 2(3); Disappearance Convention (n 114) art 1(2); UNCAT, 'General Comment no. 2' (n 106) para 5. See Naomi Roht-Arriaza, 'State Responsibility to Investigate and Prosecute Grave Human Rights Violations in International Law' (1990) 78 *California Law Review* 449, 483–88.

134 Most conventions imposing an obligation to prosecute also include an obligation to prevent the prohibited crimes. Both types of obligations are linked as the punishment of offenders is deemed essential to ensure prevention and deterrence. See Genocide Convention (n 5) art 1; Torture Convention (n 96) art 2(1); Disappearance Convention (n 114) preamble.

reasoning should be applied to the other conventions imposing a duty to prosecute. However, the possibility that the right to amnesty subsists notwithstanding a commitment to prosecute cannot be categorically excluded since states never expressly waived this right. In this regard, it must be borne in mind that states view amnesty as a sovereign prerogative enshrined in their constitution and a matter in the purview of domestic, rather than international, law. The fact that amnesties are extraordinary measures typically used to deal with situations of national emergency such as wars and political upheavals also helps explaining why states may believe that they retain this right, on an exceptional and urgent basis, even with regard to the crimes that they have otherwise undertaken to prosecute.[135]

9. The position under customary international law

Even if it is accepted that treaty-based obligations to prosecute genocide, grave breaches and torture implicitly preclude the grant of amnesty for these crimes, such a rule would only bind states parties to the relevant conventions with respect to acts meeting the restrictive definitions set out in the treaty and only when those acts were committed after the entry into force of the treaty in the relevant state. More importantly, this implicit prohibition would not cover the international crimes that have been the most widespread in recent times – crimes against humanity and war crimes committed in internal armed conflicts – since these crimes are not subject to a treaty obligation to prosecute.

These limitations of treaty law raise the question of whether there is a customary rule requiring the prosecution of core crimes under international law. While there is some evidence of *opinio juris* in support of a general obligation to prosecute international crimes, state practice does not appear to have the requisite levels of generality and consistency.[136] Therefore, scholars have generally doubted the existence of a universal obligation to prosecute crimes under

135 On this view, see Mark Freeman, *Necessary Evils: Amnesties and the Search for Justice* (CUP 2009) 55–56.

136 On evidence of *opinio juris*, see e.g. Convention on the Non-Applicability of Statutory Limitations to War Crimes and Crimes against Humanity (n 39); 'Question of the Punishment of War Criminals and of Persons Who Have Committed Crimes Against Humanity', UNGA Resolution 2712 (XXV) (15 December 1970) UN Doc A/8028; 'Principles of international co-operation in the detection, arrest, extradition and punishment of persons guilty of war crimes and crimes against humanity', UNGA Res 3074 (XXVIII) (3 December 1973) UN Doc A/9030; European Convention on the Non-Applicability of Statutory Limitation to Crimes against Humanity and War Crimes (n 42); Rome Statute of the International Criminal Court (adopted 17 July 1998, entered into force 1 July 2002) 2187 UNTS 90 (Rome Statute). On state practice, see e.g. Charles P Trumbull, 'Giving Amnesties a Second Chance' (2007) 25(2) *Berkeley Journal of International Law* 283, 295–99; Mallinder, *Amnesty, Human Rights and Political Transitions* (n 100) 129–35. See also Yasmin Naqvi, *Impediments to Exercising Jurisdiction over International Crimes* (TMC Asser Press 2010) 113–19.

international law. According to Antonio Cassese, 'no customary rule having a general purport has yet emerged imposing upon states the obligation to prosecute and punish the alleged authors of any international crime'.[137] However, there is support for the view that treaty obligations to prosecute are reflected in customary law. With regard to the Genocide Convention, the International Court of Justice has affirmed that its core principles form part of customary law.[138] As regards the Geneva Conventions, they have been ratified by virtually all states and there is extensive state practice corroborating the existence of a customary norm requiring the prosecution of grave breaches committed in international armed conflicts.[139]

The situation is less clear as regards crimes against humanity, defined in the Rome Statute as 'acts committed as part of a widespread or systematic attack directed against a civilian population'.[140] There is no comprehensive multilateral treaty instituting a repression regime for this crime. Although several international instruments prohibit it and establish the criminal responsibility of perpetrators, there is no treaty-based obligation to prosecute crimes against humanity.[141] Whether customary law imposes such a duty is controversial, primarily on account of shortcomings in state practice. According to Michael Scharf: '[t]o the extent any state practice in this area is widespread, it is the practice of granting amnesties or de facto impunity to those who commit crimes against humanity'.[142]

Even if states were to agree on an international convention requiring the prosecution of crimes against humanity, it is unlikely that a provision excluding amnesties would be accepted, as suggested by the drafting history of the Disappearance Convention. Therefore, in the context of the elaboration by international experts of a proposed international convention on crimes against humanity, Diane Orentlicher advised that '[t]he wisest course in a treaty whose aim is to assure criminal liability for crimes against humanity is to avoid explicit references to the subject of amnesties'.[143] Similarly, the International Law Commission's Special Rapporteur on crimes against humanity Sean D Murphy has,

137 Antonio Cassese and Paola Gaeta, *Cassese's International Criminal Law* (OUP 2013) 312. See also Seibert-Fohr (n 9) ch 6.

138 International Court of Justice, Advisory Opinion on Reservations to the Convention on the Prevention and Punishment of the Crime of Genocide, 1951 ICJ 15 (28 May 1951) 23.

139 Jean-Marie Henckaerts, 'The Grave Breaches Regime as Customary International Law' (2009) 7 *Journal of International Criminal Justice* 683; Yasmin Naqvi, 'Amnesty for war crimes: Defining the limits of international recognition' (2003) 85(1) *International Journal of the Red Cross* 583, 596–97.

140 Rome Statute (n 136) art 7.

141 Principles of International Law recognized in the Charter of the Nürnberg Tribunal and in the Judgment of the Tribunal (n 4); Draft Code of Crimes against the Peace and Security of Mankind, Report of the International Law Commission on the work of its 48th session, UN GAOR, 51st session, Supp. No. 10 (1996) UN Doc A/51/10; Rome Statute (n 136) art 7.

142 Michael Scharf, 'From the eXile Files: An Essay on Trading Justice for Peace' (2006) 63 *Washington and Lee Law Review* 339, 362.

143 Diane Orentlicher, 'Immunities and Amnesties' in Leila Nadya Sadat (ed), *Forging a Convention for Crimes Against Humanity* (CUP 2011) 202.

in a report from 2017, advised against the inclusion of an amnesty provision in a projected convention on crimes against humanity.[144] He recommended that national amnesty laws should be evaluated on a case-by-case basis in light of the specific treaty and customary obligations binding the enacting state, recalling that such measures would not prevent the prosecution of crimes against humanity by international criminal courts or the courts of third states.[145]

As regards war crimes committed in non-international armed conflicts, they are not subject to a repression regime akin to the grave breaches regime established by the Geneva Conventions. Article 3 of the Geneva Conventions and their Second Protocol prohibit certain acts against persons not participating or having ceased to participate in an internal armed conflict.[146] However, they do not provide for the criminal responsibility of persons infringing these rules. As a result, the question of whether serious violations of the laws of war committed in internal conflicts constitute war crimes punishable under international law remained controversial until the 1990s.[147] Doubts in this respect were dispelled by a decision of the International Tribunal for the former Yugoslavia in 1995 and there now appears to be sufficient support in *opinio juris* and state practice for a customary rule establishing the liability of war criminals in internal armed conflicts.[148] If states have the right to prosecute war crimes committed in internal conflicts, such prosecutions are not common. Indeed, crimes committed as part of civil wars, insurrections or periods of civil unrest are often covered by general amnesties, casting doubt on the existence of a customary obligation to prosecute this category of crimes.[149]

Hence, according to Claus Kreß:

> In the context of war crimes committed in non-international armed conflicts and of crimes against humanity, the view gains ground that it is more accurate to speak of an international legal presumption in favour of prosecution rather than to insist on an absolute legal duty.[150]

144 UNGA International Law Commission, Third report on crimes against humanity by Sean D. Murphy, Special Rapporteur (23 January 2017) UN Doc A/CN.4/704, para 297.

145 Ibid ('the Special Rapporteur is of the view that the present draft articles should not address the issue of amnesties under national law. Any amnesty granted by a State would have to be evaluated in light of that State's obligations under, inter alia, draft articles 9 and 14, and under customary international law as it currently exists or as it evolves in the future. Further, it should be recalled that a national amnesty would not bar prosecution of a crime against humanity by a competent international criminal tribunal or a foreign State with concurrent prescriptive jurisdiction over that crime'.)

146 Geneva Conventions (n 10) art 3; Second Protocol (n 44) arts 4 and 5.

147 La Haye (n 91) ch 4.

148 *Prosecutor v Dusko Tadic*, Decision on the Defence Motion for Interlocutory Appeal on Jurisdiction (2 October 1995) ICTY IT-94-1, para 134. See La Haye (n 91) ch 4.

149 See the Peace Agreement Amnesties Database in appendix, showing that general amnesties are frequently included in peace agreements concluding internal armed conflicts.

150 Claus Kreß, 'Reflections on the *Iudicare* Limb of the Grave Breaches Regime' (2009) 7 *Journal of International Criminal Justice* 789, 809.

Two international criminal courts have also acknowledged that state practice is not sufficiently consistent to support a customary rule requiring the prosecution of these crimes.[151] Thus, in so far as the claim that amnesties are prohibited with respect to international crimes relies on international legal requirements to prosecute, it appears to be limited to crimes which states are bound to prosecute under international conventions, at the exclusion of enforced disappearances since an amnesty prohibition was expressly rejected in this respect.

In order to make up for these lacunae, some international judges and commentators have asserted that the *jus cogens* status of international crimes entails certain consequences, including a duty to prosecute or extradite, universal jurisdiction and the non-applicability of legal impediments such as statutory limitations and amnesties.[152] With respect to *jus cogens* norms, article 53 of the Vienna Convention on the Law of Treaties provides that:

> A treaty is void if, at the time of its conclusion, it conflicts with a peremptory norm of general international law. For the purposes of the present Convention, a peremptory norm of general international law is a norm accepted and recognized by the international community of States as a whole as a norm from which no derogation is permitted and which can be modified only by a subsequent norm of general international law having the same character.[153]

International norms proscribing the crimes of genocide, torture, crimes against humanity and war crimes are widely recognised as forming part of *jus cogens* since they are universally accepted and represent fundamental values of the international community not subject to derogations. However, the question of the legal consequences of peremptory norms, beyond the invalidity of conflicting treaties, is controversial and remains unsettled.[154] Some scholars have criticised the view deriving a duty to prosecute from the peremptory status of norms prohibiting international crimes on the basis that 'the recognition of the *jus cogens* nature of international crimes, does not necessarily mean that the duty to prosecute these crimes is itself a *jus cogens* norm'.[155] According to Anja Seibert-Fohr:

151 *Prosecutor v Ieng Sary* (n 132) para 53; *Prosecutor v Kallon and Kamara* (n 132) para 71.

152 *Prosecutor v Anto Furundzija* (Judgment) ICTY-95-17/1-T (10 December 1998) paras 155–56; *Prosecutor v Kallon and Kamara* (n 132) para 71; Cassese and Gaeta (n 137) 312; M Cherif Bassiouni, 'International Crimes: Jus Cogens and Obligatio Erga Omnes' (1996) 59(4) *Law and Contemporary Problems* 63, 65–66.

153 Vienna Convention on the Law of Treaties (adopted 23 May 1969, entered into force 27 January 1980) 1155 UNTS 331, art 53.

154 See UNGA International Law Commission, Third report on peremptory norms of general international law (*jus cogens*) by Dire Tladi, Special Rapporteur (12 February 2018) UN Doc A/CN.4/714, pt III.

155 Dov Jacobs, 'Puzzling over Amnesties: Defragmenting the Debate for International Criminal Tribunals' in Larissa van den Herik and Carsten Stahn (eds), *The Diversification and Fragmentation of International Criminal Law* (Martinus Nijhoff Publishers 2012) 344.

> There is a difference between a substantive norm proscribing certain conduct and a procedural norm obliging States to prosecute or extradite persons accused of such crimes. It is one thing to say that due to the *erga omnes* character of the crime every State is entitled to investigate, prosecute and punish, or extradite those responsible, but quite another to say that there is a corresponding duty. It would be going too far to oblige every State to prosecute or extradite crimes regardless of any link simply on the basis of a prohibition.[156]

Indeed, although there is universal acceptance of the proscription of international crimes, the same cannot be said with respect to the procedural means of repression. This is shown by differences in the wording and content of treaty obligations to prosecute, and their reliance on different jurisdictional bases.

Conclusion

Amnesty has been a delicate issue to deal with in the negotiation of international treaties, partly because states apparently believe that it is a matter pertaining to domestic, rather than international, law. Thus, in multilateral negotiation processes, they have either avoided the issue or rejected formulations purporting to regulate it in a prescriptive manner. Because states do not seem prepared to allow an international instrument to restrict their amnesty prerogative, it has been suggested that it would be counter-productive to attempt including a provision prohibiting amnesties in future conventions establishing criminal responsibility for international crimes. This casts doubt upon the existence of the *opinio juris* of states in believing that an international norm prohibits amnesties for international crimes.

On the other hand, international bodies have maintained that amnesties are not acceptable with respect to crimes prohibited at the international level, particularly those that states are bound to prosecute under international law. This view started to emerge in international discourse at the turn of the 1990s and has been adopted by a growing number of international courts and expert bodies ever since, as examined in the following chapters. Thus, although there is no indication that states renounced their amnesty prerogative by ratifying international conventions requiring them to prosecute certain crimes, amnesties covering these crimes are of limited effectiveness since they may be set aside at the international level. This is especially so with respect to the crimes of genocide, grave breaches of the Geneva Conventions and torture.

Yet, the reach of treaty obligations to prosecute is limited and no such obligation exists in relation to some of the international crimes most susceptible to being amnestied in present times, including crimes against humanity and war crimes committed in internal armed conflicts. It is generally acknowledged that

156 Seibert-Fohr (n 9) 253.

the practice of states in prosecuting these crimes is not sufficiently widespread and consistent to warrant a finding that a customary norm requiring their prosecution has emerged. However, standards have been developed by international bodies to limit the possibility that amnesties may bar the prosecution of these crimes, as will be explored in the next chapters. Therefore, even if the obligation to prosecute argument on its own does not support the existence of a general ban on amnesties for international crimes, this does not settle the question as recent international developments restrict the applicability or effectiveness of amnesties with respect to these crimes.

5 International standards and state practice

Introduction

This chapter examines international standards on amnesties and whether state practice has tended to conform to these standards in recent years. The first section traces the development of the position of the UN on amnesties, from the frequent endorsement of blanket amnesties in post-conflict situations to the condemnation of all forms of amnesty preventing the prosecution of serious crimes. It also looks at expert guidelines considering the acceptability of amnesty in link with efforts to deal with mass crimes. The second section scrutinises different types of state practice in relation to amnesties. First, drawing on an original Peace Agreement Amnesties Database, it investigates whether states have tended to exclude serious crimes from pacification amnesties since 1970 and whether unlimited ones have been criticised by international peace negotiators. Second, it reviews case studies from different parts of the world examining how state authorities, particularly senior courts, have responded to legal challenges against amnesty laws extending to serious crimes. The chapter shows that, despite international pressure to comply with accountability standards, the practice of states has been far from uniform.

1. International standards

While the UN used to be supportive of peace settlements including recourse to general amnesties, it has developed a set of standards designed to combat impunity for serious crimes, including a rule rejecting the grant of amnesty for these crimes. This section traces the emergence and consolidation of this policy rule within different UN bodies and agencies. It then examines the approach adopted by international experts in policy guidelines considering the acceptability of amnesty in the wake of mass atrocities.

Development of the UN policy condemning amnesties for serious crimes

The Joinet report on amnesties (1985)

In 1983, the UN Sub-Commission on Prevention of Discrimination and Protection of Minorities requested Special Rapporteur Louis Joinet to prepare a study examining 'the importance that the promulgation of amnesty laws could have for the safeguard and promotion of human rights and fundamental freedoms'.[1] The study was based on the premise that amnesties can contribute to the promotion or protection of human rights and to the return or consolidation of democracy in three ways.[2] First, 'because the amnesty encourages national consensus in the wake of a political change brought about in a democratic framework'. Second, 'because it is the first act in the initiation of a democratic process or marks a return to democracy'. Third, 'because it is intended to block an internal crisis (non-international armed conflict) or to mark the end of an international armed conflict'. The study examined the practice of states in relation to amnesties and set out principles for the benefit of legislators and experts 'in order to enable them to better assess the impact – positive, negative or nil – of an amnesty law'.[3] Its conclusions were endorsed by the UN Commission on Human rights in 1985.[4]

This first UN study on the subject distinguished between amnesties granted for ordinary crimes and those covering political offences. The former were described as 'an expression of the relatively broad power of civil society to grant every citizen the right of oblivion, if only to facilitate his reintegration into society'.[5] They were often used to deal with prison overcrowding or for other humanitarian motives such as the protection of minors, women, disabled, old or terminally-ill people.[6] The report focused on amnesties covering political offences and identified the types of objectives for which they were most commonly granted. Those objectives included celebrating national occasions, neutralising political opposition groups, encouraging defections by insurgents, facilitating the conclusion of peace following an armed conflict, and prompting the return of exiles and refugees.[7] Amnesties issued for these purposes were viewed in a positive light since they contributed to easing tensions, fostering peace and reconciliation. By contrast, amnesties granted to agents of an outgoing authoritarian regime responsible for human rights abuses were seen as problematic because, rather than bringing appeasement, they generated tensions and instability. According to Joinet, in such cases '[w]hat is sought is not so much reconciliation as impunity'.[8]

1 UN Sub-Commission on Prevention of Discrimination and Protection of Minorities, resolution 1983/34 (6 September 1983) UN Doc E/CN.4/Sub.2/RES/1983/34.
2 UN Sub-Commission on the Prevention of Discrimination and Protection of Minorities, 'Study on amnesty laws and their role in the safeguard and promotion of human rights', Preliminary report by Mr. Louis Joinet, Special Rapporteur (21 June 1985) UN Doc E/CN.4/Sub.2/1985/16 (Joinet study) paras 7–8.
3 Ibid, paras 4, 85–86, annex p 1–2.
4 UN Commission on Human Rights (UNCHR), Report of the Sub-Commission on the Prevention of Discrimination and Protection of Minorities (4 November 1985) UN Doc E/CN.4/1986/5, 6–7.
5 Joinet study (n 2) para 23.
6 Ibid, paras 23–26.
7 Ibid, paras 27–46.
8 Ibid, para 31.

The Rapporteur also examined the types of offences for which amnesties were granted.[9] While he recommended that offences of opinion or against property should be amnestied in priority, he noted that 'an amnesty covering persons guilty of conduct involving a serious infringement of human dignity … far from encouraging national reconciliation, would only increase tension, at least initially'.[10] With regard to crimes against individuals committed in link with an armed conflict, Joinet observed that, since they are mutual and politically motivated, they would in principle be included in the scope of an amnesty.[11] However, he questioned whether violent crimes perpetrated outside military confrontations and constituting systematic human rights violations could be legitimately covered by an amnesty. The Rapporteur made a distinction between isolated acts of ill-treatment and more serious crimes amounting to crimes against humanity, considering that a decision to exclude the latter from the scope of an amnesty 'appears justified'.[12] The language used suggested that perpetrators of serious and systematic human rights violations should be excluded from the scope of amnesties.[13] In such cases, the Rapporteur considered that 'the infringement of the "human condition" is such that the right of oblivion may become a right to impunity'.[14] Therefore, he recommended that the architects and instigators of these systematic criminal practices should 'at the very least' be excluded from the scope of amnesty laws.[15]

The Joinet report is interesting because it is the first international policy document considering the status of amnesties covering serious crimes. The fact that it is considerably less assertive than subsequent UN studies on the subject indicates that there was not settled policy on amnesties at the time. The Rapporteur suggested that amnesties should exclude persons responsible for crimes against humanity or for orchestrating serious and systematic human rights violations. However, he did so in a tentative fashion and did not refer to the rationales used later on to ground the amnesty prohibition – the obligation to prosecute and the right to justice of the victims – though the legal bases for these rights and duties already existed in international law. Instead, to justify the unacceptability of amnesties extending to atrocity crimes, Joinet adopted a consequentialist reasoning stressing their negative impact on reconciliation, democracy and the protection of human rights. His approach was nuanced and catered for the specificities of different types of amnesties enjoying varying degrees of legitimacy depending on factors such as their purpose, scope, design and context of adoption. The Rapporteur did not consider that, in 1985, international law prohibited the grant of amnesty for international crimes. However, he adopted the

9 Ibid, paras 47–79.
10 Ibid, para 51.
11 Ibid, para 58.
12 Ibid, para 50–56 and 66–72.
13 Ibid, para 62.
14 Ibid, paras 67–72.
15 Ibid, para 75.

view that amnesties covering such crimes are morally wrong and unjustifiable from a policy standpoint because they create an atmosphere of impunity ill-suited to prevent the recurrence of violations, foster national reconciliation or the consolidation of democracy.

UN practice in the late twentieth century

In the late twentieth century, the UN was involved in the negotiation of a number of peace agreements containing blanket amnesty clauses. For example, in August 1987, a UN representative witnessed the signing by the Presidents of Costa Rica, El Salvador, Guatemala, Honduras and Nicaragua of the Esquipulas II peace treaty aiming to restore stability in Central America and end the war in Nicaragua.[16] The first article of this treaty provided for the adoption of an amnesty decree in each of the signatory countries, without exceptions or limitations.[17] The implementation of this provision in Nicaragua and Honduras led to the release and exoneration of numerous individuals responsible for serious crimes.[18]

A few years later, in October 1992, the Security Council welcomed the conclusion of the General Peace Agreement for Mozambique, which contained a sweeping amnesty clause including international crimes.[19] The UN also supported the Governor Island Agreement of July 1993 seeking to end the conflict in Haiti.[20] Despite the fact that this agreement extended amnesty to military leaders responsible for grave human rights violations, the Security Council approved it as 'the only valid framework for the solution of the crisis in Haiti'.[21] Other peace accords containing a blanket amnesty provision witnessed or backed by the UN in the 1990s include the Cotonou Agreement of July 1993 (Liberia), the Lusaka Protocol of November 1994 (Angola), the Abidjan Peace Agreement of November 1996 (Sierra Leone) and the General Agreement on Establishment of Peace and National Accord in Tajikistan of May 1997.[22]

16 Procedure for the Establishment of a Firm and Lasting Peace in Central America, 7 August 1987 (Esquipulas II).

17 Ibid, art 1(b).

18 Acuerdo Sapoá (Nicaragua), 23 March 1988. See John J Moore, 'Problems with Forgiveness: Granting Amnesty under the Arias Plan in Nicaragua and El Salvador' (1990–1991) 43 *Stanford Law Review* 733, 757–59.

19 General Peace Agreement for Mozambique, 4 October 1992, Protocol 6(3); UN Security Council (UNSC) resolution 782 (13 October 1992) UN Doc S/RES/782.

20 Governor Islands Accord, 3 July 1993. See Michael P Scharf, 'Swapping Amnesty for Peace: Was There a Duty to Prosecute International Crimes in Haiti?' (1996) 31(1) *Texas International Law Journal* 1; Carsten Stahn, 'United Nations Peacebuilding, Amnesties and Alternative Forms of Justice: A Change in Practice?' (2002) 84(5) *International Review of the Red Cross* 191, 193–94.

21 Governor Islands Accord (n 20) para 6; UNSC Official Records, Resolutions and Decisions of the Security Council (1993) UN Doc S/INF/49, 126.

22 Lusaka Protocol, 15 November 1994, annex 6, art 1(5); Peace Agreement between the Government of the Republic of Sierra Leone and the RUF/SL, 30 November 1996 (Abidjan

On the one hand, the UN thus frequently sanctioned the grant of blanket amnesties to facilitate peace settlements in the late twentieth century. On the other hand, a new trend started to emerge in its peacemaking practice in the early 1990s denoting a realisation of the importance of accountability in the aftermath of mass violence. In 1993 and 1994, the Security Council established two international criminal tribunals to deal with serious violations of international humanitarian law committed during the conflict in the former Yugoslavia and the genocide in Rwanda. The chapter VII resolutions creating these tribunals were based on a conviction that the prosecution of those most responsible for atrocity crimes in these contexts would contribute to end the violence, prevent its recurrence and foster sustainable peace.[23] Accordingly, the amnesties introduced by the UN-brokered peace treaties settling the conflict in the former Yugoslavia excluded serious violations of international humanitarian law within the purview of the International Criminal Tribunal for the former Yugoslavia.[24] In 1996, the UN witnessed the signing of a peace agreement in Guatemala which also expressly excluded amnesty for certain international crimes.[25]

The Joinet report on impunity (1997)

The Vienna Declaration and Programme of Action adopted in 1993 by the World Conference on Human Rights provided impetus to UN agencies for developing policy standards to combat impunity for perpetrators of human rights violations.[26] In 1996, the Sub-Commission on Prevention of Discrimination and Protection of Minorities mandated Louis Joinet to conduct a study on this subject.[27] Accordingly, the Special Rapporteur elaborated a 'set of principles for the protection and promotion of human rights through action to

Peace Agreement), art 14; General Agreement on Establishment of Peace and National Accord in Tajikistan, 29 May 1997, para 1.

23 UNSC resolution 827 (25 May 1993) preamble; UNSC resolution 955 (8 November 1994) preamble.

24 General Framework Agreement for Peace in Bosnia and Herzegovina, 21 November 1995 (Dayton Accords), annex 7, art 6; Agreement on Normalization of Relations between the Federal Republic of Yugoslavia and the Republic of Croatia, 23 August 1996, art 7.

25 Agreement on the Basis for the Legal Integration of Unidad Revolucionaria Nacional Guatemalteca, 12 December 1996, art 24.

26 Vienna Declaration and Programme of Action (25 June 1993) para 91 ('[t]he World Conference on Human Rights views with concern the issue of impunity of perpetrators of human rights violations, and supports the efforts of the Commission on Human Rights and the Sub-Commission on Prevention of Discrimination and Protection of Minorities to examine all aspects of the issue.')

27 UN Sub-Commission on the Prevention of Discrimination and Protection of Minorities, 'Question of the impunity of perpetrators of human rights violations (civil and political)', Revised final report prepared by Mr. Joinet pursuant to Sub-Commission decision 1996/119 (2 October 1997) UN Doc E/CN.4/Sub.2/1997/20/Rev.1 (Joinet report on impunity) paras 1 and 9.

combat impunity' affirming the right to know, the right to justice and the right to reparation of victims of human rights violations.[28] Explaining the importance of these rights for reconciliation, he observed that:

> [T]here can be no just and lasting reconciliation without an effective response to the need for justice; as a factor of reconciliation, forgiveness, insofar as it is a private act, implies that the victim must know the perpetrator of the violations and that the latter has been in a position to show repentance. For forgiveness to be granted, it must first have been sought.[29]

Principle 25 considered the issue of amnesty in relation to the right to justice and the right to reparation:

> Even when intended to establish conditions conducive to a peace agreement or to foster national reconciliation, amnesty and other measures of clemency shall be kept within the following bounds:
>
> (a) The perpetrators of serious crimes under international law may not benefit from such measures until such time as the State has met the obligations referred to in principle 18 [obligations to investigate, prosecute and punish];
> (b) They shall be without effect with respect to the victims' right to reparation, as referred to in principles 33 to 36 [right to reparation].[30]

This principle for the first time articulated the view that amnesties may not constitute an obstacle to the investigation, prosecution and punishment of international crimes or to the right to reparation of the victims. The Commission on Human Rights took note of the set of principles in a resolution of 17 April 1998.[31] In the afterword of the report, Joinet noted that:

> [T]hese principles are not legal standards in the strict sense, but guiding principles intended not to thwart reconciliation but to avoid distortions in certain reconciliation policies so that, once beyond the first stage, which is more concerned with 'conciliation' than reconciliation, the foundations of a 'just and lasting reconciliation' may be laid.[32]

28 Ibid, paras 17–42.
29 Ibid, para 26.
30 Ibid, principle 25.
31 UNCHR, res 1998/53 (17 April 1998) UN Doc E/CN.4/1998/53, para 5.
32 Joinet report on impunity (n 27) para 49.

The Lomé peace agreement of 1999: a turning point

The Lomé peace agreement of July 1999 acted as a catalyst for the developing UN position on amnesties. During the 1990s, advances were realised on both a practical and a theoretical level. On the one hand, some peace agreements mediated by the UN started to bar amnesty for international crimes with a view to permit their prosecution at the national or international level. On the other, amnesty came to be associated with impunity in the Joinet report of 1997 which recommended that it should not be used at the expense of the right to justice and reparation of victims. The link between both sets of developments was made on the occasion of the signing of the Lomé peace agreement, which halted a civil war in Sierra Leone and granted an unconditional amnesty to all rebel fighters implicated in the commission of grave crimes during the conflict.[33]

According to an analyst of the Lomé peace process, this amnesty 'was considered a virtual pre-condition by many of the national actors attending the peace talks, even before it was discussed by the parties'.[34] Indeed, it has been suggested that the war in Sierra Leone could not have been ended without providing guarantees to the rebel factions that they would not be prosecuted.[35] The Special Representative of the UN Secretary-General, Francis Okello, witnessed the agreement but appended a proviso to his signature specifying that '[t]he United Nations holds the understanding that the amnesty and pardon in Article IX of the agreement shall not apply to international crimes of genocide, crimes against humanity, war crimes and other serious violations of international humanitarian law'.[36] Through this disclaimer, the UN Secretariat gave practical effect and official recognition to the policy rule developed within the Commission of Human Rights. It also established a new precedent marking the change in the approach of the UN towards blanket amnesties.

In his report on the Lomé peace process, the Secretary-General stated that 'the Government and people of Sierra Leone should be allowed this opportunity to realize their best and only hope of ending their long and brutal conflict'.[37] Accordingly, there was no suggestion that the UN would refuse to sign the

33 Lomé Peace Agreement, 7 July 1999, art 9.

34 Priscilla Hayner, 'Negotiating Peace in Sierra Leone: Confronting the Justice Challenge' (December 2007) *Centre for Humanitarian Dialogue* 6.

35 Hayner has observed that 'almost none of those present, including the human rights advocates, now believe that a peace agreement would have been possible without some provision of amnesty for past crimes', ibid. See also *Witness to the Truth: Report of the Sierra Leone Truth and Reconciliation Commission* (GPL Press 2004) vol 3B, ch 6, 364–65 ([i]t was accepted, at the time of the signing of the Lomé Peace Agreement, that the RUF would not have signed the agreement if there had been any prospect of legal action being taken against its members'.)

36 Hayner (n 34) 5.

37 UNSC, 'Seventh Report of the Secretary-General on the United Nations Observer Mission in Sierra Leone' (30 July 1999) UN Doc S/1999/836, para 54.

peace agreement on account of its blanket amnesty provision. While expressing the disapproval of the UN, the disclaimer did not affect the validity of the Lomé amnesty, which was implemented in Sierra Leone through the Lomé Peace Agreement (Ratification) Act of 22 July 1999. However, when fighting resumed in 2000 in breach of the peace agreement, President Kabbah requested the Security Council to set up an international criminal court to try the persons most responsible for the commission of atrocities in Sierra Leone.[38] During the negotiation between the UN and the government on the establishment of a Special Court for Sierra Leone, the Okello reservation provided the basis for the decision of the parties to deprive the amnesty of effect with respect to persons subject to the jurisdiction of the court.[39] Accordingly, a dozen of the perpetrators considered to bear the greatest responsibility for international crimes committed during the civil war were tried by the Special Court notwithstanding the amnesty law.

A UN disclaimer was also appended to the Luena peace agreement of April 2002 which ended the civil war in Angola and contained a blanket amnesty provision.[40] Reiterating the position adopted at Lomé, Under-Secretary-General Ibrahim Gambari entered a reservation stating that amnesties applying to genocide, crimes against humanity and war crimes would not be recognised by the UN.[41] In a meeting of the Security Council, Gambari explained how this reservation was received on the ground:

> That statement of principle left some apprehension in the minds of UNITA and some people in the armed forces of Angola – as well as in some segments of civil society – who felt that this position by the United Nations may undermine the peace process, because some combatants may believe that it negates the provisions of the amnesty law that had recently been passed by the Angolan National Assembly. I went to great lengths and spent considerable time during my visit to explain and clarify the principled position of the United Nations on this issue.[42]

38 Letter dated 9 August 2000 from the Permanent Representative of Sierra Leone to the United Nations addressed to the President of the Security Council (10 August 2000) UN Doc S/2000/786. See William Schabas, 'Amnesty, the Sierra Leone Truth and Reconciliation Commission and the Special Court for Sierra Leone' (2004) 11 *University of California Davis Journal of International Law and Policy* 145, 153–54.

39 UNSC, 'Report of the Secretary-General on the establishment of a Special Court for Sierra Leone' (4 October 2000) UN Doc S/2000/915, paras 21–24. See art 10 of the SCSL Statute, annexed to the agreement between the government of Sierra Leone and the UN Secretary General on the Establishment of the Special Court for Sierra Leone (16 January 2002) 2178 UNTS 138.

40 Memorandum of Understanding, 4 April 2002 (Luena Agreement), art 2(1).

41 UNSC, 4517th meeting, 'The Situation of Angola' (23 April 2002) UN Doc S/PV.4517, 3.

42 Ibid.

As in Sierra Leone, the UN reservation appended to the Luena agreement did not affect the validity of its amnesty clause, which was implemented through a blanket amnesty law on 4 April 2002. However, since no international criminal tribunal was established in Angola and no initiatives were taken at the domestic level to investigate or prosecute the crimes of the civil war, even the most responsible perpetrators have enjoyed complete impunity.[43]

Consolidating and expanding UN standards on amnesties

The position adopted at Lomé and Luena received formal expression in the 2004 report of the Secretary-General on the rule of law and transitional justice in conflict and post-conflict societies.[44] Among the report's conclusions was a requirement that peace agreements and Security Council resolutions and mandates '[r]eject any endorsement of amnesty for genocide, war crimes, or crimes against humanity' and 'ensure that no such amnesty previously granted is a bar to prosecution before any United Nations-created or assisted court'.[45] These principles were reiterated in the 2011 follow-up report of the Secretary-General which added gross human rights violations to the crimes for which amnesty would not be recognised by the UN.[46]

In the first half of the 2000s, the Commission on Human Rights issued several resolutions on the subject of impunity emphasising that 'amnesties should not be granted to those who commit violations of international humanitarian and human rights law that constitute serious crimes'.[47] One of these resolutions requested the appointment of an independent expert to update the Joinet principles against impunity in order to reflect recent developments in international law and practice.[48] In 2005, Professor Diane Orentlicher presented the updated set of principles to the Commission on Human Rights.[49] As regards amnesties,

43 See Joris van Wijk, 'Amnesty for War Crimes in Angola: Principled for a Day?' (2012) 12 *International Criminal Law Review* 743.

44 UNSC, 'The rule of law and transitional justice in conflict and post-conflict societies', report of the Secretary General (23 August 2004) UN Doc S/2004/616.

45 Ibid, para 64(c).

46 UNSC, 'The rule of law and transitional justice in conflict and post-conflict societies', report of the Secretary General (12 October 2011) UN Doc S/2011/634, paras 12 and 67.

47 UNCHR resolution 2003/72, 'Impunity' (25 April 2003) UN Doc E/CN.4/2003/L.11/Add.7, para 2; UNCHR resolution 2004/72, 'Impunity' (21 April 2004) E/CN.4/RES/2004/72, para 3; UNCHR resolution 2005/81, 'Impunity' (21 April 2005) UN Doc E/CN.4/RES/2005/81, para 3.

48 UNCHR resolution 2004/72 (n 47) para 20.

49 UNCHR, 'Report of the independent expert to update the Set of principles to combat impunity, Diane Orentlicher' (8 February 2005) UN Doc E/CN.4/2005/102/Add.1 (Orentlicher report). See also UNCHR, 'Independent study on best practices, including recommendations, to assist states in strengthening their domestic capacity to combat all aspects of impunity, by Professor Diane Orentlicher' (22 February 2004) UN Doc E/CN.4/2004/88.

the Orentlicher report reproduced principle 25 of the Joinet report declaring that they cannot obstruct the prosecution of serious crimes under international law or the victims' rights to reparation and to know the truth.[50] The Commission took note with appreciation of the Orentlicher report but the updated set of principles was not formally adopted by a UN agency or the General Assembly.[51]

Underpinning the UN position on amnesties is, on the one hand, the obligation to prosecute international crimes and, on the other, the rights of the victims of serious human rights violations.[52] The latter were formally recognised in the Basic Principles and Guidelines on the Right to a Remedy and Reparation for Victims of Gross Violations of International Human Rights Law and Serious Violations of International Humanitarian Law (Basic Principles) adopted by the Commission on Human Rights in April 2005.[53] These principles set standards on the right to reparation and access to justice of victims of gross violations of human rights and international humanitarian law. They affirm the duty of states to investigate such violations and to 'submit to prosecution the person allegedly responsible'.[54] They also prohibit the application of statutory limitations to crimes under international law.[55] However, they are conspicuously silent as regards amnesties, despite the condemnation of these measures in previous resolutions of the Commission on Human Rights. The Basic Principles were approved by a resolution of the UN General Assembly in March 2006.[56]

In a 2009 policy paper, the High Commissioner for Human Rights recapitulated the now-settled position of the UN on amnesties:

> Under various sources of international law and under United Nations policy, amnesties are impermissible if they:

50 Orentlicher report (n 49) principle 24 ('Even when intended to establish conditions conducive to a peace agreement or to foster national reconciliation, amnesty and other measures of clemency shall be kept within the following bounds: (a) The perpetrators of serious crimes under international law may not benefit from such measures until such time as the State has met the obligations to which principle 19 refers or the perpetrators have been prosecuted before a court with jurisdiction – whether international, internationalized or national – outside the State in question; (b) Amnesties and other measures of clemency shall be without effect with respect to the victims' right to reparation, to which principles 31 through 34 refer, and shall not prejudice the right to know.')

51 UNCHR resolution 2005/81 (n 47) para 20.

52 See chs 4 and 6 in this volume.

53 UNCHR, Basic Principles and Guidelines on the Right to a Remedy and Reparation for Victims of Gross Violations of International Human Rights Law and Serious Violations of International Humanitarian Law (13 April 2005) U.N. Doc. E/CN. 4/2005/L.48.

54 Basic Principles (n 53) para 4.

55 Ibid, para 6.

56 UN General Assembly (UNGA), resolution adopting the Basic Principles and Guidelines on the Right to a Remedy and Reparation for Victims of Gross Violations of International Human Rights Law and Serious Violations of International Humanitarian Law (21 March 2006) UN Doc A/Res/60/147.

(a) Prevent prosecution of individuals who may be criminally responsible for war crimes, genocide, crimes against humanity or gross violations of human rights, including gender-specific violations;
(b) Interfere with victims' right to an effective remedy, including reparation; or
(c) Restrict victims' and societies' right to know the truth about violations of human rights and humanitarian law.[57]

It was made clear that this position entails that:

> United Nations officials, including peace negotiators and field office staff, must never encourage or condone amnesties that prevent prosecution of those responsible for serious crimes under international law, such as war crimes, genocide and crimes against humanity, or gross violations of human rights, such as extrajudicial, summary or arbitrary executions; torture and similar cruel, inhuman or degrading treatment; slavery; and enforced disappearance, including gender-specific instances of these offences, or that impair victims' right to a remedy, including reparation, or victims' or societies' right to the truth. [58]

As part of a programme of action to strengthen the rule of law at the national and international levels, a 2012 report of the UN Secretary-General reiterated the obligation of states to investigate and prosecute serious crimes and, as a corollary, not to grant or endorse amnesties for these crimes.[59] However, when it came to the view of states on these issues, expressed in the Declaration of the high-level meeting of the General Assembly on the rule of law, there was no mention of amnesties.[60] This omission reflects the lack of consensus among states on the issue of amnesty, which has been manifest in previous multilateral negotiation processes aiming towards the repression of international crimes.[61]

In a 2014 report on the promotion of truth, justice, reparation and guarantees of non-recurrence, UN Special Rapporteur Pablo de Greiff deplored that:

> Despite national and international obligations, countries in transition have been shown to be greatly tempted by amnesties, including blanket amnesties that shield perpetrators of even the worst violations from their legal

57 OHCHR, 'Rule-of-Law Tools for Post-Conflict States: Amnesties' (UN Publication 2009) 11.
58 Ibid, 27.
59 UNGA, 'Delivering justice: programme of action to strengthen the rule of law at the national and international levels', Report of the Secretary-General (16 March 2012) A/66/749, para 37.
60 UNGA, 'Declaration of the High-level Meeting of the General Assembly on the Rule of Law at the National and International Levels', resolution adopted by the General Assembly (30 November 2012) A/RES/67/1, para 22.
61 See chs 4 and 7 in this volume.

> responsibility. The Special Rapporteur expresses grave concern at such amnesties.[62]

The Rapporteur warned that, although amnesties enacted during periods of transition may pursue the legitimate aim of ending armed violence, those covering serious crimes 'have not only been shown to further entrench a culture of impunity, but also to be counterproductive as they fail in the long run to prevent the recurrence of new violations and vicious circles of violence'.[63] Accordingly, he urged states 'to refrain from adopting, and intergovernmental organizations to refrain from supporting, amnesties for genocide, war crimes, crimes against humanity and other gross violations of human rights or other serious violations of international humanitarian law'.[64]

Expert guidelines on amnesties

The 2007 Chicago Principles on Post-Conflict Justice

The Chicago Principles on Post-Conflict Justice were developed by international experts in order to assist stakeholders in designing and implementing strategies to address past atrocities.[65] They are based on an understanding that '[o]penly facing the legacy of past violence is essential for preventing future victimization, achieving peace and reconciliation, and protecting human rights'.[66] In this document, post-conflict justice is conceived as 'a comprehensive, integrated approach to addressing past atrocities' involving prosecutions, truth-telling, reparations, non-penal sanctions, memorialization, traditional mechanisms and institutional reforms.[67]

The first Chicago Principle affirms the duty of states to prosecute perpetrators of gross violations of human rights and humanitarian law.[68] On the subject of amnesties, it recommends that 'States shall not grant blanket amnesty to absolve individuals of responsibility for genocide, serious war crimes, or crimes against humanity'.[69] There is no suggestion that limited or conditional amnesties are prohibited. However, it is emphasised that amnesties should be granted in accordance with international law and only when they are necessary to negotiate

62 UN Human Rights Council (UNHRC), 'Report of the Special Rapporteur on the promotion of truth, justice, reparation and guarantees of non-recurrence, Pablo de Greiff' (27 August 2014) A/HRC/27/56, para 31.

63 Ibid.

64 Ibid, para 118(b).

65 *The Chicago Principles on Post-Conflict Justice* (International Human Rights Law Institute 2007).

66 Ibid, 2.

67 Ibid, 11.

68 Ibid, 29.

69 Ibid, 35.

the end of a conflict.[70] The first Principle also recommends that amnesties should be linked with accountability mechanisms and granted through an individualised adjudication process, keeping in mind that '[a]mnesty is more acceptable when it provides protection to low-ranking perpetrators, child soldiers, those responsible for less serious crimes, and those forced to commit violations'.[71]

The 2013 Belfast Guidelines on amnesty and accountability

The Belfast Guidelines were drafted by a group of experts on human rights and conflict resolution with a view to assist decision- and policymaking on amnesty and accountability in connection with armed conflict or repression.[72] The first part of the Guidelines lists general principles. The underlying premise is that states emerging from mass violence are under multiple obligations under international law, including a duty to investigate and prosecute serious crimes, provide redress to the victims, prevent the recurrence of violence, and protect human rights for the future.[73] Transitional states also need to work towards a number of policy objectives such as ending the conflict or repression, building democratic structures protecting the rule of law, addressing the root causes of the violence, fostering reconciliation and sustainable peace.[74] As it is often impossible to fulfil those multiple obligations and objectives 'simultaneously or rapidly', and international law offers little guidance on how they should be prioritised, the Guidelines suggest that states 'should seek to develop complementary mechanisms rather than fulfilling one legal obligation while neglecting others'.[75] Accordingly, they propose different ways in which amnesties may be designed and combined with judicial or non-judicial accountability mechanisms in order to satisfy as far as possible the various duties and policy objectives of states responding to mass atrocities.

The Guidelines emphasise that the prosecution of international crimes is required by international law and serves important policy objectives.[76] However, they note that, following situations of conflict or repression, 'there are often substantial legal, political, economic, and social challenges to pursuing widespread prosecutions' such that it is 'rarely possible or practical to prosecute all offenders'.[77] On a practical level, they explain that 'all legal systems, including international criminal law, allow for some prosecutorial discretion in deciding which suspects or which incidents to select and prioritise for prosecution'.[78] The

70 Ibid.
71 Ibid, 35–36.
72 *The Belfast Guidelines on Amnesty and Accountability* (Transitional Justice Institute, University of Ulster 2013).
73 Ibid, 6.
74 Ibid, 6–7.
75 Ibid, 6.
76 Ibid, 8.
77 Ibid.
78 Ibid.

Guidelines argue that amnesties, depending on their design and implementation, can complement selective prosecution strategies in furtherance of states' legal obligations and policy objectives.[79] In this sense, it is observed that amnesties may serve a number of legitimate goals, such as encouraging combatants to surrender, convincing authoritarian rulers to step down, facilitating peace negotiations, releasing political prisoners and permitting the return of exiles.[80] Conditional amnesties may also provide an incentive for offenders to engage with transitional justice processes. The Guidelines draw a distinction between different types of amnesties:

> In all contexts, where amnesties cover serious crimes, it is important to distinguish between illegitimate and legitimate amnesties. Illegitimate amnesties are generally unconditional and have the effect of preventing investigations and ensuring impunity for persons responsible for serious crimes. Amnesties are more likely to be viewed as legitimate where they are primarily designed to create institutional and security conditions for the sustainable protection of human rights, and require individual offenders to engage with measures to ensure truth, accountability and reparations.[81]

The second part of the Guidelines makes recommendations on the scope of amnesties. It starts by acknowledging that, while persons responsible for international crimes and gross human rights violations should be held accountable, there is no categorical prohibition of amnesties for serious crimes and some flexibility is allowed by international law.[82] A number of criteria are proposed to ensure that amnesties are consistent with states' international obligations and conducive to their transitional goals, including the limitation of the range of eligible offences or beneficiaries, and the restriction of their temporal or geographical scope.[83] The third part of the Guidelines looks at the conditions that may be included in amnesties to enhance their legitimacy and legality.[84] Requirements may be imposed on offenders either as a pre-condition for benefiting from the amnesty or, once it has been granted, to avoid its revocation. The last part makes recommendations on different ways to adopt, implement and review amnesties in order to ensure or increase their legality, legitimacy and effectiveness.[85]

79 Ibid, 8–9.
80 Ibid, 9.
81 Ibid, 9–10.
82 Ibid, 10–12.
83 Ibid, 12–16.
84 Ibid, 17–19.
85 Ibid, 19–24.

2. State practice

Several empirical studies have examined the practice of states in issuing amnesties in the recent past.[86] They reveal that over 600 amnesties have been adopted around the world since 1970 and that these measures have remained popular, particularly as a tool to end armed violence or facilitate a political transition. While these studies show that amnesties are commonplace in transitional situations, there is little empirical data measuring the extent to which amnesties have been restricted so as to exclude serious crimes since the emergence of international accountability standards.[87] Louise Mallinder, one of the few scholars having investigated this question, has found that between 1979 and 2011, 'amnesty law enactment has continued at a steady rate' and that 'throughout this period, although the number of new amnesty laws excluding international crimes has increased, so too has the number of amnesties including such crimes'.[88]

This section analyses different forms of state practice in relation to amnesties. Relying on an original Peace Agreement Amnesties Database, the first subsection investigates whether amnesties included in peace agreements have tended to exclude serious crimes since 1970. Amnesties are frequently issued in relation to an armed conflict and, when this is the case, are often introduced through a peace agreement.[89] Peace agreement amnesties are thus a representative sample of amnesties in general. Moreover, as peace agreements are often mediated by third states or intergovernmental organisations, an analysis of this particular type of amnesties permits, in addition to quantifying the practice of states in adopting pacification amnesties, to appraise the attitude of international peace negotiators towards agreements containing unlimited amnesty provisions. The second subsection considers a different type of state practice. Through case studies from different parts of the world, it examines whether states have tended to overturn or restrict amnesty laws applying to serious crimes in recent decades. It looks at how unlimited amnesty laws have been challenged in a number of countries and what has been the response of relevant domestic authorities.

86 Renée Jeffery, *Amnesties, Accountability, and Human Rights* (University of Pennsylvania Press 2014); Andrew G Reiter, 'Examining the Use of Amnesties and Pardons as a Response to Internal Armed Conflicts' (2014) 47(1) *Israel Law Review* 133; Tricia D Olsen, Leigh A Payne and Andrew G Reiter, *Transitional Justice in Balance: Comparing Processes, Weighing Efficacy* (United States Institute of Peace Press 2010); Louise Mallinder, *Amnesty, Human Rights and Political Transitions: Bridging the Peace and Justice Divide* (Hart Publishing 2008). These studies are discussed in ch 3 of this volume.

87 See Mallinder, *Amnesty, Human Rights and Political Transitions* (n 86) ch 3; Francesca Lessa, Tricia D Olsen, Leigh A Payne, Gabriel Pereira and Andrew G Reiter, 'Persistent or Eroding Impunity: The Divergent Effects of Legal Challenges to Amnesty Laws for Past Human Rights Violations' (2014) 47 *Israel Law Review* 105, 110–11.

88 Louise Mallinder, 'Amnesties' Challenge to the Global Accountability Norm? Interpreting Regional and International Trends in Amnesty Enactment' in Francesca Lessa and Leigh A Payne (eds), *Amnesty in the Age of Human Rights Accountability: Comparative and International Perspectives* (CUP 2012) 95.

89 Different types of amnesties are discussed in ch 3 of this volume.

Peace agreement amnesties

The Peace Agreement Amnesties Database documents 145 peace agreements providing for amnesty in relation to an international or internal armed conflict from 1970 to 2017.[90] It contains information on the type of amnesty introduced, its scope, whether it excludes certain crimes and whether intergovernmental organisations or third states have participated to the negotiation of the agreement.[91]

Of the 145 peace agreement amnesties identified, only 15 relate to an international armed conflict (10%), the remaining 130 concerning an internal conflict between government forces and one or more non-state armed groups. The peace agreements included in the Database involve a total of 60 countries from Africa, Asia, Europe, the Middle East, Latin America and the Caribbean. A little more than half of them (54%) relate to a conflict in Africa (78 peace agreements), 23% to a conflict in Asia (34 agreements), 13% to a conflict in Latin America and the Caribbean (19 agreements), 7% to a conflict in Europe (ten agreements) and 3% to a conflict in the Middle East (four agreements).

Peace agreement amnesties are usually formulated in broad terms applying either to all acts committed in relation to a particular conflict or, more specifically, to members of designated armed groups. Their purpose as expressed in the agreement is generally to contribute to the establishment of conditions conducive to peace, national reconciliation or to an inclusive political dialogue. The majority of peace agreement amnesties are general in that they do not contain exclusions (92 amnesties – 63%) though they sometimes apply only to certain categories of persons. Crimes under international law are the type of crimes most frequently excluded from peace agreement amnesties (29 amnesties – 20%). The second category of crimes occasionally excluded from peace agreement amnesties, in a few cases together with other types of crimes, are offences that are not motivated by, or connected to, a political objective (18 amnesties – 12%). Finally, certain peace agreement amnesties exclude specific crimes on the

90 See the Peace Agreement Amnesties Database in appendix. Peace agreement amnesties have been identified primarily on the basis of the following peace agreements databases: the UN peace agreement database (UN Peacemaker) <www.peacemaker.un.org> accessed 7 November 2018, the PA-X Peace Agreement Database Project (University of Edinburgh) <www.peaceagreements.org> accessed 7 November 2018, the Peace Accords Matrix (Krok Institute for International Peace Studies, University of Notre Dame) <www.peaceaccords.nd.edu> accessed 7 November 2018, and the Peace Agreements Digital Collection (United States Institute of Peace) <www.usip.org> accessed 7 November 2018. When consecutive agreements confirm the same amnesty provision for the same parties, only the latest one has been taken into account, excluding interim agreements.

91 Intergovernmental organisations or third states having participated to the negotiation of a peace agreement have only been included as such in the Database when they were expressly mentioned in the agreement for their role as witnesses, hosts, mediators or international observers. See Peace Agreement Amnesties Database in appendix.

ground of their seriousness but without making a link with international law (ten amnesties – 7%).

While peace agreement amnesties excluding international crimes amount to only a fifth of all amnesties included in the Database, their proportion has increased over time. Peace agreement amnesties introduced in the 1970s and the 1980s did not contain any exclusions. In the 1990s, however, seven peace agreements amnesties excluded international crimes, representing 12% of the total of peace agreement amnesties identified for that decade (59 amnesties). In the 2000s, 13 peace agreement amnesties made an exception for international crimes, amounting to 25 % of all those found in that decade (52 amnesties). Between 2010 and 2017, nine peace agreement amnesties excluded this type of crimes, representing a little over a third (35%) of all those identified in that period (26 amnesties). There has thus been a steady increase in the number of peace agreement amnesties excluding international crimes in the last two decades, though the majority of peace agreements which extended an amnesty since 2010 did so in unlimited terms.

Peace agreement amnesties limited in accordance with international standards are distributed unevenly across world regions. While the large majority relate to a conflict in Africa (22 amnesties), a few concern a conflict in Europe (five amnesties) or Latin America (two amnesties). The first African peace agreement prohibiting the grant of amnesty for an international crime was the Lusaka accord of 19 July 1999 concluded by Angola, Namibia, Rwanda, Zimbabwe, Uganda and the Democratic Republic of Congo to end the regional conflict in the latter.[92] Like most subsequent African peace agreements excluding amnesty for serious crimes, it was mediated by the UN.[93] In fact, it was adopted just a few days after the signing of the Lomé peace agreement on the occasion of which the UN for the first time publicly refused to endorse a blanket amnesty. Though many peace agreements adopted in Africa since the turn of the new millennium excluded amnesty for serious crimes in accordance with UN standards, the majority of them were general and unlimited (56 amnesties).

By contrast, none of the 34 Asian peace agreements having provided for an amnesty since 1970 made an exception for international crimes. Three of them, however, excluded serious crimes under domestic law, such as Philippines's General Agreement of October 1995 excluding 'crimes against chastity' and India's Memorandum of Agreement of July 2011 excluding persons charged with murder.[94] Only a few Asian peace accords have been brokered by international

92 Lusaka Agreement, 19 July 1999, art 3(22) and annex A (9(2)) (excluding amnesty for persons suspected of the crime of genocide).

93 Only three of the 22 African peace agreement amnesties excluding serious crimes were negotiated without UN input.

94 General Agreement for Peace between the Government of the Republic of the Philippines and the Rebolusyonaryong Alyansang Makabansa – Soldiers of the Filipino People – Young Officers' Union, 13 October 1995, art 4; Memorandum of Agreement on the Gorkha Territorial Administration (India) 18 July 2011, para 29.

organisations, which may account for the limited impact of international standards on peace negotiations in that part of the world. Recent Asian peace agreements continue to extend broad and unlimited amnesties, including Nepal's 9-Point Agreement of May 2016 and Afghanistan's peace deal with Hezb-i-Islami of September 2016.[95]

While a substantial proportion of the 19 peace agreement amnesties adopted in Latin America and the Caribbean excluded non-political offences, only two of them explicitly prohibited amnesty for crimes under international law. The most recent is the Colombian peace agreement of November 2016 containing a comprehensive list of crimes excluded according to international law.[96] As regards the ten European peace agreements included in the Database, half of them exclude amnesty with respect to international crimes, most of which were adopted in relation to the conflicts in the former Yugoslavia.[97] Lastly, none of the four peace agreements adopted in the Middle East have prohibited the grant of amnesty for international crimes.

Impact of the UN on the restriction of peace agreement amnesties

The influence of the UN on the limitation of peace agreement amnesties is clear when considering that the organisation was involved in the mediation of all but five of the 29 peace agreements prohibiting amnesty for crimes under international law. Prior to the publication of the 2009 policy paper of the High Commissioner for Human Rights instructing UN officials not to sanction amnesty for serious human rights violations, most limited peace agreement amnesties only excluded one or more core international crimes.[98] Following 2009, however, the majority of limited peace agreement amnesties also excluded serious human rights violations.

The pressure exercised by the UN during peace negotiations has manifestly brought parties to certain peace processes to adjust their expectations regarding amnesty. In several African countries, the involvement of the UN in peace talks has meant that hitherto blanket amnesty clauses became limited so as to permit the prosecution of serious crimes. For instance, while the UN was not involved in the negotiation of Mali's Framework Accord of April 2012 extending amnesty in unlimited terms, it witnessed the Ouagadougou Accords of June 2013 excluding amnesty for international crimes and gross human rights

95 9-Point Deal (Nepal) 5 May 2016; Peace agreement between the Government of Afghanistan and Hezb-i-Islami, 29 September 2016, art 9.

96 Final Agreement for Ending the Conflict and Building a Stable and Lasting Peace, 24 November 2016, ch 5, item 5.1.2 (II) paras 23 and 40–41.

97 Dayton Accords (n 24) annex 7, art 6; Agreement on Normalization of Relations between the Federal Republic of Yugoslavia and the Republic of Croatia (n 24) art 7; Interim Agreement for Peace and Self-Government in Kosovo (Rambouillet Accords), 23 February 1999, art 2(12).

98 Rule-of-Law Tools for Post-Conflict States: Amnesties (n 57) 27.

violations.[99] Similarly, whereas previous peace agreements in the Central African Republic (CAR) included a blanket amnesty clause, the first UN-brokered agreement for this country, the Libreville Accord of 21 June 2008, excluded amnesty for international crimes.[100]

The UN policy on amnesties started to be implemented in Europe. The first peace agreement to restrict its amnesty provision by reference to international law was the Quadripartite Agreement relating to the autonomous region of Abkhazia mediated by the UN High Commissioner for Refugees in 1994.[101] It provided immunity to displaced persons and refugees, except for those suspected of 'war crimes and crimes against humanity as defined in international instruments and international practice'.[102] The next peace agreements excluding amnesty for international crimes were also negotiated by the UN in relation to the armed conflicts in the former Yugoslavia and Guatemala.[103] These peace agreements prohibiting amnesty for international crimes marked a departure from the hitherto permissive attitude of the UN towards peace settlements including broad amnesties.

Since the formal condemnation of blanket amnesties at Lomé in July 1999, UN officials have generally not been involved in the negotiation of peace agreements permitting the grant of amnesty for international crimes. However, the practice of the UN has not been completely uniform as the organisation did support some peace accords notwithstanding their broad amnesty clause, such as the Bougainville Peace Agreement of January 2001 (Papua New Guinea) and the Helsinki Agreement of August 2005 (Aceh, Indonesia).[104] More recently, the UN Security Council endorsed two peace deals criticised for allowing impunity for serious human rights violations. The first was brokered by the Gulf

99 Accord cadre de mise en œuvre de l'engagement solennel du 1er Avril 2012, 6 April 2012, art 7(a); Accords de Ouagadougou (Mali), 13 June 2013, art 17.

100 Accord de Paix entre le Gouvernement de la République Centrafricaine et les Mouvements Politico-Militaires ci-après designés: FDPC et UFDR, 2 February 2007, art 4; Accord de paix de Birao, 1 April 2007, art 4; Accord de cessez le feu et de paix entre le Gouvernement de la Republique Centrafricaine et le mouvement politique et militaire Centrafricain APRD, 9 May 2008, art 4; Comprehensive Peace Agreement between the Government of the CAR and several Central African politico-military movements (APRD, FDPC and UFDR), 21 June 2008 (Libreville Accord), art 2.

101 Quadripartite Agreement on Voluntary Return of Refugees and Displaced Persons, 4 April 1994.

102 Ibid, para 3(c).

103 Dayton Accords (n 24); Agreement on Normalization of Relations between the Federal Republic of Yugoslavia and the Republic of Croatia (n 24); Agreement on the Basis for the Legal Integration of Unidad Revolucionaria Nacional Guatemalteca (n 25).

104 Bougainville Peace Agreement, 30 August 2001, para 331; Memorandum of Understanding between the Government of the Republic of Indonesia and the Free Aceh Movement, 15 August 2005, arts 3(1)-(2). The UN observer mission in Bougainville actively supported the peace process and the UN Secretary-General accepted Papua New Guinea's request of assistance for the implementation of the Bougainville agreement, see 'Letter dated 22 October 2001 from the Secretary-General addressed to the President of the Security Council'

Cooperation Council in 2011 to resolve the crisis in Yemen.[105] Despite the fact that it provided immunity to outgoing President Saleh and senior government officials allegedly responsible for widespread human rights abuses, the Security Council urged the signature and implementation of this accord.[106] The second was mediated by the Organisation for Security and Cooperation in Europe (OSCE) to end the fighting in eastern Ukraine.[107] Although it contained an unlimited amnesty provision, the Security Council approved it and required the parties to the conflict to fully implement it.[108]

The position of other intergovernmental organisations acting as peace negotiators

The practice of other intergovernmental organisations in relation to peace agreements containing an unlimited amnesty clause has been mixed. While regional organisations have co-mediated some peace agreements prohibiting the grant of amnesty for international crimes with the UN, they have also endorsed peace agreements including blanket amnesty provisions. Only four peace agreements barring amnesty for international crimes were brokered by regional organisations without UN input.[109]

Some intergovernmental organisations – the African Union (AU), the Southern African Development Community (SADC), the International Organisation of the Francophonie (OIF) and the International Conference on the Great Lakes Region (ICGLR) – have mediated more peace agreements excluding than including amnesty for serious crimes. However, other organisations – the European Union (EU), the Organisation of American States (OAS), the Economic Community of West African States (ECOWAS), the Commonwealth and the Community of Sahel-Saharan States (CEN-SAD) – have mediated more agreements including an unlimited amnesty clause than accords prohibiting amnesty for serious crimes.

(23 October 2001) UN Doc S/2001/988. See also 'Annan applauds signing of Aceh peace agreement' *UN News* (15 August 2005).

105 Agreement/Gulf Cooperation Council Initiative, 23 November 2011.

106 Ibid, para 3 ('[o]n the 29th day after the Agreement enters into force, Parliament, including the opposition, shall adopt laws granting immunity from legal and judicial prosecution to the President and those work worked with him during his time in office'); UNSC resolution 2014 (21 October 2011) UN Doc S/RES/2014.

107 Package of Measures for the Implementation of the Minsk Agreements, 12 February 2015.

108 Ibid, section 5 (calling on the parties to '[e]nsure pardon and amnesty by enacting the law prohibiting the prosecution and punishment of persons in connection with the events that took place in certain areas of the Donetsk and Lugansk regions of Ukraine'); UNSC resolution 2202 (17 February 2015) UN Doc S/RES/2202.

109 Memorandum on Measures of Providing Safety and Strengthening of Mutual Confidence between the Sides in the Georgian-Ossetian Conflict, 16 May 1996 (mediated by the OSCE); Rambouillet Accords (n 97) (mediated by the OSCE and the European Union); Political Accord of Ouagadougou (Ivory Coast), 4 March 2007 (mediated by the Economic Community of West African States); Agreement on the creation of a Truth, Justice and Reconciliation Commission in Kenya, 4 March 2008 (mediated by the African Union).

The UN position excluding amnesty for serious crimes has had some impact on the practice of other intergovernmental organisations. Since the policy change intervened at Lomé in July 1999, regional organisations have usually supported more peace agreements containing amnesties limited pursuant to international standards. For instance, while the AU brokered seven peace agreements containing a blanket amnesty provision and no agreement excluding amnesty for international crimes between 1970 and July 1999, it mediated 14 agreements excluding amnesty for international crimes and only five including an unlimited amnesty clause since the change in the UN policy. However, the practice of some intergovernmental organisations regarding pacification amnesties has not been manifestly affected by UN standards. For example, the EU brokered seven peace agreements extending amnesty in unlimited terms against five excluding amnesty for international crimes after the policy change.[110] As regional organisations have abstained from publicly condemning blanket amnesties and have tended to be supportive of peace processes even when entailing recourse to such measures, their practice does not point to the existence of a binding norm prohibiting the grant of amnesty for serious crimes in all circumstances.

The practice of states in commenting on peace agreement amnesties

The attitude of third states towards blanket pacification amnesties has been similarly inconclusive. States have generally refrained from criticising amnesties, particularly when they form part of a compromise to end a protracted armed conflict.[111] In the context of a meeting of the Security Council on the situation in Sierra Leone following the conclusion of the Lomé peace agreement, several states exceptionally commented on the agreement's blanket amnesty provision and the UN disclaimer. According to the UK delegate:

> The inclusion of a blanket amnesty for those who have committed appalling atrocities has rightly caused concern. But this was one of many hard choices that the Government and the people of Sierra Leone had to make in the interests of securing a workable agreement.[112]

The representative of Argentina similarly declared that:

> The granting of wide-ranging and general amnesty, as provided for in the Agreement, raises very important questions. Argentina's position and

110 Before the UN policy change, the EU negotiated two peace agreements extending a blanket amnesty and two agreements containing a limited one, see Peace Agreement Amnesties Database in appendix.

111 On the attitude of international actors towards amnesties, see Mallinder, *Amnesty, Human Rights and Political Transitions: Bridging the Peace and Justice Divide* (n 86) ch 8.

112 UNSCOR, 4035th Meeting (20 August 1999) UN Doc S/PV.4035, 4.

> practice in this connection have been uniform and unswerving. However, we understand that that very delicate decision can be taken only by the parties involved, which assume the historical responsibility inherent in that decision.[113]

The Gambian delegate also expressed concern about the amnesty but accepted that '[w]hile this may not foster justice, we understand the circumstances under which it was granted'.[114] Yet, he associated his country with the UN disclaimer. So did the Netherlands' representative, who defended the UN position in the following terms:

> As one of the moral guarantors of that accord, our Organization should clearly note the limits of impunity, as defined in international law, which apply to Sierra Leone as they do to any other part of the world. There can be no doubt that the atrocities committed against the civilian population of Sierra Leone ... constitute massive violations of international human rights and humanitarian law. As noted by Mr. Okello in the reservation attached to his signature on the Lomé accord, crimes against humanity, war crimes and other serious violations of international humanitarian law cannot be covered by the amnesty provisions of the accord.[115]

Some states have been inconsistent in their attitude towards pacification amnesties. For instance, the US condemned the amnesty law enacted in El Salvador in 1987, primarily on the ground that it covered human rights abuses against US citizens.[116] However, it supported the Governor Island agreement of 1993 and granted asylum to the leaders of the Haitian military junta.[117] Similarly, whereas the US opposed the grant of amnesty to war criminals implicated in the conflict in the former Yugoslavia, it supported the blanket amnesty provision of the Abidjan peace accord for Sierra Leone one year later.[118] More recently, the US justified the amnesty deal concluded in Yemen as a necessary element of the ongoing transitional process and granted immunity to ousted President Saleh when he visited the country for medical treatment.[119]

113 Ibid, 6.

114 Ibid, 10.

115 Ibid, 13.

116 Charles P Trumbull, 'Giving Amnesties a Second Chance' (2007) 25 *Berkeley Journal of International Law* 283, 297; Moore (n 18) 768–71.

117 Scharf (n 20) 5–8.

118 See Louise Mallinder, 'Retribution, Restitution and Reconciliation: Limited Amnesty in Bosnia-Herzegovina' Working Paper No. 3, *Beyond Legalism: Amnesties, Transitions and Conflict Transformation* (Queen's University Belfast, November 2009) 69–71.

119 'United States defends immunity law for Yemeni president Saleh' *The Guardian* (10 January 2012); Joshua Hersh, 'Ali Abdullah Saleh, Yemen President, To Be Granted Diplomatic Immunity Upon U.S. Arrival' *Huffington Post* (25 January 2012).

With some exceptions, states have usually confined themselves to expressing general support for peace agreements without directly addressing the issue of amnesty. For instance, on the day of the signing of the Townsville peace agreement of October 2000 ending the civil war in the Solomon Islands and containing a broad amnesty provision, the Australian foreign minister stated that:

> Implementation of the agreement is potentially of enormous benefit to all the people of the Solomon Islands, so many of whom have suffered severely and directly from the violent conflicts and other impacts of the ethnic tension over the past two years. I am delighted the facilities and support Australia has been able to provide for the conference at RAAF Base Townsville have assisted such an important and satisfying outcome.[120]

Similarly, the Portuguese President praised the Luena peace agreement of April 2002 and declared that it 'opens the way to reconciliation among Angolans and general elections'.[121] The other facilitators of the Angolan peace process – Russia, the US and the UK – also congratulated the government for this 'historic step forward' without mentioning the blanket amnesty clause included in the agreement, with respect to which the UN had entered a reservation.[122] In the same vein, several states including the US, India, China and Japan congratulated the government of Nepal on the signing of the Comprehensive Peace Accord with the Maoist rebel group in November 2006, despite the fact that it contained a vague and unlimited amnesty provision.[123]

The resolutions issued by the Security Council in relation to the 2011 peace accord in Yemen did not give rise to comments by members of the Council on the immunity granted to President Saleh. In a meeting on Yemen in 2014, the delegates of France and the US confined themselves to underscoring the need to 'turn the page on the presidency of Ali Abdullah Saleh in order to move forward in the transition'.[124] The 2015 peace agreement for Ukraine also gave rise to a Security Council resolution. In the discussion leading up to its adoption, some members mentioned the amnesty clause included in the agreement. The delegates of the UK and New Zealand stressed that this amnesty could not apply to those responsible for shooting down the Malaysian airplane in Ukraine in July 2014.[125] Yet, the representative of Lithuania was the only participant to refer to accountability for serious crimes in general terms by voicing:

120 Media Release, Australian Minister for Foreign Affairs, Alexander Downer, 'Solomon Islands: Signature of the Townsville Peace Agreement' (15 October 2000).

121 'Angolans celebrate peace deal' *BBC News* (5 April 2002).

122 Ibid. See text to n 40–41.

123 'World Reactions: We Hope It Will Work For You' *Nepal Monitor* (21 November 2006). See Renée Jeffery, 'Nepal's Comprehensive Peace Agreement: Human Rights, Compliance and Impunity a Decade On' (2017) 93(2) *International Affairs* 343.

124 UNSCOR, 7119th meeting (26 February 2014) UN Doc S/PV.7119, 3.

125 UNSCOR, 7384th meeting (17 February 2015) UN Doc S/PV.7384, 3 and 7.

> [T]he firm conviction that justice and accountability must be part and parcel of the path out of this devastating, unprovoked war against Ukraine. The perpetrators of the most serious crimes … including those responsible for the downing of Malaysia Airlines Flight MH-17, must be held to account.[126]

This language, however, was not incorporated in the resolution adopted by the Security Council.[127]

Responding to amnesty challenges

Latin America

A number of amnesty laws covering serious crimes have been challenged before international or domestic courts, usually on the basis that they were contrary to international law. There has been a higher incidence of such challenges in Latin America than in other parts of the world.[128] This can partly be attributed to the high number of amnesty laws issued in that region in the last decades of the twentieth century to shield state agents from accountability. The important role of the Inter-American system of human rights in challenging impunity for serious crimes has also been widely acknowledged.[129] Inter-American institutions have developed a consistent and detailed body of case-law on amnesties. In 2001, the Inter-American Court of Human Rights was the first international court to invalidate an amnesty law in the landmark case of *Barrios Altos v Peru*.[130] It held that amnesties designed to prevent the investigation and prosecution of serious human rights violations are incompatible with the American Convention on Human Rights.[131] The Court reaffirmed and expanded this position in several cases involving amnesty laws in Chile, Uruguay, Brazil and El Salvador, all of

126 Ibid, 9.

127 UNSC, resolution 2202 (17 February 2015) S/RES/2202.

128 Lessa, Olsen, Payne, Pereira and Reiter (n 87) 111–13. See also Francesca Lessa, Tricia D Olsen, Leigh A Payne, Gabriel Pereira and Andrew G Reiter, 'Overcoming Impunity: Pathways to Accountability in Latin America' (2014) 8 *International Journal of Transitional Justice* 75, 84–85.

129 See *Victims Unsilenced: The Inter-American Human Rights System and Transitional Justice in Latin America* (Due Process of Law Foundation 2007) 167; Brian D Tittemore, 'Ending Impunity in the Americas: The Role of the Inter-American Human Rights System in Advancing Accountability for Serious Crimes under International Law' (Tittemore 2006) 12 *Southwestern Journal of Law and Trade in the Americas* 429; Ellen Lutz, 'Responses to Amnesties by the Inter-American System for the Protection of Human Rights' in David J Harris and Stephen Livingstone (eds), *The Inter-American System of Human Rights* (Clarendon Press 1998) 346.

130 *Barrios Altos v Peru* (Merits) Inter-American Court of Human Rights Series C No 75 (14 March 2001).

131 Ibid, paras 41–44.

which were declared incompatible with the American Convention on Human Rights.[132]

Latin American amnesties have also been challenged at the domestic level, some of these actions having led to their repeal or limitation. The Peruvian amnesty law of 1995 condemned by the Inter-American Court has not been formally abrogated. However, decisions by Peru's executive and judiciary powers have recognised its ineffectiveness following *Barrios Altos* and permitted the reopening of cases in which it had been applied.[133] In Argentina, two laws of 1986 and 1987 akin to amnesties were invalidated in the early 2000s through a series of mutually reinforcing acts by the three branches of Argentina's government. This process started in the late 1990s and involved different strategies pursued by human rights and civil society organisations in order to circumvent the effects of the amnesty measures.[134] In 2003, President Kirchner eventually introduced a law nullifying them with retroactive effect and, in 2005, the Supreme Court confirmed that they were unconstitutional.[135]

Uruguay was the second Latin American country to formally repeal its longstanding amnesty law of 1986. While the law was declared unconstitutional by the Supreme Court on 19 October 2009, Uruguayan citizens rejected an initiative to repeal it through a referendum a few days later.[136] The amnesty was eventually annulled by a law of October 2011 removing barriers to accountability for the crimes perpetrated during the military dictatorship.[137] However,

132 *The Massacres of El Mozote and nearby places v El Salvador* (Merits, Reparations and Costs) Inter-American Court of Human Rights Series C No 252 (25 October 2012); *Gelman v Uruguay* (Merits and Reparations) Inter- American Court of Human Rights Series C No 221 (24 February 2011); *Gomes Lund et al. v Brazil* (Preliminary Objections, Merits, Reparations and Costs) Inter-American Court of Human Rights Series C No 219 (24 November 2010); *Almonacid-Arellano v Chile* (Merits) Inter-American Court of Human Rights Series C No 154 (26 September 2006). For an analysis of these decisions, see ch 6 in this volume.

133 A resolution of Peru's Attorney-General instructed prosecutors to request the re-opening of cases in which the amnesty had been applied and the Supreme Court confirmed that the law was no longer effective. This was accepted by the Inter-American Court in *La Cantuta v Peru* (Judgment) Inter-American Court of Human Rights Series C No 162 (29 November 2006) paras 165–89.

134 See Engstrom and Gabriel Pereira, 'From Amnesty to Accountability: The Ebb and Flow in the Search for Justice in Argentina' in Francesca Lessa and Leigh A Payne (eds), *Amnesty in the Age of Human Rights Accountability: Comparative and International Perspectives* (CUP 2012) 108–13.

135 Christine A E Bakker, 'A Full Stop to Amnesty in Argentina: The Simon Case' (2005) 3 *Journal of International Criminal Justice* 1106.

136 Francesca Lessa, 'Barriers to Justice: The Ley de Caducidad and Impunity in Uruguay' in Francesca Lessa and Leigh A Payne (eds), *Amnesty in the Age of Human Rights Accountability: Comparative and International Perspectives* (CUP 2012) 138–40, 146–48.

137 Jo-Marie Burt, Gabriela Fried Amilivia and Francesca Lessa, 'Civil Society and the Resurgent Struggle against Impunity in Uruguay (1986–2012)' (2013) 7 *International Journal of Transitional Justice* 306, 319–22; Daniel Soltman, 'Applauding Uruguay's Quest for Justice: Dictatorship, Amnesty, and Repeal of Uruguay Law No. 15.848' (2013) 12 *Washington University Global Studies Law Review* 829, 835–37.

prosecutions were halted again following a decision of the Supreme Court in February 2013 declaring that the crimes of the dictatorship were not crimes against humanity but common crimes subject to statutory limitations.[138]

The road to overcoming impunity has also been tortuous in El Salvador, where the blanket amnesty law passed in the aftermath of the civil war in 1993 was eventually annulled by the Supreme Court in July 2016.[139] Legal challenges to the law had brought the Supreme Court to declare it inapplicable in cases involving violations of fundamental rights in 2000. However, only after the 2016 decision were concrete steps taken by the Salvadoran authorities to address the crimes of the civil war, including through the creation of a commission to search for disappeared persons and the reopening of an investigation into an infamous massacre in El Mozote.[140]

Two amnesty laws issued in the late 1970s still stand in Chile and Brazil notwithstanding repeated challenges. Although the Chilean amnesty of 1978 has not been formally repealed, domestic courts have found creative ways to circumvent it, particularly since the arrest of Augusto Pinochet in London in 1998.[141] A growing number of convictions have been pronounced against agents of the military regime as the amnesty law was found inapplicable with respect to a gradually expanding set of internationally prohibited crimes.[142] However, despite judicial activism, international and civil society pressure, Chilean political actors have not been prepared to allow the revocation of the amnesty law, which still enjoys some support among certain segments of the population.[143]

Brazil is the emblematic example of resistance to this regional trend in overturning amnesty laws inherited from an authoritarian past. As attacks against its 1979 amnesty law gained momentum in 2008, the Brazilian Bar Association

138 Lessa, Olsen, Payne, Pereira and Reiter, 'Overcoming Impunity: Pathways to Accountability in Latin America' (n 128) 95; Jo-Marie Burt and Francesca Lessa, 'Recent Sentence by Uruguayan Supreme Court Obstructs Search for Truth and Justice' *Washington Office on Latin America* (28 February 2013).

139 Naomi Roht-Arriaza, 'El Salvador's Constitutional Court Invalidates Amnesty Law: Will Prosecutions Follow?' *Intlawgrrls* (19 July 2016).

140 Emily Braid and Naomi Roht-Arriaza, 'De Facto and De Jure Amnesty Laws: The Central American Case' in Francesca Lessa and Leigh A Payne (eds), *Amnesty in the Age of Human Rights Accountability: Comparative and International Perspectives* (CUP 2012) 199; Geoff Thale, 'Tracking El Salvador's Progress in Historic Human Rights Cases' *Washington Office on Latin America* (27 October 2017).

141 Marny A Requa, 'A Human Rights Triumph? Dictatorship-era Crimes and the Chilean Supreme Court' (2012) 12(1) *Human Rights Law Review* 79; Cath Collins, 'Human Rights Trials in Chile during and after the "Pinochet Years"' (2010) 4 *International Journal of Transitional* Justice 67, 75–82; Fannie Lafontaine, 'No Amnesty or Statute of Limitation for Enforced Disappearances: The Sandoval Case before the Supreme Court of Chile' (2005) 3 *Journal of International Criminal Justice* 469.

142 Ibid.

143 Lessa, Olsen, Payne, Pereira and Reiter, 'Overcoming Impunity: Pathways to Accountability in Latin America' (n 128) 90–93.

challenged its constitutionality before the Federal Supreme Court.[144] In a majority decision of April 2010, the Supreme Court upheld the law by a vote of seven to two. It reasoned that the amnesty was the result of a political agreement reached within a particular historical context and that, by contrast with other Latin American amnesties, the Brazilian measure had enjoyed broad popular support at the time of its enactment.[145] The Court considered that the amnesty law was a necessary element of Brazil's peaceful democratic transition and an integral part of the current constitutional order.[146] Notwithstanding a judgment of the Inter-American Court condemning the law in the same year, it is still in full force and consistently applied by Brazilian courts.[147]

Africa

There have been less legal challenges to amnesties outside Latin America. The most well-known relates to the South African Promotion of National Unity and Reconciliation Act adopted in 1995 following the end of apartheid. This law created a Truth and Reconciliation Commission (TRC) empowered to grant amnesty with respect to politically motivated acts, including gross human rights violations, providing that the applicant made a full disclosure of all relevant facts.[148] The TRC's amnesty-granting power was challenged before the South African Constitutional Court in 1996.[149] Explaining the rationale of the amnesty-for-truth deal underpinning the TRC, the Court stressed that, without providing the incentive of amnesty to human rights violators, 'there is nothing to encourage such persons to make the disclosures and to reveal the truth which persons in the positions of the applicants so desperately desire'.[150] It also noted that article 6(5) of the Second Protocol to the Geneva Conventions encourages the grant of amnesty at the end of internal armed conflicts, emphasising that in the wake of such conflicts, the former adversaries have to coexist within the same territory and work together on reconciliation and reconstruction.[151] Considering that the TRC amnesty

144 Fabia Fernandes Carvalho Veçoso, 'Whose Exceptionalism? Debating the Inter-American View on Amnesty and the Brazilian Case' in Karen Eagle, Zinaida Miller and DM Davis (eds), *Anti-Impunity and the Human Rights Agenda* (CUP 2016) 200; Yi Shin Tang, 'International Justice through Domestic Courts: Challenges in Brazil's Judicial Review of the Amnesty Law' (2015) 9 *International Journal of Transitional Justice* 259, 262; Nina Schneider, 'Impunity in Post-Authoritarian Brazil: The Supreme Court's Recent Verdict on the Amnesty Law' (2011) 90 *European Review of Latin American and Caribbean Studies* 39, 49.

145 Tang (n 144) 262–63; Schneider (n 144) 49–50; Veçoso (n 144) 201.

146 Ibid.

147 *Gomes Lund et al. v Brazil* (n 132); Tang (n 144) 260.

148 Promotion of National Unity and Reconciliation Act 34 of 1995, section 20.

149 *Azanian Peoples Organization (AZAPO) and Others v President of the Republic of South Africa and Others*, Constitutional Court of South Africa, Case No CCT17/96 (25 July 1996).

150 Ibid, para 17.

151 Ibid, para 31.

process did not amount to a blanket amnesty, because immunity could only be granted following a determination by a committee that the applicant fulfilled the relevant conditions, the Court upheld its constitutionality.[152]

The way in which another African amnesty has been received at the domestic level is interesting because it gave rise to a dialogue between civil society, the judiciary, the executive and the legislative powers. The Ugandan amnesty law of 2000, applying broadly to all rebel fighters ready to surrender to the government, was challenged by the Director of Public Prosecution (DPP) before the Constitutional Court.[153] In a decision of September 2011, the Court upheld the law on the basis that, on the one hand, there was no consensus in international law regarding the status of amnesties, and, on the other, the law was consistent with 'national objectives and principles of State policy and our historical past which was characterized by political and constitutional instability'.[154] It also noted that the law was not akin to a blanket amnesty since it did not cover crimes committed by state agents and an amendment of 2006 permitted the government to exclude individuals from its benefits.

Uganda's amnesty law was enacted in response to a campaign by religious and civil society leaders for the peaceful resolution of the civil war in the northern part of the country.[155] When the government decided to let the law expire in May 2012, these civil society organisations petitioned the Parliament to reinstate the law.[156] According to the Parliamentary Committee that considered this petition, the government's decision not to renew the amnesty had been influenced by international donors and agencies, including the UN, which insisted on the principle that there could be no impunity for international crimes.[157] However, the Committee agreed with the Constitutional Court that 'there is no treaty obligation applicable to Uganda, neither is there any established rule of customary international law, which prevents a state from adopting an amnesty in relation to international crimes'.[158] As the conflict in Uganda was still ongoing and

152 Ibid, para 32.

153 Amnesty Act 2000 (Uganda), sections 3(1) and 4(1).

154 *Thomas Kwoyelo alias Latoni v Uganda*, Constitutional Court of Uganda, Petition No 036/11 (21 September 2011).

155 Gilbert M Khadiagala, 'The Role of the Acholi Religious Leaders Peace Initiative (ARLPI) in Peace Building in Northern Uganda' Case Study 2 (USAID, March 2001); Louise Mallinder, 'Uganda at a Crossroads: Narrowing the Amnesty?' Working Paper No 1, *Beyond Legalism: Amnesties, Transitions and Conflict Transformation* (Queen's University Belfast, March 2009) 19–22.

156 Fairway Communique of Traditional and Religious Leaders, Civil Society and other Organisations Concerning the Decision of the Minister of Internal Affairs of Uganda to Declare, on 23rd May, 2012, the Lapse of the Amnesty Provisions of the Amnesty Act of Uganda (The Amnesty Act (Declaration of Lapse of the Operation of Part II)) Instrument, 2012 (12 June 2012).

157 Parliament of Uganda, Report of the Committee on Defence and Internal Affairs on the petition on the lapsing of part II of the Amnesty Act, 2000 (August 2013) para 9(7).

158 Ibid, para 9(36).

the amnesty process was supported by the affected communities, the Committee recommended its reinstatement and extension for a further period of two years.[159]

The next chapter of the Ugandan amnesty controversy involved an appeal by the DPP to Uganda's Supreme Court against the judgment of the Constitutional Court upholding the amnesty law. In a decision of April 2015, the Supreme Court confirmed that the law did not amount to a blanket amnesty because it only covered acts 'committed in the furtherance of war or armed rebellion'.[160] This language implied that the DPP had to verify whether every applicant qualified for amnesty. The Supreme Court observed that:

> [I]t is difficult to see how acts of genocide against a given population, or the wilful killing of innocent civilians in their homes when there is no military necessity, can be regarded as being in furtherance of the war or rebellion.[161]

Although it accepted that 'there are no uniform standards or practices in respect of amnesty', it found that 'there appears to be a minimum below which amnesty provisions may not be permitted in respect of grave crimes as recognized in international law'.[162] The Court thus ruled that the 2000 amnesty law was not applicable to international crimes. Yet, in the latest development to date, the African Commission on Human and Peoples' Rights considered that the refusal of the Ugandan government to grant amnesty to an individual charged with war crimes, in the absence of an amendment to the law to exclude serious crimes from its scope, amounted to a violation of the principle of equality before the law.[163]

Asia

In 2004, the Parliament of Indonesia adopted a law creating a truth and reconciliation commission mandated to investigate large-scale human rights violations committed during the transition to the military regime of President Soeharto in 1965.[164] The law entrusted the commission with the power to recommend

159 Ibid, paras 13(1)-(3) and 14. The amnesty law was reinstated and extended for a further period of two years in May 2013, see The Amnesty Act (Revocation of Statutory Instrument No. 34 of 2012) Instrument, 24 May 2013; The Amnesty Act (Extension of Expiry Period) Instrument, 24 May 2013.

160 *Uganda v Thomas Kwoyelo*, Supreme Court of Uganda, Constitutional Appeal No 1 of 2012 (8 April 2015).

161 Ibid.

162 Ibid.

163 *Thomas Kwoyelo v Uganda*, ACHPR Communication 431/12 (17 October 2018) para 181, discussed in ch 6 of this volume.

164 Patrick Burgess, 'De Facto Amnesty? The Example of Post-Soeharto Indonesia' in Francesca Lessa and Leigh A Payne (eds), *Amnesty in the Age of Human Rights Accountability: Comparative and International Perspectives* (CUP 2012) 280–81.

amnesty for serious human rights violations, thus prompting human rights organisations to challenge it before the Constitutional Court.[165] The amnesty provision was declared unconstitutional and, to the dismay of the petitioners, the Court decided to quash the entire law, marking the end of the projected truth commission.[166]

A similar amnesty provision was nonetheless incorporated into the terms of reference of the bilateral Commission on Truth and Friendship (CTF) created by the governments of Indonesia and East Timor in 2005 to investigate the crimes committed in connection with the referendum of independence of East Timor in 1999.[167] The CTF was empowered to 'recommend amnesty for those involved in human rights violations who cooperate fully in revealing the truth'.[168] The terms of reference also specified that '[b]ased on the spirit of a forward looking and reconciliatory approach, the CTF process will not lead to prosecution' or 'recommend the establishment of any other judicial body'.[169] Human rights organisations and the UN denounced this instrument as incompatible with international standards and boycotted the CTF.[170] However, the commission's final report released in 2008 exceeded expectations by refraining from recommending amnesties and establishing as one of its main findings that crimes against humanity had been committed in East Timor with the knowledge and support of Indonesian officials.[171]

The process of establishing a truth and reconciliation commission in Nepal pursuant to the peace agreement of 2006 which halted the conflict between the government and the Maoist rebel group, was also marred by controversies regarding the commission's power to recommend amnesty.[172] The 2013 Act creating the commission was struck out by Nepal's Supreme Court in January 2014 on account of its amnesty provision, which did not exclude serious human

165 Ibid.

166 Ibid; Decision of the Indonesian National Constitutional Court No. 006/PUU-IV/2006 (7 December 2006) 24.

167 Terms of Reference for the Commission of Truth and Friendship Established by the Republic of Indonesia and the Democratic Republic of Timor-Leste (10 March 2005). On the transitional mechanisms put in place in East Timor to deal with this violent episode, see Lia Kent, 'Beyond "Pragmatism" versus "Principle": Ongoing Justice Debates in East Timor' in Renée Jeffery and Hun Joon Kim (eds), *Transitional Justice in the Asia-Pacific* (CUP 2014).

168 Terms of Reference for the Commission of Truth and Friendship (n 167) para 14(c)(i).

169 Ibid, para 13(c) and (e).

170 UN News Centre, 'Timor-Leste: UN to boycott truth panel unless it bars amnesty for gross abuses' (26 July 2007); Megan Hirst, 'Too Much Friendship, Too Little Truth: Monitoring Report on the Commission of Truth and Friendship in Indonesia and Timor-Leste' Occasional Paper Series (International Center for Transitional Justice, January 2008).

171 Commission of Truth and Friendship (Indonesia/East Timor), *PerMemoriam Ad Spem (From Memory to Hope): Final Report of the Commission for Truth and Friendship* (March 2008) ch 8. See Kent (n 167) 188.

172 Comprehensive Peace Agreement between the Government of Nepal and the Communist Party of Nepal (Maoist) 21 November 2006, art 5.2.5. See Jeffery (n 123) 357–62.

rights violations.[173] A new law of April 2014 was quashed again by the same Court in February 2015 because it still allowed amnesty for serious crimes.[174] Throughout this process, the UN made clear to the Nepalese government that it could not condone amnesty in these terms and would not support the truth and reconciliation process if the law was not amended.[175] This stance of the UN has been criticised for depriving an institution dedicated to accountability from much-needed support.[176] In May 2016, as the commission started to function, a deal was reached between the government and the Maoist party providing for the termination of criminal proceedings and the grant of amnesty for all war-related offences.[177]

Europe

Some European states have been contradictory in their attitude towards amnesties, relying on universal jurisdiction to deny effect to foreign amnesty laws but refusing to unravel long-standing amnesties still blocking the prosecution of human rights abusers in their country. In Spain, the prosecution of international crimes committed abroad was allowed by a far-reaching law on universal jurisdiction which has since been considerably restricted.[178] On this basis, Judges Garzón and Castellón issued arrest warrants for the leaders of Chile's and Argentina's military regimes, whose prosecution at home was barred by amnesty measures.[179] In 1998, the *Audiencia Nacional* (the Spanish Court competent to deal with international crimes committed abroad) rejected a challenge based on these amnesties on the ground that they could not be effective in preventing the prosecution in Spain of crimes subject to universal jurisdiction.[180]

Spanish courts did not adopt the same accountability-oriented approach with respect to grave human rights abuses perpetrated in Spain before the democratic transition. When Judge Garzón started investigating crimes connected with the Franco regime, he was sued for overstepping his power and breaching the

173 Ordinance on Investigation of Disappeared Persons, Truth and Reconciliation Commission (March 2013) s 23.

174 Commission on Investigation of Disappeared Persons, Truth and Reconciliation Act (25 April 2014) s 26. See Jeffery (n 123) 360.

175 UN Office of the High Commissioner for Human Rights, 'Nepal: OHCHR position on UN support to the Commission on Investigation of Disappeared Persons and the Truth and Reconciliation Commission (16 February 2016).

176 Jeffery (n 123) 362.

177 'Oli, Dahal sign 9-pt deal', Nepal Republic Media (6 May 2016); Human Rights Watch, 'Nepal: 9-Point Deal Undermines Transitional Justice' (12 May 2016).

178 Art 23(4) of Organic Act No 6/1985 on the Judiciary (1 July 1985).

179 See Richard J Wilson, 'Prosecuting Pinochet: International Crimes in Spanish Domestic Law' (1999) 21 *Human Rights Quarterly* 927, 932–38.

180 Ibid, 952–56. In 2005, the *Audiencia National* convicted Adolfo Scilingo for crimes committed during military rule in Argentina, see Christian Tomuschat, 'Issues of Universal Jurisdiction in the Scilingo Case' (2005) 3 *Journal of International Criminal Justice* 1074.

Spanish amnesty law of 1977. In a decision of February 2012, the Spanish Supreme Court dismissed the charges against him but precluded future attempts to inquire into the crimes of the Franco era.[181] It upheld the amnesty law and defended it as the product of a broad social consensus having permitted reconciliation and democracy in Spain.[182] A few weeks later, the European Court of Human Rights dismissed an application from the family members of a person disappeared during the Spanish civil war on the ground that they had waited too long before petitioning the Court, without commenting on the obstacle presented by the Spanish amnesty law.[183] In April 2014, closing yet another avenue for Spanish victims, the *Audiencia Nacional* rejected an Argentine request for the extradition of former officials of the authoritarian regime.[184]

French courts have also relied on universal jurisdiction to prosecute a Mauritanian officer for acts of torture notwithstanding the amnesty law from which he benefited in his home country.[185] However, they have consistently declined to overrule an amnesty law of 1968 barring the prosecution of international crimes and gross human rights violations committed by French security forces during the Algerian War of Independence.[186] The Court of Cassation has on several occasions refused to recognise the crimes committed in Algeria and other colonial contexts as crimes against humanity on the ground that they pre-dated the entry into force of the criminal code of 1994 which introduced the prohibition of crimes against humanity into French law.[187] In two decisions of 2000 and 2003, it declared that, because the crimes committed in Algeria may not be qualified as crimes against humanity, they are covered by the amnesty law of 1968.[188] This circular reasoning has permitted French courts to uphold the 1968 amnesty law while maintaining the appearance of complying with international standards condemning amnesty for international crimes. As a result, a

181 Naomi Roht-Arriaza, 'The Spanish Civil War, Amnesty, and the Trials of Judge Garzón' (25 July 2012) 16(24) *American Society of International Law Insights* 3; Jennifer Easterday, 'Spain: 1977 amnesty law "all tied up & well tied up"' *IntLawGrrls* (6 March 2012).

182 Ibid.

183 *Gutierrez Dorado and Dorado Ortiz v Spain* App No 30141/09 (ECtHR, 27 March 2012) para 39.

184 Universal Jurisdiction Annual Review 2015, *Make Way for Justice* (Trial, ECCHR, Fidh) 5.

185 See *Ould Dah v France* (2009) 48(4) International Legal Materials 871, 872.

186 See Juliette Lelieur-Fischer, 'Prosecuting the Crimes against Humanity Committed during the Algerian War: an Impossible Endeavour? The 2003 Decision of the French Court of Cassation in Aussaresses' (2004) 2 *Journal of International Criminal Justice* 231.

187 Before the adoption of the 1994 Penal Code, crimes against humanity could only be prosecuted in France on the basis of a 1964 law recognising crimes against humanity as defined in the Nuremberg Charter as imprescriptible. In several cases against Klaus Barbie, Paul Touvier and Boudarel in the 1980s and 1990s, the Court of Cassation interpreted the notion of crimes against humanity as applying solely to acts committed in the interest of the Nazi Regime in the World War II context. See ibid; Shiva Eftekhari, 'France and the Algerian War: From a Policy of "Forgetting" to a Framework for Accountability' (2003) 34 *Columbia Human Rights Law Review* 413, 427–28.

188 Lelieur-Fischer (n 186) 241–42.

French general was able to publish a book in 2000 detailing the crimes he ordered or committed against civilians in Algeria, including torture, disappearances and summary executions, without fear of being prosecuted.

Conclusion

The UN has been the driving force in the development of an international policy rule prohibiting amnesty for international crimes and serious human rights violations. This rule forms part of a set of international standards designed to combat impunity for serious crimes including an obligation to prosecute the perpetrators, provide reparation to the victims, and a ban on statutory limitations. While UN member states have supported some of these principles, they have consistently refrained from subscribing to the rule rejecting amnesties. This may partly be explained by their continuing reliance on leniency measures in transitional contexts. Appreciating the enduring avail of amnesties following situations of mass violence, international experts have been more nuanced than the UN by acknowledging that amnesties may be acceptable in certain circumstances, notably when they are necessary to end an armed conflict and are linked to accountability mechanisms. The authors of the Belfast Guidelines, in particular, have emphasised that amnesties may play a positive role in transitional contexts by complementing prosecutorial strategies and alternative accountability mechanisms.

International standards against impunity and the efforts of the UN and human rights organisations to ensure accountability for serious crimes have had an impact on the practice of states in relation to amnesties. On the one hand, though amnesties continue to be frequently used in order to facilitate peace settlements, there has been a growing trend in excluding serious crimes from the scope of pacification amnesties in the last two decades. Indeed, since 2010, over a third of peace agreement amnesties have included an exception for international crimes. On the other hand, several amnesty laws applying to serious crimes have been overturned or circumvented in recent years as a result of domestic legal challenges. While an increasing number of amnesties have been limited a priori or a posteriori so as to exclude serious crimes, these trends have not been general or widespread. The practice of inserting exceptions for serious crimes within peace agreement amnesties has been heavily influenced by the role of the UN as peace negotiator and mostly limited to the African continent. As to the recent tendency to repeal or restrict amnesty laws covering serious crimes, it has primarily concerned Latin American amnesties previously condemned by Inter-American human rights institutions. Even within the regions where these trends have been prevalent, they have not been generalised as outliers persist.

The practice of states and intergovernmental organisations with respect to amnesty laws in the last half-century has been far from uniform. Certain international actors like the UN, human rights bodies and organisations have placed pressure on states to exclude serious crimes from the reach of amnesties and overturn blanket amnesty laws. National actors such as proactive judges and civil society groups have also in several cases taken action towards the restriction of amnesty laws so as to permit the prosecution of perpetrators of serious crimes. However, other international and domestic actors have refrained from following this trend or actively resisted it by issuing, endorsing or upholding amnesty laws covering serious crimes. Some of them have adopted an ambivalent attitude condemning blanket amnesties in general but allowing some flexibility when such measures are necessary as part of efforts to bring an end to violent conflict or repression. Even the UN has recently supported certain amnesty deals contrasting with its otherwise firm prohibitive stance. Thus, the practice of states and intergovernmental organisations in rejecting the applicability of amnesty to serious crimes has not been general or consistent, undermining the view that an amnesty ban has emerged under customary international law.

6 The right to a remedy

Introduction

This chapter examines the position of international human rights law on amnesties extending to serious crimes. General human rights treaties do not refer to amnesty or require the prosecution of human rights offenders. Nonetheless, human rights treaty bodies have derived an obligation to investigate serious human rights violations and, in some cases, to prosecute the persons responsible, from treaty provisions requiring states to protect human rights and guarantee a remedy to victims of violations. Accordingly, treaty bodies have considered that amnesties barring any form of investigation or redress for serious human rights violations are contrary to international human rights law. However, they have diverged as regards the rationale of the amnesty prohibition and the question of whether it is absolute or admits exceptions in special circumstances. The chapter analyses the parameters of this rule in the case law of the UN Human Rights Committee, the Inter-American Court and Commission on Human Rights, the European Court and Commission on Human Rights, and the African Commission on Human and People's Rights. While some of these bodies have adopted an inflexible position condemning all types of amnesties extending to human rights crimes, there is no unanimous acceptance of the existence of an absolute ban.

1. Amnesty and the right to a remedy in general human rights treaties

The only provision of a human rights treaty explicitly mentioning amnesty is article 6(4) of the International Covenant on Civil and Political Rights (ICCPR) providing that '[a]nyone sentenced to death shall have the right to seek pardon or commutation of the sentence. Amnesty, pardon or commutation of the sentence of death may be granted in all cases'.[1] This provision was introduced for humanitarian reasons in order 'to mitigate the death penalty in countries where it was still imposed by giving persons sentenced to death the right to seek

1 International Covenant on Civil and Political Rights (adopted 16 December 1966, entered into force 23 March 1976) 999 UNTS 171 (ICCPR), art 6(4).

pardon or commutation of the sentence'.[2] An earlier version of the first sentence provided that 'anyone sentenced to death shall have the right to seek amnesty, or pardon, or commutation of the sentence'.[3] However, it was though inappropriate to provide for a right 'to seek' amnesty since this measure was of a collective nature and granted by the authorities on their own initiative.[4] The reference to amnesty in the second sentence was retained to make clear that clemency measures of any kind may be granted to persons sentenced to death. The Covenant's provision on amnesty thus envisages it in a positive light, as a safeguard against the death penalty.

No general human rights treaties prohibit amnesty or impose an obligation to prosecute human rights violations. However, human rights treaty bodies have interpreted their constitutive instrument as requiring states to investigate violations of fundamental rights such as the right to life and to personal integrity and, in some cases, prosecute and punish offenders. This duty has been grounded, on the one hand, in the general provision of human rights treaties requiring states parties to protect and guarantee human rights, and, on the other hand, in the right to a remedy of victims of human rights violations. On these bases, human rights bodies have generally considered that amnesties preventing the investigation of grave human rights violations are incompatible with international human rights law.

The question of how to deal with perpetrators of human rights violations was seldom raised during the negotiation of general human rights treaties.[5] The drafting of the remedy provision of the first regional human rights convention – the European Convention on Human Rights (ECHR) – gave rise to a discussion on the type of domestic authority that should be competent to hear cases involving human rights violations.[6] Article 13 of the ECHR was modelled on article 8 of the Universal Declaration of Human Rights providing that '[e]veryone has the right to an effective remedy by the competent national tribunals for acts violating the fundamental rights granted him by the constitution or by

2 Draft International Covenant on Human Rights, Annotation prepared by the Secretary General (1 July 1955) UN Doc A/2929, para 9. See Marc J Bossuyt, *Guide to the 'Travaux Préparatoires' of the International Covenant on Civil and Political Rights* (Martinus Nijhoff Publishers 1987) 138–40.

3 Ibid.

4 Ibid.

5 Convention for the Protection of Human Rights and Fundamental Freedoms (adopted 1 November 1950, entered into force 3 September 1953) 213 UNTS 222 (European Convention on Human Rights – ECHR), art 13; ICCPR (n 1) art 2(3); American Convention on Human Rights (adopted 22 November 1969, entered into force 18 July 1978) 1144 UNTS 123 (ACHR) art 25; African Charter on Human and Peoples' Rights (adopted 27 June 1981, entered into force 21 October 1986) 1520 UNTS 217 (ACHPR), art 7(1).

6 European Commission of Human Rights, Preparatory work on article 13 of the ECHR, DH (57) 5 (Strasbourg, 10 May 1957) 2–3. See also Council of Europe, *Collected Edition of the 'Travaux Préparatoires' of the European Convention of Human Rights* (Martinus Nijhoff 1975).

law'.[7] The first drafts of article 13 accordingly prescribed that an independent tribunal or judicial authority would be competent to decide on the appropriate remedy.[8] However, the language eventually adopted in the plenary assembly merely referred to a 'national authority'.[9] This broader formulation was introduced in the Committee of Experts on Human Rights which explained that '[t]he national authority envisaged in this Article may be an administrative or legal court'.[10] No more was said on the substance of article 13 or the nature of the remedy protected. Decisions on the appropriate form of remedy and the type of institution competent to grant it were thus left to the discretion of domestic authorities.

The same issue was discussed during the drafting of the remedy provision of the ICCPR – article 2(3).[11] While the UK delegate proposed that it should refer to 'national tribunals', the US representative observed that this 'overlooked the fact that many of the rights depended upon political action and might be subject to political considerations, which was inevitable when individual rights were set against the rights of a whole people'.[12] A Belgian proposal referring to 'political, administrative or judicial' authorities was eventually adopted.[13] During the next stage of the negotiation, the advisability of retaining the reference to political authorities was called into question.[14] Some delegations believed that only judicial and, where relevant, administrative authorities should be competent to adjudicate on human rights matters. On the other hand, certain participants noted that in some countries the only form of redress available against the decisions of specific organs involved recourse to a political authority. The final version of article 2(3) provides that remedies shall be 'determined by competent judicial, administrative, or legislative authorities, or by any other competent authorities provided for by the legal system of the State'.[15] This wording allows for the grant of remedies by legislative and executive authorities without mentioning the word 'political' which some delegations found objectionable.

It does not appear that the drafters of human rights treaties intended to place an obligation on states parties to initiate criminal proceedings with respect to breaches of fundamental rights. The inclusive language used in remedy provisions rather suggests that states meant to keep the options open and leave the

7 ECHR (n 5); Universal Declaration of Human Rights, adopted by General Assembly Resolution 217A (III) of 10 December 1948, UN Doc A/810 (1948).
8 Preparatory work on art 13 of the ECHR (n 6) 5–8.
9 Ibid, 14.
10 Ibid, 11–12.
11 ICCPR (n 1).
12 UNCHR, UK amendment to art 2 (29 March 1950) UN Doc E/CN.4/374; UNCHR, summary record of the 138th meeting (6 April 1950) UN Doc E/CN.4/SR.138, para 74. See Bossuyt (n 2) 67.
13 UNCHR, summary record of the 195th meeting (29 May 1950) UN Doc E/CN.4/SR.195, para 20.
14 Bossuyt (n 2) 68–69.
15 ICCPR (n 1) art 2(3).

determination of the appropriate body and type of remedy to domestic legislation. This is consistent with the broad range of remedies available under international human rights law in response to different types of human rights violations, depending on their nature and gravity. According to Dinah Shelton:

> [S]ubstantive redress can have several aims, from victim-oriented restitutio in integrum and full compensation for pecuniary and non-pecuniary losses to deterrence of violations for the benefit of all members of society. The types of remedies will depend upon the nature of the case, but a growing consensus on minimum standards includes restitution where possible and compensation where not and the right to the truth.[16]

While it is now generally accepted that criminal proceedings are the appropriate way to respond to serious violations of fundamental rights, suggestions in this sense were scarcely made during the negotiation of human rights treaties.[17] In relation to the remedy provision of the ICCPR, the delegate of the Philippines proposed to insert a sentence requiring that '[v]iolators shall be swiftly brought to the law, especially when they are public officials'.[18] This amendment was rejected, however, suggesting that states did not understand the notion of remedy as referring exclusively to criminal justice. Since amnesties preclude the prosecution of offenders but not necessarily investigatory proceedings, civil remedies or alternative forms of reparation, not all amnesties would conflict with a literal interpretation of the remedy provisions of general human rights conventions. However, as will now be examined, each human rights court or treaty body has adopted its own interpretation of the obligations of states and the rights of the victims in response to serious human rights violations.

2. Amnesty in the case law of human rights courts and bodies

The Human Rights Committee

The Human Rights Committee (HRC) is an expert body established to monitor the implementation of the ICCPR.[19] In its general comment of 1992 concerning the right to be free from torture, it made one of the first pronouncements on the compatibility of amnesties with human rights. Noting that some states had granted amnesty in relation to acts of torture, it declared that:

16 Dinah Shelton, *Remedies in International Human Rights Law* (2nd edn, OUP 2006) 9.

17 On the drafting history of the ACHR, see Thomas Buergenthal and Robert E Norris (eds), *Human Rights: The Inter-American System* (Oceana Publications, Dobbs Ferry N.Y. 1982) pt 2.

18 UNCHR, summary record of the 195th meeting (29 May 1950) UN Doc E/CN.4/SR.195, para 24.

19 See ICCPR (n 1) pt 4.

> Amnesties are generally incompatible with the duty of States to investigate such acts; to guarantee freedom from such acts within their jurisdiction; and to ensure that they do not occur in the future. States may not deprive individuals of the right to an effective remedy, including compensation and such full rehabilitation as may be possible.[20]

By using the word 'generally', the Committee did not rule out the possibility that some amnesties might be acceptable under the ICCPR. However, it made clear that those preventing the investigation of acts of torture and depriving the victims of redress are not.

The following year, in a case brought against Jamaica by a victim of torture, the HRC held that the state was:

> [U]nder an obligation to investigate the allegations made by the author with a view to instituting as appropriate criminal or other procedures against those found responsible and to take such other measures as may be necessary to prevent similar violations from occurring in the future.[21]

While this statement seems to indicate that procedures short of criminal prosecution might be appropriate to deal with perpetrators of torture, the Committee specified in subsequent cases that 'purely disciplinary and administrative remedies cannot be deemed to constitute adequate and effective remedies … in the event of particularly serious violations of human rights'.[22] In such cases, it has considered that states are under an obligation not only to investigate but also 'to criminally prosecute, try and punish those deemed responsible'.[23] For example, in *Basilio Laureano Atachahua v Peru* (1996), the Committee urged the state to investigate a case of disappearance, compensate the victim's family and 'bring to justice those responsible for her disappearance, notwithstanding any domestic amnesty legislation to the contrary'.[24]

In its general comment on article 2 (2004), the HRC specified that a duty to bring offenders to justice arises 'notably in respect of those violations recognized as criminal under either domestic or international law, such as torture and similar

20 UN Human Rights Committee (UNHRC), 'General Comment no 20: Article 7' (3 April 1992) UN Doc HRI/GEN/1/Rev.1, para 15.

21 UNHRC, *Thomas v Jamaica*, Communication no 321/1988 (1993) UN Doc CCPR/C/49/D/321/1988, para 11.

22 UNHRC, *José Vicente et al. v Colombia*, Communication no 612/1995 (1994) UN Doc CCPR/C/60/D/612/1995, para 8.2; UNHRC, *Bautista de Arellana v Colombia*, Communication no 563/1993 (1995) UN Doc CCPR/C/55/D/563/1993, para 8.2.

23 *José Vicente et al. v Colombia* (n 22) para 8.8; *Bautista de Arellana v Colombia* (n 22) para 10; UNHRC, *Bousroual v Algeria*, Communication no 992/2001 (2006) UN Doc CCPR/C/86/D/992/2001, para 11; UNHRC, *Njaru v Cameroon*, Communication no 1353/2005 (2007) UN Doc CCPR/C/89/D/1353/2005, para 8.

24 UNHRC, *Basilio Laureano Atachahua v Peru*, Communication no 540/1993 (1996) UN Doc CCPR/C/56/D/540/1993, para 10.

cruel, inhuman and degrading treatment ... , summary and arbitrary killing ... and enforced disappearance ... '.[25] It also stressed that, when grave violations are carried out by state agents, 'the States Parties concerned may not relieve perpetrators from personal responsibility, as has occurred with certain amnesties'.[26]

Where the Committee has urged states to hold perpetrators accountable, it has usually done so on the basis that the investigation of serious violations and the prosecution of the persons responsible is necessary to give effect to the right to a remedy protected by article 2(3) of the ICCPR.[27] While it has recognised that this right entitles the victims to demand an official investigation into the circumstances of the violation as well as compensation for the harm suffered, the HRC has consistently rejected claims that the ICCPR guarantees a right to criminal justice.[28] Indeed, even in cases where it required state action towards the investigation and prosecution of human rights violations on the basis of article 2(3), it made clear that 'the Covenant does not provide that private individuals have a right to demand that the State criminally prosecute another person'.[29] This approach has been criticised by Anja Seibert-Fohr on the ground that '[i]f the Human Rights Committee requires punishment as a remedy it is inconsistent to deny a corresponding individual right'.[30]

As a justification for the duty to bring to justice perpetrators of serious violations, the Committee has also emphasised that an effective criminal law response is necessary to ensure that such violations are not repeated in the future.[31] In its concluding observations on state reports, it has repeatedly held that the absence of reaction by public authorities when fundamental rights have been violated contributes to 'an atmosphere of impunity which may undermine the democratic order and give rise to further grave human rights violations'.[32]

25 UNHRC, 'General Comment no 31: The Nature of the General Legal Obligation Imposed on States Parties to the Covenant (Art. 2)' (26 May 2004) UN Doc CCPR/C/21/Rev.1/Add.13, para 18.

26 Ibid.

27 *Basilio Laureano Atachahua v Peru* (n 24) para 10; *Bautista de Arellana v Colombia* (n 22) para 10; *Bousroual v Algeria* (n 23) para 11; *Njaru v Cameroon* (n 23) para 8. On the rationale of the obligation to bring human rights offenders to justice under the ICCPR, see Anja Seibert-Fohr, *Prosecuting Serious Human Rights Violations* (OUP 2009) 15–27.

28 'General Comment no 20: Article 7' (n 20) para 14; 'General Comment no 31' (n 25) paras 15–16; UNHRC, 'General Comment no 6: Article 6 (Right to Life)' (1982) UN Doc HRI/GEN/1/Rev.1 at 6 (1994) para 4. See Seibert-Fohr (n 27) 34–37.

29 *Sundara Arachchige Lalith Rajapakse v Sri Lanka*, Communication no 1250/2004 (2006) UN Doc CCPR/C/87/D/1250/2004, para 9.3; *José Vicente et al. v Colombia* (n 22) para 8.8; *Rodríguez v Uruguay*, Communication no 322/1988 (1994) UN Doc CCPR/C/51/D/322/1988, para 8.8; UNHRC, *HCMA v The Netherlands*, Communication no 213/1986 (1989) UN Doc Supp. No 40 (A/44/40) para 11.6.

30 Seibert-Fohr (n 27) 27.

31 'General Comment no. 31' (n 25) para 18; *Rodríguez v Uruguay* (n 29) para 12.4.

32 UNHRC, 'Concluding Observations on Uruguay' (1993) UN Doc CCPR/C/79/Add.19, para 7; UNHRC, 'Concluding Observations on El Salvador' (1994) UN Doc A/49/40, para 4; UNHRC, 'Concluding Observations on Argentina' (1995) UN Doc A/50/40, para 153;

Accordingly, the Committee has generally denounced amnesty laws extending to serious human rights violations.[33] For example, it has condemned the amnesty laws enacted in Uruguay, Chile, El Salvador, Argentina, Haiti, Yemen, Peru, Croatia, Sudan, Algeria, Spain, Colombia, Sierra Leone and Nepal.[34]

The HRC has not, however, been entirely consistent in this practice. In its reports on Uganda, Brazil, Angola and Mozambique, it refrained from criticising the broad and unlimited amnesty laws in force in those countries.[35] It is unclear whether these omissions amounted to mere oversights or resulted from a deliberate decision not to criticise amnesties considered as more acceptable on some levels.[36] In its recent report on South Africa, the Committee commended the state 'for the work of the Truth and Reconciliation Commission in investigating gross human rights violations perpetrated during the apartheid era'.[37] Although it urged South Africa to implement the recommendations of the Commission regarding the prosecution of perpetrators and the provision of reparations to victims, it did not mention the fact that the Commission granted amnesty to a number of persons responsible for grave human rights violations.[38] The avoidance of any reference to

UNHRC, 'Concluding Observations on Haiti' (1995) UN Doc A/50/40, para 230; UNHRC, 'Concluding Observations on Yemen' (1995) UN Doc A/50/40, para 252; UNHRC, 'Concluding Observations on Peru' (1996) UN Doc A/51/40, para 347.

33 Ibid; UNHRC, 'Concluding Observations on Uruguay' (1998) UN Doc CCPR/C/79/Add.90, para 7; UNHRC, 'Concluding Observations on Chile' (1999) UN Doc CCPR/C/79/Add.104, para 7; UNHRC, 'Concluding Observations on Croatia' (2001) UN Doc CCPR/CO/71/HRV, para 11.

34 Ibid. See also *Rodríguez v Uruguay* (n 29) para 12.4; UNHCR, 'Concluding Observations on Chile' (18 May 2007) UN Doc CCPR/C/CHL/CO/5, para 5; UNHCR, 'Concluding Observations on Chile' (13 August 2014) UN Doc CCPR/C/CHL/CO/6, para 9; UNHCR, 'Concluding Observations on El Salvador' (22 August 2003) UN Doc CCPR/CO/78/SLV, para 6; UNHCR, 'Concluding Observations on El Salvador' (18 November 2010) UN Doc CCPR/C/SLV/CO/6, para 5; UNHCR, 'Concluding Observations on Yemen' (23 April 2012) UN Doc CCPR/C/YEM/CO/5, para 6; UNHCR, 'Concluding Observations on Sudan' (29 August 2007) UN Doc CCPR/C/SDN/CO/3, para 9; UNHCR, 'Concluding Observations on Algeria' (12 December 2007) UN Doc CCPR/C/DZA/CO/3, para 7; UNHCR, 'Concluding Observations on Spain' (5 January 2009) UN Doc CCPR/C/ESP/CO/5, para 9; UNHCR 'Concluding Observations on Colombia' (4 August 2010) UN Doc CCPR/C/COL/CO/6, para 9; UNHCR, 'Concluding Observations on Sierra Leone' (17 April 2014) UN Doc CCPR/C/SLE/CO/1, para 17; UNHCR, 'Concluding Observations on Nepal' (15 April 2014) UN Doc CCPR/C/NPL/CO/2, para 5.

35 UNHRC, 'Concluding Observations on Uganda' (4 May 2004) UN Doc CCPR/CO/80/UGA; UNHCR, 'Concluding Observations on Brazil' (1 December 2005) UN Doc CCPR/C/BRA/CO/2; UNHCR, 'Concluding Observations on Angola' (29 April 2013) UN Doc CCPR/C/AGO/CO/1; UNHCR, 'Concluding Observations on Mozambique' (19 November 2013) UN Doc CCPR/C/MOZ/CO/1.

36 A distinctive feature of these amnesties is that they were either passed in response to public demands, as in Uganda and Brazil, or as part of a compromise between warring parties to end a protracted armed conflict, as in Mozambique and Angola, see ch 3 in this volume.

37 UNHRC, 'Concluding Observations on the Initial Report of South Africa' (27 April 2016) UN Doc CCPR/C/ZAF/CO/1, para 12.

38 Ibid, paras 12–13.

this well-known amnesty process may be seen as an implicit admission that not all types of amnesties warrant an outright condemnation.

The Inter-American system of human rights

The Inter-American Commission and Court of Human Rights are the human rights bodies having dealt with the highest number of cases involving amnesties. Their approach on issues of amnesty and accountability has gradually toughened in reaction to the climate of impunity that pervaded Latin America in the last decades of the twentieth century.[39] In that period, broad amnesties were enacted by a majority of South American and Central American states in connection with an armed conflict or regime change.[40] The grave human rights violations that were committed on a massive scale during these periods of turmoil and the generalised lack of accountability in response thereto prompted Inter-American institutions to develop robust standards on the duty to prosecute and punish human rights offenders. From these standards, a principle of unacceptability of amnesty for serious crimes was progressively derived.

Development of the duty to investigate and prosecute serious human rights violations

In its annual report of 1985–1986, the Inter-American Commission on Human Rights commented on an amnesty decreed in Guatemala upon the transfer of power from a military regime responsible for widespread human rights violations to a democratically elected government.[41] The Commission expressed concern that this amnesty could paralyse the investigation of past abuses but acknowledged the 'political limitations inherent in a country where representative

39 See generally Ellen Lutz, 'Responses to Amnesties by the Inter-American System for the Protection of Human Rights' in David J Harris and Stephen Livingstone (eds), *The Inter-American System of Human Rights* (Clarendon Press 1998); Brian D Tittemore, 'Ending Impunity in the Americas: The Role of the Inter-American Human Rights System in Advancing Accountability for Serious Crimes Under International Law' (2006) 12 *Southwestern Journal of Law and Trade in the Americas* 429; Douglass Cassel, 'Lessons from the Americas: Guidelines for International Response to Amnesties for Atrocities' (1996) 59(4) *Law and Contemporary Problems* 197.

40 For example, in the second half of the twentieth century, amnesties were issued in Chile, Argentina, Uruguay, Brazil, Bolivia, Peru, Ecuador, Colombia, Venezuela, Panama, Nicaragua, Honduras, El Salvador and Guatemala. See Leigh A Payne, Tricia D Olsen and Andrew G Reiter, *Transitional Justice Database Project* <www.tjdbproject.com> accessed 7 November 2018.

41 Inter-American Commission on Human Rights, Annual Report of 1985–1986, OEA/Ser.L/V/II.68, doc. 8, ch 4 (26 September 1986). See also Inter-American Commission on Human Rights, Report on the Situation of Human Rights in the Republic of Guatemala, OEA/Series L/V/II/61 doc.47 (1983).

democracy has just been established and where the armed forces still have a great degree of actual power'.[42]

In the report's general comment on the situation of human rights in Latin America, the Commission adopted a similarly cautious approach. It observed that the investigation and punishment of crimes committed under a previous regime is a 'sensitive and extremely delicate issue' to which international bodies' contribution can only be minimal.[43] Accordingly, it considered that 'the appropriate democratic institutions – usually the legislature – with the participation of all the representative sectors, are the only ones called upon to determine whether or not to decree an amnesty or the scope thereof'.[44] On the other hand, it stressed that 'amnesties decreed previously by those responsible for the violations have no juridical validity'.[45]

The Commission underlined the need to investigate human rights violations in order to uphold the inalienable right of societies and victims to know the truth about past events. However, it acknowledged that this right must be balanced with 'the urgent need for national reconciliation and social pacification' in countries recovering from a violent past in order to 'bring about justice rather than vengeance' and ensure that 'neither the urgent need for national reconciliation nor the consolidation of democratic government will be jeopardized'.[46] This nuanced position was reiterated in the Commission's annual report of 1993 with respect to an amnesty law enacted in Nicaragua.[47]

Velasquez Rodriguez v Honduras (1988) was the first contentious case of the Inter-American Court of Human Rights.[48] In this judgment, the Court did not consider the permissibility of amnesty laws but outlined how states must respond to allegations of human rights violations in compliance with the American Convention on Human Rights (ACHR).[49] The case concerned the disappearance of a student as part of a systematic practice carried out or condoned by the Honduran authorities. In a landmark pronouncement, the Court elaborated on the meaning of the obligation to ensure human rights under article 1(1) of the ACHR:

> This obligation implies the duty of States Parties to organize the governmental apparatus and, in general, all the structures through which public power is exercised, so that they are capable of juridically ensuring the free and full enjoyment of human rights. As a consequence of this obligation,

42 Inter-American Commission on Human Rights, Annual Report of 1985–1986 (n 41) ch 4.

43 Ibid, ch 5.

44 Ibid.

45 Ibid.

46 Ibid.

47 Inter-American Commission on Human Rights, Annual Report of 1993, OEA/Ser.L/V.85, doc.9, ch 4 (11 February 1994).

48 *Velásquez-Rodríguez v Honduras* (Merits) Inter-American Court of Human Rights Series C No 4 (29 July 1988).

49 ACHR (n 5).

> the States must prevent, investigate and punish any violation of the rights recognized by the Convention and, moreover, if possible attempt to restore the right violated and provide compensation as warranted for damages resulting from the violation.[50]

Acknowledging the difficulties states may face in investigating human rights violations, the Court indicated that this duty would not be breached merely because the proceedings do not lead to the expected outcome. However, it held that states must make a good faith effort to carry out a thorough and effective investigation into every human rights violation coming to their attention.[51] Appreciating that there might be legitimate obstacles to the prosecution of the perpetrators, it nonetheless emphasised that:

> Even in the hypothetical case that those individually responsible for crimes of this type cannot be legally punished under certain circumstances, the State is obligated to use the means at its disposal to inform the relatives of the fate of the victims and, if they have been killed, the location of their remains.[52]

Because the Honduran authorities had failed to investigate the disappearance, the Court found a violation of article 1(1) in relation to the human rights breached by this crime.[53] Although a general amnesty law had been passed following the events in question, the Court refrained from examining its compatibility with the American Convention. The measure had not been raised as a defence and the question of the obligation to prosecute under the ACHR was only subsidiary in this case since the state had failed to conduct any investigation at all.

Recognition of the right to justice of the victims

In three reports on individual petitions issued in 1992, the Inter-American Commission developed its position on amnesties. The case of *Masacre Las Hojas v El Salvador* concerned an amnesty law preventing the prosecution of Salvadoran security forces implicated in a massacre of civilians.[54] Relying on the judgment of the Court in *Velasquez Rodriguez*, the Commission found that El Salvador had failed to comply with its obligation under article 1 of the ACHR. It did not challenge the validity of the amnesty law per se but recommended that the state investigate the unlawful killings, bring those responsible to justice and provide compensation to the relatives of the victims.[55]

50 *Velásquez-Rodríguez v Honduras* (n 48) para 166.
51 Ibid, para 177.
52 Ibid, para 181.
53 Ibid, paras 182–188.
54 *Masacre Las Hojas v El Salvador*, Case 10.287, Inter-American Commission on Human Rights Report No 26/92, OEA/Ser.L/V/II.83, Doc. 14 (1993).
55 Ibid, conclusions, paras 4–5.

In *Mendoza et al. v Uruguay*, the Commission was requested to determine whether an amnesty law ratified by a national referendum and upheld by Uruguay's Constitutional Court complied with the American Convention.[56] It noted that it lacked competence to rule on the domestic legitimacy or constitutionality of the law. However, it recalled that, pursuant to the ACHR and following an established principle of international law, states may not evade their international obligations by relying on domestic legislation.[57] The Commission examined the compatibility of the amnesty law with articles 1, 8 (right to a fair trial) and 25 (right to judicial protection) of the ACHR. It found that '[o]ne of the law's effects was to deny the victim or his rightful claimant the opportunity to participate in the criminal proceedings, which is the appropriate means to investigate the commission of the crimes denounced, determine criminal liability and impose punishment on those responsible'.[58] Therefore, it concluded that the enactment and application of the amnesty law gave rise to a violation of articles 1(1), 8 and 25. It reached the same conclusion in *Consuelo et al. v Argentina* with respect to Argentine measures akin to amnesties.[59]

In *Garay Hermosilla et al. v Chile* (1997), the Commission held that a Chilean amnesty decree covering acts of enforced disappearances violated articles 1, 8 and 25 of the ACHR because it 'rendered the crimes legally without effect, and deprived the victims and their families of any legal recourse through which they might identify those responsible for violating their human rights during the military dictatorship, and bring them to justice'.[60] In its conclusions, it explicitly required the Chilean government to amend its domestic law in order to enable the investigation of the case and the prosecution of those responsible, 'thereby guaranteeing to the victims and their families the right to justice that pertains to them'.[61]

The reasoning developed by the Commission in these cases postulates that the investigation and prosecution of serious violations required by article 1(1) is essential to give effect to the rights of the victims to a fair trial and to judicial protection under articles 8 and 25, characterised as a whole as 'the right to

56 *Mendoza et al. v Uruguay*, Cases 10.029, 10.036, 10.145, 10.305, 10.372, 10.373, 10.374 and 10.375, Inter-American Commission on Human Rights Report No 29/92, OEA/Ser. L/V/II.83, Doc. 14 (1993).

57 Ibid, paras 29–32. See art 27 of the Vienna Convention on the Law of Treaties (adopted 23 May 1969, entered into force 27 January 1980) 1155 UNTS 331 (providing that '[a] party may not invoke the provisions of its internal law as justification for its failure to perform a treaty').

58 *Mendoza et al. v Uruguay* (n 56) para 40.

59 *Consuelo et al. v Argentina*, Case 10.147, 10.181, 10.240, 10.262, 10.309, 10.311, Inter-American Commission on Human Rights Report No 28/92, OEA/Ser.L/V/II.83, Doc. 14.

60 *Garay Hermosilla et al. v Chile*, Case 10.843, Inter-American Commission on Human Rights Report No 36/96, OEA/Ser.L/V/II.95, Doc. 7 rev. (1997) para 71.

61 Ibid, 111. See also *Carmelo Soria Espinoza v Chile*, Case 11.725, Inter-American Commission on Human Rights Report No 133/99, OEA/Ser.L/V/II.106, Doc. 3 rev. (1999) paras 79–91.

justice'. This was confirmed in *Ignacio Ellacuria v El Salvador* (1999) when the Commission condemned El Salvador's amnesty law because:

> [T]hat law legally removes the right to justice established by Articles 1(1), 8(1) and 25 of the American Convention, since it makes impossible any effective investigation of human rights violations, or the prosecution and punishment of all those persons involved and the reparation of damages caused.[62]

In *Castillo Paez v Peru* (1997), the Inter-American Court embraced this reasoning. It considered that a Peruvian amnesty law posed an obstacle to the investigation of a case of disappearance and ruled that articles 1(1), 8 and 25 of the ACHR require states parties 'to guarantee to all persons access to the courts, and, in particular, to a simple and rapid recourse so that, among other things, those responsible for the human rights violations may be tried and reparations obtained for the damages suffered'.[63] Even though the Court insisted on Peru's duty to prosecute and punish those responsible for the disappearance, it refrained from directly addressing the compatibility of the amnesty law with the ACHR. In *Loayza Tamayo v Peru* (1998), however, the Court responded to a defence by the Peruvian government based on the same amnesty law by stressing that:

> Under the American Convention, every person subject to the jurisdiction of a State Party is guaranteed the right to recourse to a competent court for the protection of his fundamental rights. States, therefore, have the obligation to prevent human rights violations, investigate them, identify and punish their intellectual authors and accessories after the fact, and may not invoke existing provisions of domestic law, such as the Amnesty Law in this case, to avoid complying with their obligations under international law.[64]

While the Court disregarded the effect of the Peruvian amnesty law in so far as it prevented the investigation and prosecution of the human rights violations at issue in those cases, it did not invalidate it or declare amnesties generally contrary to the ACHR. In his concurring opinion to *Castillo Paez*, Judge García-Ramírez expressed his understanding that 'the Court's Judgment does not dismiss the advisability and need of amnesty provisions that serve to restore peace, under conditions of freedom and justice, in the wake of the internal conflicts that such measures and others are intended to help to resolve'.[65] He explained that:

62 *Ignacio Ellacuria v El Salvador*, Case 10.488, Inter-American Commission on Human Rights Report No 136/99, OEA/Ser.L/V/II.106 doc. 3 rev. (1999) para 215.

63 *Castillo Paez v Peru* (Reparations and Costs) Inter-American Court of Human Rights Series C No 43 (27 November 1998) paras 105–7.

64 *Loayza Tamayo v Peru* (Reparations and Costs) Inter-American Court of Human Rights Series C No 42 (27 November 1998) para 167–68.

65 *Castillo Paez v Peru* (n 63) Concurring Vote of Judge Sergio García-Ramírez, para 6.

> [A] distinction must be made between the so-called "self-amnesty laws" promulgated by and for those in power, and amnesties that are the result of a peace process, with a democratic base and reasonable in scope, that preclude prosecution for acts or behaviors of members of rival factions but leave open the possibility of punishment for the kind of very egregious acts that no faction either approves or views as appropriate.[66]

In their concurring opinion to *Loayza Tamayo*, Judges Cançado Trindade and Abreu-Burelli also considered that self-amnesties are incompatible with the obligations of states under the American Convention.[67]

The incompatibility of amnesty laws with the American Convention on Human Rights

In *Barrios Altos v Peru* (2001), the Commission requested the Court to determine whether the Peruvian amnesty law criticised in previous cases violated articles 1, 8, and 25 of the ACHR.[68] The case concerned state-sponsored summary executions the investigation of which was blocked as a result of the amnesty law. In a watershed judgment, the Court established that amnesties and analogous measures barring accountability for serious human rights violations are incompatible with the American Convention:

> [A]ll amnesty provisions, provisions on prescription and the establishment of measures designed to eliminate responsibility are inadmissible, because they are intended to prevent the investigation and punishment of those responsible for serious human rights violations such as torture, extrajudicial, summary or arbitrary execution and forced disappearance, all of them prohibited because they violate non-derogable rights recognized by international human rights law.[69]

The Court determined that the Peruvian amnesty law violated articles 1, 8 and 25 of the ACHR because it prevented the victims from exercising their right to seek justice by obstructing the investigation and prosecution of serious human rights abuses.[70] It found that Peru had also breached article 2 of the Convention by failing to adopt measures giving effect to the rights protected therein. It declared that self-amnesty laws in general are 'manifestly incompatible with the aims and spirit of the Convention' and ruled that the Peruvian law lacked

66 Ibid, para 9.

67 *Loayza Tamayo v Peru* (n 64) Joint Concurring Opinion of Judges Cançado Trindade and Abreu-Burelli, paras 3–4.

68 *Barrios Altos v Peru* (Merits) Inter-American Court of Human Rights Series C No 75 (14 March 2001) para 1.

69 Ibid, para 41.

70 Ibid, paras 42–43.

legal effect and could not continue to bar investigations into human rights violations.[71]

Barrios Altos was the first judgment of an international court invalidating an amnesty law. In a subsequent decision interpreting this judgment, the Court went one step further by determining that the '[e]nactment of a law that is manifestly incompatible with the obligations undertaken by a State Party to the Convention is per se a violation of the Convention for which the State incurs international responsibility'.[72] As a consequence, it held that the judgment had general effects beyond the particular facts of the case and applied to all cases involving human rights violations having been closed in application of the amnesty.

In two judgments rendered in 2006, the Court considered whether investigatory mechanisms falling short of criminal prosecutions may satisfy the standards of the American Convention.[73] While it highlighted the important role which truth commissions play in revealing the truth on past abuses and providing a measure of redress to the victims, it determined that 'the "historical truth" included in the reports of the ... Commissions is no substitute for the duty of the State to reach the truth through judicial proceedings'.[74] Thus, it made clear that truth-recovery mechanisms are not valid alternatives to criminal proceedings and do not by themselves satisfy the duty of states to provide redress to victims of human rights crimes.

One of those judgments, *Almonacid-Arellano v Chile* (2006), concerned extra-legal executions qualified as crimes against humanity coming within the scope of the Chilean amnesty decree previously criticised by the Inter-American Commission.[75] In accordance with its judgment in *Barrios Altos*, the Court declared that 'States cannot neglect their duty to investigate, identify, and punish those persons responsible for crimes against humanity by enforcing amnesty laws or any other similar domestic provisions' and ruled that the amnesty decree lacked legal effect.[76] Clarifying its position on amnesties, it determined that the relevant factor for the purpose of determining their compatibility with the ACHR is their *ratio legis*, i.e. whether their aim is to prevent the punishment of serious human rights violations, rather than the type of authority or process involved in its adoption.[77] This implied that even

71 Ibid, 44.

72 *Barrios Altos v Peru* (Interpretation of the Judgment on the Merits) Inter-American Court of Human Rights Series C No 83 (3 September 2001) para 18.

73 *Almonacid-Arellano v Chile* (Merits) Inter-American Court of Human Rights Series C No 154 (26 September 2006); *La Cantuta v Peru* (Merits, Reparations and Costs) Inter-American Court of Human Rights Series C No 162 (29 November 2006).

74 *Almonacid-Arellano v Chile* (n 73) para 149–50; *La Cantuta v Peru* (n 73) para 223–24.

75 *Almonacid-Arellano v Chile* (n 73). See *Garay Hermosilla et al. v Chile* (n 60).

76 *Almonacid-Arellano v Chile* (n 73) paras 114 and 119.

77 Ibid, 120.

democratically adopted amnesty laws benefiting from some public support, as opposed to self-amnesty laws, would not be tolerated by the Court.

The Court confirmed that self-amnesties are not the only type of amnesties prohibited under the ACHR in *Gomes Lund v Brazil* (2010) and *Gelman v Uruguay* (2011).[78] In the former, it made clear that 'the non-compatibility with the Convention includes amnesties of serious human rights violations and is not limited to those which are denominated "selfamnesties"'.[79] In the latter, the Court dismissed as irrelevant the fact that the Uruguayan amnesty law at issue had been ratified in a national referendum.[80] Both the Brazilian and Uruguayan amnesties were declared incompatible with the American Convention and devoid of legal force because they precluded the investigation and prosecution of serious human rights violations.

By contrast with the amnesty laws previously invalidated by the Court, the one at issue in *The Massacres of El Mozote v El Salvador* (2012) had been enacted in connection with the settlement of a non-international armed conflict.[81] The Court therefore adapted its methodology to take into account the terms of the peace agreement and the branch of international humanitarian law dealing with internal armed conflicts, i.e. the Second Protocol of the Geneva Conventions of 1949.[82] It acknowledged that, pursuant to article 6(5) of that Protocol, 'the enactment of amnesty laws on the conclusion of hostilities in non-international armed conflicts are sometimes justified to pave the way to a return to peace'.[83] However, it considered that this allowance for amnesty as a peace-making tool is circumscribed by rules of international humanitarian law requiring the investigation and prosecution of war crimes.[84]

Following an analysis of the Salvadoran peace process and of the circumstances in which the amnesty law had been enacted, the Court concluded that:

> [T]he *ratio legis* of the [amnesty law] was to render ineffectual [a section] of the Peace Accord of 16 January 1992, and, in this way, amnesty and leave in impunity all the grave crimes perpetrated against international law during the internal armed conflict.[85]

78 *Gomes Lund et al. v Brazil* (Preliminary Objections, Merits, Reparations and Costs) Inter-American Court of Human Rights Series C No 219 (24 November 2010); *Gelman v Uruguay* (Merits and Reparations) Inter-American Court of Human Rights Series C No 221 (24 February 2011).

79 *Gomes Lund v Brazil* (n 78) para 175.

80 *Gelman v Uruguay* (n 78) para 238.

81 *The Massacres of El Mozote and nearby places v El Salvador* (Merits, Reparations and Costs) Inter-American Court of Human Rights Series C No 252 (25 October 2012).

82 Ibid, para 284; Protocol Additional to the Geneva Conventions of 12 August 1949 relating to the Protection of Victims of Non-International Armed Conflicts (adopted 8 June 1977, entered into force 7 December 1978) 1125 UNTS 609.

83 *Massacres of El Mozote v El Salvador* (n 81) para 285.

84 Ibid, para 286.

85 Ibid, para 292.

Because the law contravened articles 1(1) and 2 of the ACHR, the Court ruled that it lacked legal effect and could not continue to impede the investigation of serious crimes perpetrated as part of the conflict in El Salvador.[86]

Nuancing the right to justice in the context of efforts to end an armed conflict

In his concurring opinion to the *El Mozote* judgment, Judge Garcia-Sayán reflected on the tensions between justice and reconciliation that may arise in the context of efforts to settle a non-international armed conflict.[87] Arguing for a case-by-case approach, he expressed the view that '[t]here is no universally applicable solution to the dilemmas posed by these opposing forces, because it depends on the specific context, although there are guidelines that must be taken into account'.[88] He explained that:

> [S]everal components must be taken into consideration, both judicial and non-judicial, that are focused, simultaneously, on seeking the truth, justice and reparation. This is because the demands that arise from massive violations, the responses to the aftermath of the conflict, and the search for long-lasting peace, require both the States and society as a whole to apply concurrent measures that permit the greatest simultaneous attention to these three rights.[89]

In addition to their obligation towards the victims in these three areas, Garcia-Sayán observed that the state had, with the same intensity, 'the obligation to prevent further acts of violence and to achieve peace in an armed conflict by the means at its disposal'.[90] Indeed, he submitted that:

> Peace as a product of a negotiation is offered as a morally and politically superior alternative to peace as a result of the annihilation of the opponent. Therefore, international human rights law should consider that peace is a right and that the State must achieve it.[91]

On this basis, he advocated for a balanced approach of the obligations of states following armed conflicts:

> [I]n certain transitional situations between armed conflicts and peace, it can happen that a State is not in a position to implement fully and

86 Ibid, para 296.
87 Ibid, Concurring Opinion of Judge Diego Garcia-Sayán.
88 Ibid, para 20.
89 Ibid, para 22.
90 Ibid, para 37.
91 Ibid, para 37.

> simultaneously, the various international rights and obligations it has assumed. In these circumstances, taking into consideration that none of those rights and obligations is of an absolute nature, it is legitimate that they be weighed in such a way that the satisfaction of some does not affect the exercise of the others disproportionately. Thus, the degree of justice that can be achieved is not an isolated component from which legitimate frustrations and dissatisfactions can arise, but part of an ambitious process of transition towards mutual tolerance and peace.[92]

This opinion nuances the position of the Court with regard to amnesties adopted by states undergoing a transition from war to peace. It indicates that, even when grave crimes are concerned, the obligation to prosecute and punish is not absolute and should be balanced with the victims' right to truth and reparation, on the one hand, and the need for peace and reconciliation, on the other. Four out of the seven judges of the bench adhered to this view, suggesting that a more flexible approach could be adopted by the Court with respect to amnesties adopted as part of a peace process.

This is corroborated by the positive attitude adopted by the Inter-American Commission towards the ongoing peace process in Colombia.[93] The Colombian peace agreement of November 2016 provides for the creation of a Special Jurisdiction for Peace to deal with crimes committed during the armed conflict.[94] Perpetrators of serious crimes may, on the condition that they accept responsibility and disclose the truth, benefit from an alternative sentence entailing reparative labour and restrictions on their liberty but no prison term.[95] The Commission welcomed the peace accord and signed a cooperation agreement with the Colombian government to provide technical assistance in implementing it in accordance with the ACHR.[96] Although the transitional justice system set up by the peace agreement permits perpetrators of grave violations to avoid criminal imprisonment, it has benefited from overwhelming support by the international community, in part because it upholds the rights of the victims to truth, reparation and non-repetition of the violence. The Commission has accepted that 'the consolidation of peace is an indispensable requirement for the exercise and respect of human rights in Colombia' and it is collaborating with Colombian transitional institutions, including the Special Jurisdiction for Peace.

92 Ibid, para 38.

93 On the Colombian peace process, see ch 3 in this volume.

94 Final Agreement for Ending the Conflict and Building a Stable and Lasting Peace, 24 November 2016.

95 Ibid, item 5.1.2 (III) paras 45–47, 60, 75.

96 'IACHR Welcomes the Signing of Agreement for the Construction of Peace in Colombia' Inter-American Commission on Human Rights (IACHR) Press Release (29 August 2016); Acuerdo de Cooperación entre la Secretaría General de la Organización de los Estados Americanos y la República de Colombia para la aplicación y difusión de los instrumentos internacionales de derechos humanos (22 February 2018).

This indicates that post-conflict justice processes relying on alternative sentences to deal with perpetrators of serious crimes may satisfy Inter-American standards.[97]

The European system of human rights

The European Commission and Court of Human Rights have adopted a nuanced position on the permissibility of amnesties under the European Convention on Human Rights (ECHR).[98] While the Commission has only addressed the issue once, the Court has dealt with amnesty laws in several cases in which it developed a differentiated approach taking into account the nature of the crimes covered and the context within which the law was issued. The Court's flexible position on amnesties is in line with its reluctance to establish that the ECHR requires states parties to prosecute and punish human rights offenders in all circumstances, and its refusal to recognise that victims of violations have a right to criminal justice, in contrast with the Inter-American Court.

The possibility of amnesty for serious human rights violations

Before the abolition of the European Commission as part of a general reform of the European human rights system in 1998, that body was charged to determine the admissibility of petitions to the European Court. The first amnesty case submitted to the Court, *Dujardin v France* (1991), never reached it as it was declared inadmissible by the Commission.[99] It concerned an amnesty law enacted in France to settle conflicts between different communities in New Caledonia and prepare for the grant of self-determination to that French overseas territory. The law precluded an investigation into the murder of four policemen by a group of insurgents in the context of a politically motivated attack.[100] The victims' relatives claimed that the law violated the ECHR because it resulted in the discontinuation of criminal proceedings against the suspects in breach of article 2 (obligation to protect life).

The Commission emphasised that the right to life is one of the most fundamental rights protected by the ECHR. However, it observed that 'as with any criminal offence, the crime of murder may be covered by an amnesty'.[101] In its view, an amnesty extending to violations of the right to life would not breach the state's obligation under article 2 'unless it can be seen to form part of a general practice aimed at the systematic prevention of prosecution of the

97 'IACHR Reaffirms its Support for the Peace Process in Colombia and Is Monitoring Compliance with Inter-American Standards' IACHR Press Release (1 December 2016); 'IACHR meets with the institutions included in the Peace Agreement in Colombia' IACHR Press Release (28 June 2018).

98 ECHR (n 5).

99 *Dujardin v France* (1991) 72 DR 236.

100 Ibid, 240–41.

101 Ibid, 243.

perpetrators of such crimes'.[102] It considered that this was not the case since French law protects the right to life, *inter alia*, by criminalising murder. It also observed that the amnesty measure in question was 'entirely exceptional in character' and pursued the legitimate objective of resolving the conflicts in New Caledonia.[103] On a more general level, the Commission declared that:

> The State is justified in adopting, in the context of its criminal policy, any amnesty laws it might consider necessary, with the proviso, however, that a balance is maintained between the legitimate interests of the State and the interests of individual members of the public in having the right to life protected by law.[104]

This statement was reiterated by the European Court in *Tarbuk v Croatia* (2012) which involved a Croatian amnesty law issued in the aftermath of the armed conflict in the former Yugoslavia.[105] The Court thereby endorsed the Commission's view that an amnesty law may be acceptable, even in relation to violations of fundamental rights, as long as it is deemed necessary by the state to respond to exceptional circumstances and a balance between the legitimate interest pursued by the law and the rights of individuals is maintained.

The requirement to investigate serious human rights violations and ensure the effective functioning of the judicial system

The primary duty of states parties to the ECHR in relation to violations of fundamental rights such as the right to life and to personal integrity is the conduct of 'a thorough and effective investigation capable of leading to the identification and punishment of those responsible and including effective access for the complainant to the investigatory procedure'.[106] The Court has derived this obligation from article 1 (obligation to ensure rights) or 13 (obligation to provide a remedy) taken in conjunction with article 2 (right to life) or 3 (right to personal

102 Ibid.

103 Ibid, 244.

104 Ibid.

105 *Tarbuk v Croatia* App No 31360/10 (ECtHR, 11 December 2012) para 50 ('[T]he Convention organs have already held that, even in such fundamental areas of the protection of human rights as the right to life, the State is justified in enacting, in the context of its criminal policy, any amnesty laws it might consider necessary, with the proviso, however, that a balance is maintained between the legitimate interests of the State and the interests of individual members of the public'.)

106 *Aksoy v Turkey* ECHR 1996-VI, para 98; *Kaya v Turkey* ECHR 1998-I, para 107; *Finucane v The United Kingdom* ECHR 2003-VIII, para 69; *Bitiyeva and X v Russia* App Nos 57953/00 and 37392/03 (ECtHR, 21 June 2007) para 156; *Abdülsamet Yaman v Turkey* App No 32446/96 (ECtHR, 2 November 2004) para 53.

integrity) of the ECHR.[107] As regards violations of the right to life, it has explained that:

> The essential purpose of such an investigation is to secure the effective implementation of the domestic laws which protect the right to life and, in those cases involving State agents or bodies, to ensure their accountability for deaths occurring under their responsibility.[108]

With respect to violations of article 3, it has adopted a similar reasoning considering that an effective investigation is necessary because:

> If this were not the case, the general legal prohibition of torture and inhuman and degrading treatment and punishment, despite its fundamental importance, would be ineffective in practice and it would be possible in some cases for agents of the State to abuse the rights of those within their control with virtual impunity.[109]

The rationale of the obligation of states to investigate human rights crimes under the ECHR is thus, first and foremost, to guarantee the effectiveness of domestic norms protecting the right to life and to personal integrity by ensuring that persons violating these rights are held to account, particularly when they are state agents. Besides relying on considerations of general prevention and deterrence, the Court has highlighted that an official investigation into gross human rights violations is necessary to safeguard public confidence in the rule of law:

> [E]ven where there may be obstacles or difficulties which prevent progress in an investigation in a particular situation, a prompt response by the authorities is vital in maintaining public confidence in their adherence to the rule of law and in preventing any appearance of collusion in or tolerance of unlawful acts.[110]

107 See e.g. *McCann and Others v The United Kingdom* [GC] (1995) 21 EHRR 97, para 161; *Kaya v Turkey* (n 106) para 86; *Aksoy v Turkey* (n 106) para 98; *Assenov and Others v Bulgaria* ECHR 1998-VII, para 102; *Selmouni v France* [GC] ECHR1999-V, para 79; *Anguelova v Bulgaria* ECHR 2002-IV, paras 161 and 136; *Isayev and Others v Russia* App No 43368/04 (ECtHR, 21 June 2011) paras 136 and 186.

108 *Brecknell v United Kingdom* (2007) 46 EHRR 42, para 65; *McKerr v United Kingdom* ECHR 2001-III, para 111.

109 *Assenov and Others v Bulgaria* (n 107) para 102. See also *Ali and Ayşe Duran v Turkey* App No 42942/02 (ECtHR, 8 April 2008) para 60.

110 *Brecknell v the United Kingdom* (n 108) para 65; *McKerr v United Kingdom* (n 108) para 114; *Öneryildiz v Turkey* [GC] ECHR 2004-XII, para 96; *Abdülsamet Yaman v Turkey* (n 106) para 54; *Okkali v Turkey* ECHR 2006-XII, para 78; *Ali and Ayşe Duran v Turkey* (n 109) para 63.

To satisfy the standards developed by the Court, investigations must be effective, thorough, prompt, independent and transparent.[111] The obligation is one of means rather than result, with the consequence that 'the fact that an investigation ends without concrete, or with only limited, results is not indicative of any failings as such'.[112] However, the Court has stressed that '[a]ny deficiency in the investigation which undermines its ability to establish the cause of death or the person responsible will risk falling foul of this standard'.[113]

Where investigations lead to judicial proceedings, the Court has established that those proceedings as a whole must also satisfy a requirement of efficiency 'so that the deterrent effect of the judicial system in place and the significance of the role it is required to play in preventing violations of the right to life and the prohibition of ill-treatment are not undermined'.[114] It has also made clear that:

> While there is no absolute obligation for all prosecutions to result in conviction or in a particular sentence, the national courts should not under any circumstances be prepared to allow life-endangering offences and grave attacks on physical and moral integrity to go unpunished.[115]

Indeed, implicit in the obligation to carry out an investigation 'capable of leading to the identification and punishment of those responsible' is a requirement that there is a functioning judicial system in place including recourse to the criminal law in cases of grave crimes. The Court has considered that:

> [I]f the infringement of the right to life or to personal integrity is not caused intentionally, the positive obligation imposed by Article 2 to set up an effective judicial system does not necessarily require the provision of a criminal-law remedy in every case.[116]

Accordingly, it has accepted that civil, administrative or disciplinary proceedings may satisfy the obligation of states when serious violations are caused by negligence.[117] However, when fundamental rights have been violated by or under the responsibility of state officials, the Court has insisted on the conduct of criminal proceedings permitting the punishment of the persons responsible.[118] As with the obligation to investigate, emphasis has been placed on the effectiveness of the

111 *McKerr v. United Kingdom* (n 108) paras 111–15; *Finucane v United Kingdom* (n 106) paras 67–71. See Seibert-Fohr (n 27) 132–39.

112 *Brecknell v United Kingdom* (n 108) para 66; *Avşar v Turkey* ECHR 2001-VII, para 394.

113 *McKerr v United Kingdom* (n 108) para 113; *Avşar v Turkey* (n 112) para 394.

114 *Ali and Ayşe Duran v Turkey* (n 109) para 62. See also *Öneryildiz v Turkey* (n 110) paras 95–96.

115 *Ali and Ayşe Duran v Turkey* (n 109) para 61.

116 *Calvelli and Ciglio* [GC] ECHR 2002-I, para 51.

117 Ibid; *Öneryildiz v Turkey* (n 110) para 92; *Vo v France* [GC] ECHR 2004-VIII, para 90.

118 Ibid; *McKerr v United Kingdom* (n 108) para 121; *Yaşa v Turkey* ECHR 1998-VI, para 74.

proceedings in conformity with the criteria developed by the Court rather than on their outcome.[119]

While the Court has established that states parties to the ECHR have the responsibility to ensure that their judicial system is effective and permits the identification and punishment of persons responsible for violations of fundamental rights, it has consistently rejected the view that the victims are entitled to a right to criminal justice. In *Perez v France* (2004), it stressed that 'the Convention does not confer any right, as demanded by the applicant, to "private revenge" or to an actio popularis. Thus, the right to have third parties prosecuted or sentenced for a criminal offence cannot be asserted independently'.[120] In the same vein, in *Öneryildiz v Turkey* (2004), it held that:

> It should in no way be inferred … that Article 2 may entail the right for an applicant to have third parties prosecuted or sentenced for a criminal offence or an absolute obligation for all prosecutions to result in conviction, or indeed in a particular sentence.[121]

Thus, while states parties to the ECHR are under an obligation to investigate serious violations and, in some circumstances, ensure the prosecution and punishment of the perpetrators, there is no corresponding right of the victims to institute criminal proceedings. This limitation has been seen as a concession to state sovereignty in the criminal sphere and an acknowledgment of the principle of prosecutorial discretion based on the public interest and practical considerations such as the availability of evidence.[122] Furthermore, the Court does not seem to consider that the establishment of the guilt of human rights offenders through the criminal process is required in the interest of the victims but, rather, in the interest of society as a whole in preventing crime, deterring offenders and protecting the rule of law.[123] According to Anja Seibert-Fohr, '[t]hough the Court in individual cases calls upon States parties to criminalize and have recourse to criminal law, this is a matter of general human rights protection. Criminal punishment is not required as a remedy for the individual victim'.[124]

A differentiated approach of amnesties

In accordance with its measured position on the obligations of states in response to serious human rights violations, the European Court has developed a

119 *McKerr v United Kingdom* (n 108) para 134; *Avşar v Turkey* (n 112) paras 403–4.

120 *Perez v France* [GC] ECHR 2004-I, para 70.

121 *Öneryildiz v Turkey* (n 110) para 96. See also *Szula v the United Kingdom* [dec] App No 18727/06 (ECtHR, 4 January 2007); *Calvelli and Ciglio v Italy* (n 116) para 51.

122 Françoise Tulkens, 'The Paradoxical Relationship between Criminal Law and Human Rights' (2011) 9 *Journal of International Criminal Justice* 577, 592; Seibert-Fohr (n 27) 126.

123 See Seibert-Fohr (n 27) ch 3.

124 Ibid, 120.

nuanced body of case law on amnesties. In most of the judgments in which it referred to amnesty in relation to serious violations, it addressed the issue in the abstract alongside that of statutory limitations. In the two cases in which it was directly confronted with an amnesty law covering international crimes, the Court refused to give effect to the law but refrained from declaring an absolute prohibition. In these and other cases, it acknowledged certain limits to the general principle that amnesties for serious crimes are incompatible with the ECHR.

In a number of cases involving torture or ill-treatment at the hands of state officials, the Court stated that:

> [W]here a State agent has been charged with crimes involving torture or ill-treatment, it is of the utmost importance for the purposes of an "effective remedy" that criminal proceedings and sentencing are not time-barred and that the granting of an amnesty or pardon should not be permissible.[125]

Most of these cases concerned Turkish police officers against whom criminal proceedings had been discontinued or suspended in application of statutory limitations. Measures providing immunity to state agents responsible for violations of article 3 were criticised by the Court for creating a climate of impunity undermining the effectiveness of domestic norms protecting the right to physical integrity. Highlighting the link between impunity and recurrent criminal behaviour, the Court repeatedly observed that 'the Turkish criminal-law system, as applied, can prove to be far from rigorous and have no dissuasive effect capable of ensuring the effective prevention of unlawful acts perpetrated by State agents'.[126] Its rejection of measures shielding public authorities from accountability is consistent with the position of the European Commission in *Dujardin* to the effect that amnesties forming part of a general practice aiming to prevent the prosecution of serious crimes in a systematic manner would violate the ECHR.[127]

In *Ould Dah v France* (2009), the Court followed a different approach accounting for the different legal basis upon which the amnesty law at issue was challenged, i.e. the 1984 International Convention against Torture.[128] The case concerned a Mauritanian military officer prosecuted in France for acts of torture

125 See eg *Abdülsamet Yaman v Turkey* (n 106) para 55; *Ali and Ayşe Duran v Turkey* (n 109) para 69; *Okkali v Turkey* (n 110) para 76; *Terzi and Erkmen v Turkey* App No 31300/05 (ECtHR, 28 July 2009) para 33; *Baran and Hun v Turkey* App No 30685/05 (ECtHR, 20 May 2010) para 58; *Taylan v Turkey* App No 32051/09 (ECtHR, 3 July 2012) para 45; *Yerli v Turkey* App No 59177/10 (ECtHR, 8 July 2014) para 61; *Ateşoğlu v Turkey* App No 53645/10 (ECtHR, 20 January 2015) para 25.

126 See eg *Ali and Ayşe Duran v Turkey* (n 109) para 72; *Okkali v Turkey* (n 110) para 78; *Terzi and Erkmen v Turkey* (n 125) para 34; *Baran and Hun v Turkey* (n 125) para 60; *Yerli v Turkey* (n 125) para 60.

127 See text to n 102.

128 *Ould Dah v France* [dec] 48(4) ILM 884 (2009). See the Convention against Torture and Other Cruel, Inhuman or Degrading Treatment or Punishment (adopted 10 December 1984, entered into force 26 June 1987) 1465 UNTS (Torture Convention) 85.

committed in Mauritania, despite the amnesty from which he benefited in the latter country. French courts had proceeded on the basis of the 1984 Convention, which requires states parties to prosecute torture and entitles them to exercise universal jurisdiction over this crime.[129] The applicant was convicted in accordance with French law and complained that this violated the principle of legality protected by article 7 of the ECHR. The Court found that the conditions authorising French courts to exercise universal jurisdiction were fulfilled since the applicant had been arrested on French territory and his conviction was based on the application of the relevant international convention, which had been incorporated in French law.[130] It observed that 'the prohibition against torture is a key in all international instruments relating to the protection of human rights' and took note of its status as a *jus cogens* norm.

Concurring with other international bodies, the Court declared that amnesty laws covering torture are 'generally incompatible with the duty of states to investigate such acts'.[131] It then qualified this statement by acknowledging that 'one could not exclude the possibility of a conflict between, on the one hand, the necessity to prosecute the crimes committed and, on the other hand, the need to reconcile the social structure of a country'.[132] However, since no reconciliation process had been put in place in Mauritania, it ruled out the existence of such a conflict and held that it 'could not therefore question the obligation to prosecute such actions by allowing impunity to the perpetrator through adoption of an amnesty law, susceptible of being in violation to international law'.[133] The Court thus approved the decision of French courts to disregard the amnesty law and declared the case inadmissible.

With respect to other international crimes, such as war crimes and crimes against humanity, the Court has noted that, even though 'the public interest in obtaining the prosecution and conviction of perpetrators is firmly recognised', the fact that their commission predated the adoption of the ECHR may constitute a bar to its jurisdiction.[134] The case of *Gutierrez Dorado v Spain* (2012) concerned a forced disappearance carried out during the Spanish civil war which fell within the scope of the general amnesty law passed in 1977 as part of Spain's democratic transition. Although enforced disappearance is a crime under international law, the Court abstained from questioning the applicability of amnesty to this practice and ruled that the case was inadmissible because the applicants had waited too long before filing the case.[135] It justified this refusal to order the reopening of the case by explaining that:

129 Torture Convention (n 128) art 7.
130 *Ould Dah v France* (n 128) 894.
131 Ibid.
132 Ibid.
133 Ibid.
134 *Gutierrez Dorado and Dorado Ortiz v Spain* App No 30141/09 (ECtHR, 27 March 2012) paras 34–35; *Janowiec v Russia* [GC] ECHR 2013-V, para 151.
135 *Gutierrez Dorado v Spain* (n 134) para 39.

> Indeed, with the lapse of time, memories of witnesses fade, witnesses may die or become untraceable, evidence deteriorates or ceases to exist, and the prospects that any effective investigation can be undertaken will increasingly diminish; and the Court's own examination and judgment may be deprived of meaningfulness and effectiveness.[136]

In *Janowiec v Russia* (2013), which involved war crimes committed at the start of the Second World War, the Grand Chamber followed the same line of reasoning. It declared that 'a Contracting Party cannot be held responsible under the Convention for not investigating even the most serious crimes under international law if they predated the Convention'.[137] The Court thereby recognised that the obligation to investigate serious human rights violations under the ECHR is not absolute and may be extinguished by the passage of time. This suggests that the Court would refrain from challenging the validity of historic amnesty laws, even when they still obstruct the investigation of international crimes.

In *Marguš v Croatia* (2012), the Court had to determine whether the conviction of a Croat military officer for war crimes, with respect to which he had previously been granted an amnesty, violated article 4 of the seventh protocol of the Convention protecting the *ne bis in idem* principle.[138] Since the Croatian amnesty law expressly excluded serious breaches of international humanitarian law, the Court considered that it had been erroneously applied to the crimes committed by the applicant, which had subsequently been qualified as war crimes.[139] It determined that this error constituted a fundamental defect in the first proceedings and, therefore, that the case could be reopened in compliance with the ECHR. With regard to the permissibility of amnesty for crimes against international law, the Court declared that:

> Granting amnesty in respect of "international crimes" – which include crimes against humanity, war crimes and genocide – is increasingly considered to be prohibited by international law. This understanding is drawn from customary rules of international humanitarian law, human rights treaties, as well as the decisions of international and regional courts and developing State practice, as there has been a growing tendency for international, regional and national courts to overturn general amnesties enacted by Governments.[140]

Pursuant to a request of the applicant, the case was reconsidered by the Grand Chamber in May 2014.[141] In this judgment, the Court recalled the principle

136 Ibid, para 37.
137 *Janowiec v Russia* (n 134) para 151.
138 *Marguš v Croatia* App No 4455/10 (ECtHR, 13 November 2012).
139 Ibid, paras 75–76.
140 Ibid, para 74.
141 *Marguš v Croatia* [GC] ECHR 2014-III. In collaboration with a group of international experts, the author filed an amicus curiae with the Grand Chamber highlighting weaknesses

that state agents responsible for grave human rights violations should not benefit from immunity measures by noting that 'granting amnesty in respect of the killing and ill-treatment of civilians would run contrary to the State's obligations under Articles 2 and 3 of the Convention since it would hamper the investigation of such acts and necessarily lead to impunity for those responsible'.[142] As regards the position under international law, the Grand Chamber recognised that 'so far no international treaty explicitly prohibits the granting of amnesty in respect of grave breaches of fundamental human rights'.[143] However, after reviewing the decisions and opinions of international judicial and political bodies on the subject, it observed that '[a] growing tendency in international law is to see such amnesties as unacceptable because they are incompatible with the unanimously recognised obligation of States to prosecute and punish grave breaches of fundamental human rights'.[144] Yet, the Court nuanced this statement by acknowledging that:

> Even if it were to be accepted that amnesties are possible where there are some particular circumstances, such as a reconciliation process and/or a form of compensation to the victims, the amnesty granted to the applicant in the instant case would still not be acceptable since there is nothing to indicate that there were any such circumstances.[145]

In their concurring opinion to this judgment, three judges of the bench explained the nuanced position of the Court on the issue of amnesty:

> The adoption of international rules imposing a blanket ban on amnesties in cases of grave violations of human rights is liable, in some circumstances, to reduce the effectiveness of human rights protection ... We must acknowledge that in certain circumstances there may be practical arguments in favour of an amnesty that encompasses some grave human rights violations. We cannot rule out the possibility that such an amnesty might in some instances serve as a tool enabling an armed conflict or a political regime that violates human rights to be brought to an end more swiftly, thereby preventing further violations in the future. In any event, as we see it, the concern to ensure effective protection of human rights points in favour of allowing the States concerned a certain margin of manoeuvre in this sphere, in order to allow the different parties to conflicts engendering grave human rights violations to find the most appropriate solutions.[146]

in the view that the grant of amnesty for serious crimes is altogether prohibited by international law. The brief was cited by the Court in paras 108–113 of the judgment.

142 Ibid, para 127.
143 Ibid, para 131.
144 Ibid, para 139.
145 Ibid.
146 Ibid, Joint concurring opinion of Judges Šikuta, Wojtyczec and Vehabović, para 9.

The careful reasoning of the Grand Chamber in *Marguš* recognised the existence of a growing tendency to consider that amnesties extending to grave crimes are contrary to international law. However, it left some room for amnesties to be given deference on a case-by-case basis where they pursue a legitimate objective, such as the promotion of national reconciliation, or allow the provision of reparation to the victims. This view is consistent with the nuanced position adopted by the Court in *Tarbuk* and *Ould Dah*, where it acknowledged that some special circumstances might tip the balance in favour of an amnesty law even though it provides immunity for serious crimes.[147] Throughout its case law, the Court has distinguished between amnesties on different levels. First, it has followed a differentiated approach depending on the nature of the crimes covered – whether human rights violations or international crimes – and the type of beneficiaries – whether state agents or civilians. Second, it has taken into account the context within which and purpose for which the amnesty was adopted, whether as an exceptional measure in the context of a transitional process, or as part of a general practice aiming to shield perpetrators of grave crimes from accountability. This flexible approach reflects the uneasiness of the Court with an absolute position prohibiting all types of amnesties regardless of the particular circumstances to which they respond.

The African Commission on Human and People's Rights

Four judgments of the African Commission on Human and People's Rights have considered the issue of amnesty under the African Charter on Human and Peoples' Rights (ACHPR).[148] The case of *Malawi African Association and Others v Mauritania* (2000) concerned large-scale state-sponsored human rights violations committed against members of certain ethnic groups.[149] An amnesty law enacted by Mauritania's Parliament in 1993 barred legal actions by the victims and their relatives.[150] When assessing whether internal remedies had been exhausted for the purpose of admissibility, the African Commission held that:

> [A]n amnesty law adopted with the aim of nullifying suits or other actions seeking redress that may be filed by the victims or their beneficiaries, while having force within Mauritanian national territory, cannot shield that country from fulfilling its international obligations under the Charter.[151]

147 See n 105 and text to 132.
148 ACHPR (n 5).
149 *Malawi African Association and Others v Mauritania* (2000) AHRLR 149 (ACHPR 2000).
150 Ibid, paras 81–82.
151 Ibid, para 83.

After noting that the sheer scale of the human rights crimes committed in Mauritania and the amnesty law rendered internal remedies impracticable, it ruled that the case was admissible.[152]

The issue of amnesty was also addressed by the Commission in *Zimbabwe Human Rights NGO Forum v Zimbabwe* (2006) and *Mouvement Ivoirien des Droits Humains (MIDH) v Côte d'Ivoire* (2008).[153] The former involved a clemency order applicable to serious crimes committed in connection with a constitutional referendum and the ensuing parliamentary elections in Zimbabwe.[154] The latter involved an article of the constitution of Côte d'Ivoire extending immunity to high-ranking officials responsible for a coup.[155] In both cases, the Commission reviewed developments in international law and jurisprudence 'suggesting that the prohibition of amnesties leading to impunity for serious human rights violations has become a rule of customary international law'.[156] With regard to the amnesty measures in question, it held that:

> [B]y granting total and complete immunity from prosecution which foreclosed access to any remedy that might be available to the victims to vindicate their rights, and without putting in place alternative adequate legislative or institutional mechanisms to ensure that perpetrators of the alleged atrocities were punished, and victims of the violations duly compensated or given other avenues to seek effective remedy, the Respondent State did not only prevent the victims from seeking redress, but also encouraged impunity, and thus reneged on its obligation in violation of Articles 1 and 7(1) of the African Charter. The granting of amnesty to absolve perpetrators of human rights violations from accountability violates the right of victims to an effective remedy.[157]

The Commission thus considered that amnesties 'granting total and complete immunity from prosecution' and depriving the victims of access to any form of redress are incompatible with articles 1 (obligation to ensure human rights) and 7(1) (right to judicial protection) of the ACHPR. However, by referring to 'alternative adequate legislative or institutional mechanisms' and 'other avenues to seek effective remedy', it seemed to suggest that alternative approaches falling

152 Ibid, para 85.

153 *Zimbabwe Human Rights NGO Forum v Zimbabwe* (2006) AHRLR 128 (ACHPR 2006); *Mouvement Ivoirien des Droits Humains (MIDH) v Côte d'Ivoire* (2008) AHRLR 62 (ACHPR 2008).

154 *Human Rights NGO Forum v Zimbabwe* (n 153) paras 50–51.

155 *MIDH v Côte d'Ivoire* (n 153) para 57. See art 132 of the Constitution of Côte d'Ivoire, 2000.

156 *Human Rights NGO Forum v Zimbabwe* (n 153) para 201; *MIDH v Côte d'Ivoire* (n 153) para 91.

157 *Human Rights NGO Forum v Zimbabwe* (n 153) para 215; *MIDH v Côte d'Ivoire* (n 153) para 98.

short of criminal justice but upholding the right to a remedy of the victims might be acceptable in certain circumstances.

The recent case of *Thomas Kwoyelo v Uganda* (2018) concerned Uganda's Amnesty Act of 2000, enacted in response to a campaign by religious and civil society leaders for the peaceful resolution of the armed conflict that had ravaged northern Uganda for over a decade.[158] The Act aimed to encourage defections by rebel fighters and extended to all individuals having engaged in war or armed rebellion against the government, on the condition that they renounced violence and surrendered to the authorities.[159] Pursuant to this Act, amnesty was granted to over 26,000 returning rebel combatants irrespective of the gravity of their crimes.[160] Thomas Kwoyelo was the first and, so far, only applicant to be denied amnesty under the Act. He was charged with several counts of war crimes following his capture in 2009 and, at the time of writing, is still awaiting trial before the International Crimes Division of the Ugandan High Court.[161] This special division was established pursuant to the Juba Agreement on Accountability and Reconciliation of 2007 to prosecute persons accused of having committed serious crimes during the armed conflict.[162] In 2012, Kwoyelo filed a complaint with the African Commission alleging, inter alia, that the government's refusal to grant him amnesty violated his right to equality before the law protected by article 3 of the ACHPR.[163]

158 *Thomas Kwoyelo v Uganda*, ACHPR Communication 431/12 (17 October 2018). See Amnesty Act, 2000, discussed in ch 3 of this volume.

159 Amnesty Act, 2000 (n 158) ss 3(1) and 4(1).

160 Barney Afako, 'Undermining the LRA: Role of Uganda's Amnesty Act' *Conciliation Resources* (August 2012); Samuel Okiror, 'Forgive and forget? Amnesty dilemma haunts Uganda' *Irin* (12 June 2015).

161 See Kirsty McNamara, 'Seeking Justice in Ugandan Courts: Amnesty and the Case of Thomas Kwoyelo' (2013) 12(3) *Washington University Global Studies Law Review* 653; Paul Bradfield, 'Reshaping Amnesty in Uganda: The Case of Thomas Kwoyelo' (2017) 15 (4) *Journal of International Criminal Justice* 827; Lino Owor Ogora, 'Ten Years Later, Ugandan Court Finally Confirms 93 Charges Against Thomas Kwoyelo' *International Justice Monitor* (4 September 2018).

162 Agreement on Accountability and Reconciliation between the Government of the Republic of Uganda and the LRA/M (29 June 2007) (Juba Agreement), Annexure of 19 February 2008, s 7.

163 Kwoyelo also appealed to the Constitutional Court of Uganda which upheld the constitutionality of the amnesty law, ruled that his right to equal treatment had been violated and directed the International Crimes Division to stop the trial, see *Thomas Kwoyelo alias Latoni v Uganda*, Constitutional Court of Uganda, Petition No 036/11 (21 September 2011). However, the Director of Public Prosecution appealed against this judgment before Uganda's Supreme Court, which found that he had acted within his powers by refusing amnesty to Kwoyelo and ordered the resumption of the trial, see *Uganda v Thomas Kwoyelo*, Supreme Court of Uganda, Constitutional Appeal No 1 of 2012 (8 April 2015). Both judgments are discussed in ch 5 of this volume.

After assessing how the Amnesty Act had been applied to Kwoyelo and other amnesty applicants, and whether it covered serious human rights violations, the Commission held that:

> [I]t is clear that the Amnesty Act was applied differently to the Victim compared to the case of previous and subsequent applicants for amnesty. The Victim had satisfied all requirements in the Amnesty Act to be granted amnesty: he renounced rebellion and applied for amnesty. The fact that he was charged with grave violations of human rights is not a ground provided in the Amnesty Act for denial of amnesty.[164]

The Commission rejected the argument of the state that this difference of treatment was justified by the Juba Agreement.[165] It noted that the Amnesty Act had not been amended so as to exclude serious crimes and considered that:

> [T]he signing of the Juba Agreement without effecting corresponding and corollary amendments to the Amnesty Act is not sufficient and convincing legal ground to warrant differential treatment. It rather opens the door for varying and arbitrary interpretation and application of the Amnesty Act.[166]

The Commission thus found that, by refusing to grant amnesty to the applicant without reasonable justification, the government had violated his right to equal treatment before the law.

In an *obiter dictum* pronouncement at the end of this judgment, the Commission analysed the status of amnesties under international law in some depth in order to remedy:

> [T]he lack of clear guidance on ensuring compliance with the requirements of the African Charter when states resort to the use of amnesty as necessary means for pursuing the objectives of achieving peace and justice in times of transition from violence to peace.[167]

These comments also aimed to clarify that the finding of a violation of article 3 on account of the selective application of the amnesty law should not be interpreted as sanctioning blanket amnesties.[168] The Commission considered that blanket amnesties are contrary to international human rights and humanitarian law because they 'have the effect of excluding any form of accountability and

164 *Thomas Kwoyelo v Uganda* (n 158) para 181.
165 Ibid, paras 184–87. See Juba Agreement (n 162).
166 *Thomas Kwoyelo v Uganda* (n 158) para 187. The Constitutional Court of Uganda also ruled that the refusal to grant amnesty to Kwoyelo amounted to a violation of his right to equal treatment in *Thomas Kwoyelo alias Latoni v Uganda* (n 163).
167 *Thomas Kwoyelo v Uganda* (n 158) para 284.
168 Ibid.

hence enabling impunity'.[169] In this sense, it observed that 'unconditional amnesties with no accompanying accountability measures are particularly problematic in terms of States' compliance with international obligations, most particularly relative to their duties to respect and protect human rights'.[170] The Commission recalled its previous finding to the effect that legal measures providing complete impunity to perpetrators of gross human rights violations and depriving the victims of access to any form of remedy are contrary to the ACHPR.[171] With regard to torture, in particular, it referred to its general comment no 4 (2017) urging states not to grant blanket amnesty to persons accused of this crime.[172]

The Commission acknowledged that 'many types of amnesties have been adopted across the world', generally in circumstances characterised by 'lack of political and socio-economic stability, weak or dysfunctional institutions and diminished security'.[173] While it condemned blanket amnesties, it drew a distinction between this type of measures and conditional amnesties, described as 'those that usually offer relief from criminal conviction or criminal prosecution altogether for defined category of actors and on meeting certain preconditions including full disclosure of what they know about the conducts covered by the amnesty and acknowledgement of responsibility'.[174] The Commission suggested that conditional amnesties may be acceptable under the ACHPR in so far as they 'constitute justifiable and proportional limitations acceptable under international law'.[175] Elaborating on the requirements that should be met by conditional amnesties in order to satisfy human rights standards, it prescribed that:

> When [transitional states] resort to amnesties as necessary measures for ending violence and continuing violations and achieving peace and justice, they should respect and honor their international and regional obligations. Most particularly, they should ensure that such amnesties comply with both procedural and substantive conditions. In procedural terms, conditional amnesties should be formulated with the participation of affected communities including victim groups. Substantively speaking, amnesties should not totally exclude the right of victims for remedy, particularly remedies taking the form of getting the truth and reparations. They should also facilitate a measure of reconciliation with perpetrators acknowledging responsibility

169 Ibid, para 288.
170 Ibid, para 291.
171 See text to n 157.
172 *Thomas Kwoyelo v Uganda* (n 158) para 292. See ACHPR, General Comment on the Right to Redress for Victims of Torture and other Cruel, Inhuman or Degrading Punishment or Treatment under Article 5 of the African Charter on Human and Peoples' Rights, para 28.
173 *Thomas Kwoyelo v Uganda* (n 158) para 287.
174 Ibid, para 288.
175 Ibid, paras 287 and 291.

and victims getting a hearing about and receiving acknowledgment for the violations they suffered.[176]

This nuanced position is consistent with the flexible approach adopted by the European Court in several cases.[177] Similarly to that Court, the African Commission considers that amnesties may be acceptable when they pursue a legitimate purpose, such as ending armed violence, and do not obstruct the rights of the victims to truth and reparation. The Commission importantly adds that amnesties should be drafted taking into account the views of affected communities. It also recommends that they should be formulated so as to be conducive to reconciliation between the perpetrators and the victims through the acknowledgment of the responsibility of the former and of the suffering of the latter.

Conclusion

Human rights bodies have generally considered that amnesties covering serious human rights violations are incompatible with international human rights law. This view is based on similar provisions in different human rights treaties requiring states to protect human rights and to guarantee a remedy to victims of human rights violations. Although there is broad agreement on the general principle and its legal bases, human rights bodies have adopted distinct views on the question of whether there can be exceptions to the amnesty prohibition. Their position on this issue has evolved over time, for some towards a more absolute prohibition, for others towards an increasingly nuanced position. While certain human rights bodies have been uncompromising in their view that amnesties are not permissible under human rights law, most of them have accepted, explicitly or implicitly, that some circumstances might render such measures admissible, even when extending to serious crimes.

The question of whether the emerging prohibition of amnesty for human rights crimes admits exceptions largely depends on the rationale chosen to justify the rule, or the type of interests it aims to protect. Human rights courts have followed different approaches in this respect. On the one hand, in justifying the rule against amnesties, the Inter-American Court has placed emphasis on the right to redress of victims of human rights violations. It has established that states are under an obligation to prosecute and punish the perpetrators in order to give effect to this right, characterised by the Inter-American Commission as the 'right to justice' of the victims. On the other hand, in most of the cases in which it declared that the grant of amnesty for human rights abuses is unacceptable, the European Court focused on public interest considerations such as crime prevention, deterrence and the rule of law, rather than on the rights of

176 Ibid, para 293.

177 See *Tarbuk v. Croatia* (n 105); *Ould Dah v. France* (n 128 and text to n 132); *Marguš v Croatia* [GC] (n 141 and text to n 145).

victims. While it has also referred to the right to a remedy when criticising amnesties, it has expressly rejected the view that the ECHR confers on victims a right to criminal justice, in line with the Human Rights Committee. Thus, while the Inter-American Court has primarily grounded the amnesty prohibition in the private interest of the victims in seeing justice done, the European Court has more readily justified the rule on the basis of public interests linked to the protection of fundamental rights.

This emphasis on either private or public interests has brought human rights courts to adopt different positions on the extent of the amnesty prohibition. The Inter-American Court has made clear that all amnesties and similar measures aiming to prevent the prosecution of human rights crimes are unacceptable. It has maintained this position even with respect to amnesty laws adopted through a democratic process and ratified by public vote. Indeed, if the prohibition is based on the right to justice of the victims, all types of amnesties extending to human rights violations ought to be rejected as there seems to be no valid reason to distinguish between victims for the purpose of judicial protection. By contrast, since the European Court has placed emphasis on public interests requiring prosecution, it has accepted that competing public interests favouring amnesty might in exceptional cases outweigh the former. Thus, it has acknowledged that even amnesties extending to international crimes may be permissible if they form part of a national reconciliation process. It has also endorsed the view of the European Commission to the effect that amnesty laws may cover violations of fundamental rights as long as they pursue a legitimate public interest and maintain a balance between this objective and the protection of individual rights. The African Commission has similarly considered that conditional amnesties pursuing a legitimate objective in a proportionate manner may be acceptable under human rights law.

While they have diverged as regards the rationale and extent of the amnesty prohibition, human rights bodies have concurred on several aspects of the rule, which may be taken as the baseline of the position of amnesties under human rights law. First, all human rights bodies have recognised that states are under an obligation to investigate serious human rights violations and provide a remedy to the victims. Thus, amnesties precluding any form of inquiry into serious violations and barring the victims' access to any type of remedy would be deemed contrary to human rights law. Conversely, amnesty laws drafted so as to preclude the prosecution of human rights offenders but not investigatory proceedings and civil remedies might satisfy the obligations of states under certain human rights treaties. The European Court's approach may be construed as providing some leeway for this type of amnesties. The case law of the African Commission also allows for some flexibility as regards amnesties which do not completely close the door on accountability and are accompanied by transitional mechanisms upholding the rights of the victims to truth and reparation.

Amnesties providing for only limited penal immunity would probably not be given deference by the Inter-American Court or the Human Rights Committee since they would infringe the duty of states to prosecute and punish perpetrators under the ACHR and the ICCPR. However, it remains to be seen how the Inter-American Court would deal with an alternative sentence system of the Colombian type facilitating the discovery of the truth, inducing perpetrators to repair the harm done to the victims and ensuring a degree of accountability for serious crimes through alternative sanctions. Inter-American institutions have so far been mostly confronted with self-amnesties benefiting state agents responsible for grave abuses against civilians. They might thus adopt a less categorical attitude towards conditional amnesties extending to state opponents and complemented by accountability and reparation mechanisms. The fact that the Human Rights Committee refrained from criticising the South African truth and reconciliation process might also indicate some flexibility in this regard.

Second, there is general consensus on the view that amnesties granted by or at the instigation of a government to cover up serious crimes committed by its own agents are contrary to human rights law. Besides depriving the victims of access to a judicial remedy, amnesties shielding state officials from accountability give rise to a climate of impunity undermining the rule of law, crime prevention and deterrence. Self-amnesties are thus detrimental both to the rights of the victims and to public interests underlying general human rights protection. They have therefore been firmly condemned by the Human Rights Committee, the European Court and the Inter-American Court. In fact, the robust approach of the latter regarding the obligation to punish human rights offenders and the right to justice of the victims was developed in response to this type of amnesties. The case law of treaty bodies strongly suggests that self-amnesties applying to serious crimes are not compatible with human rights law.

Third, all treaty bodies have refused to recognise amnesty laws as a bar to their jurisdiction over serious human rights violations. While the Inter-American Court is the only one to have gone so far as to invalidate amnesty laws and declare them devoid of legal force within the domestic system in which they were enacted, all treaty bodies have rejected challenges to their jurisdiction based on amnesty laws. Their approach has usually consisted in setting aside the law in so far as it applied to serious crimes and urging the state to investigate and provide a remedy to the victims. Although there has been a tendency for treaty bodies to refuse to give effect to such laws, some amnesties were upheld or came through judicial review. For instance, the Inter-American and European Commissions endorsed amnesty laws covering serious crimes in Guatemala, Nicaragua and New Caledonia. For its part, the African Commission found that the unequal application of a Ugandan amnesty law, even with respect to persons accused of grave crimes, amounted to a violation of the ACHPR. Though not having explicitly upheld amnesty laws, the Human Rights Committee refrained from condemning such measures extending to serious human rights violations in its country reports on South Africa, Angola, Mozambique, Brazil and Uganda. The European Court also abstained from challenging Spain's amnesty law when it had an opportunity to do so.

Finally, there has been a common trend among human rights bodies to acknowledge that some flexibility may be warranted with respect to amnesties regarded as necessary as part of a peace or reconciliation process. The lack of condemnation of certain amnesty laws by the Human Rights Committee may be understood in this sense. The European Court and Commission have both explicitly recognised that the need for reconciliation is a factor to be taken into account when evaluating the acceptability of an amnesty law. The African Commission has also considered that conditional amnesties aiming to facilitate a peace process may be acceptable in so far as they fulfil certain requirements. In the same vein, the Inter-American Commission has, in early country reports, emphasised the need to balance the requirements of justice with the need for peace, reconciliation and democratisation in the aftermath of conflict or repression. The Inter-American Court has been the most stringent as regards the absolute nature of the amnesty ban. However, several Inter-American judges have been prepared to nuance the position of the Court on the obligation to punish and the right to justice in situations of armed conflicts. They have accepted that these rights and obligations may need to be weighed against the need to achieve peace, reconciliation, truth and reparation in such contexts. This higher flexibility when peace and reconciliation are at stake would arguably enable human rights bodies to support transitional strategies seeking to overcome periods of violence and division through multi-faceted approaches relying on a combination of amnesty and other mechanisms to uphold states' obligations and victims' rights to the largest extent possible.

7 The mandate of international criminal courts

Introduction

Amnesties may be seen as the antithesis of international criminal courts in so far as, whereas the latter are created for the purpose of ensuring the prosecution of certain crimes, the former are adopted in order to guarantee that certain categories of offenders will not face prosecution. This chapter analyses how international criminal courts have dealt with amnesties covering crimes within their jurisdiction and what their approaches imply for the international legality of amnesties. The first section examines whether the statutory instruments of international or hybrid criminal bodies exclude the applicability of amnesties, explicitly or implicitly. The second section reviews the case law of these bodies in order to identify the rationales underlying their refusal to give effect to amnesties. It also considers the approach of the International Criminal Court and its Prosecutor's Office regarding amnesties and alternative forms of justice. The chapter argues that, while there is general consensus on the view that amnesties cannot be effective in depriving international criminal courts of jurisdiction over persons accused of international crimes, it is not clear that this results from a general amnesty ban.

1. Amnesty in the statute of international criminal courts

This section examines how the statutory instruments of international criminal courts deal with the issue of amnesty. While the statutes of the first ad hoc tribunals and of the International Criminal Court are silent in this respect, the organic laws of most subsequent hybrid criminal courts expressly exclude amnesty as a bar to their jurisdiction. These exclusion clauses are consistent with the object and purpose of international criminal bodies, namely, to ensure accountability for alleged perpetrators of serious crimes.

The ad hoc tribunals

The International Criminal Tribunal for the former Yugoslavia (ICTY) and the International Criminal Tribunal for Rwanda (ICTR) were the first ad hoc tribunals created by the UN Security Council pursuant to its powers under Chapter 7 of the UN Charter.[1] They were established in the early 1990s to try persons responsible for serious violations of international humanitarian law committed in the contexts of the armed conflict in the former Yugoslavia and the genocide in Rwanda, respectively. The resolutions creating the tribunals affirmed that these situations constituted threats to international peace and security and determined 'to put an end to such crimes and to take effective measures to bring to justice the persons who are responsible for them'.[2] Through the tribunals, the international community intended to 'contribute to the restoration and maintenance of peace' in both contexts and 'to the process of national reconciliation' in Rwanda.[3]

The ICTY and the ICTR were competent to prosecute persons accused of war crimes, genocide and crimes against humanity.[4] Their statutes do not refer to amnesties. However, the purpose of the Security Council in establishing the tribunals would seem incompatible with a deferential approach towards leniency measures covering persons under their jurisdiction. The obligation of cooperation imposed on states by the Chapter 7 resolutions establishing the tribunals would also be inconsistent with the grant of an amnesty to such persons.[5] Moreover, since these international tribunals had primacy of jurisdiction over the national courts of all states, and their statute did not require them to defer to domestic legislation, national amnesty laws would probably not have prevented them from asserting jurisdiction over alleged perpetrators of international crimes.[6]

Corroborating this assumption, the statutes of both tribunals determine that the principle of *ne bis in idem*, prohibiting the trial of a person who has already been tried for the same facts, does not prevent them from exercising jurisdiction where 'the national court proceedings were not impartial or independent, were designed to shield the accused from international criminal responsibility, or

1 Security Council resolution 827 (25 May 1993) UN Doc S/RES/827; Security Council resolution 955 (8 November 1994) UN Doc S/RES/955. See Charter of the United Nations (adopted 26 June 1945, entered into force 24 October 1945) 1 UNTS XVI, Chapter 7.

2 Resolution 827 (n 1) preamble, paras 4–5; resolution 955 (n 1) preamble, paras 5–6.

3 Resolution 827 (n 1) preamble, para 6; resolution 955 (n 1) preamble, para 7.

4 Statute of the International Tribunal for the Prosecution of Persons Responsible for Serious Violations of International Humanitarian Law Committed in the Territory of the Former Yugoslavia since 1991, adopted by Security Council resolution 827 (25 May 1993) (ICTY statute) arts 2 to 5; Statute of the International Criminal Tribunal for the Prosecution of Persons Responsible for Genocide and Other Serious Violations of International Humanitarian Law Committed in the Territory of Rwanda and Rwandan Citizens Responsible for Genocide and Other Such Violations Committed in the Territory of Neighbouring States, between 1 January 1994 and 31 December 1994, adopted by Security Council resolution 955 (8 November 1994) (ICTR statute) arts 2 to 4.

5 Resolutions 827 (n 1) para 4; resolution 955 (n 1) para 2. See also ICTY statute (n 4) art 29; ICTR statute (n 4) art 28. All UN member states are under an obligation to comply with Chapter 7 resolutions of the Security Council pursuant to art 48(2) of the Charter of the United Nations (n 1).

6 ICTY statute (n 4) arts 9(2); ICTR statute (n 4) art 8(2).

[when] the case was not diligently prosecuted'.[7] This provision would arguably have enabled the ICTY or the ICTR to prosecute persons having been granted an amnesty with respect to an international crime since a domestic offer of amnesty would result in the crime 'not being diligently prosecuted'. As to the possibility of a person being granted an amnesty after having been convicted by one of the tribunals, another provision common to both statutes requires that '[t]here shall only be pardon or commutation of sentence if the President of the International Tribunal ... in consultation with the judges, so decides on the basis of the interests of justice and the general principles of law'.[8] Accordingly, a decision by the national authorities of a state in which a person convicted by one of the tribunals was serving his sentence to amnesty or pardon that person would need to be validated by the tribunal's authorities.

The International Criminal Court

The setting up of the ad hoc tribunals contributed to create momentum towards the establishment of a permanent international criminal court. According to Cherif Bassiouni, '[t]he events in Yugoslavia and Rwanda shocked the world out of its complacency, and the idea of prosecuting those who committed international crimes acquired a broad-based support in world public opinion and in many governments'.[9] Indeed, while initiatives towards the creation of an international criminal court date back to the 1940s, it was not until 1994 that a draft statute was formally adopted by the International Law Commission.[10] That body recommended to the UN General Assembly to 'convene an international conference of plenipotentiaries to study the draft statute and to conclude a convention on the establishment of an international criminal court'.[11] Accordingly, the General Assembly created an Ad Hoc Committee (1995) and a Preparatory Committee (1996–1998) to review the statute and prepare the work of the Rome Conference, convened in June and July 1998.[12]

The Rome statute established the International Criminal Court (ICC) as a permanent institution competent to intervene in situations involving international

7 ICTY statute (n 4) art 10(2); ICTR statute (n 4) art 9(2).

8 ICTY statute (n 4) art 28; ICTR statute (n 4) art 27.

9 M Cherif Bassiouni, *Introduction to International Criminal Law: Second Revised Edition* (Martinus Nijhoff Publishers 2014) 588.

10 UN General Assembly Official Records (GAOR), Report of the International Law Commission on the work of its 46th session (May–July 1994) UN Doc A/49/10. See ibid, 575–88.

11 Report of the International Law Commission (n 10) para 90.

12 UN General Assembly (UNGA) resolution 49/53 (17 February 1995) UN Doc A/RES/49/53; UNGA resolution 50/46 (18 December 1995) UN Doc A/RES/50/46; UNGA resolution 51/207 (16 January 1997) UN Doc A/RES/51/207; UNGA resolution 52/160 (28 January 1998) UN Doc A/RES/52/160. See Adriaan Bos, 'From the International Law Commission to the Rome Conference (1994–1998)' in Antonio Cassese, Paola Gaeta and John RWD Jones (eds), *The Rome Statute of the International Criminal Court: A Commentary* (OUP 2002, vol 1) 35.

crimes where the territorial state is 'unwilling or unable genuinely to carry out the investigation or prosecution'.[13] By contrast with the ad hoc tribunals, the ICC is complementary to national courts and can only exercise jurisdiction when the latter fail to do so. The Rome statute empowers the Court to try alleged perpetrators of genocide, crimes against humanity, war crimes and aggression.[14] A situation involving these crimes may be referred to the ICC by a state party or by the Security Council.[15] The ICC Prosecutor may also decide to initiate an investigation *proprio motu* subject to the authorisation of the Pre-Trial Chamber.[16] As a treaty-based court, the ICC may only exercise jurisdiction over crimes committed within the territory or by a national of a state party after the entry into force of the Rome statute in the state in question.[17] However, a situation involving international crimes committed in the territory of a non-party state may be referred to the Court by the Security Council acting under Chapter 7 of the UN Charter.[18] In addition to having the power of referring a situation to the ICC, the Security Council may suspend an investigation or prosecution for a renewable period of twelve months.[19]

The Rome statute does not address the issue of amnesty. The question of whether domestic amnesty processes might be accommodated by the ICC in certain circumstances was controversial during the negotiations leading up to its adoption.[20] Accordingly, the issue was generally avoided in the Preparatory Committee and the Rome Conference. The two provisions of the statute in relation to which it was raised are article 20 protecting the *ne bis in idem* principle and article 17 on admissibility.

As regards the *ne bis in idem* principle, the third paragraph of article 20 provides that:

13 Rome Statute of the International Criminal Court (adopted 17 July 1998, entered into force 1 July 2002) 2187 UNTS 90 (Rome statute) art 17.

14 Ibid, art 5(1).

15 Ibid, art 13.

16 Ibid, arts 13 and 15 and 15 bis.

17 Ibid, arts 11 and 13. The jurisdictional regime is different as regards the crime of aggression. The resolution activating the jurisdiction of the ICC over this crime only authorises state referrals and investigations *proprio motu* with respect to states parties having ratified or accepted the Kampala amendment of 11 June 2010 (resolution RC/Res.6), see ICC Assembly of States Parties, 'Draft resolution proposed by the Vice-Presidents of the Assembly: Activation of the jurisdiction of the Court over the crime of aggression' (14 December 2017) ICC-ASP/16/L.10, para 2.

18 Rome statute (n 13) art 13(b).

19 Ibid, art 16.

20 Bos (n 12) 56–57; Darryl Robinson, 'Serving the Interests of Justice: Amnesties, Truth Commissions and the International Criminal Court' (2003) 14(3) *European Journal of International Law* 481, 482–83; Mahnoush H Arsanjani, 'The International Criminal Court and National Amnesty Laws' (1999) 93 *ASIL Proceedings* 65, 67; Sharon Williams and William Schabas, 'Article 17, Issues of Admissibility' in Otto Triffterer (ed), *Commentary on the Statute of the International Criminal Court* (2nd edn, Hart Publishing 2008) 617.

> No person who has been tried by another court for conduct also proscribed under [the Rome Statute] shall be tried by the Court with respect to the same conduct unless the proceedings in the other court:
>
> (a) Were for the purpose of shielding the person concerned from criminal responsibility for crimes within the jurisdiction of the Court; or
> (b) Otherwise were not conducted independently or impartially in accordance with the norms of due process recognized by international law and were conducted in a manner which, in the circumstances, was inconsistent with an intent to bring the person concerned to justice.[21]

Amnesties, pardons and analogous measures issued before or in the course of a domestic trial for an ICC crime would presumably fall under one of the exceptions to this provision since they would result in shielding the accused from criminal responsibility and would be 'inconsistent with an intent to bring the person concerned to justice'.[22] However, where the amnesty or pardon is granted after the conclusion of the national proceedings, it would not prevent the trial and conviction of the accused, but only the execution of the sentence. During the negotiation of article 20 in the Preparatory Committee, human rights organisations suggested that the ICC should be allowed to proceed with cases tried by domestic courts in the event a clemency measure was issued to prevent the convicted person from serving his or her sentence.[23] For this purpose, the Portuguese delegation proposed the introduction of an article 19 providing that:

> [A] person who has been tried by another court for conduct also proscribed under article 5 may be tried by the Court if a manifestly unfounded decision on the suspension of the enforcement of a sentence or on a pardon, a parole or a commutation of the sentence excludes the application of any appropriate form of penalty.[24]

21 Rome statute (n 13) art 20(3).

22 See Christine Van den Wyngaert and Tom Ongena, 'Ne bis in idem Principle, Including the Issue of Amnesty' in Antonio Cassese, Paola Gaeta and John RWD Jones (eds), *The Rome Statute of the International Criminal Court: A Commentary* (OUP 2002, vol 1) 726–27; Jessica Gavron, 'Amnesties in the Light of Developments in International Law and the Establishment of the International Criminal Court' (2002) 51 *International and Comparative Law Quarterly* 91, 109–10.

23 Van den Wyngaert and Ongena (n 22) 727. See Document submitted by Human Rights Watch during the second session of the PrepCom, 'Human Rights Watch Commentary for the Preparatory Committee on the Establishment of an International Criminal Court' (August 1996).

24 Report of the Preparatory Committee on the Establishment of an International Criminal Court, Draft Statute of the International Criminal Court, UN Doc A/CONF.183/2/Add.1 (14 April 1998), 46 (art 19).

This amendment was controversial at the Rome Conference. Several delegations expressed concern that it encroached upon the principle of national sovereignty. For example, the delegate of Afghanistan emphasised that 'it was the sovereign right of States to decide on the commutation of a sentence or on a pardon, according to its national interests and crime policy'.[25] Similarly, the delegate of Israel 'had a problem with article 19, since it might imply unwarranted interference with decisions of administrative organs of a State which had already tried a person for crimes covered by the Statute'.[26] Accordingly, the British delegation submitted that while 'it understood the reasons behind the proposed text, it was unsure whether it would be possible to reach agreement on it in view of the highly sensitive and difficult issues which it raised'.[27] Most of the participants favoured the deletion of article 19.[28] The failure to retain it in the final draft has been described as 'a serious lacuna'.[29] Indeed, this provides room for national authorities to argue that the Court may not intervene in situations where a person convicted of an international crime evades punishment through a domestic offer of amnesty or pardon. This omission reflects the uneasiness of states with a treaty provision enabling an international institution to second-guess their decision to bestow clemency on convicted offenders.

Within the Preparatory Committee, the issue of amnesty was also raised in relation to the principle of complementarity.[30] During the negotiation of article 17, it was thought necessary to determine whether and how the complementarity regime would take account of 'national reconciliation initiatives entailing legitimate offers of amnesty or internationally structured peace processes'.[31] In order to promote a discussion on the subject, the US delegation circulated a non-paper reviewing a number of amnesty processes in different parts of the world and how they had been received at the national and international levels.[32] This document aimed to illustrate 'the considerable existing state practice on

25 United Nations Diplomatic Conference of Plenipotentiaries on the Establishment of an International Criminal Court Official Records (Rome, 15 June – 17 July 1998) UN Doc A/CONR183/13, vol 2, 215, para 33.

26 Ibid, 216, para 42.

27 Ibid, 215, para 34.

28 Ibid, 215–21 (the delegations of Australia, Turkey, Colombia, Venezuela, Poland, France, Iraq, Japan, Indonesia, China, Syria, India, Malawi, Algeria, Switzerland, Brazil, Jordan, Singapore, Peru, Norway, Nigeria, Egypt, Sudan, Italy, Austria, Morocco, Botswana, Vietnam, Uruguay, Oman and Iran thought that article 19 should be deleted).

29 Van den Wyngaert and Ongena (n 22) 727.

30 UN GAOR, Report of the Preparatory Committee on the Establishment of an International Criminal Court (Proceedings of the Preparatory Committee during March-April and August 1996) UN Doc A/51/22, vol 1, para 160. See also UN Diplomatic Conference of Plenipotentiaries on the Establishment of an International Criminal Court, Report of the Preparatory Committee on the Establishment of an International Criminal Court (14 April 1998) UN Doc A/CONF.183/2/Add.1, 40–41 (fn 42).

31 Ibid.

32 US Delegation Paper on State Practice regarding Amnesties and Pardon, Non-Paper/WG.3/No.7 (6 August 1997).

amnesties and pardons' and contrast different processes on the basis of 'the scope of acts covered, the nature of the negotiations that resulted in the amnesties, and the manner in which they are to be implemented'.[33] Another document bearing on the issue of amnesty submitted by Human Rights Watch underlined the reasons why cases involving ICC crimes should not be declared inadmissible on the basis of clemency measures.[34] According to Adriaan Bos, the chairman of the Preparatory Committee, the issue of amnesty 'was not profoundly discussed'.[35]

During the Rome Conference, the question of whether the statute should provide some leeway for amnesties forming part of a national reconciliation process was controversial.[36] According to Darryl Robinson, who participated in the drafting of article 17:

> Views on the matter clashed sharply, as many participants felt very strongly that prosecution is the sole appropriate response (and indeed an obligatory response), whereas others felt very strongly that alternative mechanisms were acceptable. Even among those delegations most committed to prosecution of all international crimes, many had misgivings about laying down an iron rule for all time mandating prosecution as the only acceptable response in all situations. On the other hand, creating an explicit exception allowing amnesties was equally untenable. Some delegations opposed any exception in principle, whereas others were concerned that any exception would be immediately exploited and abused.[37]

As a result of the impossibility of reaching agreement on this issue, the drafters refrained from taking any definite stance in the statute, not authorising amnesties but not excluding them either.

The question of whether there could be an amnesty exception to the jurisdiction of the ICC has been discussed extensively in the literature.[38] There is broad consensus on two points. First, commentators agree that blanket

33 Ibid, 1 (see fn).
34 Bos (n 12) 57.
35 Ibid.
36 See Robinson (n 20) 482–83; Williams and Schabas (n 20) 617.
37 Robinson (n 20) 483.
38 See Robinson (n 20); Arsanjani (n 20); Gavron (n 22); Michael P Scharf, 'The Amnesty Exception to the Jurisdiction of the International Criminal Court' (1999) 32 *Cornell International Law Journal* 507; Carsten Stahn, 'Complementarity, Amnesties and Alternative Forms of Justice: Some Interpretative Guidelines for the International Criminal Court' (2005) 3 *Journal of International Criminal Justice* 695; Richard J Goldstone and Nicole Fritz, '"In the Interests of Justice" and Independent Referral: The ICC Prosecutor's Unprecedented Powers' (2000) 13(3) *Leiden Journal of International Law* 655; John Dugard, 'Possible Conflicts of Jurisdiction with Truth Commissions' in Antonio Cassese, Paola Gaeta and John RWD Jones (eds), *The Rome Statute of the International Criminal Court: A Commentary* (OUP 2002, vol 1) 693; Naomi Roht-Arriaza, 'Amnesty and the International

amnesties are incompatible with the aim and purpose of the Rome statute and would not be respected by the ICC. The Court was established in order to put an end to impunity for 'the most serious crimes of concern to the international community as a whole' by ensuring the prosecution and punishment of the perpetrators when states fail to do so.[39] Thus, unconditional amnesties issued for the purpose of shielding perpetrators of international crimes from accountability would conflict with the very *raison d'être* of the ICC. The Prosecutor and the Court could discard measures of this type on the basis that they amount to a failure by the state to take any action towards the investigation of international crimes.

The second point on which scholars concur is that the drafters of the Rome statute left room for the ICC to be able to accommodate carefully crafted amnesty processes adhering to certain criteria in compelling circumstances. Three provisions of the statute, in particular, have been identified as potential avenues for the recognition of amnesties.

Article 17: admissibility and the principle of complementarity

Article 17 of the Rome statute sets down the scenarios in which cases may be declared inadmissible before the ICC.[40] During the negotiation of this provision, some participants questioned whether prosecutions should be seen as the only permissible response to international crimes, even at the risk of jeopardising a fragile peace or democratisation process.[41] It was argued that genuine truth and reconciliation programmes following the South African model could be an acceptable alternative to criminal justice in certain circumstances. Accordingly, a 'narrow doorway' was left in article 17 permitting deference to alternative forms of justice fulfilling certain criteria.[42]

The scenario envisaged by article 17(1)(b) refers to a situation where a case 'has been investigated by a State which has jurisdiction over it and the State has decided not to prosecute the person concerned, unless the decision resulted from the unwillingness or inability of the State genuinely to prosecute'.[43] The wording of this provision indicates that a decision by national authorities not to prosecute international crimes may be dictated by reasons other than their unwillingness or inability to do so. Indeed, the prosecution of every offender implicated in a situation of armed conflict or state repression may not be feasible

Criminal Court' in Dinah Shelton (ed), *International Crimes, Peace and Human Rights: The Role of the International Criminal Court* (Transnational Publishers 2000).

39 See Rome statute (n 13) preamble, paras 4–5.

40 The admissibility of cases under article 17 is assessed by the Prosecutor during the preliminary examination process and may be reviewed by the Court once an investigation has been opened, see arts 53(1)(b) and (2)(b), 18(2) and 19(1) to (4) of the Rome statute (n 13).

41 Robinson (n 20) 499; Williams and Schabas (n 20) 617; Dugard (n 38) 700.

42 Robinson (n 20) 499.

43 Rome statute (n 13).

in practical terms or desirable as a matter of policy where it is liable to destabilise a transitional process by provoking military backlashes, alienate critical actors in peace negotiations or otherwise leading to a resumption of violence. In such contexts, alternative mechanisms may be designed which, though falling short of criminal punishment, provide a degree of accountability and a form of compensation to the victims through the establishment of the facts, the public acknowledgment of responsibilities and reparative measures. Alternative accountability processes often rely on the grant of amnesty to certain categories of offenders subject to specific requirements.[44]

To correspond to the scenario contemplated in article 17(1)(b), alternative forms of justice would need to fulfil three conditions. First, they must include an investigatory phase permitting the facts and responsibilities to be determined in a quasi-judicial way. The provision does not require a 'criminal' investigation so that fact-finding proceedings carried out under the auspices of a truth commission could arguably satisfy this criterion. The second condition is that the national authorities decide not to prosecute, which entails that the criminal law option must be available.[45] This requirement would exclude blanket amnesties issued before any accountability process is envisaged, since the authorities would then be legally bound, and not choose, to forego prosecution. The last hurdle is that the decision in question must not result from 'the unwillingness or inability of the state genuinely to prosecute'.[46] Article 17(2) specifies that a state will be considered as unwilling when national proceedings are undertaken 'for the purpose of shielding the person concerned from criminal responsibility' or are 'inconsistent with an intent to bring the person concerned to justice'.[47] Amnesties inherently entail the exemption of offenders from criminal punishment. However, there may be room to argue that the primary goal of a particular transitional process relying on clemency measures is not to secure impunity but to establish conditions conducive to overriding public interests, such as the restoration of peace, the promotion of reconciliation and the discovery of the truth, in circumstances in which those objectives could not be attained through normal criminal proceedings.

In an informal expert paper aiming to provide guidance to the Office of the Prosecutor (OTP) as regards the application of the principle of complementarity in practice, it was acknowledged that, although the ICC is mandated to ensure that international crimes do not go unpunished, 'alternative approaches should not be summarily dismissed'.[48] The experts outlined a number of criteria to be

44 For example, the truth and reconciliation processes in South Africa, Liberia, Kenya, Guatemala, Colombia, East Timor, Indonesia, Nepal and the Solomon Islands all included an amnesty component.

45 See Robinson (n 20) 500.

46 Rome statute (n 13) art 17(1)(c).

47 Rome statute (n 13).

48 ICC OTP, 'Informal expert paper: The principle of complementarity in practice' (2003) para 72.

considered by the Prosecutor when evaluating whether alternative forms of justice or conditional amnesties are consistent with the Rome statute, including whether they apply to the most responsible perpetrators, benefit from international support, are designed and implemented through democratic processes, and permit a form of punishment to be imposed on serious offenders.[49] The experts advocated for a flexible approach of the compatibility of alternative forms of justice with the ICC framework, as long as they remain consistent with the Court's mandate. They advised the OTP not to adopt 'too precise a position' on this issue so as to be able to adapt to different contexts and circumstances, acknowledging that '[p]ast experience demonstrates that it would be arduous to attempt to develop a general doctrine on how to assess such situations'.[50]

Article 53: prosecutorial discretion and the 'interests of justice'

Article 53 lists the factors to be considered by the ICC Prosecutor when determining whether or not to proceed with an investigation or prosecution. First, she must establish that the Court has jurisdiction over the case and, second, that it is admissible on the basis of gravity and complementarity.[51] When those conditions are met, the Prosecutor may still decide not to proceed with an investigation where '[t]aking into account the gravity of the crime and the interests of victims, there are nonetheless substantial reasons to believe that an investigation would not serve the interests of justice'.[52] Pursuant to the second paragraph, the interests of justice may also ground a decision not to prosecute, which must take into account 'all the circumstances, including the gravity of the crime, the interests of victims and the age or infirmity of the alleged perpetrator, and his or her role in the alleged crime'.[53] Decisions not to proceed based solely on the interests of justice are subject to a higher standard of judicial review than those based on other considerations since they must be confirmed by the Pre-Trial Chamber.[54]

The expression 'interests of justice' is not defined in the statute and was only cursorily discussed during the negotiation of article 53.[55] A literal interpretation of the provision suggests that the interests of justice are broader than traditional prosecutorial policy grounds such as the gravity of the crime and the interests of victims. The wording of article 53(1)(c) also indicates that these interests may prevail over traditional criteria since, even when the latter prompt the Prosecutor to start an investigation, she may 'nonetheless' decide to stay proceedings if the

49 Ibid, para 73.
50 Ibid, para 74.
51 Rome statute (n 13) art 53(1)-(2).
52 Ibid, art 53(1)(c).
53 Ibid, art 53(2)(c).
54 Ibid, art 53(3)(b).
55 For a discussion of the drafting history, see William Schabas, *The International Criminal Court: A Commentary on the Rome Statute* (OUP 2010) 656–58, 663.

former so warrant. The interests of justice provisions confer on the Prosecutor 'an enormous scope for what amounts to a highly discretionary determination'.[56] On this basis, she could decide to forego an investigation or prosecution in order not to interfere with a peace process involving an amnesty programme falling short of the criteria for being declared inadmissible under article 17(1)(b). However, such a decision would be subject to the review of the Pre-Trial Chamber based on the factors enumerated in article 53, including the interests of victims. While victims are generally in favour of prosecution and punishment, it is conceivable that they would support an amnesty process if it represented the best chance of ending a protracted armed conflict, restoring stability and security.[57]

In 2007, the Prosecutor issued a policy paper making clear that the interests of justice would be interpreted restrictively by the OTP. This paper emphasises that:

> Bearing in mind the objectives of the Court to put an end to impunity and to ensure that the most serious crimes do not go unpunished, a decision not to proceed on the basis of the interests of justice should be understood as a course of last resort.[58]

It explains that there is a presumption in favour of investigation and prosecution deriving from the object and purpose of the statute, which will only be displaced in exceptional circumstances. It also specifies that there is a difference between the interests of justice and the interests of peace, the latter falling under the mandate of different institutions, primarily the UN Security Council.[59] This narrow understanding of the interests of justice has been criticised by some commentators advocating for a revision of the OTP policy in order to enable the Prosecutor to take into account the impact of ICC prosecutions on the ground, especially in the context of ongoing armed conflicts or fragile peace talks.[60]

Still, the OTP policy paper acknowledges that countervailing considerations linked to the interests of peace may inform a decision not to proceed. It recognises that, in order to mitigate the 'impunity gap' in situations involving a large number of offenders, prosecutions should be seen as only 'one part of the necessary response to serious crimes of international concern which, by itself, may prove to be insufficient'.[61] Thus, complementary measures including truth-recovery, reparation and traditional justice mechanisms are encouraged as part of

56 Ibid, 660.

57 See *Refugee Law Project*, 'Peace First, Justice Later: Traditional Justice in Northern Uganda' Working Paper No 17 (July 2005).

58 ICC OTP, 'Policy Paper on the Interests of Justice' (September 2007) 9.

59 Ibid, 1 and 8–9.

60 Maria Varaki, 'Revisiting the "Interests of Justice" Policy Paper' (2017) 15(3) *Journal of International Criminal Justice* 455; Priscilla Hayner, 'Does the ICC advance the Interests of Justice?' *Open Democracy* (4 November 2014).

61 'Policy Paper on the Interests of Justice' (n 58) 7–8.

a comprehensive strategy extending beyond the criminal justice mandate of the ICC. As regards the interests of victims, the OTP paper accepts that they include 'the victims' interest in seeing justice done, but also ... other essential interests such as their protection'.[62] In ascertaining the interests of the victims, the OTP undertakes to 'give due consideration to the different views of victims, their communities and the broader societies in which it may be required to act'.[63] Thus, some elements in the policy paper could provide support for a decision not to interfere with a grassroots transitional process involving the grant of amnesty alongside traditional or restorative justice mechanisms if such an approach was consistent with the views of the victims and affected communities as well as broader societal interests.

Article 16: deferral power of the Security Council

The third statutory route that could permit deference to an amnesty process involves the power of the Security Council to defer an investigation or prosecution pursuant to article 16.[64] Such a decision by the Council would entail a determination under Chapter 7 of the UN Charter that a situation constitutes a threat to, or a breach of, international peace and security. Thus, article 16 could only be relied on if the discontinuation of ICC proceedings was deemed necessary to maintain or restore international peace and security. While this provision would seldom be applicable, it could be used by the Council to prevent the ICC from intervening in a peace process if, for instance, an amnesty deal was seen as the only way out of a protracted and far-reaching armed conflict. In extreme circumstances, this provision could even be used to ensure the non-interference of the Court with a broad and unconditional amnesty process extending to perpetrators of serious crimes. Although such a course of action is unlikely considering the UN policy opposing the grant of amnesty for serious crimes, article 16 provides a kind of safety valve which could be activated in exceptional circumstances.[65] The caveat, however, is that a deferral request can only be effective for twelve months, subject to renewal under the same conditions, so that it could hardly serve to enforce permanent deference to an amnesty law.[66]

Hybrid courts

In the wake of the establishment of the ad hoc tribunals, several states recovering from periods of mass violence requested the UN to set up an international

62 Ibid, 5.
63 Ibid.
64 Rome statute (n 13).
65 On the UN policy on amnesties, see ch 5 in this volume.
66 See Gavron (n 22) 109.

tribunal.[67] However, the Security Council has been reluctant to use its Chapter 7 powers to create other fully international tribunals because of the considerable costs associated with these experiences. Thus, a new model of hybrid tribunal emerged, based on a mix of international and domestic elements in terms of the institutional structure, personnel and applicable law.[68] Hybrid courts have gained in popularity over the last two decades as the limitations of the ICC as a global criminal court became more apparent and international policy shifted in favour of locally grounded, rather than internationally imposed, solutions to deal with atrocity crimes.

One of the first hybrid body was created by a UN transitional administration in relation to the widespread human rights violations committed in connection with East Timor's referendum of independence from Indonesia in 1999. The UN mission established two transitional mechanisms with complementary mandates: the Serious Crimes Panels (SCP) to deal with serious offenders, and the Commission for Reception, Truth and Reconciliation to disclose the truth, promote reconciliation and facilitate the reintegration of offenders.[69] The Commission was empowered to grant immunity to offenders admitting responsibility and participating in a community reconciliation process, at the exception of those responsible for serious crimes within the jurisdiction of the SCP, i.e. genocide, war crimes, crimes against humanity, murder, sexual offences and torture.[70] While a number of East Timorese serious offenders were tried and convicted by the SCP, the most high-ranking perpetrators fled to Indonesia, which has refused to extradite them or prosecute them in its own courts.[71]

The Special Court for Sierra Leone (SCSL) was established pursuant to an agreement between the UN and the government of Sierra Leone for the purpose of ensuring the prosecution of those most responsible for atrocity crimes

67 See William Schabas, *The UN International Criminal Tribunals: The Former Yugoslavia, Rwanda and Sierra Leone* (CUP 2006) 4–7; Daphna Shraga, 'The Second Generation UN-Based Tribunals: A Diversity of Mixed Jurisdiction' in Cesare PR Romano, André Nollkaemper and Jann K Kleffner (eds), *Internationalized Criminal Courts and Tribunals: Sierra Leone, East Timor, Kosovo and Cambodia* (OUP 2004) 15.

68 Ibid; Laura A Dickinson, 'The Promise of Hybrid Courts' (2003) 97 *American Journal of International Law* 295; Sarah Williams, *Hybrid and Internationalised Criminal Tribunals, Selected Jurisdictional Issues* (Hart Publishing 2012); Bassiouni (n 9) 721–85.

69 United Nations Transitional Administration in East Timor (UNTAET) Regulation 2000/15 on the establishment of Panels with exclusive jurisdiction over serious criminal offences (6 June 2000) UNTAET/REG/2000/15; UNTAET Regulation 2001/10 on the establishment of a Commission for Reception, Truth and Reconciliation in East Timor (13 July 2001) UNTAET/REG/2001/10.

70 UNTAET Regulation 2001/10 (n 69) ss 22 to 32; UNTAET Regulation 2000/15 (n 69) s 1(3).

71 Patrick Burgess, 'De Facto Amnesty? The Example of Post-Soeharto Indonesia' in Francesca Lessa and Leigh A Payne (eds), *Amnesty in the Age of Human Rights Accountability: Comparative and International Perspectives* (CUP 2012) 272; Lia Kent, 'Beyond "Pragmatism" versus "Principle": Ongoing Justice Debates in East Timor' in Renée Jeffery and Hun Joon Kim (eds), *Transitional Justice in the Asia-Pacific* (CUP 2014) 169.

during the preceding civil war.[72] Its statute explicitly prescribes that '[a]n amnesty granted to any person falling within the jurisdiction of the Special Court in respect of [international crimes] shall not be a bar to prosecution'.[73] This provision was important in the Sierra Leonean context since a blanket amnesty law had been enacted pursuant to the Lomé peace agreement of 1999.[74] During the negotiation of this provision, the UN Secretary-General relied on a reservation appended to the Lomé agreement by his Special Representative to the effect that the UN would not recognise amnesty with respect to international crimes.[75] On this basis, a precedent was set for the inapplicability of amnesties before internationalised courts, which has generally been followed in the statutes of subsequent hybrid bodies. However, this exclusion clause had limited impact within Sierra Leone, where the amnesty law remained in full force with respect to offenders not singled out by the SCSL as the most responsible.

The Extraordinary Chambers in the Courts of Cambodia (ECCC) were created on the basis of an agreement between the UN and the Cambodian government for the purpose of prosecuting leaders of the Khmer Rouge.[76] Article 11 of this agreement provided that '[t]he Royal Government of Cambodia shall not request an amnesty or pardon for any persons who may be investigated for or convicted of crimes referred to in the present Agreement'.[77] This provision also stipulated that, with respect to an amnesty previously granted by the government to Ieng Sary, a Khmer Rouge leader, 'the scope of this pardon is a matter to be decided by the Extraordinary Chambers'.[78] The amnesty provision of the agreement, reproduced in the organic law of the ECCC, represented a

72 Statute of the Special Court for Sierra Leone, Agreement between the United Nations and the Government of Sierra Leone on the Establishment of a Special Court for Sierra Leone pursuant to Security Council resolution 1315 of 14 August 2000 (signed 16 January 2002, entered into force 12 April 2002) 2178 UNTS 137 (SCSL statute) art 1(1).

73 Ibid, art 10.

74 Peace Agreement between the Government of Sierra Leone and the Revolutionary United Front of Sierra Leone (7 July 1999) art 9, implemented through the Lomé Peace Agreement (Ratification) Act of 22 July 1999.

75 UN Security Council, Report of the Secretary-General on the establishment of a Special Court for Sierra Leone (4 October 2000) UN Doc S/2000/915, paras 23–24.

76 Law on the Establishment of the Extraordinary Chambers in the Courts of Cambodia for the Prosecution of Crimes Committed during the Period of Democratic Kampuchea, as amended on 27 October 2004, (NS/RKM/1004/006) 2329 UNTS 117 (ECCC statute); Agreement between the United Nations and the Royal Government of Cambodia concerning the Prosecution under Cambodian Law of Crimes Committed during the Period of Democratic Kampuchea, Annex to the UN General Assembly resolution 57/228B (13 May 2003) UN Doc A/RES/57/228 B.

77 Agreement between the United Nations and the Royal Government of Cambodia (n 76) art 11(1).

78 Ibid, art 11(2). See John D Ciorciari and Anne Heindel, *Hybrid Justice: The Extraordinary Chambers in the Courts of Cambodia* (University of Michigan Press 2014) 138; Shraga (n 67) 30–31; Williams (n 68) 354.

compromise between the position of the UN, which maintained that amnesty could not apply to international crimes, and the refusal of the Cambodian government to revoke the measure altogether.[79] While the amnesty was not invalidated, the determination of its scope was made subject to the discretion of the ECCC.

The founding instruments of most recent hybrid courts or tribunals also include a provision barring the applicability of amnesties. The statutes of the Special Tribunal for Lebanon (STL), created by a Chapter 7 resolution of the UN Security Council in 2007, and of the Extraordinary African Chambers (EAC), established through an agreement between the government of Senegal and the African Union in 2012, have reproduced the amnesty provision of the SCSL statute: '[a]n amnesty granted to any person for any crime falling within the jurisdiction of the [Tribunal] shall not be a bar to prosecution'.[80] These amnesty exclusion clauses cover different sets of crimes depending on the material jurisdiction of the tribunal which extends, as regards the STL, to crimes under Lebanese law including terrorist and political offences, and, as regards the EAC, to international crimes.[81] The organic law of the Kosovo Specialist Chambers (KSC) set up in 2015 with support from the European Union also bars the possibility of amnesty in the following terms:

> The jurisdiction of the Specialist Chambers shall not be subject to any amnesty granted under Article 65(15) of the Constitution. Any amnesty granted to any person for an international crime, a crime that resulted in grievous bodily injury or death, or a crime under Article 15(2), if falling within the jurisdiction of the Specialist Chambers, shall not be a bar to prosecution or punishment.[82]

The material jurisdiction of hybrid courts typically extends to international crimes and some serious common crimes. When the statute of these bodies, like those of the STL, the EAC and the KSC, excludes the applicability of amnesties for crimes falling under their jurisdiction without further distinctions, it enables them to set aside such measures regardless of the type of crimes covered,

79 ECCC statute (n 76) art 40. See Shraga (n 67) 30–31.

80 Agreement between the United Nations and the Lebanese Republic on the establishment of a Special Tribunal for Lebanon, Annex to Security Council resolution 1757 (30 May 2007) (STL statute) art 6; Statute of the Extraordinary African Chambers within the Senegalese judicial system for the prosecution of international crimes committed on the territory of the Republic of Chad during the period from 7 June 1982 to 1 December 1990, Annex to the Agreement between the Government of the Republic of Senegal and the African Union on the establishment of Extraordinary African Chambers within the Senegalese judicial system (22 August 2012) (EAC statute) art 20.

81 STL statute (n 80) art 2; EAC statute (n 80) art 4.

82 Law No.05/L-053 on Specialist Chambers and Specialist Prosecutor's Office (3 August 2015) art 18.

whether international or common crimes. This can facilitate the task of hybrid courts since they may then refuse to give effect to domestic amnesty laws without needing to engage in an analysis of the legality or legitimacy of the particular measure under international or national law.

This method was not adopted in the statute of the Special Criminal Court (SCC) established as part of the justice system of the Central African Republic (CAR) in 2015.[83] The organic law of the SCC does not mention amnesty. However, it refers to the criminal code of the CAR, which prohibits the granting of amnesty or pardon for genocide, crimes against humanity and war crimes.[84] Yet, the material jurisdiction of the SCC extends more broadly to serious violations of international humanitarian and human rights law.[85] It is unclear how this body would deal with an amnesty law applying to serious human rights violations not amounting to international crimes since such violations are not defined in its statute and do not form the object of an amnesty prohibition in domestic law.[86] Another complication is that the definitions of international crimes in the national criminal code, to which the statute refers, differ in some respects from the internationally accepted definitions, so that conducts corresponding to an international crime under international law may not be regarded as such under Central African law.[87] As two broad amnesty laws issued in the CAR in 2003 and 2008 may potentially conflict with the jurisdiction of the SCC, this body might have to face the issue of the acceptability or opposability of amnesties covering serious crimes in domestic and international law.[88]

2. Amnesty in the case law of international criminal courts

This section examines the case law of international or hybrid criminal courts dealing with the issue of amnesty. It looks at the reasons used to motivate their decisions to reject the applicability of amnesties to international crimes, in abstract or concrete cases, and what these reasons imply for the international and domestic validity or opposability of amnesty laws.

83 Loi organique No 15.003 portant création, organisation et fonctionnement de la Cour Pénale Spéciale (3 Juin 2015) (SCC Law).

84 SCC Law (n 83); Loi No 10.001 du 6 Janvier 2010 portant Code Pénal Centrafricain, art 162.

85 SCC Law (n 83) art 3(1).

86 The CAR constitution of 2016 provides that the Parliament may enact amnesties, without exceptions or restrictions, see constitution of Central African Republic (2016) art 80.

87 SCC law (n 83) art 3. See Patryk I Labuda, 'The Special Criminal Court in the Central African Republic: Failure or Vindication of Complementarity?' (2017) 15 *Journal of International Criminal Justice* 175, 181–83 and 197–99.

88 Labuda (n 87) 198.

The International Criminal Tribunal for the former Yugoslavia

The ICTY was the first international criminal tribunal to comment on the validity of amnesties in relation to international crimes. In *Prosecutor v Anto Furundzija* (1998), concerning a Croat military officer charged with torture, the ICTY Trial Chamber considered that the international norm prohibiting torture is peremptory in nature.[89] In an *obiter* comment outlining the effects of this *jus cogens* prohibition, the Court referred to amnesties as one type of national measures that would conflict with this norm:

> The fact that torture is prohibited by a peremptory norm of international law has other effects at the inter-state and individual levels. At the inter-state level, it serves to internationally de-legitimise any legislative, administrative or judicial act authorising torture. It would be senseless to argue, on the one hand, that on account of the *jus cogens* value of the prohibition against torture, treaties or customary rules providing for torture would be null and void *ab initio*, and then be unmindful of a State say, taking national measures authorising or condoning torture or absolving its perpetrators through an amnesty law. If such a situation were to arise, the national measures, violating the general principle and any relevant treaty provision, would produce the legal effects discussed above and in addition would not be accorded international legal recognition ... What is even more important is that perpetrators of torture acting upon or benefiting from those national measures may nevertheless be held criminally responsible for torture, whether in a foreign State, or in their own State under a subsequent regime.[90]

The Court thus adopted the view that the *jus cogens* status of norms proscribing international crimes entails that amnesty laws and similar measures covering these crimes are not opposable to international courts, the courts of third states or even the domestic courts of the state having enacted the measure following a change of regime. Elaborating on the link between peremptory norms prohibiting international crimes and the universality of jurisdiction over such crimes, the Trial Chamber observed that 'international crimes being universally condemned wherever they occur, every State has the right to prosecute and punish the authors of such crimes'.[91]

In *Prosecutor v Johan Tarčulovski* (2010), the ICTY declined to take into account an amnesty law passed following the end of the armed conflict in the

89 *Prosecutor v Anto Furundzija* (Judgment) ICTY-IT-95–17/1-T (10 December 1998) para 153. On the effect of *jus cogens* norms, see the Vienna Convention on the Law of Treaties (adopted 23 May 1969, entered into force 27 January 1980) 1155 UNTS 331, art 53.

90 *Prosecutor v Anto Furundzija* (n 89) para 155.

91 Ibid, para 156.

Former Yugoslav Republic of Macedonia (FYROM).[92] The accused was a police officer sentenced to twelve years of imprisonment for murder and other serious crimes. In his appeal he argued, inter alia, that the Trial Chamber had erred in its sentencing practice by failing to consider that the FYROM granted an amnesty to persons involved in the conflict in Macedonia.[93] He submitted that, since other offenders had benefited from this amnesty law, his prosecution for acts committed in the same context was contrary to basic principles of fairness. The Appeals Chamber ruled that the grant of an amnesty by the state to other persons involved in the conflict was irrelevant and did not bind the ICTY, whose statute and rules of procedure did not list amnesty as a factor to be taken into account in the determination of sentences.[94] In addition, the Court noted that the amnesty law in question explicitly excluded persons under the jurisdiction of the ICTY.[95]

The Special Court for Sierra Leone

In *Prosecutor v Kallon and Kamara* (2004), two defendants contended that the amnesty law enacted in Sierra Leone pursuant to the Lomé peace agreement of 1999 deprived the SCSL of jurisdiction over them.[96] The Appeals Chamber recalled that its statute required it not to give effect to amnesties in relation to international crimes and considered that no ground to question the validity of this provision had been advanced.[97] It then examined the position of international law on amnesties and found that it was entitled 'to attribute little or no weight to the grant of such amnesty' on the basis of three main arguments.[98]

92 *Prosecutor v Ljube Boškoski and Johan Tarčulovski* (Judgment) ICTY- IT-04–82-A (19 May 2010).

93 Ibid, para 218.

94 Ibid, para 220 (where the Court refers to article 24 of the ICTY statute (n 4) and Rule 101 of the Rules of Procedure and Evidence).

95 Ibid. However, the amnesty law was subsequently extended by Macedonia's Parliament to prevent the prosecution of four war crime cases transferred to the national authorities by the ICTY. The law as amended was upheld by Macedonia's Supreme Court in 2012. See Sinisa Jakov Marusic, 'Macedonia Abandons Hague Cases' *Balkan Insight* (20 July 2011); Sinisa Jakov Marusic, 'Macedonia PM "Agreed Amnesty for War Crimes Suspects"' *Balkan Insight* (6 April 2015).

96 *Prosecutor v Morris Kallon and Brima Bazzy Kamara* (Decision on Challenge to Jurisdiction: Lomé Accord Amnesty) SCSL-04–15-PT-060 (13 March 2004) para 1. For a detailed analysis of this decision, see Antonio Cassese, 'The Special Court and International Law, The Decision Concerning the Lomé Agreement Amnesty' (2004) 2 *Journal of International Criminal Justice* 1130; Simon M Meisenberg, 'Legality of Amnesties in International Humanitarian Law: The Lomé Amnesty Decision of the Special Court for Sierra Leone' (2004) *86 International Review of the Red Cross* 837; Sarah Williams, 'Amnesties in International Law: The Experience of the Special Court for Sierra Leone' (2005) 5 *Human Rights Law Review* 271, 279–95.

97 *Prosecutor v Kallon and Kamara* (n 96) paras 63–65 and 80–81.

98 Ibid, para 84.

First, like the ICTY, it relied on the right of states to exercise universal jurisdiction over international crimes.[99] In this regard, it observed that:

> Where jurisdiction is universal, a State cannot deprive another State of its jurisdiction to prosecute the offender by the grant of amnesty. It is for this reason unrealistic to regard as universally effective the grant of amnesty by a State in regard to grave international crimes in which there exists universal jurisdiction. A State cannot bring into oblivion and forgetfulness a crime, such as a crime against international law, which other States are entitled to keep alive and remember.[100]

Second, the Appeals Chamber noted that amnesties covering international crimes are contrary to the multilateral treaties requiring states to prosecute these crimes.[101] Third, it held that, although Sierra Leone might not have breached a customary rule by adopting the amnesty law in question, there was 'a crystallising international norm that a government cannot grant amnesty for serious violations of crimes under international law'.[102] The Court concluded that:

> Whatever effect the amnesty granted in the Lomé Agreement may have on a prosecution for [international crimes] in the national courts of Sierra Leone, it is ineffective in removing the universal jurisdiction to prosecute persons accused of such crimes that other states have by reason of the nature of the crimes. It is also ineffective in depriving an international court such as the Special Court of jurisdiction.[103]

Three other defendants contested the jurisdiction of the SCSL on the basis of the Lomé amnesty.[104] In separate decisions on these preliminary motions rendered on the same day, the Appeals Chamber rejected those challenges by reference to the reasons given in *Kallon and Kamara*. The decision in *Prosecutor v Kondewa* was supplemented by the separate opinion of Justice Robertson

99 Ibid, para 67–71.
100 Ibid, para 67
101 Ibid, paras 82 and 84.
102 Ibid. See also para 71.
103 Ibid, para 88.
104 *Prosecutor v Allieu Kondewa* (Decision on Preliminary Motion on the Invalidity of the Agreement between the United Nations and the Government of Sierra Leone on the Establishment of the Special Court) SCSL-04–14- T-128–7347 (25 May 2004); *Prosecutor v Moinina Fofana* (Decision on Preliminary Motion on Lack of Jurisdiction: Illegal Delegation of Jurisdiction by Sierra Leone) SCSL-04–14-PT-102 (25 May 2004); *Prosecutor v Augustine Gbao* (Decision on Preliminary Motion on the Invalidity of the Agreement between the United Nations and the Government of Sierra Leone on the Establishment of the Special Court) SCSL-04–15-PT-141 (25 May 2004). See Williams, 'Amnesties in International Law: The Experience of the Special Court for Sierra Leone' (n 96) 295–307.

discussing at some length the position of international law on amnesties.[105] He departed from the majority in two main respects. In the first place, relying on a common law authority, he considered that since the Lomé amnesty was tied to a peace settlement, its effectiveness was conditional upon the permanent cessation of hostilities by the parties to the conflict.[106] Therefore, if it could be proved that some of the amnesty recipients had not respected their undertaking to stop fighting, it would be possible to deny them the benefits of the amnesty.

As the Prosecution had not sought to establish a breach by the defendants of the terms of the peace agreement, but rather that a rule of international law forbids amnesties in relation to international crimes, Justice Robertson then engaged in an analysis of the status of amnesties under international law. Questioning the claim that a general amnesty ban had emerged, he recalled examples of states or international organisations offering or sanctioning the grant of amnesty to perpetrators of serious crimes.[107] He then observed that '[o]ne of the difficulties about invalidating peace settlement amnesties which apply to armies numbering tens of thousands is the practical impossibility of holding effective trials for all accused of war crimes'.[108] Accordingly, he drew distinctions between different categories of crimes and different types of perpetrators on the spectrum between foot soldiers and national leaders.[109] In his view:

> The sea change in the international community's approach to amnesty, from regarding it as the blessing of forgiveness to reproaching it as the curse of impunity, has turned on the dawning realisation of the unacceptability of amnesties for the 'authors' of crimes against humanity, i.e. those who bear the greatest responsibility. It seems to me that international criminal law has developed at least so far as to make this same distinction, namely that amnesties cannot absolve the political and military leaders who bear the greatest responsibility for genocide, torture, crimes against humanity and grave breaches of international and humanitarian law.[110]

Since the SCSL statute limited the jurisdiction of the Court to persons bearing the greatest responsibility for international crimes, rejecting the application of amnesties in their respect, Justice Robertson found that it 'neatly reflected' the rule against impunity having crystallised under international law.[111] Noting the limitations of this rule, he observed that:

105 *Prosecutor v Kondewa* (n 104), separate opinion of Justice Robertson.

106 Ibid, paras 20–29 referring to the decision of the Privy Council in *Attorney General of Trinidad and Tobago v. Lennox Phillip* [1995] 1 AC 396, PC.

107 *Prosecutor v Kondewa* (n 104) separate opinion of Justice Robertson, paras 30–31.

108 Ibid, para 33.

109 Ibid.

110 Ibid.

111 Ibid, para 49.

> The mesh of the international law dragnet may be excessively loose at this rudimentary stage of its development, but it nonetheless serves to entangle the biggest fish – those who can credibly be accused of bearing the greatest responsibility for international crimes.[112]

The Extraordinary Chambers in the courts of Cambodia

The ECCC has similarly faced a challenge to its jurisdiction based on a Cambodian amnesty decree in the case against Ieng Sary, a former Khmer Rouge leader charged with genocide, crimes against humanity and war crimes.[113] As the organic law of the Court enabled it to determine the scope of any amnesty or pardon granted before its creation, the Trial Chamber engaged in an analysis of whether international law required the prosecution of international crimes or prohibited the grant of amnesty to the persons responsible. It noted that Cambodia had ratified the international conventions prohibiting genocide, war crimes committed in international armed conflicts and torture, all of which require states parties to prosecute alleged perpetrators of the crimes in question. Accordingly, the Court considered that it was under an international obligation to construe the amnesty decree as excluding these crimes.[114] As regards other international crimes, such as crimes against humanity, it observed that:

> Although state practice in relation to other serious international crimes is arguably insufficiently uniform to establish an absolute prohibition of amnesties in relation to them, this practice demonstrates at a minimum a retroactive right for third States, internationalised and domestic courts to evaluate amnesties and to set them aside or limit their scope should they be deemed incompatible with international norms.[115]

The ECCC thus concurred with the ICTY and the SCSL in considering that amnesties covering international crimes cannot be effective before international courts or the domestic courts of third states. However, the Trial Chamber nuanced this position by recognising that state practice might not support an absolute prohibition on amnesties in relation to international crimes not subject to a treaty obligation to prosecute. It also distinguished between different types of amnesties to which different degrees of legitimacy could be ascribed. While blanket amnesties extending to international crimes were seen as incompatible with international law, the Court referred to examples of amnesties having been

112 Ibid, para 48.

113 *Prosecutor v Nuon Chea, Ieng Sary, Ieng Thirith and Khieu Samphan* (Decision on Ieng Sary's Rule 89 Preliminary Objections) 002/19-09-2007/ECCC/TC (3 November 2011).

114 Ibid, paras 38–39.

115 Ibid, para 53.

supported by the international community because they formed part of a peace or reconciliation process and imposed requirements on beneficiaries.[116] It was noted that, although blanket amnesties were previously the norm, a trend was emerging towards the enactment of more limited amnesties.[117] The Court identified a number of factors which, on a case-by-case basis, might affect the legitimacy of a particular amnesty law, including its mode of adoption, its scope and whether it is complemented by alternative accountability mechanisms.

Similarly to the SCSL in *Kallon and Kamara*, the ECCC considered that it was entitled 'in the exercise of its discretion to attribute no weight to a grant of such amnesty which it considers contrary to the direction in which customary international law is developing and to Cambodia's international obligations'.[118] Although it acknowledged that the amnesty decree 'may have contributed to restoring peace in Cambodia', the Trial Chamber observed that it had not been accompanied by transitional justice mechanisms permitting to uncover the truth about past crimes or provide a remedy to the victims.[119] It concluded that the scope of the amnesty decree should necessarily exclude genocide, war crimes committed in international conflicts and torture, and rejected its application to the other serious international crimes with which the accused was charged.[120]

The International Criminal Court

As discussed in the first section, three provisions of the Rome statute could enable the ICC to defer to a national amnesty process. Pursuant to article 16, the Security Council may request the Court not to proceed with an investigation or prosecution in a situation involving an amnesty if this was deemed necessary to maintain or restore international peace and security. The Court or the Prosecutor's Office could also decide not to interfere with a transitional process including recourse to amnesty if the process satisfied the complementarity test for genuine national proceedings under article 17. Such a scenario would entail a decision of inadmissibility before the commencement of any trial.[121] When the criteria for admissibility are met, the Prosecutor might also decide not to go ahead with an investigation or prosecution in a situation involving an amnesty pursuant to her discretionary power under article 53 to stay proceedings where they would be inconsistent with the interests of justice. While it has been suggested that this provision would enable the Prosecutor to take into account the impact of an ICC intervention on the ground, the OTP has made clear that the

116 Ibid, paras 49–52.
117 Ibid, para 51.
118 Ibid, para 54.
119 Ibid.
120 Ibid, para 55.
121 Challenges to the admissibility of a case may only be made after the commencement of the trial or subsequently with the leave of the Court on the basis of art 17(1)(c) referring to the *ne bis in idem* principle. See art 19(4) of the Rome statute (n 13).

interests of peace are not part of its mandate and that the presumption in favour of prosecution deriving from the object and purpose of the Rome statute would only be displaced in exceptional circumstances.

As a stay of proceedings on the basis of a Security Council deferral or of a decision of the Prosecutor motivated by the interests of justice would only occur in extraordinary circumstances, the most likely route through which an amnesty process might be accommodated by the ICC would be on the basis of the admissibility provision in article 17. According to articles 18 and 19, the Court may determine the admissibility of a case on its own initiative, in response to a request by the Prosecutor to authorise an investigation, or a challenge by the state having jurisdiction over the case or an accused person.[122] The admissibility of potential cases is also assessed by the Prosecutor throughout the preliminary examination process to determine if there is a reasonable basis to proceed with an investigation.[123]

The Rome statute does not set out a time limit for the completion of preliminary examinations. Thus, where national proceedings are ongoing, a situation may remain at that stage for a prolonged period of time until the OTP considers that it has sufficient information to determine whether particular cases would be admissible on the basis of complementarity.[124] A postponement by the Prosecutor of her decision to investigate a case in order to assess complementarity provides an additional route through which a transitional process involving an amnesty may be accommodated in practice. As the situation remains under the scrutiny of the OTP, this method has the advantage of maintaining pressure on national authorities to ensure that the process in question is genuine and that the most responsible perpetrators are held to account.

The situations in Uganda and Afghanistan

In an admissibility decision relating to the situation in Uganda, the Court referred to the amnesty law enacted in that country in 2000 to encourage the return of rebel fighters and end armed violence.[125] Pre-Trial Chamber II mentioned this law as part of the background of the case attesting to the absence of a legal framework enabling the investigation and prosecution of international crimes.[126] It ruled that the case was admissible since there were no relevant national proceedings at the time when the decision was made, refusing to engage in a hypothetical determination of how accountability mechanisms envisaged in ongoing peace talks might affect complementarity in the future.[127] The

122 Rome statute (n 13) arts 18(2) and 19(1)-(4).
123 ICC OTP, 'Policy Paper on Preliminary Examinations' (November 2013) paras 42–66.
124 Ibid, paras 89–90.
125 *Prosecutor v Joseph Kony et al.* (Decision on the admissibility of the case under article 19(1) of the Statute) ICC-02/04-01/05-377 (10 March 2009).
126 Ibid, para 50.
127 Ibid, paras 49–52.

approach adopted in this case indicates that, in admissibility proceedings, the Court will focus on whether concrete steps have been taken towards the investigation and prosecution of international crimes. It also suggests that, while the presence of an amnesty law may be considered as a ground for establishing the inactivity of the state, the Court will avoid engaging into an analysis of the legality or legitimacy of the measure where this would not be material to its decision.

The OTP is the ICC organ that is most likely to comment on amnesties and alternative forms of justice given its function to filter potentially admissible cases and its policy of encouraging states to carry out genuine national proceedings.[128] Situations of mass atrocities triggering the jurisdiction of the ICC often involve amnesties or analogous leniency measures. Indeed, states dealing with a legacy of widespread human rights violations typically face political and practical constraints limiting their ability to prosecute each and every offender through ordinary criminal proceedings. While it is precisely in this type of situations that the mandate of the ICC becomes relevant, alternative forms of justice are commonly envisaged in such contexts in order to relieve pressure on the justice system and foster conditions conducive to national reconciliation. Through her interactions with national actors in the preliminary examination process, the Prosecutor can provide guidance to the authorities regarding the design and implementation of a transitional justice strategy consistent with the object and purpose of the statute, so that cases need not reach the Court.[129]

The OTP's policy paper on preliminary investigations indicates that amnesty laws barring domestic proceedings for international crimes will be considered as a factor towards establishing the inactivity of the state for the purpose of the complementarity test.[130] This approach was adopted with regard to the general amnesty law passed by the Afghan Parliament in 2007, which applied to all warring parties without limitations or exceptions.[131] In her 2017 report on preliminary activities, the Prosecutor took note of this law when assessing whether national proceedings were underway in Afghanistan in relation to persons alleged to bear the greatest responsibility for ICC crimes.[132] On this and other bases, she concluded that there were no genuine national proceedings preventing the admissibility of potential cases in this situation and thus no conflict of jurisdiction with the Court.[133] In November 2017, the Prosecutor issued a request for the authorisation of the commencement of an investigation in Afghanistan.[134]

128 See 'Policy Paper on Preliminary Examinations' (n 123) paras 77 and 100–102.
129 Ibid, paras 100–102.
130 Ibid, para 48.
131 ICC OTP, 'Report on Preliminary Examination Activities 2017' (4 December 2017) para 259.
132 Ibid, paras 257–60.
133 Ibid, para 261.
134 ICC OTP, 'The Prosecutor of the International Criminal Court, Fatou Bensouda, requests judicial authorisation to commence an investigation into the Situation in the Islamic Republic of Afghanistan' (20 November 2017).

The ICC Prosecutor referred to the Afghan amnesty law as corroborating the absence of domestic proceedings for ICC crimes without elaborating on its acceptability under international law. In relation to the situation in Uganda, the Prosecutor also refrained from criticising the 2000 amnesty law, even though it applied to all returning rebel fighters irrespective of the gravity of their crimes. Those Ugandan perpetrators against whom an ICC arrest warrant was issued did not avail themselves of the amnesty law, so that there is not conflict with the jurisdiction of the Court. According to Mark Freeman, this approach suggests that 'the OTP will oppose an amnesty only to the extent it covers persons against whom the Court has actually issued arrest warrants. It likely will not oppose an amnesty that covers ICC crimes "in general"'.[135] Similarly, Dov Jacobs argues that:

> The fact that the [ICC] Prosecutor declines to acknowledge an amnesty in a specific case, where the conditions of jurisdiction are met, does not mean that the amnesty cannot apply to other individuals which are not under investigation, is not a decision of whether other amnesties granted are 'good' or 'bad', and, more generally, does not invalidate the state's whole transitional justice process.[136]

This seems to be confirmed by a statement issued by the Prosecutor in April 2016 to encourage rebel fighters to defect from the ranks of the Lord's Resistance Army (LRA), the most prominent Ugandan armed group still in activity.[137] Fatou Bensouda's communiqué emphasised that only five LRA commanders are wanted by the ICC and that many rebels have already returned home. She urged 'those still in the bush to also seize any opportunity to stop fighting and return home, where you have a chance to rebuild your lives'.[138] Uganda's amnesty law of 2000 was passed for the purpose of encouraging defections by rebel combatants, a large proportion of whom were abducted by the LRA.[139] It has been estimated that over 26,000 rebel fighters from different armed groups have been granted an amnesty certificate and a reintegration package by the Amnesty Commission created by the law.[140] When the government decided to let it expire in May 2012, civil society organisations petitioned the Parliament to reinstate the

135 Mark Freeman, *Necessary Evils: Amnesties and the Search for Justice* (CUP 2009) 84.

136 Dov Jacobs, 'Puzzling over Amnesties: Defragmenting the Debate for International Criminal Tribunals' in Larissa van den Herik and Carsten Stahn (eds), *The Diversification and Fragmentation of International Criminal Law* (Martinus Nijhoff Publishers 2012) 343.

137 ICC OTP, 'Message from the Prosecutor of the International Criminal Court, Fatou Bensouda, calling for defection by LRA fighters' (1 April 2016).

138 Ibid.

139 Amnesty Act 2000 (Uganda).

140 See Samuel Okiror, 'Forgive and forget? Amnesty dilemma haunts Uganda' Irin (12 June 2015).

law, which was extended for a further period of two years in 2013.[141] By calling on rebel fighters to return and reintegrate their communities, even though it is likely that some of them are responsible for serious crimes, and stressing that they would not be prosecuted by the ICC, without referring to the need for domestic prosecutions, the Prosecutor implicitly acknowledged the role of the Ugandan amnesty process.

The situation in Colombia

The Colombian situation has been under preliminary examination since 2004. In an interim report of 2012, the OTP concluded that there was a reasonable basis to believe that crimes against humanity and war crimes had been committed within the situation.[142] Since national proceedings were underway with respect to those crimes, the Prosecutor declined to open an investigation.[143] However, she refrained from closing the preliminary examination and continues to observe national proceedings and engage with relevant authorities to ensure that there is no impunity for the most serious crimes.[144]

The Colombian peace process, ongoing since the 1980s, has given rise to several peace agreements, some of which entailed recourse to broad amnesties.[145] The Justice and Peace Law of 2005 set out the legal framework for the demobilisation of paramilitary forces.[146] Unlike previous Colombian pacification legislation, it upheld the rights to truth, justice and reparation of victims of human rights violations. It also provided for an alternative accountability system enabling offenders to receive reduced prison sentences if they renounced violence and contributed to peace, fact-finding and reparation.[147] In a keynote speech on transitional justice in Colombia delivered in 2015, the ICC Deputy-Prosecutor clarified that reduced or alternative sentences may be acceptable under the Rome statute in the context of efforts to end an armed conflict as long as they pursue appropriate sentencing objectives and the convicted person must fulfil conditions justifying the

141 Parliament of Uganda, Report of the Committee on Defence and Internal Affairs on the petition on the lapsing of part II of the Amnesty Act, 2000 (August 2013) para 1.1, discussed in ch 5 of this volume. See Okiror (n 140).

142 ICC OTP, 'Situation in Colombia: Interim Report' (November 2012).

143 Ibid, paras 197–200.

144 'Report on Preliminary Examination Activities' (n 131) paras 149–55.

145 See Helen Alviar Garcia and Karen Engle, 'The Distributive Politics of Impunity and Anti-Impunity: Lessons from Four Decades of Colombian Peace Negotiations' in Karen Engle, Zinaida Miller and D M Davis (eds) *Anti-Impunity and the Human Rights Agenda* (Cambridge University Press 2016); Catalina Diaz, 'Colombia's Bid for Justice and Peace' in Kai Ambos, Judith Large and Marieke Wierda (eds), *Building A Future on Peace and Justice* (Springer 2009); Lisa J Laplante and Kimberly Theidon, 'Transitional Justice in Times of Conflict: Colombia's Ley de Justicia y Paz' (2006) 28 *Michigan Journal of International Law* 49.

146 Law no 975/05.

147 Ibid, arts 3, 7 and 29.

attenuation of the sentence.[148] Such requirements may include demobilisation and disarmament, an acknowledgment of responsibility, guarantees of non-repetition, the disclosure of the facts, and a ban on participation to public life, among other measures.[149] With respect to the Justice and Peace Law, the Deputy-Prosecutor observed that:

> Despite the difficulties and criticisms that the Peace and Justice process encountered, including the very low range of sentences, the Office of the Prosecutor has not found that the proceedings violated complementarity norms in the Rome Statute. I am not holding up the Peace and Justice Law as a model. I am merely pointing to it as an illustration of the wide margin that States enjoy when deciding on mechanisms designed to establish truth and that are also consistent with the Rome Statute goal of ending impunity for the most serious crimes.[150]

A peace agreement between the Colombian government and the Revolutionary Armed Forces of Colombia (FARC) was signed in November 2016.[151] Along the lines of the Justice and Peace Law, this agreement creates a comprehensive system for truth, justice, reparation and non-repetition to deal with the legacy of the conflict. As regards the justice component, the agreement provides for the establishment of a Special Jurisdiction for Peace competent to deal with serious crimes committed during the conflict. The truth component involves the creation of a Commission on Truth, Coexistence and Non-Repetition mandated to investigate the armed conflict and provide a forum for the victims. The agreement also introduces a general amnesty for political and related crimes, which explicitly excludes international crimes and serious human rights violations. Perpetrators of serious crimes may, however, receive an alternative sentence permitting them not to serve prison time if they acknowledge responsibility for their crime and commit to non-repetition at the beginning of the proceedings. Alternative sentences entail some restrictions on liberty and five to eight years of reparative labour in accordance with an individual or collective project devised in consultation with the victims and monitored by the special tribunal. Whereas offenders failing to come forward in time are liable to serve the same term under normal prison conditions, those who do not recognise their responsibility face terms of imprisonment of fifteen to twenty years.

The OTP has been supportive of the peace process with the FARC and regularly engages with national actors in a 'positive complementarity relationship'

148 ICC OTP, 'Transitional Justice in Colombia and the Role of the International Criminal Court', keynote speech by James Stewart, Deputy Prosecutor of the ICC (13 May 2015) 10–13.

149 Ibid, 12.

150 Ibid.

151 Final Agreement for Ending the Conflict and Building a Stable and Lasting Peace, 24 November 2016 (Colombian peace agreement).

aiming to ensure that the Colombian transitional process satisfies the criteria of article 17. The Prosecutor has described the process as a 'historic achievement' and a 'unique opportunity for peace'.[152] Bensouda has also commended it for providing a central place to the victims and excluding amnesty for crimes against humanity and war crimes. The amnesty law for political and related crimes passed by the Colombian Congress following the ratification of the peace deal has benefited several thousand FARC combatants.[153] The OTP has made clear that it is not concerned by amnesties of this type covering crimes which do not fall within the jurisdiction of the ICC.[154] However, the Prosecutor has stressed that amnesties extending to international crimes would indicate the inactivity, unwillingness or inability of the state to carry out genuine proceedings and thus trigger admissibility before the ICC.[155] In her 2017 report on preliminary activities, she criticised the fact that the Colombian peace agreement and the amnesty law implementing it excludes amnesty only with respect to 'serious war crimes' defined as 'systematic violations of international humanitarian law'.[156] Subscribing to the position of the OTP, the Colombian Constitutional Court recently determined that amnesty is excluded with respect to any war crime, irrespective of whether they were committed in a systematic manner.[157]

With regard to the possibility that perpetrators of international crimes benefit from an alternative sentence, including restrictions on liberty and reparative work instead of criminal imprisonment, the Prosecutor noted that:

> [T]he effectiveness of such sentences will depend on the nature and the scope of the measures that in combination would form a sanction and whether, in the particular circumstances of a case, they adequately serve sentencing objectives and provide redress for the victims. Fulfilment of those objectives would also depend on an effective implementation of the restrictions of freedoms and rights, a rigorous verification system, and whether their operationalisation with activities that are not part of the sanction, such as participation in political affairs, do not frustrate the object and purpose of the sentence.[158]

152 ICC OTP, 'Statement of the Prosecutor on the Agreement on the Creation of a Special Jurisdiction for Peace in Colombia' (24 September 2015); ICC OTP, 'Statement of ICC Prosecutor, Fatou Bensouda, on the conclusion of the peace negotiations between the Government of Colombia and the Revolutionary Armed Forces of Colombia – People's Army' (1 September 2016).

153 Law no 1820 (30 December 2016).

154 'Transitional Justice in Colombia and the Role of the International Criminal Court' (n 148) 15; ICC OTP, 'The Role of the ICC in the Transitional Justice Process in Colombia', speech by James Stewart, Deputy Prosecutor of the ICC (30 May 2018) 13.

155 'Report on Preliminary Examination Activities 2017' (n 131) para 146.

156 Ibid. See Colombian peace agreement (n 151) ch 5, item 5.1.2 (II) para 40.

157 'The Role of the ICC in the Transitional Justice Process in Colombia' (n 154) paras 127–28.

158 'Report on Preliminary Examination Activities 2017' (n 131) para 148.

Thus, although the OTP will insist on the non-applicability of amnesty to international crimes within the purview of the ICC, it is prepared to defer to alternative accountability mechanisms falling short of criminal imprisonment as long as they serve appropriate sentencing objectives and provide redress to the victims. This approach provides some leeway to transitional societies in devising innovative strategies to overcome war or authoritarian rule, while also maintaining pressure on national authorities to ensure that those responsible for the most serious crimes are held to account.

Conclusion

International criminal courts are established for the purpose of ensuring the prosecution of persons considered as most responsible for serious international crimes. Accordingly, there are strong arguments supporting the view that amnesties exonerating the very persons that these courts are mandated to prosecute cannot be effective in depriving them of jurisdiction. Thus, it has become common practice for the statutory instruments of those bodies to include a provision explicitly excluding the possibility that an amnesty may act as a bar to their jurisdiction. This practice emerged as a result of the insistence of the UN on the principle of unacceptability of amnesty for international crimes during negotiations on the establishment of early hybrid courts in Sierra Leone and Cambodia. It has subsequently been followed by other states and intergovernmental organisations in different transitional contexts. The amnesty exclusion clauses included in the statutes of some recently established hybrid bodies refer not only to international crimes but also to other common crimes within their jurisdiction. Provisions phrased as such facilitate the task of hybrid courts by permitting them to discard domestic amnesty laws without needing to embark on an analysis of their legality or opposability in relation to different types of crimes. However, these questions remain relevant for those bodies whose statute does not contain such an exclusion clause, including the ICC.

International criminal courts having dealt with the issue of amnesty have consistently found that amnesty laws may not deprive them of jurisdiction over persons accused of international crimes. Though there are some divergences among them regarding the legal bases grounding this position, there is consensus on certain points. It is generally accepted that amnesties cannot prevent the prosecution at the international level of crimes which states are required to prosecute under an international treaty, especially when the treaty establishes universal jurisdiction over the crime. This view is more controversial with regard to international crimes not subject to a treaty-based prosecutorial obligation, however, because state practice does not appear to support the existence of a customary obligation to prosecute these crimes. To obviate this difficulty, international criminal courts have considered that they are entitled not to give effect to amnesty laws covering international crimes on the basis of the *jus cogens* status of the norms prohibiting these crimes and the right of all states to prosecute the persons responsible. The implication of this reasoning is that, even if amnesty laws covering certain international crimes are not strictly prohibited by international law, they are not opposable to international or hybrid criminal courts.

Accordingly, it seems that the effectiveness of amnesties before international criminal courts is not necessarily linked to their legality under international law. These courts may refuse to give effect to an amnesty law on the basis of an explicit provision in their statute, or because of the nature of the crimes covered, without needing to demonstrate that the measure in question is contrary to international law. As a corollary, decisions of international criminal courts refusing to recognise an amnesty law as an obstacle to their jurisdiction do not necessarily indicate that the law is illegal or that all amnesties covering international crimes are prohibited by international law. These bodies are not mandated to adjudicate on the validity of domestic laws and are not empowered to do so by their statute. The approach of the ICC corroborates this view as neither the Prosecutor nor the Court have considered it necessary to engage with the legality of amnesty laws, even when they covered crimes within the Court's jurisdiction. Pronouncements in this sense would arguably overstep the mandate of international criminal courts and be superfluous since a decision not to recognise a particular amnesty as a bar to their jurisdiction would produce the same effect from the perspective of these courts.

The question of the effectiveness of amnesties before international criminal courts should also be distinguished from the validity of these measures in the domestic legal order in which they were issued. The mandate of international criminal courts is usually limited to persons identified as most responsible for serious crimes committed within a specific context. Thus, where such a court decides not to give effect to an amnesty law, this only affects the situation of persons subject to the court's jurisdiction, without depriving the law of validity at the domestic level. Accordingly, other offenders not identified as most responsible may still benefit from the measure, as happened in Sierra Leone and Uganda. In fact, national amnesty processes and transitional justice mechanisms may complement international criminal courts by placing emphasis on different objectives than those associated with the criminal law and focusing on different categories of perpetrators. As acknowledged by the OTP, in societies recovering from mass atrocities, criminal justice should be seen as only one element in a comprehensive strategy aiming to help these societies reckoning with, and moving beyond, their violent past. Besides the prosecution of serious offenders, transitional strategies may include efforts to uncover the truth about past crimes, provide acknowledgment and reparation to the victims, facilitate the reintegration of former combatants and offenders, and reconcile divided segments of a population. The ongoing peace process in Colombia illustrates how different transitional mechanisms including elements of prosecution, truth-telling, amnesty and reparation may be combined to work towards these objectives in a complementary fashion.

Conclusion

There is a high degree of continuity between ancient and modern amnesties in terms of their core characteristics, purposes and contexts of adoption.[1] Amnesty is in essence a sovereign act exempting categories of offenders from criminal punishment, generally in link with specific events affecting the nation. It is frequently introduced in relation to a period of civil unrest or political turmoil such as a rebellion, an armed conflict or a regime change. In such contexts, amnesties seek to ease tensions between adverse groups, facilitate a transitional process and permit the restoration of calm and stability. Other types of amnesties, including those granted to celebrate national events or alleviate the effect of harsh laws, perform a similar function of relief. While national authorities often ostensibly pursue this aim of relieving tensions when issuing amnesties, they may also concurrently or principally use them for self-serving purposes such as maintaining their hold on power, swaying public opinion or securing guarantees of immunity.

Amnesties used to be seen in a positive light in accordance with their function to facilitate peace settlements, release political prisoners and mitigate the effect of laws criminalising rebellion or imposing a death sentence. However, as they became associated with the notion of impunity in recent decades, they have been denounced by a growing number of policymakers, human rights bodies, organisations and advocates. This change in the perception of amnesties has mainly resulted from the development over the last century of a system of international norms which, on the one hand, proscribe conducts considered so grave that they offend against the international community as a whole and, on the other, recognise a series of fundamental human rights enforceable against state authorities. Criminal punishment is generally accepted as the most effective means of preventing and deterring serious crimes of international concern. There is also a tendency to consider that the punishment of offenders is required as a form of redress for the victims. Since amnesties preclude criminal punishment and are often resorted to in situations where serious crimes have been committed, they conflict with basic tenets of the prevailing accountability paradigm.

1 See ch 1.

Prior to the development of international criminal law and human rights law in the second half of the twentieth century, international law was not directly concerned with the rights and duties of individuals. Hence, when it authorised states to punish certain conducts infringing international rules, it did not provide for the personal responsibility of individuals but for the international responsibility of states. The idea that certain crimes threaten common values of the international community gave rise to the concept of international crimes and the emergence of the principle that persons responsible for these crimes are liable to punishment under international law.[2] This was concretised in the aftermath of World War II through the prosecution by internationally constituted tribunals of members of the defeated forces responsible for war crimes, crimes against humanity and crimes against peace. In the following decades, several multilateral treaties were adopted to prohibit certain international crimes and impose on states an obligation to prosecute alleged perpetrators.[3] The aftermath of World War II also provided momentum for the recognition that individuals have rights under international law which must be protected by state authorities. Fundamental human rights were codified in international and regional conventions requiring states to ensure their exercise by persons under their jurisdiction and guarantee a remedy to victims of violations.[4]

None of the international conventions imposing an obligation to prosecute international crimes or a duty to provide a remedy to victims of human rights violations prohibit the grant of amnesty in relation to these crimes. In the 1990s, claims started to be made by international bodies and scholars to the effect that amnesties covering serious crimes are incompatible with treaty obligations to prosecute or provide redress. However, there is no indication in the preparatory works of the relevant conventions that their drafters understood these duties as removing the possibility of amnesty in respect of the crimes in question.[5] As regards general human rights conventions, while they require states to provide a remedy to victims of violations, they do not equate the notion of remedy with criminal punishment. During their drafting history, the idea of explicitly requiring the prosecution of human rights offenders was not raised, or expressly rejected. As regards treaties instituting a repression regime for international crimes, they were adopted in order to ensure that those crimes would not go unpunished. The same purpose prompted the international community to adopt an international convention prohibiting the application of statutory limitations to international crimes and to create an international criminal court competent to prosecute alleged perpetrators when domestic authorities fail to do so. The negotiation of each of these instruments provided states

2 See ch 2.
3 See ch 4.
4 See ch 6.
5 See chs 4 and 6.

with an opportunity to outlaw amnesties in relation to international crimes. Yet, they consistently refrained from doing so.

The issue of amnesty was not mentioned during the drafting of early international conventions prohibiting genocide, grave breaches of the laws of war in international armed conflicts and torture.[6] However, it was raised in the course of the elaboration of a more recent convention prohibiting enforced disappearances.[7] Several proposals to exclude amnesty in respect of this crime were introduced but eventually rejected as some states stressed that amnesty could be a necessary element in national reconciliation processes.[8] Thus, whereas states agreed on the need to impose a duty to prosecute enforced disappearances, they could not reach consensus on a corresponding provision ruling out amnesties for this crime. This suggests that states do not consider that duties to prosecute implicitly remove the possibility of amnesty. The negotiation of the convention prohibiting statutory limitations for war crimes and crimes against humanity also presented an opportunity to prohibit amnesties.[9] Indeed, its rationale was to ban a legal mechanism having effects similar to amnesties in order to ensure the effective prosecution of international crimes. While the issue was considered, it was deliberately sidestepped.

The unwillingness of states to deal prescriptively with amnesty was also apparent during the drafting of the amnesty provision of the second protocol additional to the Geneva Conventions.[10] This provision was controversial because some states perceived it as an encroachment of international law on the discretionary prerogative of domestic authorities to decide whether or not an amnesty would be appropriate in specific circumstances. These concerns were alleviated by a general understanding that the provision was a mere recommendation devoid of binding force and was motivated by humanitarian reasons. The issue of amnesty also caused dissensions during the negotiation of the Rome statute establishing the

6 Convention on the Prevention and Punishment of the Crime of Genocide (adopted 9 December 1948, entered into force 12 January 1951) 78 UNTS 277; Geneva Conventions (adopted 12 August 1949, entered into force 21 October 1950) 75 UNTS 31/85/135/287; Convention against Torture and Other Cruel, Inhuman or Degrading Treatment or Punishment (adopted 10 December 1984, entered into force 26 June 1987) 1465 UNTS 85. Their drafting history is discussed in ch 4.

7 International Convention for the Protection of All Persons from Enforced Disappearance (adopted 20 December 2006, entered into force 23 December 2010) 2716 UNTS 3.

8 UN Commission on Human Rights (UNCHR), Report of the intersessional open-ended working group to elaborate a draft legally binding normative instrument for the protection of all persons from enforced disappearance (23 February 2004) UN Doc E/CN.4/2004/59, para 76. See ch 4.

9 Convention on the Non-Applicability of Statutory Limitations to War Crimes and Crimes against Humanity (adopted 26 November 1968, entered into force 11 November 1970) 754 UNTS 73, see ch 4.

10 Protocol Additional to the Geneva Conventions of 12 August 1949 relating to the Protection of Victims of Non-International Armed Conflicts (adopted 8 June 1977, entered into force 7 December 1978) 1125 UNTS 609, art 6(5). See ch 4.

International Criminal Court.[11] The question of whether the principle of complementarity would allow the Court to defer to alternative forms of justice or conditional amnesties forming part of a peace or reconciliation process was contentious and, in the end, no definite position was taken in the statute. While this instrument directs the Court not to give recognition to domestic decisions taken for the purpose of shielding perpetrators of international crimes from liability, it is sufficiently flexible to accommodate carefully crafted amnesties adhering to certain criteria in special circumstances.[12] Even unconditional amnesty processes could be deferred to on a temporary basis if the UN Security Council determined that this was necessary to maintain or restore international peace and security.[13]

Attempts to include an amnesty prohibition in international instruments adopted under the auspices of UN bodies similarly failed.[14] The set of principles to combat impunity, containing a rule excluding amnesties when they pose an obstacle to the prosecution of serious crimes or to the rights of victims, was not formally adopted by the UN Commission on Human Rights or the General Assembly.[15] By contrast, the basic principles on the right to a remedy, including rules imposing the prosecution of serious crimes and prohibiting statutory limitations but not amnesties, were adopted by both the Commission on Human Rights and the General Assembly.[16] The more recent declaration of the General Assembly on the rule of law, based on a report of the Secretary-General urging states not to grant or endorse amnesties in respect of serious crimes, conspicuously omits to mention this issue alongside other standards pertaining to the repression of serious crimes.[17] The attitude of states in these multilateral fora cautions against the inclusion of an amnesty provision in future accountability instruments since this is likely to decrease their chances of being formally adopted.[18]

11 Rome Statute of the International Criminal Court (adopted 17 July 1998, entered into force 1 July 2002) 2187 UNTS 90 (Rome statute).

12 See ch 7.

13 Rome statute (n 11) art 16.

14 See ch 5.

15 UNCHR, 'Report of the independent expert to update the Set of principles to combat impunity, Diane Orentlicher' (8 February 2005) UN Doc E/CN.4/2005/102/Add.1, principle 24.

16 UNCHR, Basic Principles and Guidelines on the Right to a Remedy and Reparation for Victims of Gross Violations of International Human Rights Law and Serious Violations of International Humanitarian Law (13 April 2005) U.N. Doc. E/CN. 4/2005/L.48, paras 4 and 6.

17 UNGA, 'Declaration of the High-level Meeting of the General Assembly on the Rule of Law at the National and International Levels', resolution adopted by the General Assembly (30 November 2012) A/RES/67/1. See UNGA, 'Delivering justice: programme of action to strengthen the rule of law at the national and international levels', Report of the Secretary-General (16 March 2012) A/66/749, para 37.

18 In this sense, see Diane Orentlicher, 'Immunities and Amnesties' in Leila Nadya Sadat (ed), *Forging a Convention for Crimes Against Humanity* (CUP 2011) 202; UNGA International Law Commission, Third report on crimes against humanity by Sean D. Murphy, Special Rapporteur (23 January 2017) UN Doc A/CN.4/704, para 297.

The difficulty in negotiating international instruments addressing the question of amnesty indicates the lack of any consensus among states on this issue. As a result, they have never been able to agree on a treaty norm or a policy instrument dealing with it in a prescriptive manner. The consistent refusal of states to accept any explicit limitation of their amnesty prerogative in international instruments seems to refute the claim that they implicitly consented to such limitations by adopting conventions imposing duties to prosecute or provide redress. It also casts doubt on the existence of the *opinio juris* necessary to substantiate a customary norm prohibiting amnesty for serious crimes. The unwillingness of states to permit the establishment of an international ban on amnesties may be attributed to sovereignty concerns and to the utility that is recognised to the mechanism in post-conflict or transitional situations. Indeed, amnesties are frequently relied on around the globe in order to facilitate peace processes or political transitions.[19]

Amnesty provisions have been included in peace treaties for millennia. This practice was observed in ancient civilisations and followed by European nations for several centuries starting in the late Middle Ages.[20] It denotes an age-old understanding that measures enjoining warring parties to leave the past behind are sometimes necessary to pave the way for peace. This notion still prompts belligerents to include amnesty provisions in peace settlements. Indeed, since 1970, at least 145 agreements settling international or internal armed conflicts have provided for an amnesty.[21] Pacification amnesties ordinarily cover all acts committed in link with an armed conflict. However, an increasing number of peace agreements have excluded international crimes from amnesty clauses in recent years, supporting the view that a norm excluding the grant of amnesty for these crimes is emerging under international law.[22] Yet, this trend in state practice has been limited in two respects. First, most of the peace agreements containing an amnesty provision excluding international crimes were brokered by the UN, which made clear that it would not endorse blanket pacification amnesties. Other intergovernmental organisations or third states acting as peace negotiators have been inconsistent in their practice, in some instances subscribing to the UN policy but in others expressing support for peace processes involving recourse to broad amnesties. Second, this trend has been mostly circumscribed to Africa and, even within that region, most peace agreements having extended an amnesty since 2000 did so in unlimited terms.

Another form of state practice consistent with the emergence of a norm prohibiting the grant of amnesty for serious crimes is the repeal or restriction of amnesty laws extending to such crimes by national authorities. Amnesty laws covering international crimes or gross human rights violations are often challenged before national courts by civil society groups or human rights organisations on the

19 See chs 3 and 5.
20 See chs 1 and 2.
21 See the Peace Agreement Amnesties Database in appendix.
22 See ch 5.

basis of their incompatibility with international norms and standards. Since the turn of the new millennium, several amnesty laws were overturned or circumvented by domestic courts in order to permit the prosecution of human rights abusers.[23] However, this practice has mainly concerned Latin American self-amnesties previously condemned by Inter-American human rights bodies. Although blanket amnesties have been challenged in other parts of the world, few were eventually deprived of effect at the national level. Indeed, some of these challenges backfired by prompting domestic courts to uphold and defend the validity of amnesty laws, as in South Africa and Spain, usually on the basis that they formed part of a historical consensus underpinning a national reconciliation and democratisation process.

While there have been clear trends in state practice towards the exclusion of serious crimes from amnesties, they have for the most part been circumscribed to certain regions in which international actors actively sought to promote accountability standards. The UN has been involved in the negotiation of a number of peace agreements in Africa over the last two decades and it has vigorously insisted on the exclusion of serious crimes from the scope of pacification amnesties. In Latin America, the Inter-American Court of Human Rights has adopted a forceful approach on accountability and invalidated several blanket amnesty laws. In other regions, trends towards the limitation of amnesties have not been pronounced. In Asia, for instance, only a few amnesties have been restricted in accordance with international standards and several blanket pacification amnesties have been issued in recent years. In Europe and the Middle East, recent peace agreements supported by intergovernmental organisations have provided for amnesty in broad and unlimited terms. Thus, the practice of states in excluding serious crimes from amnesties does not appear to have the requisite levels of generality and consistency to sustain the view that a prohibitive customary norm has emerged, though there are regional trends in that direction.

If the findings of this research do not support the view that a general amnesty ban has emerged under international law, they indicate that the effectiveness of amnesties in barring accountability for serious crimes is limited. In accordance with their mandate to ensure the prosecution of international crimes or protect individual human rights, international courts and bodies have generally refused to give effect to amnesty laws.[24] As domestic courts increasingly rely on the decisions of international courts when appraising the validity of amnesty laws, there is an emerging pattern towards the limitation of such measures in accordance with international standards. Thus, some amnesty laws preventing the prosecution of perpetrators of serious crimes have been repealed, circumvented or restricted at the domestic level. Others have been discarded by the courts of third states purporting to exercise jurisdiction over international crimes on the basis of an international treaty.[25] Indeed, amnesty laws protecting persons

23 Ibid.
24 See chs 6 and 7.
25 See e.g. *Ould Dah v France* [dec] 48(4) ILM 884 (2009).

responsible for crimes subject to universal jurisdiction such as torture and enforced disappearances are unlikely to be respected beyond the borders of the state in which they were issued. Hence, the effectiveness of amnesties in preventing the prosecution of serious crimes is reduced not only at the vertical level, as they will generally not be recognised by international courts, but also at the horizontal level, since they may be set aside by domestic or foreign courts.

International judicial and quasi-judicial bodies have relied on different legal bases when refusing to give effect to amnesty laws. The constitutive instruments of several hybrid criminal courts explicitly provide that amnesty may not be an obstacle to their jurisdiction.[26] These bodies may thus rely directly on their statute when setting aside amnesty laws without needing to engage in an analysis of the status of these measures under international law. However, as the jurisdiction of hybrid courts is usually limited to persons bearing the greatest responsibility for international crimes committed within a specific situation, amnesty laws will generally not be challenged by these bodies in so far as they apply to lower-level offenders not subject to their jurisdiction. For example, while the Special Court for Sierra Leone declined to give effect to an amnesty law in respect of individuals identified as most responsible for the crimes committed during the Sierra Leonean civil war, the validity of the law in securing immunity for other persons having committed serious crimes in that context was not challenged.[27]

International courts and treaty bodies have relied on other legal bases to ground their decision to set aside amnesty laws covering serious crimes. They have refused to give effect to amnesties in relation to genocide, grave breaches of the Geneva Conventions and torture on the ground that such measures are incompatible with the obligation to prosecute these crimes contained in international treaties.[28] For instance, in response to a jurisdictional challenge based on a Cambodian amnesty decree, the Extraordinary Chambers in the Courts of Cambodia considered that, since Cambodia had ratified international conventions requiring the prosecution of these crimes, it was under an international law obligation to exclude them from the scope of any amnesty law.[29] Human rights courts and treaty bodies have also criticised amnesty laws extending to treaty-based crimes.[30] Thus, while it is not clear that, by adopting treaties requiring them to prosecute certain crimes, states relinquished their right to

26 See ch 7.

27 See *Prosecutor v Morris Kallon and Brima Bazzy Kamara* (Decision on Challenge to Jurisdiction: Lomé Accord Amnesty) SCSL-04–15-PT-060 (13 March 2004).

28 See *Prosecutor v Anto Furundzija* (Judgment) ICTY-IT-95–17/1-T (10 December 1998) para 155; Decision on Challenge to Jurisdiction: Lomé Accord Amnesty (n 27) paras 82 and 84; *Prosecutor v Nuon Chea, Ieng Sary, Ieng Thirith and Khieu Samphan* (Decision on Ieng Sary's Rule 89 Preliminary Objections) 002/19–09-2007/ECCC/TC (3 November 2011) paras 38–39. These decisions are discussed in ch 7.

29 Decision on Ieng Sary's Rule 89 Preliminary Objections (n 28) paras 38–39.

30 See UN Human Rights Committee (UNHRC), 'General Comment no 20: Article 7' (3 April 1992) UN Doc HRI/GEN/1/Rev.1, para 15; *Ould Dah v France* (n 25) 894.

amnesty these crimes, the effectiveness of amnesties in preventing their prosecution is limited as these measures will not be respected by international bodies.

As regards international crimes not subject to a treaty-based repression regime, such as crimes against humanity and war crimes committed in non-international armed conflicts, international courts have declined to give them effect based on different rationales. Hybrid courts having dealt with amnesty laws covering these crimes have considered that the practice of states is not sufficiently uniform to support the existence of a customary prohibition to amnesty them.[31] However, they have subscribed to the view of the International Criminal Tribunal for the former Yugoslavia to the effect that amnesties covering international crimes, regardless of whether these crimes derive from treaty or customary law, are not opposable to international courts or the courts of third states.[32] International and hybrid criminal courts have grounded this principle of ineffectiveness of amnesties for international crimes at the international level in the *jus cogens* status of these crimes, the right of all states to prosecute alleged perpetrators and the direction in which customary law is developing.

Human rights courts and treaty bodies have primarily considered the acceptability of amnesties in relation to violations of fundamental rights such as the right to life and the right to personal integrity.[33] While there is no explicit duty to prosecute human rights offenders in general human rights treaties, these bodies have derived an obligation to investigate serious violations and, in some cases, to prosecute the persons responsible, from the duty of states to protect human rights and to guarantee a remedy to victims of violations. Accordingly, they have concurred on the view that amnesties barring any form of investigation and remedy in relation to serious breaches of fundamental rights are incompatible with human rights law. However, as a result of divergences on the extent of the obligation to prosecute and the rights of the victims, treaty bodies have adopted different approaches as regards the rationale of the amnesty prohibition and the question of whether it might admit exceptions in certain circumstances.

On the one hand, the Inter-American Court of Human Rights has considered that, in order to give effect to the right to justice of the victims, states must investigate, prosecute and punish every instance of serious human rights violations. Therefore, it has affirmed that all amnesties obstructing the prosecution of human rights offenders are unacceptable, regardless of any countervailing consideration.[34] On the other hand, the European Court of Human Rights has

31 Decision on Ieng Sary's Rule 89 Preliminary Objections (n 28) para 53; Decision on Challenge to Jurisdiction: Lomé Accord Amnesty (n 27) para 71.

32 *Prosecutor v Anto Furundzija* (n 28) para 155; Decision on Challenge to Jurisdiction: Lomé Accord Amnesty (n 27) paras 67, 82, 84 and 88; Decision on Ieng Sary's Rule 89 Preliminary Objections (n 28) para 53.

33 See ch 6.

34 See e.g. *Barrios Altos v Peru* (Merits) Inter-American Court of Human Rights Series C No 75 (14 March 2001) para 41; *Gomes Lund et al. v Brazil* (Preliminary Objections, Merits,

generally not gone further than requiring that, in response to serious violations of fundamental rights, states must conduct an effective investigation *capable of* leading to the identification and punishment of the persons responsible.[35] Like the Human Rights Committee, the European Court has also consistently rejected the view that victims of human rights violations have a right to criminal justice.[36] Thus, when criticising amnesties, it has tended to place emphasis on public interests requiring prosecution, such as crime prevention, deterrence and the defence of the rule of law, rather than on individual rights. Accordingly, the European Court has accepted that amnesties pursuing a legitimate public interest in a proportionate manner may be possible in certain circumstances, even when covering serious crimes.[37] The African Commission on Human and People Rights has also recognised that conditional amnesties justified by a legitimate objective and fulfilling certain requirements permitting to realise the rights of the victims may be consistent with human rights law.[38]

Notwithstanding these divergences, human rights treaty bodies have consistently held that amnesties shielding state agents from responsibility for grave human rights abuses are incompatible with human rights law. Indeed, self-amnesties contravene both the interests of the victims in seeing justice done and the interests of society as a whole in preventing crime, deterring perpetrators and protecting the rule of law. Human rights bodies have also generally rejected challenges to their jurisdiction over persons accused of human rights crimes based on amnesty laws. Nonetheless, the Inter-American Court has been the only one to go so far as to invalidate amnesty laws and declare them without legal effects in the domestic order in which they were enacted. Finally, most human rights bodies have acknowledged that, in situations of transition from armed conflict or state repression, prosecutorial requirements should be balanced against other considerations including the need for peace and reconciliation as well as the rights to truth and reparation of the victims.

The way in which international courts and treaty bodies have approached the issue of amnesty has varied depending on their particular mandate. For instance, from the perspective of ad hoc criminal courts and tribunals, amnesties are ineffective in so far as they cover persons bearing the greatest responsibility for

Reparations and Costs) Inter-American Court of Human Rights Series C No 219 (24 November 2010) para 175; *Gelman v Uruguay* (Merits and Reparations) Inter-American Court of Human Rights Series C No 221 (24 February 2011) para 238.

35 See e.g. *Aksoy v Turkey* ECHR 1996-VI, para 98; *Selmouni v France* [GC] ECHR1999-V, para 79; *Finucane v The United Kingdom* ECHR 2003-VIII, para 69; *Bitiyeva and X v Russia* App Nos 57953/00 and 37392/03 (ECtHR, 21 June 2007) para 156.

36 See e.g. *Sundara Arachchige Lalith Rajapakse v Sri Lanka*, UNHRC Communication no 1250/2004 (2006) UN Doc CCPR/C/87/D/1250/2004, para 9.3; *Perez v France* [GC] ECHR 2004-I, para 70; *Öneryildiz v Turkey* [GC] ECHR 2004-XII, para 96.

37 See *Tarbuk v Croatia* App No 31360/10 (ECtHR, 11 December 2012) para 50; *Marguš v Croatia* [GC] ECHR 2014-III, para 139.

38 See *Thomas Kwoyelo v Uganda*, ACHPR Communication 431/12 (17 October 2018) para 293.

international crimes. This does not necessarily imply that states are prohibited from granting amnesties in respect of international crimes, but that the perpetrators identified by these courts as the most responsible cannot rely on amnesties.[39] Alternatively, the case law of the Inter-American Court suggests that the grant of amnesty is absolutely prohibited in respect of all international crimes and serious human rights violations. By contrast, the approaches of the European Court and the African Commission provide some leeway to transitional states in devising strategies to deal with past crimes including amnesties so long as these measures are deemed necessary to achieve legitimate objectives and do not disproportionately affect individual rights. As regards the International Criminal Court, while it has considered that general amnesty laws indicate the absence of genuine national proceedings, thereby triggering the admissibility of cases before the Court, it has abstained from challenging the validity of amnesty laws not covering persons subject to its jurisdiction.[40] The Office of the Prosecutor has also recognised that alternative sentences may be acceptable, even when permitting perpetrators of serious crimes to avoid imprisonment, in so far as they pursue appropriate sentencing objectives, impose conditions on offenders justifying the attenuation of punishment and uphold the rights of the victims.[41]

Recent trends in state practice, international policy and jurisprudence denote a widely held belief that the grant of amnesty should not be permissible with respect to crimes prohibited at the international level because they offend against values of the international community. This belief is grounded in the view that measures exempting persons responsible for these crimes from punishment amount to condoning these conducts, thereby undermining their prevention and disregarding the suffering of the victims. Yet, an analysis of the reasons for which and contexts into which amnesties have been issued in the recent past shows that they may pursue legitimate objectives in transitional situations, and accordingly benefit from some degree of public support.[42] While they obstruct societal and individual demands for justice in the long term, amnesties can contribute to bring an end to situations bound to create more victims and suffering in the short term. Certain studies have also pointed to the potential of amnesties in complementing accountability and reparation efforts by enticing offenders to engage with transitional justice mechanisms.[43]

39 See ch 7.

40 International Criminal Court (ICC), Office of the Prosecutor (OTP), 'Policy Paper on Preliminary Examinations' (November 2013) para 259. The policy of the ICC regarding amnesties is discussed in ch 7.

41 ICC OTP, 'Transitional Justice in Colombia and the Role of the International Criminal Court', keynote speech by James Stewart, Deputy Prosecutor of the ICC (13 May 2015) 10–13; ICC OTP, 'Report on Preliminary Examination Activities 2017' (4 December 2017) para 148.

42 See ch 3.

43 See *The Belfast Guidelines on Amnesty and Accountability* (Transitional Justice Institute, University of Ulster 2013); Mark Freeman, *Necessary Evils: Amnesties and the Search for Justice*

In some post-conflict situations where a strict application of international standards led to the rejection or restriction of amnesties, as in Colombia and Burundi, other forms of leniency have emerged, openly or covertly, suggesting that the consolidation of an absolute ban would not lead to the disappearance of the practice.[44] Tensions between the need for peace, reconciliation and stability on the one hand, and demands for justice, accountability and redress on the other, seem inherent in situations of transition from war or repression. As shown in the case studies examined in this volume, these tensions are present in different forms between different types of actors in each particular situation, depending on an array of factors.[45] Accordingly, how best to alleviate them and ensure a degree of accountability, truth and reparation should be analysed on a case-by-case basis, taking into account a number of factors including the likelihood of military or political victory, the strength of national institutions and spoilers, the degree of international involvement, local needs and priorities.

There is growing consensus on the view that situations of mass atrocities should be addressed through comprehensive strategies incorporating different types of mechanisms placing emphasis on different transitional objectives.[46] Amnesties can make a positive contribution towards some of these objectives, particularly when designed and implemented in combination with other transitional mechanisms.[47] While the current legal and policy framework strongly discourages amnesties in relation to serious crimes, and substantially reduces the level of protection these measures afford to persons responsible for these crimes, there appears to be enough flexibility for transitional approaches involving the grant of amnesty to some categories of offenders on certain conditions to be found acceptable in compelling circumstances.

(CUP 2009) pt 2; Louise Mallinder, *Amnesty, Human Rights and Political Transitions: Bridging the Peace and Justice Divide* (Hart Publishing 2008) ch 4.

44 See ch 3.

45 See chs 3 and 5.

46 See *The Chicago Principles on Post-Conflict Justice* (International Human Rights Law Institute 2007); ICC OTP, 'Policy Paper on the Interests of Justice' (September 2007) 7–8; UN Security Council, 'The Rule of Law and Transitional Justice in Conflict and Post-Conflict Societies', report of the Secretary General (23 August 2004) UN Doc S/2004/616, 9.

47 See *The Belfast Guidelines on Amnesty and Accountability* (n 43); Tricia D Olsen, Leigh A Payne and Andrew G Reiter, *Transitional Justice in Balance: Comparing Processes, Weighing Efficacy* (United States Institute of Peace Press 2010) chs 8 and 9.

Appendix – Peace agreement amnesties database (1970 – 2017)

1. **Addis Ababa Agreement on the Problem of South Sudan (Sudan) 27 February 1972 (Intra-state)**
   - Amnesty: protocols on interim arrangements, chapter 3, articles 1–3 ('any act or matter done inside or outside the Sudan if done in connection with mutiny, rebellion or sedition in the Southern Region')
   - International mediation: Ethiopia

2. **Alvor Agreement on the Independence of Angola (Angola/Portugal) 15 January 1975 (Decolonisation)**
   - Amnesty: article 9 (no exclusions)
   - International mediation:/

3. **Tripoli Agreement (Philippines) 23 December 1976 (Intra-state)**
   - Amnesty: article 12(a) ('complete amnesty') (no exclusions)
   - International mediation: Organisation of Islamic Conference (OIC), Libya, Saudi Arabia, Senegal, Somalia

4. **Indo-Lanka Accord (India/Sri Lanka) 29 July 1987 (Inter-state)**
   - Amnesty: section 2.11 ('general amnesty') (no exclusions)
   - International mediation:/

5. **Procedure for the Establishment of a Firm and Lasting Peace in Central America (Esquipulas II) (Costa Rica/El Salvador/Guatemala/Nicaragua/Honduras) 7 August 1987 (Inter-state)**
   - Amnesty: article 1(b) (no exclusions)
   - International mediation: UN, Organisation of American States (OAS), European Economic Community

6. **Joint Declaration of the Central American Presidents (Alajuela Declaration) (Costa Rica, El Salvador, Guatemala, Nicaragua, Honduras) 16 January 1988 (Inter-state)**

   - Amnesty: para 5 (reiterated commitment to fully comply with obligations under Esquipulas II including the general amnesty)
   - International mediation:/

7. **Acuerdo Sapoá (Nicaragua) 23 March 1988 (Intra-state)**

   - Amnesty: para 5 ('amnistía general') (no exclusions)
   - International mediation: OAS

8. **The Settlement Proposals (Morocco/POLISARIO) 30 August 1988 (Decolonisation)**

   - Amnesty: paras 47(h), 70, 72 and 74 ('general and complete amnesty') (no exclusions)
   - International mediation: UN, Organisation of African Unity (OAU)

9. **Acuerdo Político entre el Gobierno Nacional, los Partidos Políticos, el M-19, y la Iglesia Católica en Calidad de Tutora Moral y Espiritual del Proceso (Colombia) 9 March 1990 (Intra-state)**

   - Amnesty: article 8 (amnesty for members of M-19) (no exclusions)
   - International mediation:/

10. **Groote Schuur Minute (South Africa) 4 May 1990 (Intra-state)**

    - Amnesty: paras 1-2 (establishment of a working group to advise on the release of political prisoners, the grant of immunity for political offences and temporary immunity for exiled members of the African National Congress) (exclusion of non-political offences)
    - International mediation:/
    - (see also Pretoria Minute of 6 August 1990 confirming the grant of a general amnesty and indemnity for political offences)

11. **Hionara Declaration on Peace, Reconciliation and Rehabilitation on Bougainville (Papua New Guinea) 23 January 1991 (Intra-state)**

    - Amnesty: article 10 ('amnesty and immunity from prosecutions') (no exclusions)
    - International mediation: Solomon Islands

12. **Acuerdo Final entre el Gobierno Nacional y el Partido Revolucionario de los Trabajadores (PRT) (Colombia) 25 January 1991 (Intra-state)**

    - Amnesty: article 5 (amnesty for members of the PRT) (exclusion of non-political crimes)
    - International mediation:/

13. **Acuerdo Final entre el Gobierno Nacional y el Ejército Popular de Liberación (EPL) (Colombia) 15 February 1991 (Intra-state)**

    - Amnesty: article 4 (amnesty for members of the EPL) (exclusion of non-political crimes)
    - International meditation:/

14. **Final Communique of the All-Liberia National Conference (Liberia) 18 April 1991 (Intra-state)**

    - Amnesty: p 35, Conference resolution (a) ('conditional amnesty') (no exclusions)
    - International mediation: Economic Community of West African States (ECOWAS), UN, OAU

15. **Acuerdo Final entre el Gobierno Nacional y el Movimieto Armado Quintin Lame (MAQL), Campamento de Pueblo Nuevo Caldono-Cauca (Colombia) 27 May 1991 (Intra-state)**

    - Amnesty: article 3(a) (amnesty for members of the MAQL) (exclusion of non-political crimes)
    - International mediation:/

16. **Memorandum of Understanding between the Government of the Republic of South Africa and the United Nations High Commissioner for Refugees on the Voluntary Repatriation and Reintegration of South African Returnees (South Africa) 16 August 1991 (Intra-state)**

    - Amnesty: para 3 (exclusion of non-political offences)
    - International mediation: UN High Commissioner for Refugees (UNHCR)

17. **Protocol between President Jean-Bertrand Aristide and the Parliamentary Negotiating Commission to find a Definitive Solution to the Haitian Crisis (Haiti) 23 February 1992 (Intra-state)**

    - Amnesty: article 5(1) ('general amnesty') (exclusion of common crimes)
    - International mediation:/

18. **Chapultepec Peace Agreement (El Salvador) 16 January 1992 (Intra-state)**

    - Amnesty: chapter 6
    - International mediation: UN

19. **Acuerdo entre los Comandos Ernesto Rojas (CER) y el Gobierno Nacional (Colombia) 20 March 1992 (Intra-state)**

    - Amnesty: articles 3-4 (amnesty for members of the CER) (no exclusions)
    - International mediation:/

20. **General Peace Agreement for Mozambique (Mozambique) 4 October 1992 (Intra-state)**

    - Amnesty: protocol I(I) (no exclusions)
    - International mediation: UN, Italy, US, UK, France, Portugal

21. **Memorandum of Settlement (Bodo Accord) (India) 20 February 1993 (Intra-state)**

    - Amnesty: article 18(ii) (exclusion of heinous crimes)
    - International mediation:/

22. **Governor Islands Accord (Haiti) 3 July 1993 (Intra-state)**

    - Amnesty: article 6 (no exclusions)
    - International mediation: UN, OAS

23. **Cotonou Agreement (Liberia) 25 July 1993 (Intra-state)**

    - Amnesty: article 19 ('general amnesty') (no exclusions)
    - International mediation: ECOWAS, UN, OAU

24. **Constitution of the Republic of South Africa Act 200 of 1993 (South Africa) 18 November 1993 (Intra-State)**

    - Amnesty: chapter 16 (exclusion of non-political crimes)
    - International mediation:/

25. **Quadripartite Agreement on Voluntary Return of Refugees and Displaced Persons (Georgia/Abkhazia/Russia/UNHCR) 4 April 1994 (Inter-state)**

    - Amnesty: para 3(c) (exclusion of war crimes, crimes against humanity and serious non-political crimes)
    - International mediation: UNHCR

26. **Acuerdo Político Final Gobierno Nacional Corriente de Renovación Socialista (CRS) (Colombia) 9 April 1994 (Intra-state)**
    - Amnesty: chapter 5 (amnesty for members of the CRS) (exclusion of non-political crimes)
    - International mediation:/

27. **Agreement on the Gaza Strip and the Jericho Area (Cairo Agreement) (Israel/Palestine) 4 May 1994 (Inter-state)**
    - Amnesty: article 20 (no exclusions)
    - International mediation: US, Russian Federation (RF), Egypt

28. **Acuerdo para la Paz y la Convivencia Ciudadana, Gobierno Nacional, Departamental y Municipal y Melicias Populares del Pueblo y para el Pueblo, Milicias Independientes, de Valle de Aburra y Milicias Metropolitanas, de la Ciudad de Medellin (Colombia) 26 May 1994 (Intra-state)**
    - Amnesty: chapter 4 (amnesty for militia members) (exclusion of non-political crimes)
    - International mediation:/

29. **Acuerdo Político Final entre el Gobierno Nacional y Frente Francisco Garnica de la Coordinadora Guerrillera (FFG) (Colombia) 30 June 1994 (Intra-state)**
    - Amnesty: chapter 2(1-3) (amnesty for members of the FFG) (exclusion of non-political crimes)
    - International mediation:/

30. **Memorandum of Settlement between the Government of Mizoram and the Hmar People's Convention (HPC) (India) 27 July 1994 (Intra-state)**
    - Amnesty: article 6(2) (no exclusions)
    - International mediation:/

31. **Honiara Commitments to Peace on Bougainville (Papua New Guinea) 3 September 1994 (Intra-state)**
    - Amnesty: para 4 (no exclusions)
    - International mediation: Solomon Islands

32. **Accord de Paris (Gabon) 7 October 1994 (Intra-state)**
    - Amnesty: p 30(14) ('amnistie générale') (no exclusions)
    - International mediation: European Union (EU), OAU, France, RC, Benin, Germany, Canada

33. **Lusaka Protocol (Angola) 15 November 1994 (Intra-state)**

- Amnesty: annex 6(I)(5) (no exclusions)
- International mediation: UN, US, RF, Portugal

34. **Accord de paix et de réconciliation nationale (Djibouti) 26 December 1994 (Intra-state)**

- Amnesty: title 7 ('amnistie générale') (no exclusions)
- International mediation:/

35. **Joint Agreement of the Government of the Republic of the Philippines and the National Democratic Front on Safety and Immunity Guarantees (Philippines) 24 February 1995 (Intra-state)**

- Amnesty: article 2 ('immunity guarantees' for acts in link with the peace negotiations)
- International mediation:/

36. **Accord établissant une paix définitive entre le Gouvernement de la République du Niger et l'Organisation de la Résistance Armée (Niger) 15 April 1995 (Intra-state)**

- Amnesty: article 15 ('amnistie générale') (no exclusion)
- International mediation: Algeria, Burkina Faso, France

37. **Waigani Communiqué (Papua New Guinea) 18 May 1995 (Intra-state)**

- Amnesty: articles 1-3 (no exclusions)
- International mediation:/

38. **Israeli-Palestinian Interim Agreement on the West Bank and the Gaza Strip (Oslo II) (Israel/Palestine) 28 September 1995 (Intra-state)**

- Amnesty: article 16 (no exclusions)
- International mediation: EU, US, RF, Egypt, Jordan, Norway

39. **General Agreement for Peace between the Government of the Republic of the Philippines and the Rebolusyonaryong Alyansang Makabansa – Soldiers of the Filipino People – Young Officers' Union (Philippines) 13 October 1995 (Intra-state)**

- Amnesty: article 4 ('general and unconditional amnesty') (exclusion of crimes against chastity and other crimes committed for personal ends)
- International mediation:/

40. **General Framework Agreement for Peace in Bosnia and Herzegovina (Dayton Accords) (Bosnia-Herzegovina/Serbia/Croatia) 21 November 1995 (Inter-state)**

- Amnesty: annex 7, article 6 (exclusion of serious violations of international humanitarian law and common crimes)
- International mediation: UN, EU, US, RF, UK, Germany, France

41. **Decree of the President of the Russian Federation on the Resolution of the Chechen Crisis (Yeltsin's peace plan) 31 March 1996 (Intra-state)**

- Amnesty: article 2 (exclusion of grave crimes)
- International mediation:/

42. **Memorandum on Measures of Providing Safety and Strengthening of Mutual Confidence between the Sides in the Georgian-Ossetian Conflict (Georgia) 16 May 1996 (Intra-state)**

- Amnesty: article 4 (exclusion of military crimes and crimes against civil people)
- International mediation: Organisation of Security and Cooperation in Europe (OSCE), RF

43. **Agreement on Normalization of Relations between the Federal Republic of Yugoslavia and the Republic of Croatia (Croatia/Serbia) 23 August 1996 (Inter-state)**

- Amnesty: article 7 (exclusion of 'the gravest violations of humanitarian law having the nature of war crimes')
- International mediation: UN

44. **Peace Agreement between the Government of the Republic of Sierra Leone and the RUF/SL (Abidjan Accord) (Sierra Leone) 30 November 1996 (Intra-state)**

- Amnesty: article 14 (no exclusions)
- International mediation: UN, OAU, Commonwealth, Ivory Coast

45. **Agreement on the Basis for the Legal Integration of Unidad Revolucionaria Nacional Guatemalteca (Guatemala) 12 December 1996 (Intra-state)**

- Amnesty: articles 21-24 (exclusion of crimes not connected with a political objective and 'crimes which, under domestic law or the international treaties ratified or signed by Guatemala, are imprescriptible or are not subject to an extinction of criminal liability')
- International mediation: UN

46. **Agreement between the President of the Republic of Tajikistan and the Leader of the United Tajik Opposition (Tajikistan) 23 December 1996 (Intra-state)**

 - Amnesty: para 4 ('universal amnesty and reciprocal pardoning') (no exclusions)
 - International mediation: UN

47. **Preliminary Agreement on a National Reconciliation Pact (Central African Republic – CAR) 18 January 1997 (Intra-state)**

 - Amnesty: Appendix 6(I)(6) (no exclusions)
 - International mediation: Gabon, Burkina Faso, Chad, Mali

48. **Sudan Peace Agreement (Sudan) 21 April 1997 (Intra-state)**

 - Amnesty: chapter 1(B)(3), chapter 6(8)(ix) and annex 2 ('general and unconditional amnesty') (no exclusions)
 - International mediation:/

49. **Acuerdo de Paz entre Gobierno y Frente Norte 3-80 (Acuerdo de Managua) (Nicaragua) 30 May 1997 (Intra-state)**

 - Amnesty: article 6 (amnesty for members of the Frente Norte 3–80) (no exclusions)
 - International mediation: OAS

50. **General Agreement on the Establishment of Peace and National Accord in Tajikistan (Tajikistan) 27 June 1997 (Intra-state)**

 - Amnesty: annex I, para 2 ('mutual forgiveness and amnesty') (no exclusions)
 - International mediation: UN

51. **Results of the Third Round of Direct Talks (Lisbon Compromise) (Morocco) 29 August 1997 (Decolonisation)**

 - Amnesty: article 3 (reaffirmation of amnesty envisioned in 1988 Settlement Proposals) (no exclusions)
 - International mediation: UN

52. **Conakry Peace Plan (Sierra Leone) 23 October 1997 (Intra-state)**

 - Amnesty: annex 2, article 8 ('unconditional immunities and guarantees from prosecution') (no exclusions)
 - International mediation: ECOWAS, UN, OAU

53. **Protocole d'accord additionnel entre le Gouvernement de la Republique du Niger et l'Union des Forces de la Resistance Armee (FPLS, MUR, FAR) et les Forces Armees Revolutionnaires du Sahara (Niger) 23 November 1997 (Intra-state)**

- Amnesty: article 8 ('amnistie générale') (no exclusions)
- International mediation: Algeria

54. **Chittagong Hill Tracts Accord (Bangladesh) 2 December 1997 (Intra-state)**

- Amnesty: D (Gha), paras 14-16 ('general amnesty') (no exclusions)
- International mediation:/

55. **Lincoln Agreement on Peace Security and Development on Bougainville (Papua New Guinea) 23 January 1998 (Intra-state)**

- Amnesty: article 10 (no exclusions)
- International mediation: Solomon Islands, New Zealand

56. **Acuerdo final entre el Gobierno Nacional y el Movimiento Independiente Revolucionario Comandos Armados (MIR-COAR) (Colombia) 29 July 1998 (Intra-state)**

- Amnesty: chapter 3(6) ('indultos y amnistías') (pardons and amnesties to members of the MIR-COAR)
- International mediation:/

57. **Accord de N'Djaména entre le Gouvernement de la République du Niger et le Front Démocratique pour le Renouveau (FDR) (Niger) 21 August 1998 (Intra-state)**

- Amnesty: article 7 ('amnistie générale') (no exclusions)
- International mediation: Chad

58. **Interim Agreement for Peace and Self-Government in Kosovo (Rambouillet Accords) (Kosovo) 23 February 1999 (Intra-state)**

- Amnesty: article 2(12) (exclusion of serious violations of international humanitarian law)
- International mediation: EU, OSCE, US, RF, UK, France, Italy, Germany

59. **Wunlit Dinka Nuer Covenant (South Sudan) 8 March 1999 (Intra-state)**

- Amnesty: para 2 (no exclusions)
- International mediation:/

60. **Peace Agreement between the Government of Sierra Leone and the RUF (Lomé Peace Agreement) (Sierra Leone) 7 July 1999 (Intra-state)**

- Amnesty: article 9 ('absolute and free pardon and reprieve') (no exclusions)
- International mediation: UN, OAU, ECOWAS, Commonwealth, Togo, Ghana, Liberia, Libya, Mali, Nigeria, UK, US

61. **Loi sur la concorde civile (Algeria) 13 July 1999 (Intra-state)**

- Amnesty: chapter 2 (exemption from prosecution) (exclusion of offences having led to the death or permanent disability of the victim, rape and those involving the use of explosives in public places)
- International mediation:/

62. **Lusaka Agreement (Angola/Namibia/Rwanda/Zimbabwe/Uganda/ Democratic Republic of Congo - DRC) 19 July 1999 (Inter-state)**

- Amnesty: article 3(22) and annex A(9.2) (exclusion of perpetrators of genocide)
- International mediation: UN, OAU, Southern African Development Community (SADC), Zambia

63. **Dialogue inter-togolais: accord cadre de Lomé (Togo) 29 July 1999 (Intra-state)**

- Amnesty: p 8 (extension of 1994 amnesty law) (no exclusions)
- International mediation: EU, Organisation Internationale de la Francophonie (OIF), France, Germany

64. **Waat Lou Nuer Covenant (South Sudan) 6 November 1999 (Intra-state)**

- Amnesty: second point of declaration (no exclusions)
- International mediation:/

65. **Accord de cessation des hostilitiés en République du Congo (RC) 16 November 1999 (Intra-state)**

- Amnesty: para 3(2) (no exclusions)
- International mediation: Comité de Suivi de l'Appel de Douala, Conseil Mondial de la Paix

66. **Agreement between the Governments of Sudan and Uganda (Nairobi Agreement) (Sudan/Uganda) 8 December 1999 (Inter-state)**

- Amnesty: para 10 (no exclusions)
- International mediation: Kenya

67. **Accord de cessez-le-feu et de cessation des hostilités entre le Haut Commandement de la Force Publique et le Haut Commandement des Forces d'Autodéfense de la Résistance (Accord de Pointe Noire) (RC) 29 December 1999 (Intra-state)**

- Amnesty: article 5 ('amnistie générale') (no exclusions)
- International mediation: Gabon

68. **Accord cadre de réforme et de concorde civile (Djibouti) 7 February 2000 (Intra-state)**

- Amnesty: article 5 (no exclusions)
- International mediation:/

69. **Liliir Covenant on Peace and Reconciliation (South Sudan) 15 May 2000 (Intra-state)**

- Amnesty: para 3 (no exclusions)
- International mediation:/

70. **Arusha Peace and Reconciliation Agreement for Burundi (Burundi) 29 August 2000 (Intra-state)**

- Amnesty: protocol 3, article 26(1)(l) (exclusion of acts of genocide, crimes against humanity, war crimes and acts of participation in coup d'état)
- International mediation: UN, OAU, EU, OIF, Uganda, Kenya, Tanzania, Zambia, Rwanda, DRC, Ethiopia

71. **Townsville Peace Agreement (Solomon Islands) 15 October 2000 (Intra-state)**

- Amnesty: part 2, article 3 ('general amnesty') (no exclusions)
- International mediation: Commonwealth, Australia

72. **Peace Agreement between the Republic of the Philippines and the Rebolusyonaryong Partido NG Manggagawa – Pilipinas/Revolutionary Proletarian Army/Alex Boncayao Brigade (Philippines) 6 December 2000 (Intra-state)**

- Amnesty: articles 3-4 (no exclusions)
- International mediation:/

73. **Agreement between the Government of the State of Eritrea and the Government of the Federal Democratic Republic of Ethiopia (Eritrea/Ethiopia) 12 December 2000 (Inter-state)**

- Amnesty: article 2 (general prisoner release) (no exclusions but a Claims Commission was set up pursuant to article 5(1) to 'decide

through binding arbitration' of claims resulting from violations of international humanitarian law – under article 5(8), claims not submitted within one year of the signature of the agreement 'shall be extinguished')
- International mediation: UN, OAU, EU, US, Algeria

74. **Program for the Solution of the Crisis in the Pcinja District (Covic Plan) (Serbia) 1 February 2001 (Intra-state)**

- Amnesty: annex 5b, para 4 ('Amnesty of criminal responsibility for terrorism') (exclusion of persons responsible for 'concrete acts of violence')
- International mediation: UN

75. **Marau Peace Agreement (Solomon Islands) 7 February 2001 (Intra-state)**

- Amnesty: article 6 (extension of amnesty introduced by 2000 Townsville Peace Agreement) (no exclusions)
- International mediation:/

76. **Implementation of the Good Friday Agreement: Proposals by the Two Governments (Ireland/United Kingdom) 1 August 2001 (Inter-state)**

- Amnesty: para 20 (exemption from prosecution in specific cases)
- International mediation:/

77. **Bougainville Peace Agreement (Papua New Guinea) 30 August 2001 (Intra-state)**

- Amnesty: para 331 (extension of the general amnesty introduced by 1998 Lincoln Agreement) (no exclusions)
- International mediation:/

78. **Peace Agreement between the Government of the Republic of Chad and the Movement for Democracy and Justice in Chad (Chad) 7 January 2002 (Intra-state)**

- Amnesty: article 2 ('general amnesty') (no exclusions)
- International mediation: Community of Sahelo-Saharan States (CEN-SAD)

79. **Memorandum of Understanding (Luena Agreement) (Angola) 4 April 2002 (Intra-state)**

- Amnesty: chapter 2, article 2.1 (general amnesty) (no exclusions)
- International mediation: UN, US, RF, Portugal

80. **Chukudum Crisis Peace Conference (South Sudan) 20 August 2002 (Intra-state)**

    - Amnesty: resolution 3.1-3.3 (general amnesty) (no exclusions)
    - International mediation:/

81. **Global and Inclusive Agreement on Transition in the Democratic Republic of Congo (Pretoria Agreement) (DRC) 16 December 2002 (Intra-state)**

    - Amnesty: part 3, article 8 (exclusion of war crimes, genocide and crimes against humanity)
    - International mediation: UN, African Union (AU)

82. **Peace Agreement between the Government of the Republic of Uganda and the National Rescue Front II (Yumbe Peace Agreement) (Uganda) 24 December 2002 (Intra-state)**

    - Amnesty: articles 3(2) and 4(2) (extension of 2000 amnesty law to members of the National Rescue Front) (no exclusions)
    - International mediation:/

83. **Linas-Marcousis Agreement (Ivory Coast) 23 January 2003 (Intra-state)**

    - Amnesty: article 3(i) and annex, article 7(5) (exclusion of serious economic violations and serious violations of human rights and international humanitarian law)
    - International mediation: UN, ECOWAS, AU, EU, OIF, World Bank, International Monetary Fund, France

84. **Memorandum of Settlement on Bodoland Territorial Council (India) 10 February 2003 (Intra-state)**

    - Amnesty: article 12(1) (no exclusions)
    - International mediation:/

85. **Accords de Paix et de cessation des hostilités dans le département de Pool (RC) 17 March 2003 (Intra-state)**

    - Amnesty: para 4 (extension of amnesty law contemplated in the 1999 Accord de Pointe Noire) (no exclusions)
    - International mediation:/

86. **Inter-Congolese Negotiations: The Final Act (Sun City Agreement) (DRC) 2 April 2003 (Intra-state)**

    - Amnesty: 22 resolution no DIC/CHSC/02 (1) and 33 resolution no DIC/COR/04 (8) (setting up a National Truth and Reconciliation Commission empowered to grant amnesty to persons confessing their

crimes when their primary motivation was political, except for genocide and crimes against humanity)
- International mediation: UN, AU, SADC, EU

87. **Joint Declaration of the Defence and Security Forces of Côte d'Ivoire and the Armed Forces of the Forces Nouvelles (Ivory Coast) 4 July 2003 (Intra-state)**
    - Amnesty: para 8 (reference to amnesty provided in 2003 Linas Marcousis Agreement, excluding serious economic violations and serious violations of human rights and international humanitarian law)
    - International mediation: UN, ECOWAS and France

88. **Peace Agreement between the Government of Liberia, the Liberians United for Reconciliation and Democracy (LURD), the Movement of Democracy in Liberia (MODEL) and the Political Parties (Accra agreement) (Liberia) 18 August 2003 (Intra-state)**
    - Amnesty: article 34 ('recommendation for a general amnesty') (no exclusions)
    - International mediation: UN, AU, ECOWAS, EU, Ghana and Nigeria

89. **Pretoria Protocol on Outstanding Issues of Political, Defence and Security Power Sharing in Burundi (Burundi) 2 November 2003 (Intra-state)**
    - Amnesty: article 2 (temporary immunity for all leaders and combatants of the CNDD-FDD, the security forces and some civilians serving sentences when so determined by a Joint Commission) (reaffirmation of the 2000 Arusha peace and reconciliation agreement excluding amnesty for international crimes and providing for the creation of an international criminal tribunal)
    - International mediation: South Africa

90. **Peace Agreement between the Government of Chad and the Mouvement pour la démocratie et la justice au Tchad (Chad) 14 December 2003 (Intra-state)**
    - Amnesty: article 2 ('general amnesty') (no exclusions)
    - International mediation: Burkina Faso

91. **Zinguinchor Peace Agreement between the Government of Senegal and the MFDC (Senegal) 30 December 2004 (Intra-state)**
    - Amnesty: article 1 (extension of amnesty law in effect) (no exclusions)
    - International mediation:/

92. **Comprehensive Peace Agreement between the Government of Sudan and the SPLM/SPLA (Sudan) 9 January 2005 (Intra-state)**

   - Amnesty: article 1(8) and 27(2) (general prisoner release) (no exclusions)
   - International mediation: Kenya

93. **Memorandum of Understanding between the Government of Mizoram and the Bru National Liberation Front (BNLF) (India) 26 April 2005 (Intra-state)**

   - Amnesty: para 6 (no exclusions)
   - International mediation:/

94. **Charte pour la paix et la réconciliation nationale (Algeria) 14 August 2005 (Intra-state)**

   - Amnesty: part 2 (exclusion of mass killings, rape and attacks using explosives in public places)
   - International mediation:/

95. **Memorandum of Understanding between the Government of the Republic of Indonesia and the Free Aceh Movement (Helsinki Agreement) (Indonesia) 18 August 2005 (Intra-state)**

   - Amnesty: articles 3(1) and 3(2)(1) (no exclusions)
   - International mediation: Finland

96. **Juba Declaration on Unity and Integration between the Sudan People's Liberation Army (SPLA) and the South Sudan Defence Forces (SSDF) (South Sudan) 8 January 2006 (Intra-state)**

   - Amnesty: point 5 ('general amnesty') (no exclusions)
   - International mediation:/

97. **25-Point Ceasefire Code of Conduct Agreed between the Government of Nepal and SPN (Maoist) (Nepal) 25 May 2006 (Intra-state)**

   - Amnesty: point 16 (no exclusions)
   - International mediation:/

98. **Dar-es-Salaam Agreement on Principles Towards lasting Peace, Security and Stability in Burundi (Burundi) 18 June 2006 (Intra-state)**

   - Amnesty: article 2(1) (provisional immunity for members of the Palipebutu-FNL and general prisoner release) (no exclusions)
   - International mediation: UN, AU and South Africa

- (see also the Comprehensive Ceasefire Agreement between the Government of the Republic of Burundi and the Palipehutu-FNL of 7 September 2006: reiteration of the provisional immunities in Annexure I (2.1.5) and Annexure II (3.1))

99. **Memorandum of Peace and Understanding in Cabinda Province (Angola) 1 August 2006 (Intra-state)**
    - Amnesty: chapter 2(B)(1) and annex 3/4 of annex 4 (no exclusions)
    - International mediation:/

100. **Dialogue inter-togolais: accord politique global (Togo) 20 August 2006 (Intra-state)**
    - Amnesty: article 2(4) (Commission charged to take measures to facilitate pardon and national reconciliation) (no exclusions)
    - International mediation: EU and ECOWAS

101. **Comprehensive Peace Agreement between the Government of Nepal and the Communist Party of Nepal (Maoist) (Nepal) 22 November 2006 (Intra-state)**
    - Amnesty: article 5.2.7 (exclusion of non-political offences)
    - International mediation:/

102. **Accord Cadre pour la Paix en Ituri entre le Gouvernment de la Republique Democratique du Congo et les Groupes Armes de l'Ituri (MRC, FNI, et FRPI) (DRC) 26 November 2006 (Intra-state)**
    - Amnesty: article 1(1) (same exclusions as in 2003 Sun-City Agreement: genocide and crimes against humanity)
    - International mediation: UN

103. **Accord de Paix entre le Gouvernement de la République Centrafricaine et les Mouvements Politico-Militaires ci-après designés: FDPC et UFDR (CAR) 2 February 2007 (Intra-state)**
    - Amnesty: article 4 ('amnistie générale') (no exclusions)
    - International mediation:/

104. **Accord Politique de Ouagadougou (Ivory Coast) 4 March 2007 (Intra-state)**
    - Amnesty: article 6(3) (extension of amnesty law introduced by the Linas-Marcousis Agreement excluding serious economic violations and serious violations of human rights and international humanitarian law)
    - International mediation: ECOWAS and Burkina Faso

105. **Accord de paix de Birao (CAR) 1 April 2007 (Intra-state)**

- Amnesty: article 4 ('amnistie générale') (no exclusions)
- International mediation:/

106. **Agreement between the Government of Nepal and Madheshi Janadhikar Forum (Nepal) 30 July 2007 (Intra-state)**

- Amnesty: para 3 (no exclusions)
- International mediation:/

107. **Agreement between the Government of Nepal and Chure Bhawar Pradesh Ekta Samaj (Nepal) 13 September 2007 (Intra-state)**

- Amnesty: para 1 (no exclusions)
- International mediation:/

108. **Accord de paix entre le gouvernement du Tchad et les mouvements UFDD, RFC, CNT, UFDDF (Accord de Syrte) (Chad) 25 October 2007 (Intra-state)**

- Amnesty: article 3 ('amnistie générale') (no exclusions)
- International mediation: CEN-SAD, Libya and Sudan

109. **23-Point Agreement between the Top Leaders of the Seven-Party Alliance (Nepal) 23 December 2007 (Intra-state)**

- Amnesty: para 14 (no exclusions)
- International mediation:/

110. **Actes d'Engagement – North and South Kivu (DRC) 23 January 2008 (Intra-state)**

- Amnesty: article 4(1) (exclusion of genocide, war crimes and crimes against humanity)
- International mediation: UN, EU, AU, US, International Conference on the Great Lakes Region (ICGLR)

111. **Doha Agreement (Yemen) 1 February 2008 (Intra-state)**

- Amnesty: para 2 (general amnesty and release of prisoners) ('except for those charged in cases turned over to the general prosecutor or under consideration by the courts')
- International mediation: Qatar

112. **Kenya National Dialogue and Reconciliation – Truth, Justice and Reconciliation Commission (Kenya) 4 March 2008 (Intra-state)**

- Amnesty: p 1 (amnesties may be granted by the Commission in exchange for the full truth) (exclusion of genocide, war crimes and crimes against humanity)
- International mediation: AU Panel of Eminent African Personalities

113. **Accord de cessez le feu et de paix entre le Gouvernement de la Republique Centrafricaine et le mouvement politique et militaire Centrafricain APRD (CAR) 9 May 2008 (Intra-state)**

- Amnesty: article 4 ('amnistie générale') (no exclusions)
- International mediation: Economic Community of Central African States (ECCAAS), Gabon

114. **Constitution of 2008 (Myanmar) 29 May 2008 (Intra-state)**

- Amnesty: section 445 (immunity for government officials) ('in respect of any act done in the execution of their respective duties')
- International mediation:/

115. **Comprehensive Peace Agreement between the Government of the CAR and several Central African politico-military movements (APRD, FDPC and UFDR) (Libreville Accord) (CAR) 21 June 2008 (Intra-state)**

- Amnesty: article 2 (reiteration of the commitment for a general amnesty law) (exclusion of crimes within the jurisdiction of the ICC)
- International mediation: UN, CEN-SAD, CEMAC, OIF and Gabon

116. **Peace Agreement between the Government and the CNDP (DRC) 23 March 2009 (Intra-state)**

- Amnesty: article 3 (amnesty in conformity with international law)
- International mediation: UN, AU, ICGLR

117. **Acuerdo de San José para la reconciliación nacional y el fortalecimiento de la democracia en Honduras (Honduras) 22 July 2009 (Intra-state)**

- Amnesty: article 2 ('amnistía general') (exclusion of non-political crimes)
- International mediation: Costa Rica

118. **Accord de paix entre le gouvernement de la République du Tchad et le Mouvement National (Chad) 25 July 2009 (Intra-state)**

- Amnesty: article 3 ('amnistie générale') (exclusion of common crimes)
- International mediation: CEN-SAD, Libya

119. **Charte de la Transition (Madagascar) 9 August 2009 (Intra-state)**

- Amnesty: articles 25-30 (exclusion of genocide, crimes against humanity, war crimes and grave human rights violations)
- International mediation: UN, AU, SADC and OIF
- (see also 'Accord no 1 de Maputo sur l'annulation des charges relatives aux évènements de 2002 à Madagascar', 'Accord no 2 de Maputo sur le cas du Président Marc Ravalomanana' and 'Accord no 3 de Maputo sur l'annulation des poursuites et des condamnations prononcées contre les personnalités politiques et civiles ou militaires durant le régime de Ravalomanana' signed on 8 August 2009)

120. **Framework Agreement to Resolve the Conflict in Darfur between the Government of Sudan and the JEM (Sudan) 23 February 2010 (Intra-state)**

- Amnesty: article 2 (no exclusions)
- International mediation: UN, AU, Qatar

121. **Framework Agreement to Resolve the Conflict in Darfur between the Government of Sudan and the LJM (Sudan) 18 March 2010 Intra-state**

- Amnesty: article 3 (no exclusions)
- International mediation: UN, AU, Qatar

122. **Agreement between the Government of Nepal and Akhil Terai Mukti Morcha (Sansthapan Paksha) (Nepal) 7 May 2010 (Intra-state)**

- Amnesty: para 3 (amnesty for members of Akhil Terai Mukti Morcha) (exclusion of non-political offences)
- International mediation:/

123. **Agreement between the Government of the Federal Democratic Republic of Ethiopia and the Ogaden Liberation Front (ONLF) on the Termination of the State of Insurgency (Ethiopia) 12 October 2010 (Intra-state)**

- Amnesty: article 2 (in accordance with the constitution which excludes amnesty for crimes against humanity)
- International mediation:/

124. **Memorandum of Agreement on the Gorkha Territorial Administration (India) 18 July 2011 (Intra-state)**

- Amnesty: para 29 (exclusion of persons charged with murder)
- International mediation:/

125. **Doha Documents for Peace in Darfur – Framework for the comprehensive peace process in Darfur (Sudan) 14 July 2011 (Intra-state)**

- Amnesty: article 60 ('amnistie générale') (exclusion of war crimes, crimes against humanity, crimes of genocide, crimes of sexual violence and gross violations of human rights and humanitarian law)
- International mediation: UN, AU, Arab Ligue

126. **Roadmap for Ending the Crisis in Madagascar - Commitments by Malagasy Political Stakeholders (Madagascar) 13 September 2011 (Intra-state)**

- Amnesty: paras 18 and 20 (exclusion of genocide, war crimes, crimes against humanity and gross violations of human rights)
- International mediation: UN, AU, SADC, OIF and OIC

127. **Agreement/Gulf Cooperation Council (GCC) Initiative (Yemen) 23 November 2011 (Intra-state)**

- Amnesty: para 3 ('immunity from legal and judicial prosecution') (limited amnesty for the President and senior officials) (no exclusions)
- International mediation: Gulf Cooperation Council, EU

128. **Accord cadre de mise en œuvre de l'engagement solennel du 1er Avril 2012 (Mali) 6 April 2012 (Intra-state)**

- Amnesty: article 7(a) ('amnistie générale') (no exclusions)
- International mediation: ECOWAS, Nigeria, Ivory Coast, Burkina Faso

129. **Ceasefire Agreement between the Government and the Chin National Front (CNF) (Myanmar) 7 May 2012 (Intra-state)**

- Amnesty: point of agreement no 12 ('complete immunity' for members of CNF) (no exclusions)
- International mediation:/

130. **Acte d'adhésion de la CPJP à l'accord de paix global de Libreville (CAR) 25 August 2012 (Intra-state)**

- Amnesty: Declaration no 2 (adherence to 2008 Libreville Accord including amnesty law passed accordingly) (exclusion of crimes within the jurisdiction of the ICC)

- International mediation: UN, AU, Forces Multinationales des Etats d'Afrique Centrale

131. **Agreement between the Chin National Front (CNF) and Union-Level Peace Working Committee at the 2nd Round of Peace Talks (Myanmar) 9 December 2012 (Intra-state)**

- Amnesty: article 4 (no exclusions)
- International mediation:/

132. **Agreement between the Government of the Republic of South Sudan (GRSS) and the South Sudan Democratic Movement/Army (SSDM/A) 27 February 2013 (South Sudan) (Intra-state)**

- Amnesty: article 2(a) ('renewed amnesty for the SSDM/A group') (no exclusions)
- International mediation:/

133. **Agreement between the Government of Sudan and the Justice and Equality Movement-Sudan on the Basis of the Doha Document for Peace in Darfur (Sudan) 6 April 2013 (Intra-state)**

- Amnesty: article 24 ('general amnesty') (exclusion of war crimes, crimes against humanity, genocide, sexual violence and gross violations of human rights and humanitarian law in accordance with 2011 Doha Documents)
- International mediation: UN, AU, Qatar

134. **Accords de Ouagadougou (Mali) 13 June 2013 (Intra-state)**

- Amnesty: article 17 (exclusion of war crimes, crimes against humanity, genocide, sexual violence and gross violations of human rights and humanitarian law)
- International mediation: UN, AU, ECOWAS, EU, France, Suisse, Algeria, Mauritania, Niger

135. **Outcome Documents from the Conclusion of the Kampala Dialogue between the Government of the Democratic Republic of the Congo and the M23 (DRC) 12 December 2013 (Intra-state)**

- Amnesty: article 1 (exclusion of genocide, war crimes, crimes against humanity and other massive violations of human rights)
- International mediation: UN, ICGLR and Uganda

136. **Framework Agreement on the Bangsamoro, Annex on Normalization (FAB) (Philippines) 25 January 2014 (Intra-state)**

- Amnesty: article J(2) (general amnesty) (no exclusions)
- International mediation: Malaysia

137. **Joint Geneva Statement on Ukraine (Ukraine, Russia, EU, United States) 17 April 2014 (Inter-state)**

- Amnesty: para 4 (exclusion of capital crimes)
- International mediation: EU, OSCE, US

138. **Projecto de Lei de Memorando de Entendimento (Mozambique) 25 August 2014 (Intra-state)**

- Amnesty: p 1-2, paras f-g (general amnesty) (no exclusions)
- International mediation:/

139. **Package of Measures for the Implementation of the Minsk Agreements (Ukraine-Russia) 12 February 2015 (Inter-state)**

- Amnesty: para 5 ('pardon and amnesty') (no exclusions)
- International mediation: OSCE

140. **National Ceasefire Agreement (Myanmar) 15 October 2015 (Intra-state)**

- Amnesty: chapter 6 (b-c) (release and withdrawal of charges) (no exclusions)
- International mediation: UN, EU, China, India, Japan, Thailand

141. **Libyan Political Agreement (Sukhairat Agreement) (Libya) 17 December 2015 (Intra-state)**

- Amnesty: p 21, article 11 (exclusion of war crimes, crimes against humanity and other crimes under international law)
- International mediation: UN

142. **9-Point Deal (Nepal) 5 May 2016 (Intra-state)**

- Amnesty: withdrawal of cases and granting of clemency (no exclusions)
- International mediation:/

143. **Peace agreement between the Government of Afghanistan and Hezb-i-Islami (Afghanistan) 29 September 2016 (Intra-state)**

- Amnesty: article 9 (no exclusions)
- International mediation:/

144. **Final Agreement for Ending the Conflict and Building a Stable and Lasting Peace (Colombia) 24 November 2016 (Intra-state)**

- Amnesty: chapter 5, item 5.1.2 (II) para 23 ('the broadest possible amnesty') and paras 40-41 (exclusion of common crimes, crimes

against humanity, genocide, serious war crimes, hostage taking or other serious deprivations of freedom, torture, extrajudicial executions, forced disappearances, rape and other forms of sexual violence, child abduction, forced displacement and the recruitment of minors)
- International meditation: UN, Cuba, Norway

145. **Joint Declaration of the Chairman of the Presidential Council of the Government of National Accord, Fayez Al Sarraj, and the commander of the Libyan National Army, Khalifa Haftar (Libya) 25 July 2017 (Intra-state)**

- Amnesty: article 1 (no exclusions)
- International mediation: France

Bibliography

Books

Abtahi H and Webb P, *The Genocide Convention: The Travaux Préparatoires* (Martinus Nijhoff Publishers 2008)

Aguilar P, *Memory and Amnesia: The Role of the Spanish Civil War in the Transition to Democracy* (Berghahn Books 2002)

Allen T and Vlassenroot K (eds), *The Lord's Resistance Army, Myth and Reality* (Zed Books 2010)

Allmand C, *The Hundred Years War* (Cambridge University Press 1988)

Ambos K, Large J and Weirda M (eds), *Building a Future on Peace and Justice* (Springer 2009)

Balogh E, *Political Refugees in Ancient Greece: From the Period of the Tyrants to Alexander the Great* (Witwatersrand University Press 1943)

Barahona De Brito A, González Enríquez C and Aguilar P (eds), *The Politics of Memory and Democratization: Transitional Justice in Democratizing Societies* (Oxford University Press 2001)

Bass GJ, *Stay the Hand of Vengeance: The Politics of War Crimes Tribunals* (Princeton University Press 2000)

Bassiouni MC, *Crimes against Humanity in International Criminal Law* (Martinus Nijhoff Publishers 1992)

—— *Introduction to International Criminal Law: Second Revised Edition* (Martinus Nijhoff Publishers 2014)

—— and Wise EM, *Aut Dedere Aut Judicare: The Duty to Extradite or Prosecute in International Law* (Martinus Nijhoff Publishers 1995)

—— et al., *The Chicago Principles on Post-Conflict Justice* (International Human Rights Law Institute 2007)

Beigbeder Y, *Judging War Criminals: The Politics of International Justice* (Palgrave Macmillan 1999)

Bonet H, *The Tree of Battles* (Liverpool University Press 1949)

Boraine A, *A Country Unmasked: Inside South Africa's Truth and Reconciliation Commission* (Oxford University Press 2000)

Bossuyt MJ, *Guide to the 'Travaux Préparatoires' of the International Covenant on Civil and Political Rights* (Martinus Nijhoff Publishers 1987)

Braud S, *Seneca: De Clementia* (Oxford University Press 2009)

Buergenthal T and Norris RE (eds), *Human Rights: The Inter-American System* (Oceana Publications, Dobbs Ferry N.Y. 1982)

Burgers JH and Danelius H, *The United Nations Convention against Torture: A Handbook on the Convention against Torture and Other Cruel, Inhuman, or Degrading Treatment or Punishment* (Martinus Nijhoff Publishers 1988)

Cassese A and Jones JRWD (eds), *The Rome Statute of the International Criminal Court: A Commentary* (Oxford University Press 2002)

—— and Gaeta P, *Cassese's International Criminal Law* (Oxford University Press 2013)

Ciorciari JD and Heindel A, *Hybrid Justice: The Extraordinary Chambers in the Courts of Cambodia* (University of Michigan Press 2014)

Cobban H, *Amnesty after Atrocity? Healing Nations after Genocide and War Crimes* (Paradigm Publishers 2007)

Contamine P, *War in the Middle Ages* (Blackwell 1984)

Council of Europe, *Collected Edition of the 'Travaux Préparatoires' of the European Convention of Human Rights* (Martinus Nijhoff Publishers 1975)

Crowe DM, *War Crimes, Genocide, and Justice: A Global History* (Palgrave Macmillan 2014)

Davis JM and Tremmel GB, *Parole, Pardon, Pass and Amnesty Documents of the Civil War: An Illustrated History* (McFarland and Company 2014)

de Vattel E, *The Law of Nations, or, Principles of the Law of Nature, Applied to the Conduct and Affairs of Nations and Sovereigns* (Liberty Fund 2008)

de Visser MW, *Ancient Buddhism in Japan Sutras and Ceremonies in Use in the Seventh and Eighth Centuries AD and their History in Later Times* (Librairie Orientaliste Paul Geuthner, Paris 1928)

Doher M, *Proscrits et exilés après Waterloo* (J Peyronet & Cie, Paris 1965)

Domenico R, *Italian Fascists on Trial 1943–1948* (University of North Carolina Press 1991)

Dorjahn AP, *Political Forgiveness in Old Athens: The Amnesty of 403 B.C.* (Northwestern University Studies in the Humanities No 13, Evanston 1946)

Dorris JT, *Pardon and Amnesty under Lincoln and Johnson* (University of North Carolina Press 1953)

Dowling MB, *Clemency and Cruelty in the Roman World* (University of Michigan Press 2006)

Duparc P, *Origines de la grâce dans le droit pénal romain et français du Bas-Empire à la Renaissance* (Librairie du Recueil Sirey, Paris 1942)

Engle K, Miller Z and Davis DM (eds) *Anti-Impunity and the Human Rights Agenda* (Cambridge University Press 2016)

Foviaux J, *La rémission des peines et des condamnations: Droit monarchique et droit moderne* (Presses Universitaires de France, Paris 1970)

Freeman M, *Necessary Evils: Amnesties and the Search for Justice* (Cambridge University Press 2009)

Frei N, *Adenauer's Germany and the Nazi Past: The Politics of Amnesty and Integration* (Columbia University Press 2002)

Gacon S, *L'amnistie. De la Commune à la guerre d'Algérie* (Editions du Seuil, Paris 2002)

Garrisson J, *L'édit de Nantes: chronique d'une paix attendue* (Fayard, Paris 1998)

Ginsburgs G and Kudriavtsev VN (eds), *The Nuremberg Trial and International Law* (Martinus Nijhoff Publishers 1990)

Godechot J, Hyslop BF and Dowd DL, *The Napoleonic Era in Europe* (Holt, Rinehart and Winston 1971)

Grotius H, *The Rights of War and Peace* (Cambridge University Press 1853)
—— *De jure belli ac pacis libri tres* (A C Campbell tr, Hyperion Press 1979)
Hammond NGL, *A History of Greece to 322 B.C.* (3rd edn, Clarendon Press 1986)
Hayner PB, *Unspeakable Truths: Transitional Justice and the Challenge of Truth Commissions* (Taylor & Francis 2010)
Heller KJ and Simpson G (eds), *The Hidden Histories of War Crimes Trials* (Oxford University Press 2013)
Henckaerts J-M and Doswald-Beck L (eds), *Customary International Humanitarian Law* (Cambridge University Press 2005)
Humbert WH, *The Pardoning Power of the President* (American Council on Public Affairs, Washington D.C. 1941)
Huntington SP, *The Third Wave: Democratization in the Late Twentieth Century* (University of Oklahoma Press 1991)
Hurnard ND, *The King's Pardon for Homicide before AD 1307* (Clarendon Press 1969)
Israel FL (ed), *Major Peace Treaties of Modern History 1648 – 1967* (Chelsea House Publications 1967)
Jeffery R, *Amnesties, Accountability, and Human Rights* (University of Pennsylvania Press 2014)
Jensen C, *The Pardoning Power in the American States* (University of Chicago Press 1922)
Johnson JT, *Just War Tradition and the Restraint of War* (Princeton University Press 1981)
Joughin JT, *The Paris Commune in French Politics, 1871–1880: The History of the Amnesty of 1880* (Johns Hopkins Press 1955)
Keen M, *The Laws of War in the Late Middle Ages* (Routledge & Kegan Paul 1965)
Klüber JL, *Droit des gens moderne de l'Europe* (Librairie de J G Cotta, Stuttgart 1819, vol 1)
Kovachi AJ, *Prelude to Nuremberg, Allied War Crimes Policy and the Question of Punishment* (University of North Carolina Press 1998)
Krentz P, *The Thirty at Athens* (Cornell University Press 1982)
Kritz NJ (ed), *Transitional Justice: How Emerging Democracies Reckon with Former Regimes* (Unites States Institute of Peace 1995)
La Haye E, *War Crimes in Internal Armed Conflicts* (Cambridge University Press 2008)
Largeaud J-M, *Napoléon et Waterloo: la défaite glorieuse de 1815 à nos jours* (Boutique de l'histoire, Paris 2006)
Larsen SU (ed), *Modern Europe after Fascism, 1943–1980s* (Columbia University Press 1998)
Lesaffer R (ed), *Peace Treaties and International Law in European History* (Cambridge University Press 2004)
Lessa F and Payne LA (eds), *Amnesty in the Age of Human Rights Accountability: Comparative and International Perspectives* (Cambridge University Press 2012).
Levie HS, *Terrorism in War: The Law of War Crimes* (Oceana Publications, Dobbs Ferry N.Y. 1993)
Linforth IM, *Solon the Athenian* (University of California Press 1919)
Loening T, *The Reconciliation Agreement of 403/402 B.C. in Athens: Its Content and Application* (Steiner, Stuttgart 1987)
Loraux N, *The Divided City: On Memory and Forgetting in Ancient Athens* (Zone Books 2002)

Mallinder L, *Amnesty, Human Rights and Political Transitions: Bridging the Peace and Justice Divide* (Hart Publishing 2008)

—— et al., *The Belfast Guidelines on Amnesty and Accountability* (Transitional Justice Institute, University of Ulster 2013)

Maogoto JN, *War Crimes and Realpolitik: International Justice from World War I to the 21st Century* (Lynne Rienner Publishers 2004)

Mattei J-M, *Histoire du droit de la guerre (1700–1819): introduction à l'histoire du droit international* (Presses Universitaires d'Aix-Marseilles 2006)

McAdams J, *Transitional Justice and the Rule of Law in New Democracies* (University of Notre Dame Press 1997)

McKnight BE, *The Quality of Mercy: Amnesties and Traditional Chinese Justice* (University Press of Hawaii 1981)

Meron T, *Henry's Wars and Shakespeare's Laws: Perspectives on the Law of War in the Later Middle Ages* (Clarendon Press 1993)

Mertz B, *Temples, Tombs and Hieroglyphs: A Popular History of Ancient Egypt* (Brockhampton Press 1999)

Monteil J, *La grâce en droit français moderne* (Librairies techniques, Paris 1959)

Murray RB, *Legal Cases of the Civil War* (Stackpole Books 2003)

Naqvi YQ, *Impediments to Exercising Jurisdiction over International Crimes* (TMC Asser Press 2010)

Neff SC, *Justice in Blue and Grey: A Legal History of the Civil War* (Harvard University Press 2010)

Novak A, *Comparative Executive Clemency: The Constitutional Pardon Power and the Prerogative of Mercy in Global Perspective* (Routledge 2016)

Nowak M and McArthur E, *The United Nations Convention Against Torture: A Commentary* (Oxford University Press 2008)

O'Donnell G and Schmitter PC, *Transitions from Authoritarian Rule: Tentative Conclusions about Uncertain Democracies* (John Hopkins University Press 1986)

Olsen TD, Payne LA and Reiter AG, *Transitional Justice in Balance: Comparing Processes, Weighing Efficacy* (United States Institute of Peace Press 2010)

Oppenheim LFL, *International Law: A Treatise* (6th edn, Longmans 1944)

—— *International Law: A Treatise* (7th edn, Longmans 1948)

O'Shea A, *Amnesty for Crime in International Law and Practice* (Kluwer Law International 2002)

Patterson RF (ed), *Plutarch's Lives of Solon and Nicias* (Blackie and Son Limited 1930)

Parry C (ed), *The Consolidated Treaty Series* (Oceana Publications, Dobbs Ferry N.Y. 1969–1986)

Phillips CL and Axelrod A, *Encyclopaedia of Historical Treaties and Alliances* (Fitzroy Dearborn 2001)

Pictet JS (ed), *Commentary I: Geneva Conventions for the Amelioration of the Condition of the Wounded and Sick in Armed Forces in the Field* (International Committee of the Red Cross 1952)

Pike LO, *A History of Crime in England* (Smith Elder and Co 1873)

Rocard M, *L'art de la paix, l'édit de Nantes* (Janine Garrisson ed, Editions Atlantica, Biarritz 1997)

Roht-Arriaza N and Mariezcurrena J, *Transitional Justice in the Twenty-First Century: Beyond Truth versus Justice* (Cambridge University Press 2006)

Root RK, *Transitional Justice in Peru* (Palgrave Macmillan 2012)
Russel FH, *The Just War in the Middle Ages* (Cambridge University Press 1975)
Sandoz Y, Swinarski C and Zimmermann B (eds), *Commentary on the Additional Protocols of 8 June 1977 to the Geneva Conventions of 12 August 1949* (Martinus Nijhoff Publishers 1987)
Sarkin J, *Carrots and Sticks: The TRC and the South African Amnesty Process* (Intersentia 2004)
Schabas W, *The UN International Criminal Tribunals: The Former Yugoslavia, Rwanda and Sierra Leone* (Cambridge University Press 2006)
—— *Genocide in International Law: The Crime of Crimes* (Cambridge University Press 2009)
—— *The International Criminal Court: A Commentary on the Rome Statute* (Oxford University Press 2010)
Schindler D and Toman J, *The Laws of Armed Conflicts* (Martinus Nihjoff Publisher 1988)
Schwarzenberger G, *International Law as Applied by International Courts and Tribunals* (Stevens & Sons Limited 1968)
Scott JB (ed), *The Hague Conventions and Declarations of 1899 and 1907* (Oxford University Press 1915)
Scovazzi T and Citroni G, *The Struggle against Enforced Disappearance and the 2007 United Nations Convention* (Martinus Nijhoff Publishers 2007)
Seibert-Fohr A, *Prosecuting Serious Human Rights Violations* (Oxford University Press 2009)
Shelton DL, *Remedies in International Human Rights Law* (2nd edn, Oxford University Press 2006)
Skeat WW, *An Etymological Dictionary of the English Language* (new edn, Oxford University Press 1924)
Sikkink K, *The Justice Cascade: How Human Rights Prosecutions Are Changing World Politics* (WW Norton 2012)
Sitze A, *The Impossible Machine: A Genealogy of South Africa's Truth and Reconciliation Commission* (University of Michigan Press 2013)
Spitz R and Chaskelson M, *The Politics of Transition: A Hidden History of South Africa's Negotiated Settlement* (Hart Publishing 2000)
Taylor H, *A Treatise on Public International Law* (Callaghan and Company 1901)
Turner LCF, *The First World War* (Frederick Warne & Co 1967)
Tutu D, *No Future without Forgiveness* (Rider, London 1999)
United Nations War Crimes Commission, *History of the United Nations War Crimes Commission and the Development of the Laws of War* (HM Stationary Office 1948)
Van den Wyngaert C, *The Political Offence Exception to Extradition: The Delicate Problem of Balancing the Rights of the Individual and the International Public Order* (Kluwer, Deventer 1980)
van Sliedregt E, *The Criminal Responsibility of Individuals for Violations of International Humanitarian Law* (TMC Asser Press 2003)
Williams S, *Hybrid and Internationalised Criminal Tribunals: Selected Jurisdictional Issues* (Hart Publishing 2012)
Willis JF, *Prologue to Nuremberg: The Politics and Diplomacy of Punishing War Criminals of the First World War* (Greenwood Press 1982)
Wolff C, *Jus Gentium Methodo Scientifica pertractatum* (Clarendon Press 1934)

Contributions to edited books

Allmand C, 'The War and Non-Combatants' in Fowler (ed), *The Hundred Years War* (Mac Millan Press 1971) 163–83

Beer S, 'Hunting the Discriminators: Denazification in Austria, 1945–1957' in Hálfdanarson (ed), *Racial Discrimination and Ethnicity in European History* (Edizioni PLUS 2003) 177–88

Boniece SA, 'Brest-Litovsk, Peace of (1918)' in Wolfrum (ed), *The Max Planck Encyclopedia of Public International Law* (Oxford University Press 2012) 1051–54

Boraine A, 'Truth and Reconciliation in South Africa: The Third Way' in Rotberg and Thompson (eds), *Truth v. Justice: The Morality of Truth Commissions* (Princeton University Press 2000) 141–57

Coetzee M, 'An Overview of the TRC Amnesty Process' in Villa-Vicencio and Doxtader (eds), *The Provocations of Amnesty: Memory, Justice and Impunity* (Africa World Press 2003) 181–94

Curry A, 'The Military Ordinances of Henry V: Texts and Contexts' in Given-Wilson, Kettle and Scales (eds), *War, Government and Aristocracy in the British Isles, C. 1150–1500* (Boydell Press 2008) 214–49

De Zayas AM, 'Amnesty Clause' in Bernhardt (ed), *Encyclopaedia of Public International Law* (Max Planck Institute for Comparative Public Law and International Law 1992, vol 1) 148–51

—— 'Westphalia, Peace of (1648)' in Bernhardt (ed), *Encyclopaedia of Public International Law* (Max Planck Institute for Comparative Public Law and International Law 2000, vol 4) 1465–69

Honwana A, 'Children of War: Understanding War and War Cleansing in Mozambique and Angola' in Chesterman (ed), *Civilians in War* (Lynne Rienner Publishers 2001) 123–42

Jacobs D, 'Puzzling over Amnesties: Defragmenting the Debate for International Criminal Tribunals' in van den Herik and Stahn (eds), *The Diversification and Fragmentation of International Criminal Law* (Martinus Nijhoff Publishers 2012) 305–45

Keen M, 'The Jurisdiction and Origins of the Constable's Court' in Gillingham and Holt (eds), *War and Government in the Middle Ages* (Boydell Press 1984) 159–69

—— 'Richard II's Ordinances of War of 1385' in Archer and Walker (eds), *Rulers and Ruled in Late Medieval England* (Hambledon Press 1995) 33–48

Kent L, 'Beyond "Pragmatism" versus "Principle": Ongoing Justice Debates in East Timor' in Jeffery and Kim (eds), *Transitional Justice in the Asia-Pacific* (Cambridge University Press 2014) 157–94

Lutz E, 'Responses to Amnesties by the Inter-American System for the Protection of Human Rights' in Harris and Livingstone (eds), *The Inter-American System of Human Rights* (Clarendon Press 1998) 345–70

Martin I, 'Justice and Reconciliation: Responsibilities and Dilemmas of Peace-Makers and Peacebuilders' in Hankin (ed), *The Legacy of Abuses: Confronting the Past, Facing the Future* (Conference Report, The Aspen Institute 2002) 81–90

Münch F, 'Vienna Congress (1815)' in Bernhardt (ed), *Encyclopaedia of Public International Law* (Max Planck Institute for Comparative Public Law and International Law 2000, vol 4) 1286–89

Orentlicher D, 'Immunities and Amnesties' in Sadat (ed), *Forging a Convention for Crimes against Humanity* (Cambridge University Press 2011) 202–22

Robson E, 'The Seven Years War' in Lindsay (ed) *The New Cambridge Modern History* (Cambridge University Press 1957, vol 7) 465–86

Roht-Arriaza N, 'Amnesty and the International Criminal Court' in Shelton (ed), *International Crimes, Peace and Human Rights: The Role of the International Criminal Court* (Transnational Publishers, Ardsley N.Y. 2000) 77–82

Schabas W, 'No Peace Without Justice? The Amnesty Quandary' in Schabas (ed), *Unimaginable Atrocities: Justice, Politics and Rights at the War Crimes Tribunals* (Oxford University Press 2012) 173–98

Seibert-Fohr A, 'Amnesties' in Wolfrum (ed), *The Max Planck Encyclopaedia of Public International Law* (Oxford University Press 2012) 358–65

Shraga D, 'The Second Generation UN-Based Tribunals: A Diversity of Mixed Jurisdiction' in Romano, Nollkaemper and Kleffner (eds), *Internationalized Criminal Courts and Tribunals: Sierra Leone, East Timor, Kosovo and Cambodia* (Oxford University Press 2004) 15–38

Van den Bogaert S, 'Berlin Congress (1878)' in Wolfrum (ed), *The Max Planck Encyclopedia of Public International Law* (Oxford University Press 2012) 900–906

Villarán de la Puente S, 'Peru' in *Victims Unsilenced: The Inter-American Human Rights System and Transitional Justice in Latin America* (Due Process of Law Foundation 2007) 95–126

Williams S and Schabas W, 'Article 17, Issues of Admissibility' in Triffterer (ed), *Commentary on the Statute of the International Criminal Court* (2nd edn, Hart Publishing 2008) 605–25

Articles

Aguilar A, 'Collective Memory of the Spanish Civil War: The Case of the Political Amnesty in the Spanish Transition to Democracy' (1997) 4(4) *Democratization* 88

Akhavan P, 'The Lord's Resistance Army Case: Uganda's Submission of the First State Referral to the International Criminal Court' (2005) 99 *American Journal of International Law* 403

—— 'Are International Criminal Tribunals a Disincentive to Peace? Reconciling Judicial Romanticism with Political Realism' (2009) 31(3) *Human Rights Quarterly* 624

Arsanjani MH, 'The International Criminal Court and National Amnesty Laws' (1999) 93 *American Society of International Law Proceedings* 65

Bakker CAE, 'A Full Stop to Amnesty in Argentina: The Simon Case' (2005) 3 *Journal of International Criminal Justice* 1106

Bassiouni MC, 'International Crimes: Jus Cogens and Obligatio Erga Omnes' (1996) 59 *Law and Contemporary Problems* 63

—— 'Searching for Peace and Achieving Justice: The Need for Accountability' (1996) 59(4) *Law and Contemporary Problems* 9

Battini M, 'Sins of Memory: Reflections on the Lack of an Italian Nuremberg and the Administration of International Justice after 1945' (2004) 9(3) *Journal of Modern Italian Studies* 349

Binningsbø HM et al., 'Armed Conflict and Post-Conflict Justice, 1946–2006: A Dataset' (2012) 49(5) *Journal of Peace Research* 731

Bradfield P, 'Reshaping Amnesty in Uganda: The Case of Thomas Kwoyelo' (2017) 15(4) *Journal of International Criminal Justice* 827

Branch A, 'Uganda's Civil War and the Politics of ICC Intervention' (2007) 21 *Ethics and International Affairs* 179

Burke-White WW, 'Reframing Impunity: Applying Liberal International Law Theory to an Analysis of Amnesty Legislation' (2001) 42 *Harvard International Law Journal* 467

Burt J-M, Amiliviay GF and Lessa F, 'Civil Society and the Resurgent Struggle against Impunity in Uruguay (1986–2012)' (2013) 7 *International Journal of Transitional Justice* 306

Cassel D, 'Lessons from the Americas: Guidelines for International Response to Amnesties for Atrocities' (1996) 59(4) *Law and Contemporary Problems* 197

Cassese A, 'The Special Court and International Law, the Decision Concerning the Lomé Agreement Amnesty' (2004) 2 *Journal of International Criminal Justice* 1130

Collins C, 'Human Rights Trials in Chile during and after the "Pinochet Years"' (2010) 4 *International Journal of Transitional Justice* 67

Dadrian VN, 'The Turkish Military Tribunal's Prosecution of the Authors of the Armenian Genocide: Four Major Court-Martial Series' (1997) 11 *Holocaust and Genocidal Studies* 28

D'Amato A, 'Peace vs Accountability in Bosnia' (1994) 88(3) *American Journal of International Law* 500

Davis L, 'Power Shared and Justice Shelved: The Democratic Republic of Congo' (2013) 17(2) *International Journal of Human Rights* 289

—— and Hayner P, 'Difficult Peace, Limited Justice: Ten Years of Peacemaking in the DRC' (March 2009) *International Center for Transitional Justice*

Dickinson LA, 'The Promise of Hybrid Courts' (2003) 97 *American Journal of International Law* 295

Doria J, 'Angola: A Case Study in the Challenges of Achieving Peace and the Question of Amnesty or Prosecution of War Crimes in Mixed Armed Conflicts' (2002) 5 *Yearbook of International Humanitarian Law* 3

Dugard J, 'Reconciliation and Justice: The South African Experience' (1998) 8 *Transnational Law and Contemporary Problems* 277

—— 'Dealing with Crimes of a Past Regime: Is Amnesty Still an Option?' (1999) 12 *Leiden Journal of International Law* 1001

Duker WF, 'The President's Power to Pardon: A Constitutional History' (1977) 18(3) *William and Mary Law Review* 475

Eftekhari S, 'France and the Algerian War: From a Policy of "Forgetting" to a Framework for Accountability' (2003) 34 *Columbia Human Rights Law Review* 413

Encarnacion OG, 'Reconciliation after Democratization: Coping with the Past in Spain' (2008) 123(3) *Political Science Quarterly* 435

Focardi F and Klinkhammer L, 'The Question of Fascist Italy's War Crimes: The Construction of a Self-Acquitting Myth (1943–1948)' (2004) 9(3) *Journal of Modern Italian Studies* 330

Garner JW, 'Punishment of Offenders against the Laws and Customs of War' (1920) 14 *The American Journal of International Law* 70

Gavron J, 'Amnesties in the Light of Developments in International Law and the Establishment of the International Criminal Court' (2002) 51 *International and Comparative Law Quarterly* 91

Goldstone R, 'Exposing Human Rights Abuses: A Help or Hindrance to Reconciliation' (1995) 22 *Hastings Constitutional Law Quarterly* 607

—— and Fritz N, '"In the Interests of Justice" and Independent Referral: The ICC Prosecutor's Unprecedented Powers' (2000) 13(3) *Leiden Journal of International Law* 655

Graybill LS, 'Pardon, Punishment, and Amnesia: Three African Post-Conflict Methods' (2004) 25(6) *Third World Quarterly* 1117

Grupp S, 'Some Historical Aspects of the Pardon in England' (1963) 7 *The American Journal of Legal History* 51

Hayner PB, 'Negotiating Peace in Sierra Leone: Confronting the Justice Challenge' (December 2007) *Centre for Humanitarian Dialogue*

—— 'Negotiating Justice: Guidance for Mediators' (February 2009) *Centre for Humanitarian Dialogue*

—— 'Does the ICC Advance the Interests of Justice?' (4 November 2014) *Open Democracy*

Henckaerts J-M, 'The Grave Breaches Regime as Customary International Law' (2009) 7 *Journal of International Criminal Justice* 683

Igreja V, 'Multiple Temporalities in Indigenous Justice and Healing Practices in Mozambique' (2012) 6 *International Journal of Transitional Justice* 404

—— 'Amnesty Law, Political Struggles for Legitimacy and Violence in Mozambique' (2015) 9 *International Journal of Transitional Justice* 239

Jeffery R, 'Nepal's Comprehensive Peace Agreement: Human Rights, Compliance and Impunity a Decade On' (2017) 93(2) *International Affairs* 343

Jorgensen JN, 'Clemency and Pardons Note' (1992–1993) 27 *University of Richmond Law Review* 345

Kaufman Z, 'Transitional Justice for Tōjō's Japan: The United States Role in the Establishment of the International Military Tribunal for the Far East and Other Transitional Justice Mechanisms for Japan after World War II' (2014) 27 *Emory International Law Review* 755

Kobil DT, 'The Quality of Mercy Strained: Wresting the Pardoning Power from the King' (1991) 69 *Texas Law Review* 569

Kreß C, 'Reflections on the Iudicare Limb of the Grave Breaches Regime' (2009) 7 *Journal of International Criminal Justice* 789

Labuda PI, 'The Special Criminal Court in the Central African Republic: Failure or Vindication of Complementarity?' (2017) 15 *Journal of International Criminal Justice* 175

Lafontaine F, 'No Amnesty or Statute of Limitation for Enforced Disappearances: The Sandoval Case before the Supreme Court of Chile' (2005) 3 *Journal of International Criminal Justice* 469

Langdon S and Gardiner AH, 'The Treaty of Alliance between Hattusili, King of the Hittites, and the Pharaoh Ramesses II of Egypt' (1920) 6(3) *The Journal of Egyptian Archaeology* 179

Laplante LJ, 'Outlawing Amnesties: The Return of Criminal Justice in Transitional Justice Schemes' (2009) 49 *Virginia Journal of International Law* 915

—— and Theidon K, 'Transitional Justice in Times of Conflict: Colombia's Ley de Justicia y Paz' (2006) 28 *Michigan Journal of International Law* 49

LCK, 'The Power of the President to Grant a General Pardon or Amnesty for Offences against the United States' (1869) 17(10) *The American Law Register* 577

Leclercq S, 'Injustice through Transitional Justice? Subversion Strategies in Burundi's Peace Process and Postconflict Developments' (2017) 11 *International Journal of Transitional Justice* 525

Lelieur-Fischer J, 'Prosecuting the Crimes against Humanity Committed during the Algerian War: An Impossible Endeavour? The 2003 Decision of the French Court of Cassation in Aussaresses' (2004) 2 *Journal of International Criminal Justice* 231

Lessa F, Olsen TD, Payne LA, Pereirayy G and Reiter AG, 'Persistent or Eroding Impunity: The Divergent Effects of Legal Challenges to Amnesty Laws for Past Human Rights Violations' (2014) 47 *Israel Law Review* 105

—— 'Overcoming Impunity: Pathways to Accountability in Latin America' (2014) 8 *International Journal of Transitional Justice* 75

Lutz E and Sikkink K, 'The Justice Cascade: The Evolution and Impact of Foreign Human Rights Trials in Latin America' (2001) 2 *Chicago Journal of International Law* 1

Malamud-Goti J, 'Transitional Governments in the Breach: Why Punish State Criminals' (1990) 12(1) *Human Rights Quarterly* 1

Mallinder L, 'The End of Amnesty or Regional Overreach? Interpreting the Erosion of South America's Amnesty Laws' (2016) 65 *International and Comparative Law Quarterly* 645

McNamara K, 'Seeking Justice in Ugandan Courts: Amnesty and the Case of Thomas Kwoyelo' (2013) 12(3) *Washington University Global Studies Law Review* 653

Meisenberg SM, 'Legality of Amnesties in International Humanitarian Law: The Lomé Amnesty Decision of the Special Court for Sierra Leone' (2004) 856 *International Review of the Red Cross* 837

Méndes JE, 'Accountability for Past Abuses' (1997) 19 *Human Rights Quarterly* 255

Migliore DM, 'Amnesty: An Historical Justification for Its Continuing Viability' (1972–73) 12 *Journal of Family Law* 63

Miller RH, 'The Convention on the Non-Applicability of Statutory Limitations to War Crimes and Crimes against Humanity' (1971) 65 *American Journal of International Law* 476

Moore JJ, 'Problems with Forgiveness: Granting Amnesty under the Arias Plan in Nicaragua and El Salvador' (1990–1991) 43 *Stanford Law Review* 733

Naqvi YQ, 'Amnesty for War Crimes: Defining the Limits of International Recognition' (2003) 85(1) *International Journal of the Red Cross* 583

Nino CS, 'The Duty to Punish Past Abuses of Human Rights Put into Context: The Case of Argentina' (1991) 100 *Yale Law Journal* 2619

Ogren K, 'Humanitarian Law in the Articles of War Decreed in 1621 by King Gustavus II Adolphus of Sweden' (1996) 36(313) *International Review of the Red Cross* 438

Orentlicher DF, 'Settling Accounts: The Duty to Prosecute Human Rights Violations of a Prior Regime' (1991) 100 *Yale Law Journal* 2537

Osiel MJ, 'Why Prosecute? Critics of Punishment for Mass Atrocity' (2000) 22 *Human Rights Quarterly* 118

Parker P, 'The Politics of Indemnities, Truth Telling and Reconciliation in South Africa: Ending Apartheid without Forgetting' (1996) 17 *Human Rights Law Journal* 1

Quinn RJ, 'Will the Rule of Law End? Challenging Grants of Amnesty for the Human Rights Violations of a Prior Regime: Chile's New Model' (1994) 62 *Fordham Law Review* 905

Reiter AG, 'Examining the Use of Amnesties and Pardons as a Response to Internal Armed Conflicts' (2014) 47(1) *Israel Law Review* 133

Requa MA, 'A Human Rights Triumph? Dictatorship-Era Crimes and the Chilean Supreme Court' (2012) 12(1) *Human Rights Law Review* 79

Robinson D, 'Serving the Interests of Justice: Amnesties, Truth Commissions and the International Criminal Court' (2003) 14(3) *European Journal of International Law* 481

Roht-Arriaza N, 'State Responsibility to Investigate and Prosecute Grave Human Rights Violations in International Law' (1990) 78 *California Law Review* 449

—— 'The Spanish Civil War, Amnesty, and the Trials of Judge Garzón' (25 July 2012) 16(24) *American Society of International Law Insights*

—— 'After Amnesties are Gone: Latin American National Courts and the New Contours of the Fight against Impunity' (2015) 37(2) *Human Rights Quarterly* 341

—— and Gibson L, 'The Developing Jurisprudence on Amnesty' (1998) 20 *Human Rights Quarterly* 843

Roniger L and Sznajder M, 'The Legacy of Human Rights Violations and the Collective Identity of Redemocratized Uruguay' (1997) 19 *Human Rights Quarterly* 55

Rose C, 'Looking beyond Amnesty and Traditional Justice and Reconciliation Mechanisms in Northern Uganda: A Proposal for Truth-Telling and Reparations" (2008) 28(2) *Boston College Third World Law Journal* 344

Schabas W, 'Amnesty, the Sierra Leone Truth and Reconciliation Commission and the Special Court for Sierra Leone' (2004) 11 *University of California Davis Journal of International Law and Policy* 145

Scharf MP, 'The Letter of the Law: The Scope of the International Legal Obligation to Prosecute Human Rights Crimes' (1996) 59(4) *Law and Contemporary Problems* 41

—— 'Swapping Amnesty for Peace: Was There a Duty to Prosecute International Crimes in Haiti?' (1996) 31(1) *Texas International Law Journal* 1

—— 'The Amnesty Exception to the Jurisdiction of the International Criminal Court' (1999) 32 *Cornell International Law Journal* 507

—— 'From the eXile Files: An Essay on Trading Justice for Peace' (2006) 63 *Washington and Lee Law Review* 339

Schneider N, 'Impunity in Post-Authoritarian Brazil: The Supreme Court's Recent Verdict on the Amnesty Law' (2011) 90 *European Review of Latin American and Caribbean Studies* 39

Schwarzenberger G, 'The Judgment of Nuremberg' (March 1947) 21(3) *Tulane Law Review* 329

Sculier C, 'Négociations de paix au Burundi: Une justice encombrante mais incontournable' (May 2008) *Centre for Humanitarian Dialogue*

Sebba L, 'The Pardoning Power: A World's Survey' (1997) 68(1) *Journal of Criminal Law and Criminology* 83

Slye RC, 'The Legitimacy of Amnesties under International Law and General Principles of Anglo-American Law: Is a Legitimate Amnesty Possible?' (2002) 43 *Virginia Journal of International Law* 173

Smith G, 'The Prytanaeum in the Athenian Amnesty Law' (1921) 14 *Classical Philology* 345

Smith HS, 'A Note on Amnesty' (1968) 54 *The Journal of Egyptian Archaeology* 209

Snyder EC, 'The Dirty Legal War: Human Rights and the Rule of Law in Chile 1973–1995' (1995) 2 *Tulsa Journal of Comparative and International Law* 253

Snyder J and Vinjamuri L, 'Trials and Errors: Principle and Pragmatism in Strategies of International Justice' (2004) 28(3) *International Security* 5

Soltman D, 'Applauding Uruguay's Quest for Justice: Dictatorship, Amnesty, and Repeal of Uruguay Law No. 15.848' (2013) 12 *Washington University Global Studies Law Review* 829

Speck PK, 'The Trial of the Argentine Junta: Responsibilities and Realities' (1987) 18 *University of Miami Inter-American Law Review* 491

Stahn C, 'United Nations Peacebuilding, Amnesties and Alternative Forms of Justice: A Change in Practice?' (2002) 84(5) *International Review of the Red Cross* 191

—— 'Complementarity, Amnesties and Alternative Forms of Justice: Some Interpretative Guidelines for the International Criminal Court' (2005) 3 *Journal of International Criminal Justice* 695

Stedman SJ, 'Spoiler Problems in Peace Processes' (1997) 22 *International Security* 5

Sutil JG, 'Dealing with past Human Rights Violations: The Chilean Case after Dictatorship' (1992) 67 *Notre Dame Law Review* 1455

Tang YS, 'International Justice through Domestic Courts: Challenges in Brazil's Judicial Review of the Amnesty Law' (2015) 9 *International Journal of Transitional Justice* 259

Thornton WW, 'Pardon and Amnesty' (1885) 6(4) *Criminal Law Magazine* 457

Tittemore BD, 'Ending Impunity in the Americas: The Role of the Inter-American Human Rights System in Advancing Accountability for Serious Crimes under International Law' (2006) 12 *Southwestern Journal of Law and Trade in the Americas* 429

Tomuschat C, 'Issues of Universal Jurisdiction in the Scilingo Case' (2005) 3 *Journal of International Criminal Justice* 1074

Tulkens F, 'The Paradoxical Relationship between Criminal Law and Human Rights' (2011) 9 *Journal of International Criminal Justice* 577

Trumbull CP, 'Giving Amnesties a Second Chance' (2007) 25 *Berkeley Journal of International Law* 283

Vandeginste S, 'Bypassing the Prohibition of Amnesty for Human Rights Crime under International Law: Lessons Learned from the Burundian Peace Process' (2011) 29(2) *Netherlands Quarterly of Human Rights* 189

—— 'Burundi's Truth and Reconciliation Commission: How to Shed Light on the past while Standing in the Dark Shadow of Politics?' (2012) 6 *International Journal of Transitional Justice* 355

—— 'Museveni, Burundi and the Perversity of *Immunité Provisoire*' (2016) 10(3) *International Journal of Transitional Justice* 1

van Wijk J, 'Amnesty for War Crimes in Angola: Principled for a Day?' (2012) 12 *International Criminal Law Review* 743

Varaki M, 'Revisiting the "Interests of Justice" Policy Paper' (2017) 15(3) *Journal of International Criminal Justice* 455

Vinjamuri L and Boesenecker AP, 'Accountability and Peace Agreements, Mapping Trends from 1998 to 2006' (September 2007) *Centre for Humanitarian Dialogue*

von Elbe J, 'The Evolution of the Concept of the Just War in International Law' (1939) 33 *American Journal of International Law* 665

Weisman N, 'A History and Discussion of Amnesty' (1972) 4 *Columbia Human Rights Law Review* 529

Williams S, 'Amnesties in International Law: The Experience of the Special Court for Sierra Leone' (2005) 5 *Human Rights Law Review* 271

Wilson RJ, 'Prosecuting Pinochet: International Crimes in Spanish Domestic Law' (1999) 21 *Human Rights Quarterly* 927

Zalaquett J, 'Balancing Ethical Imperatives and Political Constraints: The Dilemma of New Democracies Confronting past Human Rights Violations' (1992) 43 *Hastings Law Journal* 1425

Index